State Banking in Early America

State Banking in Early America

A New Economic History

HOWARD BODENHORN

UNIVERSITY PRESS

2003

OXFORD
UNIVERSITY PRESS

Oxford   New York
Auckland   Bangkok   Buenos Aires   Cape Town   Chennai
Dar es Salaam   Delhi   Hong Kong   Istanbul   Karachi   Kolkata
Kuala Lumpur   Madrid   Melbourne   Mexico City   Mumbai   Nairobi
São Paulo   Shanghai   Taipei   Tokyo   Toronto

Published by Oxford University Press, Inc.
198 Madison Avenue, New York, New York 10016

www.oup.com

Oxford is a registered trademark of Oxford University Press

Library of Congress Cataloging-in-Publication Data
Bodenhorn, Howard.
State banking in early America : a new economic
history / by Howard Bodenhorn.
    p.   cm.
Includes bibliographical references and index.
ISBN 0-19-514776-6
1. Banks and banking—United States—State supervision.   2. Banks and
banking—United States—History.   I. Title.
HG1778.U5 B63 2002
332.1'224'097309034—dc21   2002029005

9 8 7 6 5 4 3 2 1

Printed in the United States of America
on acid-free paper

For Pam,
who insisted that I write it

Preface

It has been more than forty years since the publication of Bray Hammond's *Banks and Politics from the Revolution to the Civil War* and more than fifty years since the appearance of Fritz Redlich's *The Molding of American Banking*. Conceived and written in the aftermath of the Great Depression, both works sprang from the fundamental premise that decentralized, lightly regulated financial markets and banking systems were inherently unstable. Good policy and good practice required a strong, centralized regulatory structure.

These two books' conclusions provided a historical justification, which meshed neatly with many economists' beliefs about the instability of financial markets, for broadening the Federal Reserve's supervisory powers. Hammond's and Redlich's books deeply influenced economic theory and banking history and, thus, banking policy. It is notable in this regard, however, that neither book focuses on the economics of early American banking in the sense that it explicitly employs economic models and economic reasoning in the study of economic issues. Redlich's book is more intellectual biography than economic history. It focuses on the development of banking philosophies and frequently notes how practice strayed from theory. The historical lesson was that an outside agency was needed to keep bankers on the straight and narrow. Hammond, on the other hand, traces the connection of politics and banking in early America and shows how political discourse intersected with and influenced banking practice. The lesson that emerged from Hammond's book was that regulatory and supervisory powers were best divorced from the political process. The twin pillars of postdepression-era banking policy were a *strong* and *independent* supervisory power.

Subsequent volumes, such as Larry Schweikart's *Banking in the American South from the Age of Jackson to Reconstruction*, have mostly provided similar interpretations while focusing on shorter periods or specific places. Other histories, such as Benjamin Klebaner's *American Commercial Banking* or Paul Trescott's *Financing American Enterprise*, cover 300 years of banking history in about 200 pages, which means that the economics of early American banking is given inadequate attention.

It is time for a new, genuinely economic study of early American banking markets. This book represents the first full-length treatment of early American banking in over forty years. During that time, economic historians have offered many new interpretations of several important developments in antebellum banking policy and practice. Such features of early American financial history as free banking, branch banking, deposit insurance, and microbanking have been reinterpreted since the works of Redlich and Hammond. Moreover, economic theory has made significant advances, and this book incorporates these theoretical insights into the interpretation of several important periods. The so-called information-theoretic approach links the chapters into a unified whole. Early sections of each chapter synthesize the extant research; later sections present extensions, new findings, and new interpretations. This is not, then, a narrow scholarly monograph intended for a specific audience. My hope is that it can inform the opinions and research of readers from any number of fields.

The pages that follow represent the culmination of an intellectual journey that began more than a decade and a half ago. My interest in early American banking was piqued in Eugene White's graduate U.S. economic history course, and it was reinforced in his European economic history course where I wrote a comparative paper on Irish and U.S. free banking. My gratitude to Eugene runs deep. Through his kindness and generosity, he has eased my transition from student to colleague to coauthor and, ultimately, to friend. One day I hope to repay him, somehow.

I also owe a deep intellectual debt to Michael Bordo and Hugh Rockoff. For the past five years, Mike and Hugh have included me as a regular participant in the Money, History and Finance workshop at Rutgers. Mike runs a relaxed seminar and pays for lunch, the Holy Grail of academe. Hugh offers insightful and polite comments on my work and gives endless encouragement. I thank them both for their intellectual generosity. Of all the people associated with the Monday workshops, perhaps no two people deserve more recognition than Dorothy Rinaldi and Laura Ford, who have patiently helped me negotiate the labyrinth that is the Rutgers' parking authority. If you have never visited New Brunswick, you cannot imagine.

Many other people deserve thanks for reading all or part of the manuscript as it has progressed over the past decade or so. I offer special thanks to Mike Bordo, Charles Calomiris, Richard Grossman, Mike Haupert, Steve Horwitz, John James, Naomi Lamoreaux, Kerry Odell, Hugh Rockoff, Richard Sylla, Eugene White, Robert Wright, a host of conference and seminar attendees, and two or three dozen anonymous referees, who all offered gentle comments and sometimes not-so-gentle criticisms along the way. In the end, all the comments and criticisms improved the quality of the effort.

I am indebted to Paul Donnelly at Oxford University Press whose enthusiasm for and encouragement of this project kept me going. Frank Fusco and Robin Miura are to be thanked for their shepherding the manuscript through to completion. An anonymous reader made several useful suggestions that improved the quality of the exposition; his or her efforts are appreciated.

I also thank Cambridge University Press for permission to reprint large parts of my article, "Making the Little Guy Pay: Payments-System Networks, Cross-Subsidization, and the Collapse of the Suffolk System," *Journal of Economic History* 62:1 (March 2002), which appears in chapter 5. Many of the ideas discussed in chapter 7 first appeared as "Zombie Banks and the Demise of New York's Safety Fund," *Eastern Economic Journal* 22:1 (Winter 1996). My thoughts on the Safety Fund have changed somewhat since 1996, however, and chapter 7 more accurately represents the current state of my beliefs on the subject.

I thank the John M. Olin Foundation, the Economic History Association, the Robert King Mellon Foundation, and Lafayette College for research support. It was during the term of my Olin Faculty Fellowship in 1995/96 that the idea for this book emerged and early versions of chapters 4, 5, 6, and 9 were sketched out. Through the Cole Grant-in-Aid program, the Economic History Association financed two trips to archives that generated the data underlying chapter 3. The Robert King Mellon Foundation's funding of Lafayette College's summer fellowship program provided the time and resources to focus on my work. I thank them all without implicating any for the results.

Finally, I thank Pam for being an incredibly able research assistant who remained patient as I struggled through the writing of this book. Whatever its remaining shortcomings, this book would be a mere shadow of what it is absent her assistance and counsel.

H. B.

Contents

1. Introduction   3

2. Establishment and Governance of the Antebellum Bank   11

3. Banking Theory and Banking Practice in Antebellum America   44

4. New England: Small Banks and Familial Ties   72

5. The Rise and Fall of the Suffolk System   95

6. Middle Atlantic: Conservatism and Experimentation   123

7. New York's Safety Fund System: America's First Bank Insurance Experiment   155

8. Free Banking: The Populist Revolt Takes Root in New York   183

9. Banking in the South and West: Banks and the Commonweal   219

10. Property Banking, Free Banking, and Branch Banking   249

11. Assessing America's Early Banks   287

Notes   297

Bibliography   323

Index   345

State Banking in Early America

1

Introduction

An outpouring of recent theoretical and empirical research places financial intermediaries center stage in the process of economic growth and development. Through their dealings with customers as depositors, borrowers, consignors, entrepreneurs, and shareholders, financial intermediaries have an advantage over other market participants in gathering and processing information on the likelihood of success for at least some entrepreneurial projects.[1] The better financial intermediaries are at gathering and processing information, the better the overall economic performance. Scarce capital will be directed to its most productive uses and the gap between potential and actual aggregate output (or income) will be narrower than if financial intermediaries are less productive. Indeed, a number of recent cross-country empirical studies show that countries with more advanced financial sectors tend to experience faster economic growth.[2]

In an earlier study, I showed that the U.S. experience in the first half of the nineteenth century was consistent with the cross-country empirical studies.[3] States with more banking facilities per capita in 1830 experienced greater rates of economic growth up to 1860 than states with less-developed banking sectors. While the state-level evidence was consistent with the so-called convergence hypothesis—that wealthier states grow more slowly and poorer states grow more quickly so that per capita income should converge through time—it also showed that more financially deep economies, which also tended to be the wealthier economies, grew faster.[4] Consider just the 1850s. A 10 percent increase in the initial stock of money per capita in 1850 increased the annual average rate of real economic growth over the decade by 41.3 percent. Alternatively, a 10 percent increase in the initial stock of bank loans per capita increased the annual average rate of real growth over the decade by 23.4 percent.

In this instance, modern economic and statistical techniques have uncovered a process appreciated, if only abstractly, by contemporary observers and commentators. Writing in 1831, Nathan Appleton provided a prescient statement of the link between finance and economic development. "Bank capital," wrote Appleton, "consists of money, which the proprietors do not choose to employ themselves, but have established a fund, to be employed by the active and enterprising classes of society. It is thus placed where those classes can command it, at their pleasure. Abundance of such capital is, in its highest degree, favorable to public prosperity, by exciting industry and extending trade."[5] While modern economists may disagree with some of Appleton's word choices, many are in broad agreement with his hypothesis, namely, that banks play a pivotal role in the process of economic development. Although some continue to question the importance of banks qua banks, they tend to agree with the broader proposition that financial services, more generally, have a role to play in economic development.

It is important, however, not to claim too much. While banking was pivotal, financial intermediation was not the wellspring of any country's, any region's, or any state's economic growth. A well-functioning financial sector may contribute to economic growth, but even a well-conceived and well-regulated financial sector will not overcome unfavorable resource endowments, low rates of human and physical capital accumulation, suboptimal population growth rates, low labor force participation rates, or inefficient and counterproductive government policies outside the financial sector. At the same time, even a poorly designed, inefficient financial sector will not bring an otherwise vibrant economy to a standstill. The early American experience is consistent with the notion that states that promoted financial development—through liberal chartering as in Massachusetts, through free banking as in New York, or through state-supported, broad-based branch banking as in Virginia—consistently experienced moderate to high rates of economic growth. Despite the seeming differences in these three states' approaches to bank chartering and regulation, the common thread was financial liberalism. When the public outcry for more banking facilities grew loud, these states allowed the sector to grow. Not all states followed this policy, and some paid a heavy price.

It is typically unwise to argue by example, but two examples stand out. After poor government policy choices in Pennsylvania in the 1810s and 1830s undermined the state's banking sector, the state effectively stopped chartering banks until the 1850s. As a result, Philadelphia's banks fell behind New York's in their ability to accommodate growing credit demands. There were a host of factors that led to New York displacing Philadelphia as the nation's financial and commercial center, but it is possible that lagging banking facilities played a part. Similarly, Louisiana's restrictive banking policies in the 1840s have been cited as a cause of the decline in the share of Mississippi and Ohio river basin produce moved through New Orleans and financed by New Orleans banks.[6] The steamboat, the Erie Canal, and the railroad all acted to redirect traffic away from New Orleans and toward New York, but declining credit facilities also influenced trade patterns.

This book will not explicitly consider the connection between financial development and economic growth. I have covered that material elsewhere. Instead, this book explores regional differences in banking structures, which bear indirectly on the connection between financial and economic development.

To the extent that a single theme emerges from a work that considers regional differences, it is that the United States benefited from its free banking philosophy. Although I adopt the term "free banking," it should not be confused with free banking in the sense that Austrian economists, such as Lawrence White and George Selgin, and others use the term.[7] They have in mind a very specific set of laissez-faire conditions, facilitating the emergence of a spontaneous order of inside and outside money. Austrian free banking theorists assume that the government defines neither the unit of account nor the medium of exchange. Both arise endogenously from the free contracting between banks and their customers. Early American banks, no matter how liberal the chartering requirements, were not free banks in this sense. The federal government defined the base money (gold and silver) and the unit of account (the dollar). State legislatures required and courts enforced dollar-denominated bank contracts. Banks unable or unwilling to redeem their banknotes in gold or silver were typically considered bankrupt and closed down. Banks and banknote holders could not write legally enforceable contracts in something other than the government-defined base money.

Within the narrower U.S. context, *free banking* is generally used to refer to a very specific set of legal conditions for opening a bank defined by a New York state law of 1838. Under the terms of the 1838 law, a prospective banker could open a bank wherever and whenever he chose once he registered with the state comptroller and deposited a specified quantity of state or federal bonds as a guarantee against fraud and failure. Instead of free banking, a better description of this process would be "bond-secured note issue" banking, which admittedly flows less trippingly off the tongue. Regardless of the term used to describe it, New York's law proved versatile, exportable, and popular, and some variant was eventually adopted in 21 states.

As I use the term here, I have in mind neither of these narrow constructions of free banking and I use it only because there is no good synonym. I use free banking to reflect the workings of the early American Madisonian polity, in which state governments ceded as little power to the federal government as seemed practicable. This decentralized federalism provided state legislatures with a great deal of flexibility in their approach to economic issues. Individual states decided whether or not to underwrite the construction of basic infrastructure (e.g., roads, canals, harbor clearing, banks). If a state's citizens decided that the state might have a role, then they were free to define the limits. Thus, Massachusetts and Rhode Island chartered banks liberally, but they tended not to take an activist role. Neither provided much capital to new banks, neither put insinuative government officials onto the boards of directors of banks, and neither state offered any implicit guarantees to the banks' customers. In Virginia, the state provided one-fifth of the Bank of Virginia's initial capital, appointed directors, and inspected the books, but it left most of the decisions to the board of directors elected by the private shareholders. Kentucky, Tennessee, Illinois, and others stepped in when private investors would not and formed wholly state-owned banks, which provided banking services as the state endeavored to attract settlers and push the frontier westward.

Thus, this book is a study of the financial experimentation that took place in the United States between 1790 and 1860. Some experiments succeeded; others failed. The important lesson to be learned from this history is not that some bad ideas, which caused financial hardship for some, were adopted. Rather, it is that there was no one best banking system. Where branch banking succeeded in Virginia, it failed in Alabama. Bond-secured note issue succeeded in New York, but it failed in Michigan and Minnesota. A state-owned bank thrived in South Carolina; another imploded in Illinois. The lesson—one that is important for modern developing countries who may too quickly attempt to imitate the banking structures of the developed world—is that a successful banking system is one that is flexible, predictable, and incentive-compatible; one that meets the needs of borrowers, depositors, and shareholders; and one that reduces downside risks to a generally agreed-upon level. This implies that we cannot a priori define an optimal, one-size-fits-all banking system. We need to know something about the formal and informal institutions underlying an economy and something about the risk preferences of its citizenry.

Historically, outsiders view Americans as experimenters and risk takers. Nowhere is that more apparent than in their early banking policies.

Plan of the Work

Chapter 2 turns to the establishment and governance of early American banks. Early banks could not legally open for business until they received a charter from a state legislature. After the American Revolution, there was a large, pent-up, derived demand for investment funds and banks seemed a good way to supply them. High demand for loanable funds, and low supply, meant that the profit potential was great. Legislators recognized this and used it to their own, and sometimes the state's, advantage. The chartering process became a method of rent extraction. For those aspiring bankers capable or fortunate enough to get a charter, the issue was establishing a corporate structure that met public demands for credit, legislative demands for transparency, and shareholder demands for accountability and profitability. In response, banks developed simple but effective corporate hierarchies to channel instructions down and information up the chain of command. Chapter 2 uses the modern theory of the firm and principles of corporate finance to show that bankers built relatively sophisticated corporate structures that mitigated numerous principal-agent problems. In general, compensation policies and managerial practices aligned officer and shareholder incentives.

Chapter 3 then sheds light on several long-unanswered questions: What did early American banks do on a daily basis? How did they lend? Too whom did they lend? For how long? And, what sorts of projects did they finance? Most interpretations of the period emphasize the so-called real-bills doctrine. The doctrine held that banks should lend only to the most creditworthy borrowers and only at very short terms, generally 30 to 60 days. The premise underlying this theory was that people who had met their previous commitments to whom the banks made loans would meet the banks' commitments. Traditional studies recognize that many early U.S. banks did not slavishly follow real-bills prescriptions, and they scold them for not doing so. Chapter 3 agrees with the traditional histories in that early banks did not adhere to strict real-bills policies, but it offers a different, more sanguine, interpretation of the banks' choices. Early American banks were socially beneficial engines of growth precisely because they violated the precepts of the doctrine. Bankers were just as innovative and entrepreneurial as leaders in other sectors and they underwrote and financed industrial experimentation.

While chapters 2 and 3 draw a portrait of a typical antebellum bank in broad strokes, chapters 4 through 10 fill in the details of regional differentiation in state banking. Chapters 4 and 5 chronicle the development of state banking in New England from its colonial antecedents through the Civil War. Chapter 4 discusses recently emphasized features of the region's banks: their small size and familial organization. New England banks were not impersonal dispensers of credit in anonymous markets. Rather, they were formed by and served as the financial arms to extended kinship networks of artisans, traders, and manufacturers.

Chapter 5 then offers a new interpretation of the other defining characteristic of New England's banking structure: the Suffolk system. The Suffolk Bank of Boston operated a regional clearinghouse for banknotes, thereby facilitating the use of currency in trade. While traditional interpretations emphasize the benefits accruing to the public from the operation of the system, chapter 5 shows that the Suffolk used intimidation and coercion to put and keep the clearing system in place. The system is analyzed using modern theories of networks, including the inherent externalities of increased membership and appropriate pricing rules. Because the Suffolk mis-priced its services, an alternative network was established and the system collapsed.

Chapters 6 through 8 highlight the notable features of banking in the Middle Atlantic region. Chapter 6 discusses American banking's inauspicious beginnings. America's first commercial bank, the Bank of North America, was chartered by the Continental Congress to assist war finance. After the war, the bank came under attack in the Pennsylvania legislature, its charter was revoked, and the bank nearly removed to Wilmington, Delaware. Within a short time, its charter was restored, but Pennsylvania chartered a rival institution. The political antagonism surrounding the charter mongering that took place in Middle Atlantic state houses expressed itself in cutthroat competition in Philadelphia, New York City, and Baltimore. Economists generally view such competition favorably, but it inhibited these banks from cooperating in the face of common threats. Distrust inhibited the establishment of clearinghouses until the 1850s. Moreover, state demand for credit and the insistence that banks finance the construction of canals and other internal improvement projects undermined bank stability and placed them in harm's way during economic downturns.

Chapter 7 offers a fresh interpretation of the New York Safety Fund, America's first experiment in bank liability insurance. The panic of 1819 and the wave of bank failures that followed induced legislators to seek out alternatives to shareholder liability as a means of protecting noteholders and depositors from losses due to bank failure. New York legislators debated several proposals between 1819 and 1827 before they finally settled on the suggestion of a Syracuse lawyer. While the legislature did not accept the details of his mutual guaranty system, it established a coinsurance scheme similar to the modern Federal Deposit Insurance Corporation. Each bank paid insurance premiums to a common fund from which noteholders of failed banks were reimbursed. The safety fund was innovative and ahead of its time in some regards, but the system collapsed just nine years after its establishment when 11 banks failed in rapid succession. Using many of the insights developed in studies of the savings and loan crisis of the 1980s and the failure of the Federal Savings and Loan Insurance Corporation in 1989, chapter 7 shows that the safety fund's bankruptcy resulted from a host of contributing factors, including excessive risk-taking, adverse selection, fraud, and inadequate supervisory oversight.

Free banking may be the most discussed feature of early American banking. On one side, free banking is seen as the culmination of radical laissez-faire philosophies that influenced mid-nineteenth-century business policy. While free and open competition may be appropriate in other lines of business, it can be and usually is disastrous when allowed in banking markets. The other side views free entry and open competition in banking in the same favorable light as competition in every other industry. Chapter 8 traces the political and intellectual development of the free banking debate. It then turns to modern interpretations. The evidence shows that the U.S. experience can be interpreted to support either position, depending on the period focused on. Free banking created a sort of gold-rush mentality in 1837 Michigan and 1838 New York. Massive entry was followed by widespread failure. Later experience, however, was generally more favorable. After 1845, failure rates among free banks fell dramatically and occurred at about the same rate as traditionally chartered banks. The remainder of chapter 8 highlights the modern debate and provides new interpretations of the period, including discussions of the so-called note-issue paradox and the perverse seasonality of note issues that also appeared during the post–Civil War National Banking Era. Because postbellum federal banking law was modeled on New York's antebellum free banking laws, it is not surprising that bankers in both eras faced similar incentives.

Chapters 9 and 10 constitute the final substantive section of the book. The former details the development of banking in the South and West. Although these two regions were culturally distinct, they adopted similar banking policies. In both regions, banks received large state subsidies, they became embroiled in various public infrastructure projects, and they operated in accordance with what historians have labeled the "commonwealth ideal." That is, banks were expected to promote social welfare and the common good. The final section of chapter 9 reinterprets the commonwealth ideal in economic terms. Building on the seminal insights of Joseph Schumpeter and Alexander Gerschenkron, the chapter shows that southern and western banks were designed to help late-developing economies catch up with early developers. A secondary role of these institutions was to insulate the regional economy from the potentially devastating effects of financial panics, extended recessions, and debt-deflation cycles. In effect, these banks reinflated depressed economies, which slowed or stemmed a rising tide of personal and business bankruptcy.

Chapter 10 then details the defining features of southern and western banking systems. It turns first to the so-called plantation banks of the Deep South. In an effort to encourage immigration and commercial agriculture, these state-subsidized banks simultaneously monetized agricultural economies and provided long-term mortgage credit for farm purchase and improvement. In the end, this experiment failed, but not as much from of an inherent inconsistency between the two objectives as from bad timing. Six of seven plantation banks, with a combined capital in excess of $20 million, were established in the mid-1830s and had inadequate opportunity to establish themselves on a sound footing before the panics of 1837 and 1839 devolved into an extended commercial depression. The chapter then turns to a discussion of these regions' notable banking import, namely, free banking. In general, the western experience with free banking was not as good as New York's, but it was not as bad as some earlier writers suggested either. Banks failed, and this section offers a critical assessment of several competing theories. The final section of chapter 10 discusses how branch banking promoted financial stability. Where the large number of small unit banks in the northeastern United States inhibited the formation of effective mutual guaranty coalitions, the small number of large branch banks in the South and West encouraged the establishment of such coalitions. There was, however, an arduous learning process. New evidence shows that interbank coalitions formed in the late 1830s were neither as effective nor as stable as those formed in the late 1850s. The lessons learned in the earlier period translated to success 20 years later.

Finally, chapter 11 places the U.S. banking system within the context of the early nineteenth-century macroeconomy. The available evidence shows that banking services grew in accordance with overall growth in the economy. One exception was the mid-1830s, when a speculative wave poured over the United States and banking grew faster than most economic indicators. High credit demand drove up bank profitability, which induced entry and increased bank capital and specie leverage ratios. The bubble burst when actions at the Bank of England sharply drove up short-term interest rates, which diminished bank profitability and pushed some into insolvency. After 1843, bank lending and private investment moved together up to the outbreak of the Civil War. Federal policy during the war, particularly the National Banking Acts of 1863 and 1864, rationalized U.S. banking structure and diminished the importance of state banking and the differences inherent in a decentralized federalism.

2

Establishment and Governance of the Antebellum Bank

The effects of information asymmetries and risk on financial contracts have been evident since the first banks were formed in the United States. The influences of information and risk problems, in fact, weighed heavily in the creation of the banks themselves, the forms they took, and their internal structures. In the late eighteenth and early nineteenth centuries, corporations represented a financial innovation, a significant break with the well-known individual money lender and private banker. Few knew what the immediate consequences of incorporation would be; even fewer could have envisioned the sweeping changes that widespread incorporation would bring to finance and industry.

Contemporaries were thus wary, perhaps justly, of the corporation. It was given life independent of its creators. Its organizers and initial stockholders could come and go, live and die, succeed and fail, and the bank continued without them. The corporate firm was ceded some of the more important rights of the individual, like the right to sue and be sued in its own name, but it was given rights not available to proprietorships and partnerships, the most obvious being limited liability and perpetual life.

Partly as a result of these concerns, Americans placed heavy restrictions on their earliest corporations. The state had to authorize and license them, and it did so by way of a charter. Before potential shareholders could establish a corporate bank, they first had to convince a legislature of the merit of their proposal, demonstrate their commitment to the project, and produce evidence of their capabilities as bankers. These were not easy tasks and only a small proportion of charter requests were ever granted.

Despite the reservations of many and the several hurdles placed in the path of potential corporate bankers, quite a few commercial banks were chartered. In 1790, there were three—one each in Philadelphia, Boston, and Baltimore—by all accounts progressive, commercially active entrepôts. By 1835, there were 584; large cities may have had a dozen or more, small towns two or three, and not a few crossroad villages had their own bank. All this activity suggests that contemporaries, while wary of potential corporate excesses, recognized the powerful wealth-generating possibilities of the corporation.

Corporations tapped the savings of many, accumulated capitals larger than those that even the wealthiest would have risked in a single enterprise, and operated on a scale not captured by any partnership. The wealth-creating potential of a commercial bank far exceeded that of any other contemporary enterprise.

But with its immense size and great promise, the corporate bank arrived with a host of new threats and organizational problems. So large a firm, relatively speaking, might deceive and defraud on a grand scale. As we shall see in later chapters, however, individual cases of fraudulent behavior were infrequent; widespread fraud was downright rare. Thus, the underlying structure of internal and external incentives facing contemporary banking firms must have aligned the bankers' and the public's interests.

The first part of this chapter outlines the intricate, arcane, and sometimes inefficient legislative procedures bankers were forced to navigate before they were granted a license to operate. While the system was flawed in some respects, its ultimate purpose was to ensure that bankers had an incentive to actually provide the services they promised. The second section shows that committed bankers demonstrated their commitment in numerous ways. They developed the first truly hierarchical, internal managerial structures to limit managerial opportunism. A hierarchical structure protected not only the shareholders, but also the public from managerial shirking and dishonesty. The second section also shows how spontaneously arising markets helped control bank behavior and, in so doing, how they aligned managerial, shareholder, and debt holder incentives. The monitoring of bank managers, then, devolved not just to legislative oversight committees, but to a host of market participants, including bank employees, shareholders, and the public. In effect, America's earliest banks developed internal and external practices that addressed a host of corporate governance issues.

Getting Started

Obtaining a Charter

Before a bank's managers could settle down to the task of running a bank, its promoters faced the often slippery business of obtaining a charter (a license to operate). Because charters were granted by state legislatures, obtaining one hinged on the promoters' political clout. Aspiring bankers needed the support of one or more legislators willing to shepherd an authorizing act through a byzantine committee system. Sometimes even constant attention by a diligent legislator did not guarantee success.

With most legislative sessions swamped with charter petitions, committee members weeded through them to determine which, if any, were deserving. "[I]t is the duty of the Legislature," said one contemporary, "to ascertain by competent testimony, whether the amount of business and capital in the place where the bank is to be established, are such, as to require the accommodation; and above all, whether those who ask the privilege, are men of unsuspected character."[1]

Even deserving bank promoters had no assurance that their petition would be viewed favorably by either the committee or the legislative body as a whole. Sectional and partisan disputes often flared up during discussions on authorizing acts and more often determined the proponent's fate than ability or merit. Throughout the antebellum era, skill at navigating political waters remained key in obtaining a charter. Banks, as organizations, were believed to harbor and act on the party sympathies of both their promoters and the legislative majority at the time the charter act was passed. Many believed that banks accommodated only those of similar political persuasion. Some banks actually behaved that way.

Proposed banks, too, were expected to claim allegiances and many were formed expressly in response to preferences (real and imagined) shown by existing banks. In 1803 Philadelphia, young Republican merchants complained that the existing Federalist-controlled banks—the Bank of North America, the Pennsylvania Bank, and the First Bank of the United States—discriminated against them. In response, Philadelphia Republicans, then in possession of a legislative majority, formed their own.[2]

They took up $1 million in stock subscriptions to create the Philadelphia Bank and petitioned for a charter after the bank was all but a fait accompli. Fierce opposition to the interloper quickly arose. The existing banks argued that another was superfluous and would only impair their specie holdings, hence their strength and stability.[3] When that argument failed to move the legislature against the upstart bank, a rumor was circulated that the bank had fallen under the influence of Aaron Burr. Such animosity may have developed because the new bank was known to have Jeffersonian leanings and promised to upset the established Federalist mercantile aristocracy by providing credit to Republican merchants. It was more likely that a new bank simply threatened the profits of the existing oligopoly.

Pennsylvania was not alone in its uncomfortable marriage of banks and politics. The Browns of Providence, Rhode Island, had chartered the Providence Bank in 1791 and were the only bankers in the city until 1800. In that year, a potential competitor (to be named the Exchange Bank) petitioned the legislature for a charter. The Browns fought the charter and considered punishing the Exchange Bank's promoters by calling their outstanding loans. Once they realized the new bank's charter was inevitable, the

Browns backed off to avoid open warfare. Their reputation and economic clout notwithstanding, the Browns' attempt to quash the upstart failed because they were Federalists, and the Republican "tone of the state government at that time was not favorable to them."[4]

Although the federal government did not charter banks (except the First and Second Banks of the United States), federal politics also affected a would-be banker's prospects. In 1803, the Roger Williams Bank was chartered in Rhode Island and it, too, was known to harbor Republican dispositions. Although he generally held banks in low regard, President Thomas Jefferson wrote the following to Treasury Secretary Albert Gallatin: "as to the patronage of the republican [Roger Williams] bank in Providence, I am decidedly in favor of making all the banks republican by sharing [government] deposits amongst them in proportion to the dispositions they show."[5] While the benefits of aligning a bank with an administration were potentially large, the costs could be too. In return for its deposits, the federal treasury expected reciprocation when it came calling for loans. Recognizing the quid pro quo conditions, only three Rhode Island banks were brought into Gallatin's fold.[6]

If political savvy or personal clout could not elicit a charter, there were more pedestrian methods of acquiring it. One was surreptitious bribery of one or more influential legislators; another was to exploit chronic budgetary concerns and, in effect, overtly bribe the entire legislature.

During the 1833 Ohio General Assembly session, a group petitioned for a bank to be called the Franklin Bank of Cincinnati. A letter from a legislator to one of the petitioners revealed a thinly disguised bribe. "[I]f the 'people' will only attend to my notes [debts]," he informed one of the bank's promoters, "I assure them that they shall have the best of my exertions here . . . at least until the fate of the Franklin Bank is decided."[7]

Ohio's legislative assembly was certainly not the only one to give in to blatant charter mongering. New York's assembly was involved in several unseemly chartering shenanigans. The charters of the State Bank of Albany (1803), the Merchants' Bank of New York City (1805), and the Bank of America of New York City (1812) were all tainted by "especially scandalous" corruption.[8] The Merchants' Bank scandal represented perhaps the most audacious assault on sometimes loose legislative morals. Agents for the bank literally patrolled the halls of assembly, eavesdropped on committee debates on the charter, and promised favors to garner support.[9] Three legislators were promised shares in the new bank with the guarantee that they would be quickly repurchased at 25 percent over par. Another was authorized to subscribe 30 shares and promised an advance of £5 (about $25) on each. Yet another was offered 50 shares with a promise that they would be repurchased whenever he chose, with a guarantee of at least a $1,000 profit. All the activity surrounding the chartering bills raised such partisan acrimony that one of the bill's opponents physically attacked one of its advocates in the assembly chamber. Once the extent of the bribery became public, the governor prorogued the assembly and the attorney general was instructed to prosecute all those involved. Only one charge of perjury was ever brought before a grand jury, however, and that case was dismissed.

In other instances, prospective bankers openly bribed the entire legislature with the promise of a chartering "bonus." In return for a charter, these banks promised to fill the state treasury, sometimes with a onetime payment, sometimes with a promise to lend at preferential rates, sometimes by ceding a block of shares to the state so that it would reap a stream of dividends. Southern legislators typically preferred the latter two options. Virginia chartered the Bank of Virginia in January 1804; the state reserved the right to subscribe to one-fifth ($300,000) of its shares, and the bank was required to underwrite the subscription by lending the state its $300,000 capital subscription.[10] Subsequent charters were less generous. Instead of reserving the right to buy shares at a discount, Virginia demanded them gratis. The Farmers Bank of Virginia, chartered in 1812, ceded 3,334 shares to the state, and most later charters contained similar provisions.[11]

Bribery on this scale offends modern sensibilities, tainting early bank charters and making these banks' promoters appear nefarious and their motives sinister. Contemporary partisans on both sides of the aisle exploited this appearance when it served their purposes. Bray Hammond argued that the Jeffersonian banking impetus grew out of the Federalist character of many early banks.[12] Republicans claimed that the Federalist banks were tainted by bribery, corruption, and charter mongering. But because these charters were irrevocable, the best the Republicans could do was charter their own partisan banks, which, of course, elicited Federalist howls of protest.

Even if corruption and charter mongering forced both sides to the transaction into legal and moral gray areas, the resulting organizations may best be judged not by their beginnings but by their subsequent actions. If the only way a prospective banker could get a foothold was to grease the legislative wheels, so much the better for society's borrowers that he did so. Moreover, if the bank ultimately grew into a creditable and creditworthy institution, everyone benefited.

Naomi Lamoreaux and Christopher Glaisek found that younger men who promoted banks in the 1830s had, by the 1860s, accumulated taxable wealth rivaling that of the old guard in charge of the older elite banks.[13] These were not shady characters opening fly-by-night organizations. Besides, many of these new banks grew as large and as respectable as their older rivals once the political brouhaha surrounding their charters drifted from memory. Later generations of borrowers benefited because an earlier generation of bankers engaged in some graft.

The sheer size of the bribes and bonuses and the eagerness with which they were handed out demonstrated the profits to be had in banking, especially for the first to obtain a charter in a community. Existing banks often countered lobbying efforts by potential rivals by offering bonuses in return for not chartering another—a measure, perhaps, of the discounted value of expected future monopoly profits. More often than not, however, upstarts outbid their future rivals for the right to compete.

If entry into banking had been as free as it was into textiles or flour milling, any entrepreneur correctly perceiving an opportunity in banking would have been rewarded with profits—monopoly profits if he was the only one willing or able to exploit the opportunity. The persistence of these profits, however, would quickly attract entry, which would benefit consumers through increased output and lower prices and result in diminished profits for the incumbent banker.

Entry was not free. Because a charter required a license from the state, the person obtaining one was not necessarily the best banker. Rather, he was the most persuasive lobbyist. It is not clear that these two skills overlapped. This was one potential source of inefficiency in banking. Unless the best lobbyist and the best banker were one and the same, the bank might fail to capture any available technical efficiencies. Furthermore, with limited competition, an X-inefficient banker faced few incentives to change. Licensing-induced rent seeking provided at least some communities with inefficient banks.[14]

In the limiting case, rent seeking costs could be substantial. If, for example, a group of prospective bankers believed that the discounted net present value of the stream of monopoly profits from banking was $1 million, each applicant would have invested an amount marginally less than the product of the probability of receiving the monopoly grant and the discounted stream of monopoly rents in obtaining a charter.[15] If there were ten applicants, each with an equal probability of obtaining the charter, each would spend up to $100,000, and the expected monopoly rents would be completely expended in the race to obtain the property right.

Clearly, the winner benefited because he spent only $100,000 to get the rights to an expected $1 million, but the players as a group spent $1 million to obtain $1 million. Society was no better off because the expected net social return was zero. Events in New York in 1836 seem consistent with this model of rent seeking. The legislature received 93 petitions for bank charters; only 12 were granted. Surely, the 81 unsuccessful petitioners spent significant amounts in their unsuccessful lobbying activities.

A second potential source of inefficiency arose when a banker was given an initial right to provide intermediary services for a given community then discovered too late that the right was not ceded in perpetuity. English tradition held that when Parliament granted a monopoly right, they rarely infringed on it.[16] United States practice in this regard represented yet another break from English tradition.

In the United States, what the state gave, the state very often took away. Recognizing this proclivity among legislators, aspiring bankers rarely allowed an incumbent banker to enjoy his monopoly uncontested. Prospective bankers offered numerous enticements for the state to abrogate its previous monopoly grant. Incumbent banks were then forced to revisit a battle previously won. Each round of charter petitions elicited new rounds of rent seeking so that potentially much more than $1 million could be spent in an effort to capture the $1 million in rents.

The case of the Philadelphia Bank demonstrates both the amounts played for and the potential for waste. When the Philadelphia Bank petitioned the legislature for a charter in December 1803, its prospects were grim. The state already held a significant share in the Pennsylvania Bank and several legislators feared, as the Pennsylvania Bank's managers contended, that chartering a new bank would impair the state's existing financial interests. To allay these fears, the Philadelphia Bank offered several alternative "bonus" schemes. The one finally agreed on consisted of a $135,000 cash gratuity, an exchange of $300,000 in its stock for depreciated U.S. 6 percent bonds, the right to purchase an additional $200,000 in capital at par after four years and a similar amount after eight years, and an obligation to lend the state $100,000 at 5 percent for up to ten years.[17] All this from a bank with a capital of just $1.3 million.[18]

To derail the charter of the Philadelphia Bank, the Pennsylvania Bank made a series of increasingly generous offers to the state. It first offered a $100,000 interest-free loan to be repaid in depreciated U.S. 6 percents. Its final offer was a sweeping package estimated to have been worth $440,000. Even this amount failed to sway the legislature, and the Philadelphia Bank was chartered in January 1804.

Although legislative chartering, and the rent seeking that attended it, generated inefficiencies, it also served a potentially useful purpose. The state's principal concern was devising a mechanism that minimized the banker's incentives to cheat and defraud the public. In medieval Europe, for example, it was not unusual to execute a failed banker after his assets had been confiscated and turned over to his creditors.[19]

Threats of execution may have induced good behavior, but positive reinforcements tend to be more effective at eliciting sought-after behavior than negative consequences. One such inducement was to promise the banker a stream of economic rents as long as he behaved. By restricting competition, the state created monopoly or oligopoly rents that remained available only as long as the banker remained in business. This gave the banker the incentive to behave if the discounted value of the rents exceeded the short-term benefits of absconding. Recognizing the banker's incentive, the public was willing to hold the banker's notes and deposits, thereby encouraging the expansion of the financial sector.

Furthermore, the state, having brought about a transfer from depositors (in lower interest rates on deposits) and borrowers (higher loan rates) to the banker, seized some of those rents and transferred them back to the public. Taxes, dividends, or bonuses paid into the state treasury by banks were ultimately expended in some other pursuit. Clearly, in the absence of information asymmetries and with costless enforcement mechanisms, less costly transfer mechanisms could have been devised. But information asymmetries and costly enforcement mechanisms were the rule, so it is not clear that a readily superior method of simultaneously inducing good behavior and augmenting the state's coffers existed.

Subscribing Shares and Paying in Capital

Having navigated the political currents, entrepreneurs next faced the challenge of organizing their bank: selling shares, sitting a board of directors, hiring a management team, and resolving a host of corporate governance issues.

Selling shares seemed a relatively straightforward process. Most charters required that a newly chartered bank open subscription books at convenient places—taverns, coffee houses, city halls, and existing banks being the most popular—where prospective investors could record their name and the number of shares desired. If more than the available number of shares were subscribed, the largest subscribers had their allocations reduced so that share ownership could be spread as widely as possible.

Many states, too, attempted to democratize bank ownership by limiting stockholder votes. Typically, owners of five or fewer shares retained one vote per share. Those owning more than five shares were awarded one vote for each of the first five shares and one vote for each additional five shares, so an owner of 35 shares could cast 11 votes. Charter regulations and bylaws often imposed a maximum number of votes as well.

Limiting clauses served two purposes: to provide a disincentive for bank shares to fall into a few hands; and to limit the relative power of large shareholders if they did. If successful, these restrictions could undermine what might have otherwise been an effective corporate governance mechanism. The most direct method of aligning management and control is to concentrate share holdings, either with one majority shareholder or with a handful of minority shareholders with relatively large stakes.[20] Substantial minority shareholders reduce the classic free rider problem because they have incentives to collect information and monitor management as most of the benefits of monitoring accrue to the monitors themselves rather than to a group of dispersed shareholders. Large shareholders, argue Andrei Shleifer and Robert Vishny, improve managerial behavior because large shareholders not only desire profit maximization, but they have "enough control over the assets of the firm to have their interests respected."[21]

Diluting the voting rights of large shareholders, as early bank charters did, undermined shareholder control and managerial monitoring. Majority ownership was effective only to the extent that the voting mechanism worked so that the majority could come together, form alliances, and exercise control over management. Again, with a single majority shareholder, there was little wiggle room. His dictates were followed or the managers were punished. With large minority shareholders, matters were complicated because managers may have been able to interfere with the formation of effective alliances. Moreover, once a coalition was formed, management could play one faction against another, thereby reducing its effectiveness in monitoring and policing managerial behavior.[22]

Although limiting the voting rights and control powers of large shareholders reduced potential monitoring gains, limiting voting rights also reduced the possibility that large shareholders could control the firm at the expense of small shareholders, managers, creditors, and employees.[23] The potential for large shareholders to direct bank funds to pet projects, regardless of underlying merit, increased the probability of bank failure and reduced the willingness of the public to hold the bank's debt. Additionally, overly close supervision and the possibility of abrupt dismissal may have meant that there were fewer expected firm-specific rents for managers and employees and therefore diminished incentives to invest in firm-specific human capital. Finally, if large shareholders could expropriate returns at the expense of small shareholders, incentives to invest were reduced, shrinking the pool of savings (or external finance) available to the firm.

Thus, legislators faced a tradeoff with only normative reasons for preferring one type of bank ownership to the other a priori. On one hand, encouraging dispersed ownership and restricting voting rights reduced the likelihood that a bank would fall under the control of one or a few self-seeking shareholders that might defraud the public. On the other, it reduced incentives to monitor managerial behavior. Such structures deserve more theoretical attention, but it is possible that legislators weighed these incentives and developed voting schemes that, they believed, would equalize the costs at the margin.

Despite concerted efforts to encourage dispersed share ownership, many, perhaps even most, banks fell into the hands of a few shareholders. Although some historians contend that bank stock was the favored investment for guardians, trustees, and widows, the simple fact was that stock ownership was beyond the means of most early nineteenth-century Americans.[24] Early bank shares typically had a par value of $400 or $500 (and often sold at a 10 to 20 percent premium). In addition, investing in one of the earliest banks required some degree of courage because these were largely unknown and untested enterprises.

It was not until the end of the antebellum era that the early nineteenth-century vision of widespread bank share ownership was approached, even approximately. Rhode Island's experience, while not completely representative, was indicative of the general trend. Shares in the Providence Bank (the state's oldest) had a par value of $400.[25] Most of the banks formed in the next two or three decades had par values of $100. By the 1840s and 1850s, however, par values declined to as little as $25, opening up share ownership to the middle class. Despite this trend, wealthy merchants still provided the bulk of bank capital.

The wealth and social prominence of bank stockholders notwithstanding, few banks opened with their capital subscriptions fully paid in. Typically paid in installments, a bank's capital was raised over a period of one to four years. The practice of paying in a corporation's capital in installments dated back at least to 1613 and the charter of the English East India Company.[26] The company's £100 shares were payable in four equal installments. Paying capital in installments offered at least four benefits. First, the arrangement committed investors and provided a schedule for cash infusions, which would generate confidence in the company's ability to meet its obligations. Second, the practice encouraged investors to plow back early profits in anticipation of future calls. Third, it allowed subscribers to limit their exposure in the event that the firm failed early.

The fourth, and perhaps the most important, benefit of installment payments was that capital could be raised by tapping the savings of the upper-middle class of artisans and merchants of modest means. Few individuals could afford a $100 share, fewer still a $400 one, but many could afford four annual or semiannual payments of $25. Allowing investors to pay for their shares over an extended period benefited both parties. More people were given an opportunity to effectively diversify their portfolios, and the bank was able to tap a larger pool of savings.

Par values, installment amounts, and payment schedules represented a balancing act, reflecting the promoter's preferred shareholder profile and the need to attract capital. Two monthly installments of $50 might attract the right kind of shareholder, but too few of them. On the other hand, a schedule of 20 installments of $5 might get the banker into previously untapped pools of savings, but it might also attract unsuitable shareholders. Moreover, such an easy policy could unleash a speculative frenzy, which occurred with John Law's Compagnie des Indes.[27] An initial investment of only 10 percent with the remainder payable in 19 monthly installments evoked a rush of investment from all classes. Aristocrats and their valets were caught up in a speculative frenzy that ended with the bursting of the South Sea Bubble.

Another potential shortcoming of the installment procedure was that it was not uncommon for subscribers to pay their first installment in specie with subsequent calls paid in heavily depreciated government bonds or promissory notes drawn by the stockholder on the bank itself (so-called stock notes). Using the subscribed shares as collateral, the shareholder borrowed from the bank to pay the calls designed to provide the bank with its capital.

Critics claimed that the use of stock notes undermined the very premise of capital itself, namely, the protection of the bank's creditors in the event of its failure. In 1824, Maine's bank commissioners found that 65 percent of the Bangor Bank's capital was made up of stock notes; the Bath Bank, 80 percent; the Hallowell and Augusta Bank, 43 percent; the Kennebec Bank, 76 percent; the Passamaquoddy, 67 percent; and the Waterville Bank, 82 percent.[28] Even though critics had little difficulty in uncovering the use and potential abuse of stock notes, Gallatin argued that their use was "extremely rare."[29]

Like the public generally, state bank commissioners were ambivalent toward the use of stock notes. In 1831, New York bank commissioners believed the practice dangerous. "It was a common thing," they reported, "to put a bank in operation upon a small part of its capital being paid in."[30] The perceived danger, of course, was that the bank's capital was generated through its own (fictitious) credit rather than firmly established by a vault full of specie. It was feared that this practice allowed men of limited means and dubious character (the bank commissioners thought the two groups nearly coincident) to abuse the practice, take control of a weak bank, and practice fraud upon its shareholders and the public.

In 1835, a different group of commissioners held a different opinion. "[T]here can be no objection," they wrote, "to the loan of moderate amounts in anticipation of funds not immediately available, by persons who are able and intending to hold the stock."[31] Without the records of individual banks to expose the extent of the use of stock notes, we will never know just how widespread it was. In 1836, the bank commissioners continued to discuss their use, noting simply that it had "sometimes" been done.[32]

Other states imposed various restrictions to reduce the use of stock notes, but most proved ineffective. Some states required paying in at least one half of the bank's capital before it could begin lending. The charter of the Nantucket Bank was typical of others in that it forbade stockholder borrowing until the capital was fully paid in.[33] In the 1850s, Massachusetts required all banks to hold at least one half of their capital as vault cash. Even this seemingly straightforward requirement was open to interpretation. One observer noted:

> Some years ago, when an out-of-town bank was about to go into operation, an acquaintance of mine, of high legal attainments as well as good sense, was appointed one of the commissioners to go through with what I must call the farce of counting the money, &c. As soon as finished, he saw preparations making to cart the money away again;— "but," he said, "this money is to remain in the bank as part of the capital." "Yes," said they, "but *our* vault is in the city"! [sic] In later days, no such excuses are made; the money is rolled in, and rolled out, and the law seems to be satisfied.[34]

Even had these varied attempts eliminated the use of stock notes, there was nothing to stop extensive shareholder borrowing once the capital was paid in.

Buying into a bank by way of stock notes, while subject to abuse, was not the unmitigated evil that some banking historians have made it out to be. The use of stock notes provided benefits that may well have outweighed their costs. In the early nineteenth century, specie was scarce, which forced banks to operate on something other than a pure specie (100 percent) reserve basis. Moreover, some contemporaries mistakenly believed that the capital, once paid in, remained as so much idle specie laying in the vault. It wasn't, nor should it necessarily have been.

Lamoreaux and Glaisek argue that banks became "vehicles of mobility."[35] Young entrepreneurs, strapped for cash, could establish a bank based on stock notes and provide credit primarily to themselves until their mercantile or manufacturing businesses generated the profits to pay off the stock notes. At this point, these bank shares no longer represented highly speculative securities. Rather, they became "a leading, possibly one of the best then available, investment grade securities."[36] Facing a ready market, the bank's promoters could then decide whether or not they preferred to maintain an interest in the organization.

Even Hammond praises the Yankee ingenuity of stock notes. He argues that complaints about their use were "unrealistic and inconsistent," given that they reflected American pragmatism in overcoming difficult problems.[37] If Americans had allowed the chronic shortage of capital and specie to impede the formation of banks, the circle of capital shortages and underdevelopment observed in so many other places would have operated in the United States. The pretense of paying capital was forgivable because it invited banking services that stimulated trade and growth.

Sitting a Board of Directors and Selecting Managers

Once subscriptions were taken and the capital paid, it was time to elect a board of directors and install a management team. Because many, if not most, shareholders were merchants, bank boards were overwhelmingly drawn from the merchant class.[38] It was widely held that directors should be "of undoubted credit, great experience, and extensive business."[39] Selecting established merchants was advantageous in that they understood current business practice, kept a watchful eye on the market, and were privy to the gossip circulating in the taverns and coffeehouses. Established and well-known merchants were, therefore, in a position to assess loan requests. "Such men," it was said, "would attract to [their bank] numerous customers like themselves."[40]

Although prominent merchants brought prestige to a new bank, making them directors came with costs. Because they rarely received direct compensation, they often took it in indirect ways. It was taken as a matter of course that bank directors, their families, their friends, and their business associates had first claim to a bank's resources.[41] As president of the Bank of the United States, Nicholas Biddle preferred to appoint well-to-do businessmen who traded on their own funds and rarely made use of bank credit. Biddle replaced board members who borrowed habitually. Small-town, state-chartered banks could rarely be as discriminating.

Another difficulty in making merchants directors was that their mercantile interests were taken more seriously than their board responsibilities. When the two conflicted, banking matters invariably took a back seat. The minute book of the Citizens Bank of Louisiana is replete with the president's complaints of poor attendance and the lack of quorums that delayed business. On 6 August 1838, five of thirteen directors in attendance resolved that "absent members be informed that the business of the Bank is delayed for want of a quorum and that they be invited to attend the meetings of the Board."[42] The invitation went unanswered, as only six directors attended the next regular meeting of the board. Only seven or eight directors made regular appearances.

The Massachusetts Bank of Boston faced similar problems. When it opened in 1784, the bank's bylaws designated seven of twelve directors a quorum. Within two years, the number required for a quorum was reduced to five; in 1809, it was further reduced to just three.[43] To N. S. B. Gras, this trend indicates that the bank had fallen under the influence of a small group of self-interested directors. It was just as likely that the changing quorum requirements were a pragmatic response to the chronic absence of directors and the board's need to conduct business.

We should not be overly harsh in assessing a director's failure to appear at board meetings. As Walter Bagehot notes, bank directors could not attend to the affairs of one organization while ignoring the affairs of another, principally their own.[44] If they ignored their own, they ran the "risk of ruin," and a ruined director would be dismissed from the board. A director's real function, then, was to bestow some of his own trustworthiness and creditworthiness to his bank. It was hoped that banks administered by men of high standing and good character would reflect these same traits.

With their mercantile experience, bank directors often knew about trade and commerce, but few qualified as entrepreneurial bankers. This is why Fritz Redlich claims that individual directors sometimes became influential, but boards as a whole rarely did.[45] Bagehot writes, "A board of upright and sensible merchants will always act according to what it considers 'safe' principles . . . according to the *received* maxims of the mercantile world then and there."[46] It would be extraordinary if merchants had developed informed and original insights into banking because banking was a specialized trade and few merchants were trained in it.

This deficiency was overcome by hiring specialized bank managers known as cashiers, who were trained in the business and who devoted their professional energies exclusively to bank management. As the first professional bank managers, most cashiers received their training through informal apprenticeships and on-the-job training. They often began as tellers, clerks, or bookkeepers and worked their way up through the ranks.

Redlich argues that the profession in America can very nearly be traced back to a single individual—Tench Francis, the first cashier of the Bank of North America, the first bank chartered in the United States.[47] When the Massachusetts Bank of Boston was preparing to open, it sent its head bookkeeper to Philadelphia to train under Francis while a director of the Philadelphia bank traveled to Boston to assist the Bostonians in their enterprise. Similarly, Alexander Hamilton sent William Seton to Philadelphia to train under Francis before he was made the cashier at the Bank of New York. Because the next generation of cashiers was drawn from the subordinate ranks at ongoing banks, the methods developed by Francis through trial and error were, with modifications to meet new times and different circumstances, widely adopted.

A cashier's duties included countersigning banknotes; observing and monitoring the conduct of subordinate employees; examining, usually daily, the cash accounts of the bank; taking in and recording loan requests; notifying loan applicants of the disposition of their requests; laying before the board of directors a current statement of all accounts when requested; corresponding with debtors, creditors, and other banks; and attending weekly meetings of the board of directors, sometimes acting as recording secretary. Cashiers spent their day attending to the bank's affairs. Many could not even escape the bank in the evening; some were allowed, others required, to live in quarters above the bank's offices.

The cashier's responsibilities placed him in a position of trust and temptation. The potential gains from fraud were substantial, especially if the board failed to be observant, something that was constantly complained of by contemporary critics. In 1837, Maine's bank commissioners claimed to have found a bank operated by the cashier with practically no board supervision.[48] Without proper supervision, the possibility for fraud increased.

Fraud, however, was relatively rare. The reasons were manifold. Morality and conscience were probably sufficient deterrents in most instances, but shareholders also required guarantee bonds from cashiers. Cases arose, of course, in which cashiers defrauded their institutions and slipped out under cover of darkness just prior to being discovered. But given that these cases were few and far between, early American banks must have solved at least some of the stickier corporate governance issues that still plague hierarchical organizations. The next section discusses the basic principles of corporate governance and how early banks applied these principles.

Issues of Corporate Governance

Internal Governance Systems: Theory

Use of the corporate form has been extensive and has generated enormous wealth in the United States. It has many benefits: Dividing equity claims into small shares facilitates the accumulation of much larger amounts of capital than relying on the capital of a few very wealthy people. Separating ownership from control also widens the pool of potential managers by inducing the emergence of a class of managers who specialize in running the firm while shareholders, specialize in risk bearing. Moreover, creating small-denomination shares simplifies investor diversification because investors can hold shares in many different firms. Finally, the emergence of thick markets enhances investor liquidity, which further stimulates demand. By reducing both systemic and liquidity risks, the corporate form lowers the cost of capital and promotes entrepreneurship.

The corporation, however, comes with costs. Since Adam Smith, economists have argued that markets punish inefficient behavior. Producers making shoddy products will lose out to producers who make quality products; sellers who cheat customers will lose out to honest sellers, and so on. But even Smith recognized that markets may not correct all inefficient behavior. Market failures in the form of monopolies, externalities, transactions costs, and information asymmetries are clear examples of the inefficacy of the market in certain instances. Another is that the market may not have much bearing on the internal operations of the firm itself, or it may affect them only with a substantial lag. Ronald Coase, in fact, shows us that firms are, by their very nature, mechanisms designed to avoid at least some costly market transactions and may thus be insulated from some punishments that the market might otherwise mete out.[49]

Thus, the corporate form generates agency costs that must be resolved. Coase's elegant argument notes that the firm grows until the relevant costs of markets and internal transactions are equalized. But the internalized costs discussed by Coase are internal to the firm, not to the people working in the firm. If those people within the firm all pursued their own objectives, trying to cheat and shirk to the fullest extent possible, "the productive efficiency of the firm would be deeply problematic."[50] Once we establish a firm capable of internalizing production and transaction costs, it has to be organized in such a way as to mitigate employee cheating, shirking, and other forms of self-interested behavior inconsistent with wealth creation or profit maximization.

An internal governance structure, then, must be one that resolves most of the issues markets would resolve if corporations were the atomistic firms of elementary economic theory. Those issues include: Who controls what? Who makes the decisions? Who defines the objectives? Who has the responsibilities to see that actions consistent with those decisions and objectives are taken? Who has claims against the assets and cash flows of the firm? How each of these questions is answered creates incentives for those people involved with or employed by the firm. The central concern of corporate governance is to align each party's incentives so that the firm will deploy its resources efficiently. At the same time, governance structures should not be so cumbersome as to inhibit timely decision making and action.[51]

An agency relationship is a contract under which one group (the principals) engage another group (the agents) to perform some service on the principals' behalf.[52] Effective performance of this service typically requires that the principals delegate at least some decision-making authority to the agents. If both groups are composed of self-interested utility maximizers, there is good reason to believe that the agents will sometimes pursue their own interests that directly conflict with the principals' interests. Principals can limit agents from straying too far from expected norms by establishing incentives and monitoring. In some instances, it may even benefit the agent to demonstrate his willingness to pursue the principals' interests by expending his own resources (bonding) to ensure his continued good behavior. The important point, however, is that these relationships are not costless. Developing and implementing incentive schemes, monitoring, and bonding are all costly activities. Even with incentives, monitoring, and bonding, some agents will still subordinate the principals' interests to their own.

Interpretations of the corporation dating back to Smith, but detailed in Adolph Berle and Gardiner Means's classic 1932 study, focus on the agency problems that arise when management control (agent) is effectively separated from ownership (principal).[53] Berle and Means insist that the interests of owners "most emphatically will not be served by a profit-seeking controlling group."[54] The controlling group is more likely to profit at the expense of the corporation than to make profits for it. Many economists still proceed from Berle and Means's characterization of the corporation.[55]

Recent interpretations of the corporation, like those of Eugene Fama, Fama and Michael Jensen, Frank Easterbrook, and others, accept the effective separation of management and ownership, but they begin from a slightly different premise.[56] Instead of asserting the possibility of a classic entrepreneur, their models see the firm as a locus of contracts between naturally separate groups of managers and risk bearers, with the firm directly and its managers indirectly disciplined through internal competition among managers for advancement, through direct external competition with other firms, and through indirect external competition with management teams ready to replace shirking incumbents.[57]

Beginning from first principles, the Fama-Jensen model identifies four basic steps in any corporate decision process: (1) initiation, or the generation of proposals for resource use and the structuring of contracts; (2) ratification, or the choice of which of several competing initiatives to implement; (3) implementation, or the execution of ratified decisions; and (4) monitoring, or the measurement of performance of agents and the paying of rewards.[58] Steps (1) and (3) are usually retained by managers; steps (2) and (4) are reserved for risk bearers. The problem is that this four-step process creates agency costs, so controlling the agency problems is a vital part of the decision process. As long as incentives differ, it is imperative that steps (2) and (4) remain in the hands of those not involved in steps (1) and (3). Some agents may be involved, to a greater or lesser degree, at all stages, but effective control requires the two groups to be separate.

A hierarchical structure is a common way to separate management [stages (1) and (3)] and control [(2) and (4)]. Hierarchical structures capture three important facets of effective managerial monitoring and control.[59] First, hierarchies are structured such that the decisions of low-level agents are passed on to higher-level agents for ratification and monitoring. Second, boards of directors who often hold a significant ownership position in the firm ultimately ratify and monitor the organization's most important decisions and retain the power to hire, fire, and compensate top-level decision makers, namely, presidents and chief executive officers. Third, the hierarchical structure creates incentives encouraging mutual monitoring among low-, middle-, and high-level decision agents.

Two markets monitor and control managerial behavior. One is the external market. External markets limit shirking because existing managers recognize that others are waiting in the wings, ready to take their places. Monitors also know this, so they will readily punish excessive shirking by replacing incumbent managers with qualified fresh talent. At the same time, outside competitive pressures force firms to maintain competitive salaries and responsive systems. Firms with unresponsive systems lose their managers, and the best managers are the first to exit.

The other managerial market is the internal market, the specifics of which will be unique to each firm and will generally evolve to provide effective managerial monitoring. One component common to most is that any manager's job is to monitor and evaluate the performance of underlings, so a hierarchical firm will naturally develop a top-down system of performance monitoring. A less well-appreciated structural element of most systems is the bottom-up system that also develops in most hierarchies. Managers lower in the hierarchy are generally interested in moving up, and they will endeavor to expose and replace shirking or incompetent equals and superiors. Fama notes that in the "locus of contracts" approach to the firm, managers at all levels face incentives to point out and punish shirking at all levels.[60] Because each manager's compensation is indirectly tied to the performance of all other managers, each has an incentive to monitor others both above and below. Although the effect is greatest for the highest-level managers, all managers also recognize that their external opportunity wage will be dependent on the overall performance of the firm. Managers in a poorly performing firm will not be in as great of a demand as managers of a highly successful firm. Thus, all the incentives, both internal and external, elicit monitoring *of* all levels *at* all levels.

Internal Governance Systems: Practice

Figure 2.1 presents a highly stylized organizational chart for a typical antebellum bank. Shareholders, of course, retained the ultimate decision-making power in the firm. Shareholder meetings were held at least once per year and shareholders were expected to attend and vote. Given the potentially large costs and modest benefits of attending meetings and casting

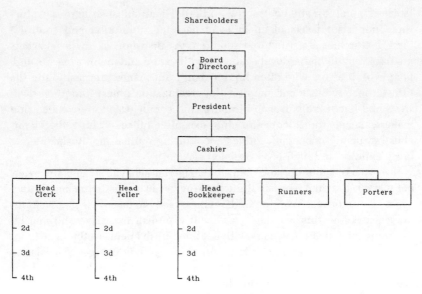

Figure 2.1 Organizational Chart—Antebellum Bank

votes, even by proxy, few shareholders cast their ballots and even fewer attended meetings.

This meant that effective control, particularly ratification [step (2) above] and monitoring [step (4)], devolved to the board of directors. Except in cases in which the state took a stake in a bank and retained the right to appoint outsiders to the board, directors were generally required to be shareholders themselves and elected by their peers.[61] The charter of the Bank of Kentucky, for example, mandated that only those shareholders who had held 25 or more shares for more than three months were eligible for directorships.[62] Like many other banks, it required that at least three directors be replaced each year.

Steps (1) (initiation) and (3) (implementation) were delegated to a president, who was elected to the board and selected from among its members; a chief executive officer, known as a cashier; and any other officers, employees, or agents authorized or appointed by the board. Figure 2.1 reproduces an organizational chart for a large city bank, which might employ as many as a half-dozen clerks and a handful of tellers and bookkeepers. Smaller banks were considerably less hierarchical. The simplest structure consisted of a president, cashier, and clerk.

In either big or small banks, boards were expected to provide close supervision of the bank and its managers. Early bank bylaws provided for specific discount days, those days on which the bank actually extended loans to borrowers. The Philadelphia Bank's discount days were Mondays and Thursdays; the Bank of Chester County's were Tuesdays and Saturdays.[63] The cashier was to collect the notes and bills of exchange offered for discount and submit with them any directly relevant information concerning the borrowers' creditworthiness (e.g., deposit ledgers, bill books, etc.) to the board for acceptance or denial. The board would meet on its appointed discount day and vote yea or nay on each offered note or bill. Cashiers then implemented the board's choices, extending credit to discounters offering accepted notes and bills; they simply returned refused bills to their offerers.

As previously noted, this procedure quickly became onerous for many directors who ran substantial businesses of their own. At the first 33 board meetings of the Bank of Chester County, an average of six (of thirteen) sitting board members attended.[64] While some boards allowed repeated absences, the president of the Memphis branch of the Bank of Tennessee insisted on regular attendance. On 11 October 1860, President James Lenow declared Director E. M. W. King's seat vacant because he had not attended a weekly meeting since 23 August 1860, and the board selected a replacement to complete King's unexpired term.[65] Similarly, the Bank of East Tennessee at Knoxville experienced substantial director turnover because the president was apparently unforgiving of repeated absences from board meetings. At each of three consecutive board meetings in September 1851, a director resigned. Only one was immediately replaced.[66]

Regardless of a president's leniency toward directors who missed board meetings, the reality was that most directors were not inside the bank often enough to provide informed monitoring. Some banks solved this problem by appointing a committee of board members (most often three) committed to their supervisory and oversight responsibilities and investing them with some of the powers of the board as a whole. Others simply allowed the president and cashier to become de facto managers who were given most of the daily decision-making authority originally invested in the board.

The latter alternative was adopted at small country banks and at older, established urban banks where the cashier had a long record and the president provided effective daily oversight. At the latter banks, retaining the practice of having the board pass judgment on all notes simply became too cumbersome relative to the benefits of constant board supervision. By the 1850s, banks had abandoned the practice of twice-weekly discount meetings because borrowers now faced daily movements in interest and exchange charges and demanded more timely decisions.

At some banks, the discount clerk took in hundreds of notes and bills each day, many of them for small amounts needed for routine business by repeat borrowers. In these instances, it was simply more cost effective to allow the cashier to exercise his judgment. Most boards, however, retained their practice of meeting once or twice per week at which time the cashier would lay out a statement of loans made during the previous week. At these meetings, the board determined if the aggregate volume of loans was appropriate, but it spent little time on the particulars of the loan portfolio.

Boards also retained the right to approve large loans or other exceptional transactions, just as they instituted new or altered existing policies. At the 30 May 1836 meeting, for example, the board of the Citizens Bank of Louisiana implemented new policy when it instructed the cashier to enter into an arrangement with the Hunstville branch of the Bank of the State of Alabama so that each would accept bills of exchange drawn on the other.[67] Similarly, at its next meeting, it instructed the cashier that he could discount bills drawn against warehoused and insured sugar and cotton in amounts up to two-thirds the current market value of the produce.[68] Clearly, the board had relinquished daily operation of the bank, but its actions remained consistent with Fama and Jensen's stylized four-step process. The cashier was responsible for *initiation* of some and *implementation* of most decisions, but the board retained its *ratification* prerogative and *monitored* the cashier's activities.

Also consistent with Fama's multilevel monitoring thesis, antebellum banks were organized so that high-level managers supervised lower-level managers and low-level managers monitored other low-level managers and even higher-level managers. This cross-level monitoring was crucial in a business where defalcations could be quick and disastrous. Both cashiers and presidents, for example, were required to number and countersign all banknotes put in circulation. Many larger banks, moreover, hired a bookkeeper who maintained the banknote ledger, which recorded the number, denomination, date issued, and date destroyed of all notes issued by the bank. This policy reduced the likelihood that either the president or the cashier could fraudulently issue a significant volume of banknotes. At lower levels in the hierarchy, a clerk was responsible for the vault cash, but a bookkeeper maintained the vault ledger. To deter a fraudulent complicity between them, a committee of directors regularly took possession of the ledger, counted the contents of the vault, and reconciled any discrepancies.

Although organizational hierarchies were designed to facilitate monitoring and limit agency costs, this structure represented only one component of a wider system of punishments and incentives designed to elicit appropriate behavior on the agent's part. Banks required employees to demonstrate a commitment to prudence and honesty by forcing them to post substantial bonds. In 1814, the Bank of Chester County (Pennsylvania) required its cashier to post a $20,000 bond with sureties acceptable to the board. The clerk was asked to post a $2,500 bond and the porter (whose responsibilities included messenger and delivery services), $500. By way of comparison, the cashier was paid $600 per annum; the clerk, $300; and the porter, $250.[69] Each, however, had easy access to the bank's assets. A cashier, left unattended or inadequately supervised, could easily abscond with $5,000 or $10,000 in specie. An unsupervised clerk could easily walk out the door with several hundred to a few thousand dollars.

When the president and the board failed to take their monitoring responsibilities seriously, the bank sometimes paid dearly. One morning in 1840, the first teller of the Bank of Virginia failed to report for work and was not at home when the cashier sent someone to make inquiries. His sudden disappearance raised suspicions and a committee was appointed to examine his books. They soon uncovered a deficit of $544,116.47.[70] A loss of this magnitude was enough to bankrupt most contemporary firms, but in January 1840, the Bank of Virginia carried more than $3.6 million in capital and had accumulated $485,892.37 in retained earnings.

The bank's shareholders bore the loss. The legislature required the bank to write off its losses, to reduce its authorized and paid-in capital to $2.5 million, and to reduce the par value of its shares from $100 to $70. Although a legislative committee blamed the president and board of directors for not having monitored the teller more closely, the shareholders reelected the president and the entire board to another term.

Compensation systems, too, were structured to induce good behavior. Aidan Hollis and Arthur Sweetman developed a model that predicts that bank shareholders and directors face incentives to compensate managers well enough that most are unwilling to sacrifice the discounted value of future wages to capture the onetime payoff of fraud.[71] Moreover, the model predicts that the greater the potential agency costs or the more difficult it is to provide effective supervision, the greater the "good behavior" wage premium.

Although no systematic study of bank salaries exists, scattered evidence from antebellum banks is consistent with the Hollis and Sweetman hypothesis. Table 2.1 provides salaries at selected banks for several levels in the bank hierarchy. Presidents and cashiers of large urban banks were paid handsomely. In 1803, the president of the Merchants' Bank of New York City was paid $3,000 per annum; the cashier, $2,500 plus an unspecified housing allowance. By 1860, these salaries had doubled in nominal terms and increased 2.5 times in real terms.[72] In 1803, these men were paid about 7 times as much as a skilled artisan. By 1860, they were earning 12 times as much.

Without more information on the men, their duties, and their backgrounds, it will be impossible to break these salaries into returns to general human capital, returns to firm-specific human capital, and agency cost avoidance premiums. It is clear, however, that these wages exceeded simple returns to education. A cashier, who might have earned as much as $4,000 in the 1840s, was paid considerably better than George Tucker, the first professor of political economy at the University of Virginia, who was paid $1,125 in 1844/45.[73] Banks were not, however, in the general habit of overcompensating employees. Watchmen, those bank employees who brought

Table 2.1 Officers' Salaries at Selected U.S. Banks in Selected Years

A: Urban Center Banks

Job Title	Merchants Bank of New York (1803)	Mass. Bank of Boston (1814)	Bank of State Alabama Mobile (1834)	Bank of State Missouri St. Louis (1840)	Merchants Bank of New York (1857)
President	$3,000	—	$2,000	$3,000	$6,000
Cashier	2,500[a]	$2,000	2,500	3,000	6,000
First Teller	1,250	1,300	1,600	1,400	2,500
Second Teller	900	—	—	—	2,100
First Bookkeeper	900	1,400	1,500	1,300	2,100
Second Bookkeeper	750	—	1,200	1,250	—
Discount Clerk	750	1,350	1,200	1,250	1,700
Runner	700	—	650	—	—
Porter	350	—	—	600	800
Urban Artisan	450	500	525	600	500
Urban Laborer	225	300	200	265	330

B: Rural and Small-Town Banks

Job Title	Farmers Bank of Lancaster Pa. (1810)	Bank of Pittsburgh (1819)	Mechanics and Mfrs Trenton (1834)	Bank of Delaware County Pa. (1842)	State Bank Indiana Indianapolis (1853)
President	$ 300	$ 250	$ 800	$ 300	$1,000
Cashier	1,200	1,000	1,000	1,025	1,600
Clerk	800	750	700	600	1,000
Porter	—	200	250	—	300
Ag. Laborer	180	200	—	—	—
Unskilled Laborer	—	—	275	275	310

Notes: Excludes housing allowance of unspecified value. Annual wages of urban artisans, urban laborers, agricultural laborers, and unskilled laborers calculated from average daily wages assuming 300 working days per annum.

Sources: Panel A. Bank officer salaries: column 1, Hubert, *Merchants' National Bank,* p. 14; column 2, Gras, *Massachusetts First National Bank,* pp. 535–36; column 3, Brantley, *Banking,* vol. 1, appendix; column 4, Cable, *Bank,* p. 207; column 5, Hubert, *Merchants' National Bank,* pp. 143–44. Artisan and laborer wages: columns 1 and 2, Adams, "Wage Rates," p. 406; columns 3–5, Margo and Villaflor, "Growth," pp. 894–95. Panel B. Bank officer salaries: columns 1, 2, and 4, Holdsworth, *Financing,* pp. 223, 274, 362; column 3, Godfrey, *Mechanics Bank,* p. 50; column 5, Indiana, *Report,* p. 23. Agricultural and unskilled laborer wages: columns 1 and 2, Adams, "Some Evidence," p. 517; columns 3–5, Margo and Villaflor, "Growth," pp. 894–95.

the fewest skills and for whom agency problems would be smallest, were paid about the same as urban laborers and janitors at the University of Virginia.[74]

Jensen and William Meckling argue that the extent to which a firm's managers deviate from profit maximization will depend on the outside market for managers.[75] The divergence from optimality is directly related to the cost of replacing a manager. If his responsibilities require little firm-specific human capital, if his performance is easily monitored, and if replacement costs are modest, then divergence will be small. Any significant divergence on the part of the manager is punished with swift replacement. Furthermore, the manager's salary will diverge little from that of an outsider with similar generalized human capital.

The seemingly significant divergence between the salaries of bank managers and those of greater educational attainments suggests three possibilities. The first is that bank managers had developed extensive firm-specific human capital that was valuable not only to the manager himself but to the bank. If he had extensive personal knowledge of the creditworthiness of most of the bank's borrowers, for example, his exit would represent a serious loss to the firm. Second, the bank may have offered supracompetitive remuneration in an effort to elicit a greater work effort than he might have provided otherwise. The threat of losing these supracompetitive payments if shirking were detected may have elicited greater effort. Third, and most likely, was that both factors operated. Banks compensated firm-specific human capital and paid a wage premium to elicit desired behavior.

Employees at each level knew that there were others who desired these well-paying jobs and would quickly replace a malingerer. Moreover, the firm-specific human capital loss could be minimized if shirking managers were replaced with a direct underling who already possessed an intimate knowledge of the firm and firsthand knowledge of the task. Thus, the external labor market elicited the desired behavior, but internal competition did so as well.

Banks developed potentially complex systems of managerial control to mitigate shirking and outright fraud. Hierarchical structures imposed top-down, bottom-up, and lateral discipline. High-level managers monitored lower-level employees, and low-level employees kept a sharp eye on their superiors. Even tellers, clerks, and bookkeepers at equivalent levels in the structure, who otherwise reported to the same superior, kept watch on each other. Recognizing, however, that monitoring would prove inadequate to the task of completely eliminating the principal-agent problem, banks developed pecuniary incentive structures to further reduce it. Bonding encouraged outside monitoring of agents by one group of outsiders, namely, their bondsmen. What bondsman, after all, would accept responsibility for an unqualified or dishonest manager? The salary structure elicited monitoring from a second set of outsiders, namely those desirous of the managers' jobs. The general, but not certain, effect was to rein in the most egregious forms of managerial misbehavior. These controls did not exhaust the universe of solutions to the agency cost problem. Another way to limit agency costs was for shareholders to elicit the assistance of yet another group of potential monitors, namely, debt holders.

Corporate Governance and the Debt-Equity Mix: Theory

In 1958, Franco Modigliani and Merton Miller published an article that substantively altered the approach to corporate finance.[76] They argue that the value of the firm should depend on its real assets, not on the specific mix of debt and equity used to finance those assets. As many subsequent writers point out, however, the Modigliani-Miller theorem holds only if capital markets are "perfect," if debt and equity are taxed similarly, and if the costs of bankruptcy are nil.[77] Of course, neither of the latter two conditions is regularly met, and critics argue that a "perfect" capital market is one in which the Modigliani-Miller theorem holds.[78]

For two to three decades after publication of their article, economists argued that the optimal capital structure was neither all equity nor all debt, but a mix that satisfied a tradeoff based on shareholder preferences between debt's lower tax costs and the risk of its pushing a firm into bankruptcy.[79] Failure to repay creditors typically results in bankruptcy. Failure to pay dividends, on the other hand, might elicit howls of protest at shareholder meetings, but it doesn't end in bankruptcy hearings.

Financial economists developed the so-called pecking order theory of corporate finance.[80] Besides debt and equity, most corporate managers face a third financing choice, namely, retained earnings. The pecking order hypothesis states that businesses first seek to finance their operations out of retained earnings. When that source is exhausted, management issues debt. Only as a last resort will managers issue new equity to finance ongoing projects.[81]

A stylized version of the hypothesis states that managers prefer to provide equity investors with a constant stream of dividends to avoid the loss of investor confidence consequent upon reduced payments.[82] Thus, shareholder demands provide managers with a limited and inelastic supply of retained earnings. Managers are forced to solicit outside investment to finance new or expanded projects. New equity issues are typically ruled out because: (1) the decision of better-informed insiders to sell additional shares may imply that shares are currently overpriced; or (2) the choice to sell additional shares may signal management's expectations that the project may not generate enough revenue to meet the repayment obligations of new debt flotations. The pecking order hypothesis predicts that debt becomes the residual source of finance, and firm size is constrained by management's taste for risk. Moreover, debt financing pushes some of the risk of project failure on to debt holders, while shareholders reap all of the residual profits from project success.

In the 1980s, Modigliani and Miller's explanations for observed variances in corporate debt-equity mixes gave way to the view that differences in leverage arise from information asymmetries and monitoring capabilities. Shareholders and debt holders take distinct and separate stakes in the firm. Shareholders provide funds in return for residual claims on future profits; debt holders provide funds in return for contractual covenants promising specific payouts at specific dates. Shareholders can do things debt holders can't; debt holders can do things shareholders can't.[83] Thus, each retains a different, but specific, role in corporate governance.

Information-based theories of capital structure still accept the pecking order hypothesis, but they offer an alternative explanation for the practice of simultaneously paying dividends and taking on new debt. Easterbrook argues that there are two principal agency costs: the previously discussed problem of dispersed share ownership and ineffective monitoring of managers; and a second, less obvious, cost of excessive risk aversion by managers.[84]

Manager portfolios are usually poorly diversified because their single most valuable asset is their firm-specific human capital. Having most of their wealth tied up in a firm, managers have less interest than shareholders, who can hold diversified equity portfolios, in pursuing risky projects. Left to their own devices, managers select overly safe investment projects that have relatively low expected returns. Investors prefer the opposite strategy.

Even if shareholders successfully induce managers to pursue riskier projects, managers may still reduce the firm's overall risk exposure, at shareholder expense, by altering its dividend policy. From the managers' point of view, the lower the debt-equity ratio, the better. Lower debt ratios imply a lower probability of being forced into default and, perhaps, bankruptcy. So even after shareholders force managers to adopt a riskier strategy, managers can reduce the effective risk by paying less in dividends. The result is more retained earnings and a lower risk of default, but this managerial policy transfers wealth from shareholders to debt holders who now receive the contracted-for interest rate without bearing the contracted-for risk.

Easterbrook argues that the most cost-efficient solution to the twin agency costs of monitoring and managerial risk aversion is to constantly force the firm into the capital market.[85] A constant stream of new debt issues brings with it constant monitoring by debt holders. This solves the shareholders' monitoring problem while simultaneously resolving the risk-aversion problem. By demanding regular dividend payments and allowing new equity issues only in exceptional circumstances, shareholders ensure that managers do not transfer wealth to debt holders by moving significantly away from the shareholders' preferred risk position and debt-equity mix.

Previous sections demonstrated that banks, as corporations, develop internal governance structures designed to limit managerial opportunism. This section shows that corporations also use their debt-equity mix to promote managerial monitoring. By continually forcing managers into debt markets, those managers' actions are under the constant scrutiny of informed creditors who have a parallel interest in limiting managerial opportunism. The fundamental difference between shareholders and debt holders, however, is the nature and timing of their control powers. Mathias Dewatripont and Jean Tirole argue that debt holders are too prone to interfere with managers, while shareholders are too passive.[86] Nevertheless, it is optimal to cede contingent control to one of these two groups to discipline managers. As long as the firm experiences good realizations on its projects, managers are rewarded by having passive shareholders in control. The managers satisfy shareholders with dividends, and shareholders allow managers limited use of the firm as a mechanism for generating personal utility and firm-specific human capital rents. If the firm experiences particularly bad realizations, however, debt holders take control and impose tough standards. Thus, managers have incentives to avoid bad outcomes.

Corporate Governance and the
Debt-Equity Mix: Practice

Economists often argue that banks are different from ordinary firms. Because they hold information-intensive portfolios that outsiders can value only imperfectly and only at great expense, banks may face incentives to underproduce or misrepresent information. Instead of investing in information-gathering technologies, a banker might simply acquire assets randomly (some good, and some "bad"), represent them all as "good" and profit to the degree that he does not expend as much on assets and information as he would if, in fact, he engaged in the monitoring he claims to have engaged in.[87]

With the potential for cheating and misrepresentation, regulators typically require banks to be corporations and to place a sizable amount of owner-contributed equity at stake. A large equity stake is designed to impose expected losses on the banker if he misrepresents or underproduces information. "Investors will only invest in intermediaries which have large enough endowments to verify their reliability."[88] But a large capital alone may not guarantee good behavior on the part of managers. The capital could be dissipated within a short period, with the investors left holding the bag. Moreover, early banks were relative unknowns and bankers needed to adopt policies that would encourage share ownership. One such practice was the regular payment of dividends.

Although regular dividend payments by early banks surely went toward resolving Easterbrook's twin agency cost problem, the simple fact was that they assuaged nervous shareholders. Whatever other purpose they might serve, dividend payments are a sign of organizational health.[89] A regular and relatively smooth stream of dividends is potentially a more reliable indicator of health than an impressive income statement, balance sheet, or pronouncement from some legislative oversight committee, all of which are manipulable to an extent.

The Modigliani-Miller theorem has been assailed from several angles, the most common being that the differential tax treatment of debt and equity does not adequately explain variations in the debt-equity mix. Nearly as common has been the assertion that capital markets are not perfect. While modern markets may not be perfect, early equity and debt markets were most assuredly not so. Not only firms but also whole industries lacked track histories. Markets were thin; information, while always scarce, was downright sparse and often unreliable; and the status of debt and equity holders was still undergoing legal interpretation. In such an environment, the promise of a constant stream of dividends may have provided the liquidity necessary to encourage equity ownership in thin and erratic markets.[90]

In the earliest capitalist organizations, investors were not indifferent between alternative debt-equity mixes. The combination of high risks and limited information, as well as greater legal protection of creditors, meant that most investors, if given a choice, would have preferred creditor status. As previously noted, corporate law was in its infancy in early nineteenth-century America, but existing law gave clear preference to debtors. Moreover, legal protection of creditors was more effective than that of shareholders because default was an easily verified violation of a debt contract.[91]

Furthermore, debt holders were better protected than shareholders against dishonesty and incompetency among a bank's managers, employees, and agents. Though the issue deserves greater scrutiny, even a brief excursion into antebellum Tennessee's banking law demonstrates the greater protection granted debt holders. In *Union Bank v. Campbell*, the board loaned against a promissory note fraudulently issued by a bankrupt and dissolved partnership.[92] Two of the bank's directors knew the partnership was broken yet failed to notify the board as a whole. It was later discovered that one director allowed the note to be discounted because part of the proceeds would be used by the broken partnership to repay a debt owed to that director. The bank's attorney argued that the directors had perpetrated a fraud on the bank and should be held personally liable. Tennessee's highest court rejected his argument. The directors acted as agents of the bank, regardless of whether they had done so in good faith, which made the bank's shareholders ultimately responsible for the directors' fraud.

The Bank of East Tennessee's charter was typical in that Section 12 required that if the directors violated another charter requirement, they might be held personally liable for the bank's debts. In the mid-1850s, the bank's directors were sued under the terms laid down in Section 12 for unspecified policies that directly violated the bank's charter.[93] In *Marr v. Bank of West Tennessee*, the state's appellate court held in cases of insolvency that "bill holders and stockholders have each, equitable claims; but those of the bill

holders [creditors] possess, as I conceive, a prior *exclusive* equity."[94] The
doctrine that creditors be paid first, argued the court, was "so firmly settled,
upon the plainest principles of . . . authority, that it cannot be shaken or
brought into doubt."[95]

Debt holders were not only better protected against duplicity and inep-
titude, but they also held more liquid positions because of the fixed payoff
implicit in a typical debt contract.[96] Debt contracts, too, carried a specific
maturity date; equity did not. Both features made debt more marketable
than equity in early financial markets. Jonathan Baskin and Paul Miranti
argue that some early American banks, faced with a limited ability to finance through long-term debt, did the next best thing. They tried to make
their equity behave like debt. By smoothing dividends even in the face of
volatile profit streams, these banks gave their equity the debtlike feature of
fixed payoff streams. In pursuing a dividend-smoothing strategy, early banks
made their equity more attractive to investors and effectively widened the
market for capital and lowered its costs.

Early commentators argued that smoothed dividends were more important the further removed shareholders were from the business. Knowledge-
able and informed shareholders could be treated like partners, but uninformed investors needed the assurances provided by a constant stream of
dividends.[97] For most investors, then, it was the prospect of dividends that
mattered. The longer the history of uninterrupted dividends, and the higher
the dividends as a percentage of par share values, the better. Whatever the
merits of this approach, it made sense. Lacking reliable information on the
internal operations of the firm, the one easily observable signal of organizational health was dividend payouts.

It is relatively easy to find early banks that smoothed dividends even
though interest rates, earnings, and profits fluctuated widely. Figure 2.2 provides a representative example that supports the Baskin and Miranti thesis.
The Exchange Bank of Providence, Rhode Island, provided its investors
with nearly level payouts between 1835 and 1860 despite low earnings during the panics of 1837 and 1857 and the recession of 1848. It is easy to
identify other Rhode Island banks that pursued similar strategies. The coefficient of variation of dividends at the Providence Bank was 0.12; the
coefficient of variation of profits was 0.27.[98] At the Phoenix Bank of Providence, they were 0.13 and 0.19. Dividends at these banks, at least, were
considerably less volatile than profits.

In their study of nineteenth-century manufacturing stocks, Jeremy Atack
and Peter Rousseau challenge Baskin and Miranti's dividend-smoothing hypothesis.[99] Atack and Rousseau admit that information asymmetries provided incentives for firms to pay substantial dividends to encourage equity
holding, but they found little evidence of dividend smoothing. Although
some banks followed a smoothing policy, there is little evidence that banks
as a group smoothed dividends. Dividend and profit rates were calculated
from a sample of 50 New England banks in continuous operation between

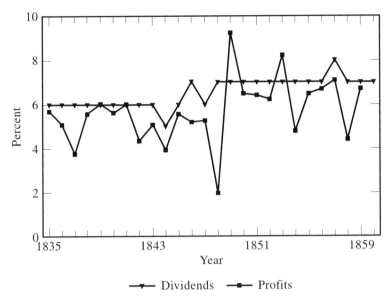

Figure 2.2 Dividends and Profits, Exchange Bank of Providence. Sources: Rhode Island, *Acts and Resolves*, 1835–1860, and author's calculations

1835 and 1860, and the time-series coefficient of variation of average dividends (0.0088) and the coefficient of variation for average profit rates (0.0092) were practically the same. Across the industry as a whole, dividends were not substantially less volatile than profits.

What was true about most banks' dividend policy was that they rarely retained a substantial volume of earnings. Once a bank established a modest retained earnings fund (called a "contingent fund" in contemporary balance sheets) totaling, perhaps, about 10 percent of the paid-in capital account, most profits were paid out to equity holders. This dividend policy may have provided one mechanism for monitoring bank managers. As the previous section made clear, effective corporate governance often demands both share and debt holdings. One important element of a modern bank's business is the provision of deposits or transaction services, which are paid for indirectly by depositors forgoing returns on deposits. Deposits are a liability—a debt—for the bank, and banking has evolved a contractual "structure involving deposits that, like all redeemable claims, allow the depositors to affect the resources under management control."[100] In other words, depositors are creditors and may, like other creditors, provide valuable monitoring services.

Many scholars, however, do not believe that depositors can be or will be effective bank monitors. Dewatripont and Tirole are characteristic, in many respects, because they argue that the "distinctiveness of banks . . . is the nature of the debt-holders, who are small dispersed depositors, typically unable meaningfully to exert residual rights of control."[101] Although banks have many creditors, they each may take a smaller stake in the bank than its equity holders. Thus, creditors-cum-depositors closely resemble small equity holders in that each has few incentives to monitor or to involve themselves in the management of the firm. The solution is to substitute depositor monitoring with outside monitoring. Some argue that independent rating firms like Moody's, who place their reputations at risk, may provide effective, market-based oversight.[102] Others argue that, given banks' opaque, hard-to-value portfolios, prudential oversight requires the intervention of a regulator with the legal power to discipline and punish.[103]

Charles Calomiris and Charles Kahn, on the other hand, believe that depositors can be effective bank monitors.[104] They developed a model wherein the first-come, first-serve constraint creates incentives for at least some depositors to monitor. Because banks issue debts redeemable at par on demand, yet hold only fractional reserves against those debts, a sudden and pervasive demand for liquidity implies that only those depositors at the head of the queue will be able to fully cash out. Calomiris and Kahn convincingly argue that immediate par redemption combined with the first-come, first-serve constraint creates incentives for some depositors to monitor and to take control of a poorly performing institution before its net worth is fully dissipated. Though only a few, presumably large, depositors bear the costs of monitoring, they capture the benefits by being first in the queue. A declining bank's monitors cash out first, receiving full and immediate par redemption. Nonmonitors take their lead from monitors, cashing out only when they observe monitors cashing out. In accepting a later position in the queue, nonmonitors accept a lower expected payout. In effect, nonmonitors compensate monitors by allowing monitors to cash out first and fully.

Although antebellum banks held deposits, their principal demandable debt instruments were banknotes. Banknotes were noninterest-bearing promissory notes payable on demand at par at the issuing bank or authorized agency. Banknotes, like deposits, provided liquidity and exchange services. The question is: did they resemble other forms of debt and serve debt's corporate governance role by encouraging outside monitoring of management behavior?

Studies by Gary Gorton and Howard Bodenhorn suggest that they did.[105] Specialized traders in banknotes, known as banknote brokers, made markets in banknotes by standing ready to purchase them at varying discounts from par. Gorton's model predicts that the market price of a banknote should have reflected the cost of redeeming it, which should have increased the further a banknote was from its issuing bank, plus a risk premium, reflecting the perceived probability that the issuing bank might fail or suspend before the note could be returned and redeemed. His model presumes that early American banknote brokers gathered and processed information on the riskiness of different banks and then bought notes at efficient, competitively determined prices.

Any test using banknote prices is then a joint test of both the monitoring and efficient pricing hypothesis. Gorton tests the hypothesis by considering the time-series trajectory of note prices among newly formed banks.[106] He finds that the discounts on the notes of ultimately successful young banks are initially large and trend downward as these banks establish themselves and prove their viability. Reputation formation is a slow and costly process and prices in efficient markets will fully reflect new information.

Instead of reputation formation, Bodenhorn focuses on reputation deterioration.[107] He tests the hypothesis that the price brokers paid for banknotes decreased as the issuing bank's condition worsened. Bodenhorn gathered information on the prices brokers paid for the notes of a sample of failing banks. Five years prior to failure, prices of the notes of failing and nonfailing banks were nearly identical. About two years prior to failure, however, average prices in the two samples began to diverge markedly. The price of soon-to-fail banks' notes decline sharply and collapse at the time of failure. Moreover, because some banks were closed before their net worth was completely dissipated, the average price increased modestly after closure. This increase, if efficient, should have reflected the expected banknote redemption rate (cents on the dollar) as brokers, regulators, and court-appointed administrators assessed the quality of the bank's remaining assets.

In a related study, Bodenhorn finds that market participants efficiently analyze different aspects of a bank's debt-equity mix.[108] Economists since Smith have argued against the extensive use of small-denomination banknotes.[109] Small-denomination notes are more likely to be used by the poor and those least able to ascertain the quality of these notes. Moreover, small-denomination notes encouraged counterfeiting, the costs of which, of course, would also fall disproportionately on the poor and laboring classes. Smith and subsequent advocates of this position assume that people are unable to discriminate between different issuers. But Bodenhorn shows that banks that relied more on small notes witnessed a reputational pricing effect.[110] Banks issuing larger volumes of small notes saw their notes sink in price, after controlling for redemption costs.

Dewatripont and Tirole identify three corporate governance scenarios: (1) as long as the managers' actions result in good performance, control remains with passive shareholders; (2) marginal results trigger limited intervention by activist shareholders; and (3) poor performance triggers excessively interventionist creditor control.[111] Gorton's and Bodenhorn's evidence on banknote markets suggests that this governance schematic is an appropriate way of thinking about corporate governance practice among early American banks in that troublesome managerial policies led informed banknote brokers to downgrade the bank's debt, which potentially triggered intervention by activist shareholders.

It is also important to note that not every bank whose notes declined in market price failed. There were dozens (possibly hundreds) of instances in which banknote prices recovered a few months after an initial decline. If the market was as efficient as Gorton's and Bodenhorn's studies imply, this is not an unexpected finding. Effective monitors, having uncovered potential problems at a bank, would inform the market of their lowered assessment of management's strategy by lowering the price they paid for its debt. Banknote price reductions provided signals to activist shareholders who demanded a change in management policy or, perhaps, a change in the management team itself. As in modern corporations, debt holders and equity holders took distinct, but complementary, roles in monitoring, rewarding, and punishing the actions of the banks' managers.

Concluding Remarks

As corporations, and corporations without much in the way of past lessons to learn from, America's early banks were forced to grapple with the issue of how to develop internal and external structures capable of limiting managerial opportunism without developing systems so cumbersome that they interfered with routine operations or the possibility of exploiting unexpected innovative opportunities. The evidence implies that, by and large, banks were successful. Although Alfred Chandler and his followers focus on the complex hierarchical structures developed in the post–Civil War industrial corporation, early banks developed their own internal hierarchies.[112] Granted, these banks' hierarchies were not as tall, nor as laterally complex as those instituted and exploited by national and international transportation and industrial enterprises, but they were nevertheless just as innovative and equally successful in controlling managerial opportunism. With a little digging, we can uncover a dozen or so instances of extraordinary managerial fraud, like that perpetrated against the Bank of Virginia in 1840. The striking thing, however, is that we can easily uncover only about a score of such instances when there were tens of thousands of cashiers, tellers, clerks, and bank presidents employed between 1790 and 1860. For every instance in which a system failed, there were a hundred instances of success.

Banks devised internal structures that encouraged monitoring by creating incentives for a diverse group of people to monitor. As previously noted, top-down supervisory systems limited the ability of subordinate employees to shirk, cheat, and steal. Less well appreciated were the complex systems of bottom-up and lateral monitoring imposed by many banks. Ambitious underlings faced incentives to uncover, document, and report incompetence or shirking by superiors. Similarly, lateral monitoring was designed to expose unwanted behavior.

Internal structures were developed by the visible hand of management to control managerial opportunism and generally proved equal to the task.

External monitoring structures, on the other hand, resulted from the operation of the invisible hand of the market. Modern corporate finance recognizes the importance of a firm's debt-equity mix in aligning shareholder and managerial interests. By forcing managers to continually contract with creditors, shareholders elicit the assistance of debt holders who evaluate management's project choices and monitor the outcomes. Shareholders and boards of directors are thereby provided with an additional piece of information, the market price of debt, that allows for informed decision making.

Among modern corporations, debt takes many forms, from marketable commercial paper to gilt-edge bonds to junk bonds to trade credit, and the price of each provides shareholders and the public with valuable information about the activities of the firm's management. Antebellum banks had less sophisticated debt-equity mixes. Nearly all of a bank's debt was short term (primarily deposits and banknotes), and outside markets developed only in banknotes. Nevertheless, the available evidence suggests that these markets efficiently priced bank debt, and theory suggests that demandable debt resolves exactly the sorts of governance issues faced by corporations in other industries.

Bodenhorn and Michael Haupert show that antebellum banks relied excessively on banknote issues even after deposit banking became relatively more lucrative.[113] This seemingly irrational behavior may, in fact, have been quite rational. Because secondary markets never developed in deposits, shareholders may have forced managers to fund the bank's portfolio with debt that was publicly traded. In doing so, the shareholders elicited the monitoring of the managers' actions by a group of informed outsiders, namely, banknote brokers.

The end result of both the internal and external monitoring structures was that banks became more trusted; eventually, they were even viewed as a piece of basic industrial infrastructure like roads, canals, bridges, and the like. Small-town boosterism in the antebellum era usually revolved around turnpike, canal, and, later, railroad construction and bank formation. Because they could be trusted, banks ultimately provided an impetus to economic growth by supplying communities with much-needed credit. The next chapter details the lending practices of America's early banks and shows how they promoted trade, commerce, and industrialization.

3

Banking Theory and Banking Practice in Antebellum America

Modern theories of financial intermediation begin from the premise that small and young firms will not be able to convey credible information about themselves and their prospects or establish publicly observable reputations that will allow them access to arm's-length or public debt markets.[1] Foreclosed from commercial paper or bond markets, small firms must rely on financial intermediaries for the bulk of their financing because owner-contributed equity and retained earnings are insufficient to finance continuing operations. Banks, then, loom large in the economy if most business is small business as it was in early America. For banks to have mattered to economic development, it was imperative that their owners and managers were far-sighted, risk-taking innovators, and that they sought out similar individuals engaged in nonfinancial pursuits.

If most banks followed the dominant banking theory of the period, the so-called real-bills doctrine, it is not clear that they would have mattered very much. Real-bills policies prescribed a passive banking sector, one that responded and reacted to events rather than one that anticipated events, shrewdly seeking out new opportunities. A prototypical nineteenth-century bank did not approach potential borrowers in emerging industries and initiate relationships. Rather, it catered to established businessmen involved in safe, predictable trades. An unimaginative merchant who generated unimpressive, but consistent, profits period after period was a more preferred customer than an entrepreneur who might reap supernormal profits from an innovative product or process.

This chapter shows that early nineteenth-century banks were not the prototypical banks described by contemporary real-bills theorists. Moreover, it argues that not following a pure real-bills policy led to a positive result. Banks deviated from real-bills prescriptions in several regards—namely, by lending to farmers, manufacturers, and other nonmercantile firms—but in so doing, they quickened the pace of economic development. In other respects—namely, short-term loans subject to renewal under certain conditions—banks adopted policies that mimicked real-bills policies. Adopting these aspects of the policy was consistent with mitigating moral hazard problems discussed in chapter 2. In short, banks loaned to emerging sectors and innovative firms because doing so was profitable when banks forced these firms to recontract at regular intervals. Banks, then, performed their principal information-producing functions by gathering information before making the loan, monitoring during the loan period, and enforcing terms at the loan's maturity.

Effective ex ante, interim, and ex post monitoring was made easier through the development of long-term relationships. Knowing they could cultivate profitable relationships with potentially profitable young firms and sustain them for long periods, banks faced incentives to do so. Evidence from antebellum American banking markets implies that long-term relationships benefited both parties. Because continuing associations lowered monitoring and risk costs, banks could offer long-term customers attractive loan terms, namely, lower interest rates, fewer collateral requirements, and larger lines of credit. Banks, it seems, did what modern theories say they should have done and, in the process, made everyone better off. Consistent with evidence from the previous chapter, the bank's shareholders were better off because they earned higher returns. Debt holders were better off because the loan portfolio was less risky than it otherwise might have been. Society, as a whole, was better off because the bank's actions promoted economic growth and development, increasing both the size and the composition of the pie.

Contemporary Theory and Practice

Promissory Notes, Bills of Exchange, and the Real-Bills Doctrine

Various theories about what constituted proper banking circulated in the late eighteenth and early nineteenth centuries. Some held that banks should extend only mercantile credit, eschewing agricultural and industrial entanglements. Others held that land and personal property were appropriate bases for credit. Still others promoted lending backed by government securities.[2] It was the first approach in the guise of the real-bills doctrine that was championed by nearly every notable contemporary writer.

The real-bills doctrine held that business credit should be extended in the form of short-term loans used to finance the production and shipment of goods. Within a relatively short period, sale of the goods provided the borrower with the wherewithal to repay the loan. A bank's function was to provide working capital to "bridge the gap between seedtime and harvest, between the purchase of raw materials and the sale of the finished product," between purchase in one place and sale in another.[3] Because shipment and sale of a commodity typically required several weeks, banks provided interim credit to finance transportation and warehousing costs. Real bills, if limited to strictly commercial transactions in amounts less than the current market value of the goods, were self-liquidating in that the revenues generated in the transaction exceeded the loan. The real-bills doctrine, therefore, prescribed a passive role for banks, and it was a long-standing belief that banks should provide just enough credit to satisfy the "needs of trade" and no more. The banking system would thus reflect the level of commercial activity, expanding and contracting the supply of credit in concert with the changing rhythms of the economy.[4]

Underlying the doctrine was a belief that adherence to it fostered liquidity and guaranteed solvency in both financial and real sectors of the economy. George Tucker, the first professor of political economy at the University of Virginia and contemporary real-bills advocate, argued that if banks directed credit toward those engaged in regular and profitable businesses; if they refused "accommodation to the rash, adventurous, and oversanguine, and above all, to those who were disposed to live ostentatiously; and if they would check their [lending] whenever they saw the spirit of speculation abroad, they might do much" to curb the recurrent business cycle, which was often attributed to recurrent swings in the volume of bank-supplied credit.[5]

A prudent banker, wrote Tucker, provided credit at 60 days to merchants of noted acumen and unquestioned character. By lending to high-quality borrowers, bankers virtually guaranteed timely repayment. In equilibrium, moreover, one-ninth of the bank's loan funds was granted each week, just as one-ninth was repaid.[6] A constant turnover implied a continual replenishment of the bank's reserves, which allowed it to meet its usual banknote redemption demands. Furthermore, if redemption demands became unusually great, the continual loan turnover allowed the banker to painlessly augment his reserves in a relatively short time simply by refusing new loans as old ones were repaid.

The doctrine remained popular well into the late nineteenth and early twentieth centuries. Naomi Lamoreaux found late-nineteenth-century New England bankers committed to the doctrine. If anything, they took it to its next level by developing proportional prescriptions. A preferred portfolio included 20 percent in high-grade bonds, another 20 percent in open market commercial paper, and the remaining 60 percent in locally generated real bills.[7] H. G. Moulton argued that the 1913 Federal Reserve Act was based on a nineteenth-century real-bills theory.[8] Even as late as 1929, Charles Dunbar argued that it was easy for banks to arrange the purchase of bills with respect to maturity "so as to provide for a steady succession of payments to the banks, and thus to facilitate the reduction in business, if necessary, or [alter] its direction into new channels, as prudence or good policy may require."[9]

To the extent that antebellum bankers adopted some type of real-bills policy, they did so not because contemporary commentators believed it the best policy, but because it made sense. Bray Hammond notes that when the directors of the Bank of North America began extending credit, they forged ahead "on the basis of their experience as merchants" and loaned on a "common sense" basis.[10]

Although lending was based on common sense, was the doctrine itself sensible? Modern theories split on this question, depending on what the theory attempts to explain. Viewed from the perspective of the individual lender, real-bills prescriptions are logical. Douglas Diamond, for example, analyzes the tradeoff between short-and long-term debt in a two-period model with asymmetric information and incomplete contracts, and he shows that a type of real-bills rule acts as a revelation or sorting mechanism.[11] He argues that entrepreneurs who know that their projects are profitable will finance with short-term debt and refinance later when new information arrives. Entrepreneurs with potentially unprofitable projects prefer to finance with long-term debt. The reason is that entrepreneurs with good projects are willing to accept the risk that new profitability information will be adverse and their projects will not be refinanced. Entrepreneurs with bad projects will not accept the risk because the good outcome is almost never observed.

Viewed from a macroeconomic perspective, however, Thomas Sargent and Neil Wallace argue that real-bills prescriptions are unattractive. They developed a model designed to mimic a real-bills doctrine and show that it actually amplifies macroeconomic cycles.[12] Moreover, the theory was built on a fallacy of composition often unappreciated by contemporary writers and many subsequent historians. What appeared to be sound practice to an individual bank in good times (short-term lending on only unquestioned security) and bad times (refusing renewals, demanding repayment, and bolstering reserves) was not a desirable response by the system as a whole.

Not every contemporary theorist failed to see the theory's essential flaw. Writing in 1802, Henry Thornton recognized that a true real-bills policy would produce an indeterminant price level because the issue of every additional dollar was anchored to another dollar, not to a unit of a physical commodity like gold.[13] As Thornton noted, a rising price level would generate a growing demand for loans to finance the same volume of real transactions. Growing loan demands would expand the money supply, which would raise prices, which would increase demand, and so forth ad infinitum. A strict real-bills policy would fail to limit the quantity of money. In an expanding economy, the inflation would fuel itself. In a recessionary economy, the deflation would also accelerate. Facing panicky note holders anxious to redeem their notes into base money, the banks' concerted and simultaneous effort to contract had the paradoxical effect of undermining their own solvency.

Credit crunches and deflations, as Ben Bernanke and his coauthors demonstrate, have macroeconomic consequences because they hasten and magnify the deterioration of borrowers' balance sheets.[14] Deflation increases the real cost of debt repayment (Irving Fisher labeled this the "debt-deflation problem"), which diminishes borrowers' net worth.[15] Some borrowers are pushed into bankruptcy, and this causes a deterioration in the banks' balance sheets. As the banks' debtors come to recognize the banks' worsening position, they cash out in ever greater amounts. The real-bills driven response, then, set in motion a vicious downward spiral that was typically broken by the banks' suspension of specie payments. Suspensions stemmed runs but further frustrated any attempt to quickly rehabilitate the suspending banks' reputations. Even had adherence to the policy created an elastic currency that met the "needs of trade," the resulting encouragement of long-swing cycles (monetary and credit expansion during the boom; contraction feeding the bust) was undesirable.[16]

How was the doctrine translated into practice and implemented by those banks willing to follow its tenets? Nineteenth-century banks extended credit not so much by loans as by discounts. The difference between the two is in the timing of the interest payment. Modern loans (like mortgages and automobile loans) are often amortized over their life: the borrower makes monthly installment payments that include both principal and interest. With nineteenth-century discounts, as with most modern notes and commercial paper, the interest payment was deducted up front and the borrower repaid the face value of the debt at maturity. If a merchant presented a banker with a $100 note payable in 30 days, he received $99.50 in funds if the note carried a 6 percent interest charge. In 30 days, he repaid $100.

So-called single- and double-name paper constituted the bulk of most banks' discounts; for a real-bills bank, double-name paper was clearly preferred. Single-name paper (sometimes simply called promissory notes) represented a simple credit extended to an individual or business secured only by the real or personal property of the note's drawer.[17] Real-bills advocates objected to single-name paper on two grounds. First, realizing on the collateral was slow and costly in the event of borrower default. Second, the supply of credit and, more important, money lost its connection to the needs of trade. This "overtrading" inevitably resulted in inflation. "The bill business," wrote the directors of the Bank of Kentucky, "is limited by the actual operation of commerce; the accommodation [single-name paper] business is as limitless as the want of money, the rage of speculation, or the spirit of gambling."[18]

Double-name paper, unlike single-name paper, resulted from and represented a specific commercial transaction. To replenish his inventory, a retail dry-goods merchant typically offered the wholesaler a note, payable at his place of business or at a local bank; to complete the transaction, the wholesaler would take the note, write the word "Accepted" across its face, endorse the reverse, and then carry it to a bank to have it discounted. The wholesaler thereby received immediate payment for his goods, and the retailer indirectly received credit from a bank. Promissory notes such as these were called double-name paper because they carried the guarantee of both the drawer (the retailer) and the acceptor (the wholesaler). If the maker or drawer failed to meet his obligation at maturity, the bank (or a subsequent rediscounter if the bank sold the note to another) had legal recourse against any and all endorsers. The bank carried the dishonored note to a local magistrate or notary, who recorded it as "protested" for nonpayment and then notified all endorsers by mail that the note was dishonored and that they stood potentially liable. Banks preferred double-name paper for the obvious reason that it was better secured than single-name paper, which was secured only by the personal collateral of the maker.

A common form of double-name paper was the bill of exchange, an unconditional order made by one person (the drawer or maker) instructing a second person (the drawee) to pay, on a specific date, a certain sum to a specific person or bearer (the payee) at a specific place. The substantive difference between a promissory note and a bill of exchange was the place of payment. A promissory note was typically made payable at the drawer's home, place of business, or local bank. A bill of exchange was payable at a specific distant location (again, typically a bank or place of business) designated on the face of the bill. The drawer or drawee was required to have funds available at that place to meet the bill at maturity.

Before a bill became a legally recognized financial instrument, the drawee was required to accept and endorse it. Once he had, the bill was called an "acceptance" or "trade acceptance" and the drawee became the acceptor. Like promissory notes, bills or acceptances were freely transferable. If a bearer didn't want to hold the bill to maturity, he could sell it to a fourth party (recall that the first three are drawer, acceptor, and payee), who acknowledged the sale by attaching his endorsement beneath that of the acceptor. In the early nineteenth century, the most common fourth parties were wealthy capitalists, private bankers, and commercial bankers with interregional connections who sought short-term investments for their idle funds. By the end of the antebellum era, firms began specializing in the transfer and collection of bills of exchange, and commercial banks became significant buyers and sellers of bills of exchange.[19]

Bills of exchange came in two types: clean bills and documentary bills. Loans made on goods in transit or storage gave rise to documentary bills because they carried an attached bill of lading. A bill of lading was a document produced by a shipper or warehouseman acknowledging receipt of goods for shipment or storage. Because the terms of many long-distance contracts were cash on receipt or even 90 days after receipt, the seller-shipper often waited several months before payment was received. By tendering a bill of lading attached to a bill of exchange, a seller-shipper received advances secured by the goods in transit, and in many instances, the advances were used to finance the shipping costs themselves.

An attached bill of lading made the documentary bill an attractive investment because the bill of lading allowed the borrower to take possession of the good listed on the bill to secure payment in the event of default. Clean bills, on the other hand, did not carry the attached documentation and, therefore, carried no more guarantee than the personal warranty of the drawer and drawee. Clean bills were to documentary bills of exchange what single-name accommodation notes were to double-name notes. Clean bills, however, were considerably rarer than single-name promissory notes. Only established and well-known traders in commodities with wide markets (like cotton and tobacco) could find a ready market for their clean bills.[20]

Bills of exchange were used throughout the United States, but they were ubiquitous in the Atlantic cotton trade. William Gouge provided a detailed description of the trade:

> A merchant from Natchez repairs to New York, and purchases one hundred thousand dollars' worth of goods, giving his notes or bills for the same. The New York merchant has these notes or bills discounted by a bank, and with the proceeds purchases bills of exchange on England, through which he pays on old debt due in that country, or procures a fresh supply of foreign commodities. The Mississippi merchant carries the goods to Natchez, and there disposes of them to neighboring planters, in expectation of being paid out of the growing crop of cotton. In due season he receives the cotton, and sends it to a factor in New Orleans. In the interval, the notes or bills he gave to the New York merchant have been sent to the Commercial Bank of Natchez for collection. They are now due. He draws on the factor at New Orleans. The Commercial Bank discounts these drafts, and with what he thus receives, the Natchez merchant pays the notes or bills he gave to the New York jobber or importer. Here are still several accounts unsettled. The New Orleans factor is in debt to the Commercial Bank of Natchez, and the latter is in debt to the Bank of America at New York. But the factor has, in cotton consigned to him, the means of paying his debt to the bank at Natchez, and thereby enabling it to settle accounts with the bank at New York. The factor ships cotton to Liverpool, and draws a bill of exchange on England, which bill he sells, and with the proceeds pays the New Orleans agent of the Commercial Bank of Natchez, which agent will suppose to be the Union Bank [of New Orleans]. The Bank of America at New York, draws on the Commercial Bank at Natchez; the latter draws on the Union Bank of Louisiana, in favor of the bank at New York; the Union Bank sends the foreign bill of exchange to New York; the Bank of America receives it there, and sells it to an importing merchant, who transmits it to Europe, perhaps in payment for the very dry goods he had the year before sold to the Mississippi merchant. . . . About the same time it [the bill of exchange] reaches the city [Liverpool], the cotton on which

it is founded arrives; and thus the accounts between England and the United States are adjusted.[21]

Although Gouge's explanation can be confusing, figure 3.1 reduces it to a simple quadrilateral flow diagram. Cotton and manufactured goods flow counterclockwise around the outside of the diagram, and the real flows are financed by two clockwise triangular flows around the inside of the quadrilateral. Reduced to their essence, the transactions proceeded in the following steps: (1) Cotton moved down the Mississippi River from Natchez merchants to New Orleans factors and on to Liverpool's textile mills; (2) the shipment of manufactured goods from Liverpool's burgeoning industrial sector flowed from Liverpool wholesalers to New York jobbers to Natchez retailers; (3) financing the transatlantic shipment of cotton was a triangular flow of finance in which New Orleans factors drew bills of exchange in favor of Liverpool merchants on sterling balances held in New York banks;[22] (4) financing the transatlantic flow of manufactured goods was an equivalent triangular flow of dollar-denominated bills in which Natchez retailers drew bills on New York merchants, whose bankers ultimately drew funds on New Orleans bankers and factors who underwrote cotton transactions.

The sheer complexity of these transactions, and the apparent ease with which they were carried out, demonstrates that early American financial

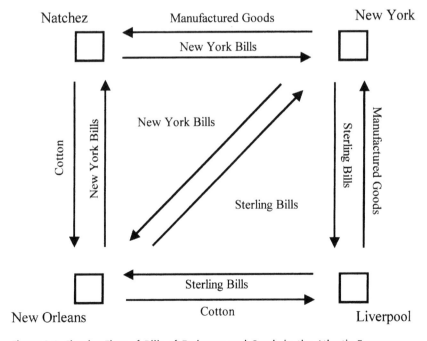

Figure 3.1 Circular Flow of Bills of Exchange and Goods in the Atlantic Economy

markets were more sophisticated than often believed. Moreover, in assisting long-distance trade, banks indirectly widened markets, fostered specialization, and promoted economic growth and development.

An issue that has been debated for the better part of two centuries is the extent to which contemporary bankers adhered to the real-bills doctrine, or a reasonable facsimile thereof. Some writers refer to policy statements offered by contemporary bankers to draw conclusions. In 1784, both the Bank of New York and the Massachusetts Bank (Boston) adopted unequivocal real-bills policies: the Bank of New York's bylaws set a 30-day loan with a no-renewal policy; the Massachusetts Bank limited discounts to 30 days on mercantile bills and 60 days on promissory notes secured by merchandise collateral, and neither type was eligible for renewal.[23]

Within a decade, the Bank of New York's policy had changed considerably. Single-name paper collateralized by such things as public debt, corporate securities, bullion, mortgages, and warehoused merchandise had become common and so much a part of the bank's everyday business that it established a separate department just to manage these transactions.[24] Contemporary economists remarked on a continuing trend among Philadelphia's banks to extend credit on longer terms and with less security. This sort of anecdotal evidence, combined with an unshakable belief that religious adherence to real-bills policies would have staved off most of the antebellum era's financial panics, leads Fritz Redlich to conclude that "banking reached its moral and managerial nadir" in the 1820s and 1830s.[25] Because they failed to follow real-bills prescriptions, Redlich determines that the bank of the 1830s "was still steering without a compass."[26] Hammond offered a simple but highly effective criticism when he wrote that it was "notorious that this doctrine was professed long after it had become otiose."[27]

Contemporary Banking Practice: New Evidence and New Interpretations

Although many questions surround antebellum banking, there are two broad questions of particular interest to economic historians. First is the extent to which banks followed the prescriptions of the real-bills doctrine, which implies a host of subsidiary questions. Did early U.S. banks lend at short term? Did they focus on mercantile credit secured by goods in transit? Did they generally refuse renewals? A second and potentially more important question is whether antebellum banks acted as Schumpeterian financiers and engines of growth.[28] Was it even possible to be both?[29]

If bankers adopted real-bills policies, then it is not immediately clear that they could simultaneously promote industrial development. Recall Tucker's sentiment that a real-bills banker should not lend to adventurers as well as the typical characterization of a real-bills system as passive, expanding and contracting in response to the underlying rhythms of the economy.

Joseph Schumpeter's idealized banker stood in stark contrast to the prototypical real-bills banker.[30] Schumpeter envisioned capitalist development beginning in an equilibrium state in which households and firms exchanged factors of production and final goods in the familiar circular flow. True economic development required a disruption of the circular flow. It required the introduction of an innovation and an unexpected or surprise shift in the production function. Realizing this productive shift required two things: a competitive environment that elicited an entrepreneurial search for new products and processes expected to yield a short-lived competitive advantage; and the existence of financiers (typically bankers) willing to interrupt the equilibrium circular flow by channeling credit (or venture capital) to promising but unproved enterprises.

Development demanded bank credit and Schumpeter's banks, to be initiators of growth, had to *occasionally* behave quite unlike real-bills bankers. The real-bills banker was a paragon of prudence; he carefully weighed costs and benefits and avoided unnecessary risks. Schumpeter's banker, on the other hand, also recognized the line between risk and uncertainty. The difference between Schumpeter's and Tucker's bankers was that the former more often crossed the line. Schumpeter's idealized banker, like his entrepreneur, was a "distinctly heroic figure, prepared (unlike most mortals) to venture forth boldly into the unknown."[31] Reducing the entrepreneurial process to a precise and careful comparison of alternatives with known probability distributions was a wholly unrealistic view of the process, and it eliminated the very necessary human qualities of boldness, audacity, and imagination.[32] This is not to imply that a Schumpeterian banker was rash or careless. Even his banker spent most of his day avoiding risk, but he was sometimes persuaded to set aside his rational, calculating manner and follow his intuition into the realm of uncertainty.

Richard Sylla argues that both Redlich and Hammond shunted discussions of antebellum banking onto an unfortunate siding by focusing inordinate attention on the extent to which early American banks engaged in pure, short-term mercantile lending.[33] A careful reading of the contemporary real-bills literature, however, reveals an ambivalence and hesitancy that Redlich and Hammond do not show. Instead of stating rigid rules, the theory actually said that banks *should mainly* lend on commercial paper and *largely* avoid industrial and agricultural credit.[34]

The era's bankers, if not the era's banking theorists, recognized that banks could safely hold some noncommercial, long-term loans as part of a balanced portfolio. Many commentators mistakenly associated real-bills lending with wholesaling, where stock was thought to turn over regularly and predictably. But Moulton rightly noted a similar regularity in the turnover of many manufacturers' inventories of raw materials and finished goods.[35]

It was possible, therefore, that loans to manufacturers were just as "commercial" as loans extended to wholesalers who marketed manufacturers' output. To differentiate a manufacturer's or artisan's notes and bills from a wholesaler's based solely on their different economic functions was to establish a false dichotomy between transforming a good's physical properties and transforming its physical location. Both were risky processes, both could be uncertain, both were productive, and both changed the essential nature of the good. In some instances, drawing a distinction was useful; in others, it was not.

It seems clear that pure real-bills theories were ill-founded in fact and ignored in actual practice. In the twentieth century, banks commonly renewed loans so that they often ran for months or even years. Moreover, Moulton estimated that about 30 percent of all bank loans, circa 1915, though nominally at short term, extended over long periods and financed fixed capital investment.[36] Another 30 percent financed manufacturers' working capital. In short, late nineteenth-and early twentieth-century commercial banks were one "of the most important of the institutions related to the process of capital formation."[37]

How important were they to capital formation and economic growth in the first half of the nineteenth century? To date, only scant attention has been paid to this issue, but the limited evidence suggests that early American banks preferred to loan at short term but did not eschew industrial finance. In his study of Stephen Girard's Philadelphia private bank, Donald Adams finds loans that averaged 90 to 120 days; he also finds artisans and manufacturers among the bank's more prominent clients.[38] Lance Davis, too, uncovers compelling evidence that antebellum bankers underwrote industrial development through the provision of short-term credit.[39] Davis reports that more than 90 percent of the credit extended to New England's largest textile mills between 1840 and 1860 was provided by banks. While these studies provide indirect evidence of potential for banks to influence the pattern of economic development, they do not systematically or directly study lending patterns and credit policies at America's earliest banks.

Table 3.1 presents evidence on one aspect of lending practices at eight antebellum banks.[40] The table reports average loan maturities, the standard deviation of loans, and the percent of notes renewed. Given previous interpretations of early American banking, the results are really quite remarkable. Among these eight banks, which represent a broad cross section, loan maturities averaged about 80 days. The private banking house of Thomas Branch & Sons of Petersburg consistently offered the longest terms, about 110 days. Yet, these were not exceptionally long compared to an 86-day average maturity at the Black River Bank, an 87-day maturity at the Bank of Gallatin and the State Bank of New Brunswick, or the 90-day maturity at the Bank of Cape Fear.

Data from the Black River Bank of Watertown, New York, facilitates a modest test of a real-bills effect. It is possible that the average loan terms

Table 3.1 Loan Features at Eight Antebellum Banks for Selected Years, 1815–1860; Average Maturity in Days; (Standard Deviation); {Percent Renewed}

Year	Bank of Cape Fear (N.C.)	Bank of Chester County (Pa.)	Bank of Gallatin (Tenn.)	Black River Bank (notes) (N.Y.)	Black River Bank (bills) (N.Y.)	Branch & Sons (Va.)	State Bank New Brunswick (N.J.)	Bank of Tenn. Memphis (Tenn.)
1815	92.6 (3.1) {42.2}	na (na) {74.4}						
1825	91.8 (4.7) {97.8}		86.7* (9.3) {na}					
1835	92.0 (12.7) {76.0}							
1845	90.4 (6.2) {100.0}			85.5 (21.6) {na}	72.3 (30.2) {na}	112.8 (41.9) {na}		
1850				85.6 (27.1) {na}	75.6 (33.4) {na}	116.9 (67.2) {0.0}		
1855				73.2 (49.8) {4.9}	58.0 (25.5) {0.8}	104.4 (56.1) {0.0}	87.0 (35.1) {na}	77.6 (29.6) {na}
1860				77.9 (40.8) {6.2}	62.3 (27.7) {4.5}			85.1 (41.9) {na}

Notes: First number listed in each year/bank cell is arithmetic average maturity of all loans reported. Second number (in parentheses) is the standard deviation. Third number (in braces) is percent of discounts renewed. For the Black River Bank, bills were distinguished from notes by reported place of payment. Any discount payable outside the immediate locale of Watertown, New York, was treated as a bill of exchange. The principal places of payment were New York City, Albany, and Boston. Black River Bank 1860 values from 1859; Branch & Sons 1845 values from 1847; Memphis branch of Bank of Tennessee 1855 values from 1858; State Bank of New Brunswick 1855 values from 1852/53. Values for State Bank of New Brunswick are for only 228 notes protested for nonpayment in 1852/53. It is assumed that the maturity structure of protested notes was not substantially different from those of notes paid at maturity.

Sources: Bank of Cape Fear, *Records, 1815–1846;* Bank of Chester County, *Discount Book, 1815–1819;* Bank of Gallatin, *Discount Book, 1822–1824;* Black River Bank, *Discount Book #2, Discount Book #3;* Branch & Company Records, *Bill Books, 1845–1858;* State Bank of New Brunswick, *Protested Notes, 1852–1853;* Bank of Tennessee, *General Check Ledger, 1858–1862.*

mask a fundamental division between bills of exchange and promissory notes. It could be that legitimate bills ran for short periods while promissory notes (or accommodation paper) ran for longer periods, and combining the two conceals poor practice. The Black River Bank's clerk clearly distinguished between locally payable promissory notes and bills of exchange, and table 3.1 separately reports the summary statistics. From 1845 to 1860, bills ran about 13 fewer days to maturity than notes, a statistically significant difference in every year.[41] It should be noted, however, that a difference as small as 6 days is statistically significant.

Although these banks maintained loan portfolios with similar average maturities, each arrived at that average in its own unique way. The Bank of Cape Fear loans, for example, were closely distributed around the mean with a standard deviation of only about 3 days in 1815. Moreover, its minimum maturities rarely fell below 30 days, and its maximums rarely exceeded 100. The Bank of Gallatin apparently followed similar practice, but only two years' data make firm conclusions impossible.

Practices at the Black River Bank and Branch & Sons differed dramatically. Maturities at these institutions were widely variable, with standard deviations around their respective means commonly in excess of 20, even 30, days. Additionally, these banks offered demand loans (callable without prior notice, effectively a zero-day maturity), as well as a handful of loans with maturities of a year or more. In 1855, the owner of the Black River Bank gave his youngest (and reportedly most troublesome) son a large loan with a five-year maturity and sent him to Ohio to seek his fortune.[42] Although these sorts of long-term, noncommercial loans were sometimes made, they were rare.

A second fundamental aspect of real-bills lending was the banks' refusal to renew loans. Real-bills bankers expected repayment at maturity and frowned on renewals because a continually renewed loan quickly devolved into accommodation lending secured only by the personal collateral of the borrower. Again, the evidence in table 3.1 shows wide disparities in bank behavior. The Bank of Cape Fear, for example, often renewed more than 90 percent of its notes. Occasionally, the percent dipped as low as 40, but this even exceeded most other banks. In fact, the Black River Bank and Branch & Sons adopted an opposite policy and were loath to renew. Thomas Branch rarely renewed a note or bill; the Black River Bank typically renewed less than 5 percent of its loans.

The relatively high renewal rates at the Bank of Cape Fear in rural North Carolina (about 90 percent) and the Bank of Chester County in rural Pennsylvania (about 75 percent) may follow from the predominance of agricultural loans in these banks' portfolios.[43] Faced with few legitimate alternatives, banks in small towns may have quickly exhausted the supply of mercantile paper and filled out their portfolios with farm loans. Many farm loans surely financed farm improvements, were repeatedly renewed, and thus represented de facto long-term, fixed-capital bank finance. Other farm loans financed crop planting and would not be repaid until after the harvest. A 90-day loan, then, quickly became a 180-day or even a 270-day loan because it was renewed at maturity until the crop was sold through a factor and the proceeds were realized by the farmer or planter.

Long extensions and repeated renewals did not indicate that these loans were used for fixed investment or that the underlying loans were doubtful. They could just as easily represent a continuous need for working capital. It may have been less costly for a bank to extend a loan than to make a new one, and it may have been more convenient for the borrower to extend the loan than to settle and borrow again in a day or two. It is probable, however, that a large percentage of renewed loans was devoted to fixed investment.[44]

While agricultural loans were excoriated by real-bills advocates, they made an important contribution toward contemporary economic growth. The first stage of economic development is the commercialization of agriculture, which generally requires specialization, as well as increases in scale. Bank loans facilitated both and promoted economic growth, a fact that was not lost on contemporaries. Some banks, in fact, like the Farmers and Mechanics Bank of Philadelphia, were chartered explicitly to provide credit to the agricultural sector. Because the city's existing banks refused to loan to farmers, the Farmers and Mechanics Bank was required to extend an amount equal to 10 percent of its capital stock as long-term credit to farmers secured by mortgages.[45]

Mortgage lending of this sort clearly violated the fundamental precepts of real bills, but it surely promoted agricultural development and therefore represented a justifiable departure from accepted practice as long as it represented part of a balanced portfolio.[46] But agricultural lending, per se, did not have to represent a significant departure from "commercial" lending. Loans used to finance the harvesting of crops, the fall fattening of livestock, or driving that stock to market were essentially commercial and short term.[47] In each case, the loan underwrote a marketable output with a value in excess of the value of the loan, and this was not substantially different from financing the harvesting and shipment of cotton and tobacco to European markets, or the shipment of cotton textiles from New England to the Old Northwest, or the production and shipment of iron farm implements from Pennsylvania foundries to southern plantations.

Evidence from four urban banks shows that antebellum banks, like late nineteenth- and early twentieth-century banks noted by Moulton, provided industrial credit while maintaining a real-bills appearance by lending short term with few renewals. Table 3.2 reports the sectoral distribution of borrowing at the Black River Bank of Watertown, New York; the Memphis branch of the Bank of Tennessee; the Bank of Charleston, South Carolina; and Branch & Sons of Petersburg, Virginia. For each of the reported years, each bank's borrowers were linked with a city directory or a manuscript census to determine the borrower's principal occupation. Generally, about one-third of the borrowers were matched, but as long as the unmatched

Table 3.2 Sectoral Composition of Bank Borrowers, Percent of Loans by Dollar Value, Selected Years

				Sector				
Year	Ag	Con	Mer	Mfg	Ser	Tran	Misc	Unknown
Black River Bank								
1855	0.2%	0.2%	33.9%	3.7%	20.7%	0.0%	0.3%	39.1%
1856	0.2	0.2	23.1	13.0	4.5	0.0	0.1	58.8
1857	0.3	0.2	22.0	10.4	5.8	0.0	0.1	61.1
1858	0.1	0.1	37.4	13.4	5.8	0.5	0.0	42.7
1859	5.8	4.3	15.8	19.2	12.1	12.1	30.7	
Memphis Branch of the Bank of Tennessee								
1858	1.1%	1.0%	23.1%	7.6%	26.8%	0.4%	10.9%	29.0%
1859	1.5	4.7	28.7	8.3	27.2	4.2	4.3	21.2
1860	0.0	2.1	37.2	5.6	16.8	15.3	5.3	17.6
1861	0.3	2.5	44.8	2.9	16.5	2.3	3.8	26.9
Bank of Charleston								
1863	0.2%	0.6%	49.2%	6.3%	6.0%	1.1%	1.1%	35.6%
Branch & Sons								
1850	10.9%	0.0%	12.7%	46.0%	8.0%	0.9%	1.3%	20.2%
1851	14.4	0.0	21.6	20.6	9.1	1.0	0.4	33.0
1852	12.3	0.0	25.1	38.3	4.8	1.5	0.5	17.5
1853	11.1	0.0	13.2	39.2	13.3	0.8	0.0	22.4
1854	6.6	0.0	31.6	17.9	13.7	1.5	0.0	28.1
1855	11.7	0.0	18.3	13.6	22.4	0.8	0.3	32.9

Notes: For sectoral definitions, see text. Occupations and sectors were determined by matching the borrower to either a manuscript census or a city directory or both closest to loan date.

Sources: Black River Bank: Jefferson County Historical Society, *Black River Bank Records* (1855–1859); *Watertown . . . Directory for 1856–57;* U.S. Census Office, Eighth Census (1860), manuscript census for Jefferson County New York; New York State Census (1855), manuscript for Watertown city. Memphis Branch of the Bank of Tennessee: Tennessee State Library and Archives, *Bank of Tennessee, 1838–1865; Williams' Memphis Directory* (1860); U.S. Census Office, Eighth Census (1860), manuscript for Shelby County, Tennessee. Bank of Charleston: *Records; Directory of the City of Charleston* (1860). Branch & Company: Virginia Historical Society, *Branch & Company Records; First Annual Directory; Second Annual Directory; Richmond, Petersburg . . . Directory;* U.S. Census Office, Eighth Census (1860), manuscript for various Virginia counties.

borrowers were randomly distributed, the resulting figures in the occupational categories should fairly represent the underlying industrial distribution of these banks' loan portfolios.[48]

Consider first the two large southern banks, namely, the Bank of Charleston and the Memphis branch of the Bank of Tennessee. A widely accepted historical interpretation, based largely on contemporary observations (and complaints), is that southern banks eschewed both agricultural and industrial lending. The evidence on these banks' borrowers is generally consistent with this characterization. The Bank of Charleston, in particular, shows a marked preference for mercantile lending. Nearly one-half of its loans went to merchants, while only about 6 percent went to manufacturers and artisans. Another 6 percent went to those employed in service industries, mostly attorneys.

A different picture emerges for the two banks located in emerging regional, commercial, and industrial centers. In 1860, Petersburg ranked as the forty-ninth largest industrial city in the United States and the third largest among southern cities. The private banking house of Thomas Branch & Sons loaned to many emerging manufacturers. Throughout most of the early 1850s, as much as one-third to one-half of Branch & Sons' lending went to manufacturers and artisans. The reason for the rapid decline in the mid-1850s has yet to be determined. It may have been that Branch & Sons' practice of rediscounting notes at the Petersburg branch of the Bank of Virginia and the Farmers Bank of Virginia ultimately undermined his entrepreneurial advantage. Once the city's commercial banks determined the quality of the industrial bills and notes discounted by Branch & Sons, they approached these borrowers themselves and dealt with them directly instead of through Branch & Sons, agency.[49] An alternative, and equally plausible, explanation is that with the increase in the number of unidentified borrowers, the bank continued to act as a niche provider of venture capital to young, entrepreneurial manufacturers who were not large enough or prominent enough to be listed in Petersburg's city directories.

Just as Petersburg was emerging as a regional, even national, manufacturing center, Watertown, New York, was strategically located near the convergence of the St. Lawrence River, Lake Ontario, and the Erie Canal. It, too, emerged as a smaller, regional commercial and manufacturing center. Like Branch & Sons, the Black River Bank was quick to exploit opportunities to lend to manufacturers. Though the Black River Bank's portfolio never absorbed the same relative proportion of manufacturing paper as Branch & Sons, it regularly extended 10 to 20 percent of its credit to manufacturers and artisans.

Figures 3.2 and 3.3 also suggest that both banks held portfolios representative of the industrial mix of the local economy. Figure 3.2 compares the percentage of independent businesses listed in a Watertown city directory of 1856–57 by sector with the percentage of credit extended to each sector by the Black River Bank. Merchants and manufacturers received credit in proportion to their general representation in the local economy. Those employed in services were underrepresented, while construction businesses and farmers were modestly overrepresented, among the bank's customers.

Figure 3.3 paints a similar portrait of the Branch & Sons lending policies

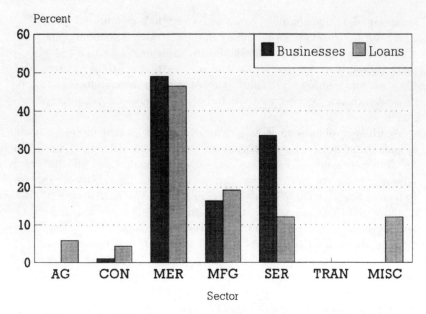

Percent

Figure 3.2 Loan Distribution by Sector and Percentage of Firms by Sector: *Watertown, New York.* Sources: Black River Bank, *Discount Book #3; Watertown . . . Directory for 1856–57.* From "An Engine of Growth: Real Bills and Schumpeterian Banking in Antebellum New York" by Howard Bodenhorn, *Explorations in Economic History* 36 (1999), figure 3, p. 294. © Reprinted with the permission of Academic Press.

and Petersburg's industrial mix. Merchants and manufacturers received credit in about the same percentage as their representation in the local economy. Construction firms were underrepresented among the bank's borrowers even while service sector workers (notably clerks and attorneys) and planters were modestly overrepresented.

Finding that banks provided short-term working capital to manufacturers in the early stages of American industrialization reveals the necessity of reinterpreting the importance of finance in the Industrial Revolution. Many economic historians have argued that Anglo-American banks offered few advantages to the emerging industries of the nineteenth century. T. S. Ashton, for example, writes that "it is doubtful whether the banking system was a principal source of the capital by which the new technique was applied to manufacture."[50] Similarly, Robert Puth writes: "Commercial banks [were] imperfect devices for meeting some of the financial needs of new industries."[51]

The shortcoming of these interpretations, however, is that they focus inordinate attention on fixed capital in manufacturing and the unwillingness of Anglo-style banks to finance or underwrite it. Yet, a great deal of recent

Percent

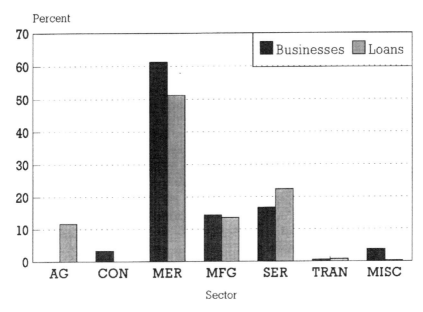

Figure 3.3 Loan Distribution by Sector and Percentage of Firms by Sector: Petersburg, Virginia. Sources: Branch & Company Records, *Bill Book: Second Annual Directory for Petersburg*

research suggests that fixed capital played a small role in the earliest stages of economic development. Adam Smith's analysis places working capital, not fixed capital, at center stage of the incipient capitalism he describes.[52] Contemporary estimates of early nineteenth-century British capital stock led one historian to conclude that it was not obvious "that the nation's economic activity was appreciably more [fixed] capital intensive" midway through the Industrial Revolution than previously.[53]

As late as the 1850s, investments in the kinds of fixed capital commonly associated with economic modernity absorbed a small share of most firms' total capital requirements. Even in large-scale enterprises, the ratio of fixed to working capital was little different from that of many small-scale manufactories. In iron and copper forges, the ratio of fixed to total capital averaged about 11 percent; in textiles, between 8 and 17 percent; in brewing, 10 percent or less.[54] Even in the most capital-intensive, state-of-the-art cotton textile mill circa 1830, fixed capital represented only about one-half of invested capital. There was, writes Phyllis Deane, "no signs of a dramatic leap in the capital formation ratio or a sharp discontinuity in the nature of capital itself."[55]

What of the United States with its more capital-intensive "American system" of manufacturers? Using information collected for the *McLane Report* of 1832 (a survey of manufacturers in the northeastern United States), Kenneth Sokoloff estimates that working capital absorbed a much greater percentage of most manufacturers' invested capital than fixed capital.[56] Including accounts receivable, the working capital share of total capital absorbed from 40 to 90 percent of manufacturing capital. Yet, this total may overstate the fixed capital requirements of most manufactories. Outside the textile industries, machinery and tools made up a small percentage of total capital. For most industries, fixed capital–to–total capital ratios fell between 1 and 12 percent. Moreover, the lion's share of this fixed capital was tied up in land and buildings. G. S. Callender's conclusion, "the amount of capital necessary to establish a manufacturing industry was not large, and could be easily supplied by a few men," seems accurate.[57]

Because early manufactories were so heavily reliant on working capital, they were more concerned with securing steady sources of short-term rather than long-term credit. Fixed capital investments could be satisfied with a modest initial investment supplemented with regularly plowed-back profits. Manufacturers and artisans, then, faced financing decisions and problems not unlike those facing merchants whose fixed capital requirements might be small, but whose inventory and work-in-progress represented a significant investment financed with short-term credit. And, as seen above, banks provided both merchants and manufacturers with short-term (if not real-bills) credit generally proportional to their representation in the local community.

Finding banks willing to lend to manufacturers, as well as merchants, in conjunction with research showing that a preoccupation with large-scale fixed investment is misplaced, opens up the possibility of an entirely new interpretation of the role of Anglo-style banks in promoting economic development. Under the established view, bank lending policies failed to meet the needs of the emerging industrial sector and, thus, failed to assist economic development. Mounting evidence that access to working capital and trade credit were more crucial to industrial success than fixed capital implies that the traditional interpretation was incorrect. American banks did not inhibit growth by refusing long-term credit demands because little long-term credit was needed (at least among merchants and manufacturers; farmers may represent an exception). "What was needed," writes Sidney Pollard, "was a sufficient injection of short-term credit into the system to allow the mutual extension of credit to be developed. For the rest, banks merely had to provide a smooth transfer mechanism."[58] It seems that they did.

Financing Entrepreneurship and Innovation

Although the industrial distribution of loans at several antebellum banks suggests that they were not tied exclusively to mercantile lending, it does not show that they were innovative Schumpeterian banks that interrupted static equilibria. As Moulton notes, real-bills banking (in its broadest sense) was consistent with lending to manufacturing and agriculture. Providing working capital by way of short-term nonrenewable loans was "commercial" banking regardless of the exact economic function of the borrower, so simply lending to manufacturers does not necessarily imply innovative, risk-taking banking. It does, of course, imply that banks could be of direct and immediate use to manufacturers and could, therefore, play an essential role in economic development, but Schumpeterian banking requires taking that extra step.

Unfortunately, testing Schumpeter's hypothesis is fraught with difficulties. How do we measure innovative thinking and foresight? How can we determine whether one banker saw outside the box while another remained trapped inside it? As Sylla points out, we may derive (as some have) macroeconomic tests of Schumpeter's hypothesis, but "in the end, the Schumpeterian hypothesis pertains to microeconomic relationships between individual banks and the enterprises they financed."[59]

Thomas Branch was clearly one of Schumpeter's visionary bankers. From its inception, his private banking house loaned to the city's tobacco factories, cotton factories, and flour mills. One instance of Branch's foresight stands out, however. Uriah Wells opened the Petersburg Iron, Bell, and Brass Foundry in 1847, was noted as much for his mechanical genius as his ability as a founder, and was sometimes called the city's "father of foundries."[60] In 1853, Wells decided to expand into the production of railroad cars and increased his facilities from one plant employing 60 hands to three plants employing as many as 400 hands.[61] "Although agricultural implements and carriages were still important products, the Wells plant looked to the ever increasing and expanding railroads for the bulk of its business and concentrated on the manufacture of locomotives, box cars, and flat cars."[62]

Such an expansion surely required larger lines of credit than he had carried before, and Wells turned to all sources of capital. Branch & Sons accommodated him for the first time with loans in 1853 and 1854 to purchase the coal needed to fire his furnaces. In 1855, Branch simply discounted his personal notes.[63] Although this is the only readily documented story of Branch assisting entrepreneurship, there must have been others.

Loveland Paddock, president and principal shareholder of the Black River Bank, also fit the Schumpeterian mold. In 1848, Moses Eames, a cheese maker in Rutland, New York, recognizing the value of large-scale steam engines, came up with the idea of a small-scale steam engine generating only a few horsepower.[64] He reasoned that such an engine would be useful to farmers, artisans, and small-scale manufacturers. When Eames had some work done on his cheese vats at George Goulding's machine shop, Eames mentioned his idea to Gilbert Bradford, Goulding's shop foreman. Bradford recommended Eames's idea to Goulding, noting that the development of the machine might benefit local industry and generate additional profits for the firm. Goulding opposed the idea. Rather than assist farmers, Goulding argued, a portable steam engine was more likely to "kill every farmer there is around here."[65]

Bradford ignored his employer's advice and spent his spare time building prototypes in Goulding's own machine shop. In 1849, Bradford constructed a working model that generated about one-half horsepower. He demonstrated its usefulness by installing it in a local newspaper office where it powered the printing press. Bradford applied to Goulding for financial and mechanical assistance. Goulding refused, still considering the machine more dangerous than practical. In 1850, Horace Greeley visited Watertown to deliver a public address, at which time he observed the little engine. Impressed by its ingenuity, Greeley wrote of it in a column in the *New York Tribune* in July 1850 and mentioned it in his capacity as a U.S. commissioner at the Crystal Palace exhibition in 1851.[66]

Despite Greeley's admiration, Bradford could find neither financing nor technical assistance. In 1851, he convinced fellow machinist Charles Hoard to enter into a partnership and they set up shop. They immediately turned to the Black River Bank for financial assistance, and the bank responded with a number of small loans. Over the next two years, the bank discounted about a half-dozen notes for the firm of Hoard & Bradford. By 1857, the firm employed 150 machinists working nights and weekends to fill orders for portable steam engines. In 1898, the firm still existed as the Portable Steam Engine Manufacturing Company and remained one of the "leading industrial concerns of northern New York."[67]

Although it is impossible to know whether the Black River Bank's actions were necessary for the firm's success, the bank's actions do provide something of an object lesson regarding the connection between visionary entrepreneurs and visionary bankers. The bank demonstrated a combination of caution and boldness, the very qualities Schumpeter prized. Although the bank offered Hoard & Bradford financial assistance, it did so in a limited way. The last half-dozen notes discounted by Hoard, when he was still operating his machine shop, averaged about $325; the first half-dozen notes discounted by Hoard & Bradford averaged about $63.[68]

Several other instances exist of the Black River Bank offering financial assistance to fledgling enterprises. Benjamin Hotchkin established a tannery and harness manufactory in late 1854; by January 1855, he was discounting notes at the Black River Bank.[69] In 1853, J. D. Crowner began construction of the Crowner House Hotel, a three-story brick building capable of accommodating more than 100 guests. By October of that year, Crowner was discounting notes at the Black River Bank. Similarly, I. N. Remington established the Remington Paper Mill in 1853 and the Black River Bank was discounting his notes by July of that year.[70] The bank was, in Schumpeter's terms, interrupting the circular flow, directing funds to enterprises not yet putting anything back into the flow. This was the very essence of financial entrepreneurship.

Short-Term Loans and Long-Term Relationships

Information Asymmetries and
Banking Relationships

On 13 January 1855, James Colwell (a carriage maker) and L. S. Rice (a merchant) each offered a $100 note payable in 90 days to the Black River Bank for discount. The bank discounted both notes. Colwell paid an effective interest rate of 6.43 percent; Rice paid 7.22 percent. On 19 August 1858, Benjamin F. Dill offered a $600 note for discount at the recently opened Memphis branch of the Bank of Tennessee. A few weeks later, he discounted a second note for the same amount. In 1859, after he repaid his first two notes, Dill discounted seven more notes with an average value of $1,000. In 1860, he discounted five more averaging $2,100. The bank's treatment of Dill was not unique. In 1859, D. L. Greer's average discounted note was $867; in 1860, $1,475; and in 1861, $2,000.

While there were, undoubtedly, myriad factors that influenced the Black River Bank's discount rates, one immediate factor was the length of the bank-customer relationship. Colwell was a longtime customer who had previously discounted (and repaid) 92 notes. Rice was a relative newcomer who had previously discounted only 9 notes. The managers of the Black River Bank presumably knew a great deal more about James Colwell than about L. S. Rice, and the higher price paid by Rice reflects the greater risk or uncertainty surrounding his loan.

Similarly, the Bank of Tennessee's pattern of offering relatively small loans to first-time customers and larger loans to longtime customers is consistent with the hypothesis that long-term bank-customer relationships allay some asymmetric information problems. It is not surprising that banks increased a repeat customer's line of credit because longer relationships afforded the bank more opportunities to make judgments about the prospective borrower's creditworthiness.

In autumn 1856, three borrowers approached the Black River Bank with $5,000 promissory notes (more than five times the average loan amount). One note was discounted for the Potsdam & Watertown Railroad; the second for O. & E. L. Paddock, commission merchants (general wholesalers); and the third for Charles F. Symonds, a merchant miller. Each was a 60-day note; each paid about 7 percent interest. What differentiated the notes was the number of endorsers. The Paddocks' note had a single endorser, Symonds' note had two endorsers, and the railroad's note carried ten endorsements.

When loan amounts and interest rates were held constant, among borrowers whose bank relationships differed in length, the bank found a different margin along which to change the terms of the agreement to further insure itself against the risk of default. Because it did not, perhaps could not given New York's usury law, alter the other terms of the loan, the bank protected itself by demanding that the relative newcomer—the Potsdam & Watertown Railroad—provide more guarantors than longtime borrowers.

The asymmetric information approach to financial intermediation argues that intermediaries exist because they mitigate moral hazard and adverse selection problems that naturally arise in financing uncertain entrepreneurial projects. Intermediaries capture economies of scale or exploit other comparative advantages in the production of information about borrowers.[71] Banks differ from other financial intermediaries in two respects. First, they specialize by catering to borrowers too small to economically invest in publicly observable reputational capital, so relevant information is acquired only at considerable expense.[72] Second, banks bundle transactions and clearing services with lending.[73] Joint provision affords the lender more detailed information about a borrower's past choices and present condition. By providing deposit services, for example, a bank observes a firm's cash flows, which provide the bank with information about the firm's investment opportunities and financial capabilities.

In addition to gathering and assessing information, banks typically engage in three distinct monitoring activities to mitigate problems arising from information asymmetries. Ex ante evaluations and screening reduce adverse selection problems. Interim monitoring involves observing and, perhaps, supervising behavior in the interval between when the loan is made and when it is repaid. Ex post monitoring consists of costly state verification in which the project's outcome is ascertained.[74] If a good outcome is observed, the bank-borrower relationship continues. If a bad outcome is observed, the bank determines the reason. If it was the result of postcontractual opportunistic behavior on the borrower's behalf, the relationship is terminated. If the bad outcome was the result of events beyond the borrower's control, the loan may be renegotiated and the relationship may continue, albeit on a different footing. This sequence of ex ante, interim, and ex post monitoring fosters the development of long-term relationships between banks and borrowers, like those outlined above, particularly with those borrowers whose projects prove profitable more often than not.

Several studies have modeled the association between the length or strength of the bank-borrower relationship and the time path of loan rates. Mitchell Petersen and Raghuram Rajan argue that adverse selection and moral hazard problems have significant effects on the borrowing abilities of inexperienced and small firms.[75] By developing a relationship with a bank, the young or small firm can provide the lender with ample opportunity to observe and monitor the firm, thereby lowering the firm's borrowing costs. The longer the relationship, the lower the bank's costs and risks, so loan rates decline and credit availability increases as the relationship matures. Loan rates, then, should be inversely related to the firm's age and, more important, to the duration of the specific bank-borrower relationship. Similarly, Arnould Boot and Anjan Thakor show that collateral requirements are negatively correlated with the length of the relationship.[76] Borrowers are asked to pay higher rates and pledge more collateral early in the relationship. As the borrower experiences repeated project success, loan rates and collateral requirements decline.

These conclusions stand in sharp contrast to the implications of Steven Sharpe's model.[77] Sharpe argues that long-term relationships exist not because banks treat repeat customers well, but because borrowers become "informationally captured." Although many financial economists argue that insider information, monitoring, enforcement, and long-term relationships mitigate information asymmetries and allow for a more efficient allocation of loanable funds, Sharpe's model implies that the banks' informational advantages lead to allocational distortions.

In Sharpe's model, competing banks initially offer excessive loan amounts at below equilibrium prices to attract customers so that they can capture them. In later periods, the bank extracts its monopoly rents. First-time borrowers are given too much capital at inefficiently low rates and second-time borrowers are given too little credit at a rate in excess of the informationally advantaged rate. Longtime customers cannot move to other lenders because they find it costly to convey credible information about themselves to other lenders. Moreover, adverse selection makes it difficult for one bank to draw off another's good customers (to skim the cream, if you will) without also attracting some of its bad customers.[78]

Others, like Rajan and Mitchell Berlin, argue that the competitive character of the local banking market or the availability of nonbank financing influences the time path of loan rates.[79] Rajan, for example, argues that information-intensive borrowers will generate rents sufficient to provide a bank with a normal return on its investment in information in the long run, but neither party can fully commit to this mutually beneficial contract because of the incompleteness and unenforceability of some contractual arrangements.[80] From the bank's perspective, it would be optimal to offer first-time borrowers relatively low interest rates to avoid adverse selection problems, then recoup this early-period subsidization by charging rates slightly in excess of competitive, informationally advantaged rates.

Banks cannot follow this otherwise optimal strategy if nonbank financing (bonds or commercial paper) is widely available. Once a firm has demonstrated repeated project success, it will turn to lower cost, arm's-length markets. Even in the absence of nonbank alternatives, competitive banking markets can distort capital allocation. In markets with little effective competition, the probability of one bank pilfering another's better customers is low. In this case, the bank can take the entirety of the future relationship into account when determining its current loan pricing policy. A bank can simultaneously avoid the adverse selection problem and charge a below-market (risk-adjusted) loan rate to attract potentially profitable customers knowing that it will increase its rates later in the relationship after the borrower has more fully revealed its true risk characteristics.

In competitive banking markets, mature, successful firms can seek out banks other than its current one to get better loan terms. Because the first-mover bank cannot write or enforce contractual commitments by borrowers to maintain the relationship, the first-mover bank suffers losses by offering low loan rates early. Thus, competition limits a bank's ability to engage in long-term subsidization. Moreover, competitive banking markets inhibit banks' abilities to foster long-term relationships, so young and small firms will have a more difficult time attracting capital.

The Petersen-Rajan and Boot-Thakor theories posit that loan rates fall as the bank-borrower relationship matures, the Sharpe hypothesis posits a rising loan rate, and the Rajan and Berlin hypotheses are inconclusive but consistent with a flat time path of loan rates in competitive banking markets. The modern empirical literature has yet to provide a strong or compelling case for any of these theories. Evidence from antebellum banking markets, however, provides qualified support for the first hypothesis, namely, that bank loan rates decline as bank-borrower relationships mature, holding constant the competitive environment.

Employing the records of the Black River Bank, figure 3.4 presents an estimated trajectory of loan rates as the bank-borrower relationship progresses.[81] The evidence is consistent with the Petersen-Rajan and Boot-Thakor hypotheses that loan rates diminish as the relationship matures.

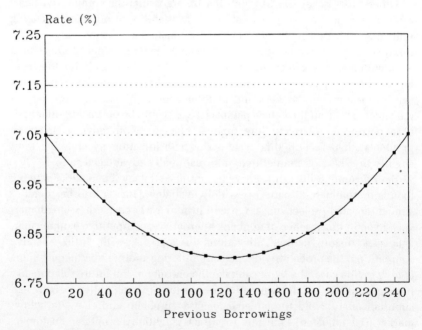

Figure 3.4 Trajectory of Loan Rates and the Length of the Lending Relationship. Source: Calculated from information in Black River Bank, *Discount Book #3*.

First-time borrowers at the bank in 1855 paid an estimated 7.05 percent on loans. A customer who had borrowed 50 times paid 15 fewer basis points on his loan. One who had borrowed 120 times paid 25 fewer basis points. Were these large enough reductions to make exclusive relationships valuable to borrowers? That is, were these economically significant differences? Yes, they were. In modern financial markets, a move of 25 basis points in interest rates is considered large; it would certainly get the attention of both commentators and borrowers. In antebellum America, it was rather substantial as well. At the Black River Bank in 1855, the average borrower paid 7.15 percent, while the prime rate on high-grade commercial paper averaged 6.77 percent, or 0.38 percent (38 basis points) lower. A long-term borrower, then, who paid 25 fewer basis points on a loan paid a rate closer to the prime rate than the average bank rate. In modern financial markets, only the best (lowest risk) borrowers pay equivalently low bank rates, so it is likely that only similarly low-risk borrowers paid similarly low rates.

Beyond about 120 borrowings, loan rates actually increased. It is possible that frequent borrowers became, from the bank's point of view, too-frequent borrowers; recurrent borrowing may have implied firm weakness, insufficient owner-contributed equity, or overly risky projects. But it seems unlikely that habitual borrowers were considerably riskier than other borrowers; otherwise, their loan rates would have been higher, not lower, than average. The more likely explanation is that if a single borrower borrowed 20 or 30 times each year, the bank's portfolio became effectively less diversified and its realizations grew more closely tied to the realizations of a few borrowers' entrepreneurial projects. With an average maturity of 80 days, 30 annual borrowings implied that 7 loans were outstanding at a given time. The bank responded by raising rates, which reflected the increased risk to the bank due to less portfolio diversification and the increased risk of postcontractual opportunistic behavior by the borrower. With several large loans outstanding, the borrower's incentive to default may have increased.

The length of the bank-borrower relationship also bore directly on loan sizes. Figure 3.5 plots the estimated trajectory of loan amounts as the banking relationship matured. First-time borrowers at the Black River Bank borrowed an average of $250.[82] A proprietor or partnership that had borrowed 90 times borrowed nearly twice as much. A firm that had borrowed 200 times borrowed an average of $665. But like loan rates that began to increase for very frequent borrowers, loan amounts for recurrent borrowers fell after about 200 borrowings. The reason is probably analogous to the explanation for higher rates for habitual borrowers: 30 borrowings per year implied that 7 were outstanding at a given time, and 7 large loans simply diminished the bank's ability to diversify its portfolio. It was costly to lend excessive amounts to a few large borrowers. An effectively diversified portfolio implied a large number of small loans to a cross section of the local business community. What is good for modern mutual funds was no less beneficial

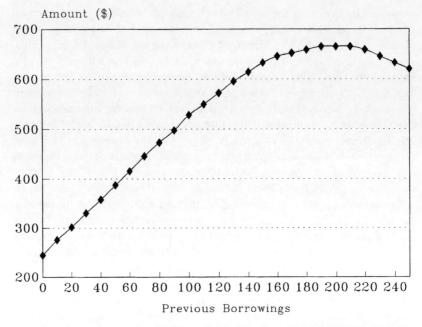

Figure 3.5 Trajectory of Loan Amounts and the Length of the Lending Relationship. Source: Calculated from information in Black River Bank, *Discount Book #3*.

for mid-nineteenth-century banks. Broad diversification across geographies and industries smoothed returns and reduced risks.

Concluding Remarks

Reduced loan rates, larger loan amounts, and reduced collateral demands for longtime borrowers is consistent with the theoretical finance literature. This literature argues that reputation effects are important in both arm's-length debt markets (bonds and commercial paper) and private bank transactions. The models developed in this literature predict that a lender's ability to accumulate information over the life of its relationship with a borrower allows it to refine the terms of its loans. Forming and maintaining relationships are economically important activities because information asymmetries make small and young firms more reliant on bank financing than large and established firms with publicly observable reputations.

There is a general sentiment, historically at least, that many of the more notable technological breakthroughs occurred within small and young firms. Modern corporate research and development have reduced the relative importance of small-firm innovation in some industries, but small-firm innovation remains important in others (non-Microsoft computer software comes to mind), and small firms were an important element of nineteenth-century technological advancement.[83] Early American banks, from the proprietorial Black River Bank in northern New York state to the Memphis branch of the Bank of Tennessee and most of the rest in between, directly supported small-firm technological and entrepreneurial breakthroughs. If long-term relationships with borrowers made bankers more willing to support potentially significant entrepreneurial projects, they were unarguably economically important.

But banks did not have to demonstrate Schumpeterian insights in every loan they made. By adopting a real-bills policy in that loans were short-term and regularly renegotiated, banks protected themselves from the most egregious forms of borrower moral hazard. Even routine loans promoted development if bankers provided routine credit to emerging sectors and industries. The evidence reported above suggests that banks were valuable sources of credit to incipient industrialists. Although most bankers eschewed long-term credit to finance fixed-capital investment, American manufacturing was not short-circuited for lack of long-term credit. Manufactories typically had small fixed-capital requirements that could be met by the pooled savings of one or two partners. What weighed heavily on manufacturers was short-term working capital, and this was exactly the type of credit Anglo-American banks provided.

4

New England

Small Banks and Familial Ties

Generations of monetary and banking historians have held up New England banks as models of probity.[1] Many attributed these banks' conservatism to the social and economic standing of their promoters. Cities such as Boston and Providence were well-established commercial centers when the first commercial banks appeared, and families such as the Bowdoins of Boston and the Browns of Providence were the guiding forces behind the earliest New England banks.[2] The men were successful merchants with established reputations and valuable international trading connections, and they recognized both the usefulness of banks as creators of credit and the potentially large costs of staking a soon-tarnished bank. Above all, they understood that bad banking was bad for business, their own and everyone else's.

Though historians generally defend these early bankers' prudence, their conservatism was not always lauded or applauded by contemporaries. When the New Haven Bank of Connecticut proved more conservative than its two local competitors in extending credit, it drew bitter complaints from disappointed would-be borrowers, and pamphleteers condemned its restraint. "[A]s to the slow, timid, formal, grinding, patriotic New Haven Bank, wrote one pamphleteer," its glory is eclipsed, "it goes on in the old jog of its early fame, loaning its money in the fashion of ancients . . . it brags less of its liberality and it is more steadily pinching and penurious than its patriotic neighbors with their large investments."[3] Such was the fine line antebellum bankers were forced to tread. Liberality might endanger a bank's continuance; penuriousness might endanger the frustrated borrower's. Credit was the lifeblood of trade and, if doled out in miserly portions, banks were of little consequence.

Despite their reputed conservatism, New England banks were not inconsequential. As the region's agricultural sector declined, labor moved into cities and towns and found employment in emerging industries.[4] Mill towns such as Lowell, Lawrence, Haverhill, and Worcester arose along fast-moving rivers and exploited cheap water power. As the mills expanded and the mill towns grew, banking facilities mushroomed. In 1840, Lowell claimed two banks; Haverhill, two; Worcester, four. Twenty years later, Lowell supported six banks; Lawrence, two; Haverhill, three; and Worcester, six. And these banks surely played an important part in the region's industrial development. Lance Davis reports that banks provided nearly 100 percent of the short-term capital used by eight important New England textile mills in 1840. As late as 1860, 90 percent of these mills' short-term capital was bank-supplied.[5]

Local sources of credit, while certainly important, were often less critical to success in commerce or manufacturing than was usually imagined. Lacking access to a local bank, mill operators and other manufacturers could and did borrow in Boston's and even New York City's short-term capital markets. Financial capital was an unusually fungible resource, and a respected, established, profitable enterprise could find willing lenders even at great distances. Start-up firms and commercial neophytes, on the other hand, had more idiosyncratic risks and were more dependent on personal relationships and local sources of credit. It was important, for this reason, that banks in different circumstances acted differently. One-size-fits-all credit facilities were uneconomic in many, if not most, circumstances.[6]

We saw previously that this was generally the case. Rural and city banks, large and small, held different portfolios and catered to different clienteles. But this was their great strength, not their great weakness. Nearly a century ago, Howard Kemble Stokes wrote that "the development of banking was to a large degree a normal adaptation of banks to the business of their respective communities."[7] This chapter provides an overview of how local differences and adaptations to them influenced New England's banking system. These adaptations, in turn, gave rise to several phenomena distinct to New England banks, which influenced the extent to which they promoted growth in the regional economy.

Colonial Antecedents

When the colonies threw off British rule, New England was viewed as the most commercially sophisticated, most economically developed region. Its city streets were filled with merchant shops and counting houses, its ports bustled around both seagoing and coastwise trades, and its craftsmen engaged in artisan-style manufacturing. Independence unleashed a pent-up demand for reliable sources of capital, both foreign and domestic, to finance the continued expansion of these pursuits. This demand for capital was satisfied in two ways. One was through the sale of long-term debt and equity, which New Englanders everywhere purchased and held. Winifred Rothenberg found among the effects of decedents shares in bridge companies, turnpikes, canals, aqueducts, insurance companies, foundries and iron works, textile mills, and a hat manufactory.[8] The second source of credit was through the agency of commercial banks. Amid all the clamor surrounding the chartering of limited-liability corporations, no industry attracted more equity capital in the first two or three decades following independence than the financial industry.[9]

Despite the region's diversifying and developing economy, America's first commercial banks were not located in New England. The nation's first banks opened in Philadelphia in 1782 and New York in 1784. New England, though, was home to three of the next four: the Massachusetts Bank of Boston in 1784, the Providence Bank of Rhode Island in 1791, and the Hartford Bank of Connecticut in 1792.[10] The fourth, the Bank of Maryland chartered in 1790, served Baltimore.

New Englanders' desire for banks predated independence and the chartering of the Massachusetts Bank by about a century. The first documented private bank scheme dated to at least 1686, when John Blackwell proposed a "Bank of Credit, Lumbard, and Exchange of Moneys by persons of approved integrity, prudence, and estate in this country."[11] His proposed bank was to issue bills of credit secured by real estate, personal property, and nonperishable merchandise. Blackwell's land bank involved a rather sophisticated governance structure. He proposed 21 principal managers, several deputy managers, a treasurer, an accountant, a clerk, and a London agency. Each of the 21 principal managers was to advance £500 in cash, mortgages, or merchandise to establish an initial paid-in capital of £10,500 as security for the bank's note issues. The colonial council approved the scheme, but it appears that Blackwell could not gain the support of 21 persons capable of supplying the initial capital. He abandoned the project in July 1688.

It was not until 1714 that the next attempt to form a privately owned bank with the privilege of note issue arose. In early February, advertisements appeared in Boston newspapers announcing the plan of a bank and calling for subscriptions. The plan was modeled after Blackwell's abortive plan of 1686. This bank was to have seven trustees, seven directors, a treasurer, and two clerks. Its capital was to be limited to £300,000 with each subscriber tendering a mortgage on real estate to secure its circulating notes. Individuals could borrow at rates not exceeding 5 percent. In addition, £400 of its annual net profits were earmarked for the support of a charity school in Boston provided that the city's freeholders elected to accept the bank's notes in the payment of municipal taxes. The plan also offered an unspecified stipend to Harvard College. Unlike the 1686 proposal, the legislature defeated this scheme because they feared that the bank's issues might reduce the attractiveness of the colony's own bills of credit. The legislature's refusal fueled a heated pamphlet debate for several years that just as abruptly disappeared.[12]

Both of these bank schemes were designed to mitigate the ill effects of the shortage of quality specie in the colonies. Colonial coinage consisted of a cumbersome mixture of English, French, Spanish, and Portuguese coins that never circulated in great quantity and tended to be low quality. Most of the coins were badly worn or clipped and formed the basis of constant complaint. It was not until 1737 that the first coins were minted in the colonies, at John Higley's Granby copper mines in Connecticut.[13] Higley's coins were made of pure copper and the first striking carried the inscription "Valued at Three Pence." They apparently failed to maintain their stated value in circulation, however, as later strikings carried the inscription "Value Me As You Please." But jewelers found the coins of high-enough quality that they were melted down for use as gold alloy. It is unlikely that Higley's coins significantly reduced the colony's chronic shortage of coins. They certainly did not alleviate the merchant's or artisan's need for credit.

Colonial complaints about the shortage of currency have been read skeptically by economic historians, many of whom probably took their cue from Adam Smith. Smith dismissed colonial complaints: "No complaint, however, is more common than that of the scarcity of money. Money, like wine, must always be scarce with those who have neither the wherewithal to buy it, nor the credit to borrow it."[14] But recent research has suggested that colonial complaints were legitimate and that it was concerns about the currency shortage that prompted the banking scheme of 1714.[15] The 1714 proposal, in fact, would have imposed a 40-shilling penalty on the bank for each £100 in specie taken in and withdrawn from circulation.[16]

The next documented bank scheme arose in Connecticut in the early 1730s. In 1730, a group of merchants petitioned the provincial legislature for a charter granting them the right to issue, among other things, bills of credit but their petition was denied because their issues would have interfered with the colony's own. In 1732, the plan was revived, and in May, a petition was laid before the legislature requesting a charter for the New London Society for Trade and Commerce. Its stated purpose was "promoting and carrying on trade and commerce to Great Britain and his Majesty's islands and plantations in America, and to other of his Majesty's dominions; and the encouraging of the fishery, *etc* . . . as well as for the common good as their own private interests."[17]

The provision allowing note issue in the 1730 petition was removed and replaced with the "common good" and "private interest" clauses in the 1732 incarnation. This amendment removed the legislative stumbling block. The charter passed and the society immediately began lending against mortgage security and issuing its own notes. Connecticut's colonial government was "alarmed" at the society's actions and the governor called a special session of the colonial council to clear it up. In February 1733, the society's charter was revoked, its mortgages assumed by the state, its notes (about £10,000 to £15,000) called in, and its affairs settled. The bank's organizers (all of whom suffered considerable losses) met on 5 June 1735, voting to dissolve the short-lived bank.

Because of the region's continued inability to solve the persistent shortage of money and credit, the Massachusetts General Court adopted a resolution in 1739 soliciting serious proposals for augmenting the existing medium of exchange. The resolution elicited two proposals: one, a Land Bank proposed by John Colman, who had been interested in the 1714 scheme, based on real estate security; the other, a Silver Bank whose notes were to be redeemable in silver at a future date with graduated redemption values proportional to the time a note remained in circulation. The intent, of course, was to provide incentives for the public to hold its notes for long periods. Notes received quickly would be redeemed at the current exchange rate between colonial issues and silver (about 28 paper shillings per ounce of silver). Notes redeemed in 1755 would be exchanged at the rate of 20 shillings per ounce.

Subscribers to the Land Bank were to borrow and circulate £150,000 in notes proportionate to their subscriptions. The only initial payment required of its subscribers was 40 shillings per £1,000 for organizational expenses. Its notes were payable in 20 years and their redemption was guaranteed by the subscribers paying 3 percent interest and one-twentieth of the principal in the bank's own notes or in hemp, flax, bar iron, or several other enumerated goods.[18] A joint legislative committee report recommended rejection of the Land Bank and laid the Silver Bank proposal over for the next session. In the interim, neither was to commence operations.

At the next legislative session, battle lines were quickly drawn. The governor and council favored the Silver Bank; the house largely favored the Land Bank but a slim majority also reported favorably on the Silver Bank. Eventually, both proposals were reported to another joint committee, but council and house members refused to meet with one another. Feeling the need to break the deadlock, the house resolved by a vote of 59 to 37 that "persons concerned in the said [Land Bank] scheme should *not* be forbidden to issue bills or notes of hand."[19] Upon adoption of this resolution, the governor issued a proclamation urging Bostonians not to accept the notes of either bank until the appropriate enabling acts had passed. Notwithstanding the governor's cautioning, both banks organized and the Silver Bank began issuing notes by 1 August 1740. Within a short time, the Land Bank issued its proposed maximum of £150,000; the Silver Bank issued £120,000.

Battle lines over the banks' extralegal actions were as sharply drawn among Boston's populace as in the colonial legislature. Boston merchants generally supported the Silver Bank and opposed the Land Bank; farmers supported the latter. Pamphleteers published long essays supporting their favored institution and attacking the other. Boston merchants openly expressed their inclinations as they placed advertisements declaring whether they would or would not accept the Land Bank's notes. For those harboring reservations about either or both banks, wild rumors and official proclamations certainly increased their discomfiture. Samuel Adams' father, one of the Land Bank's directors, was accused of refusing to accept the bank's notes. He offered a reward of £5 to any person providing the name of the party responsible for the rumor. The guilty party was eventually found out and the false rumor exposed, but the damage was done. More important, perhaps, was the governor's proclamation that any colonial official found accepting or passing the banks' notes would be dismissed and attorneys found passing its notes were barred from appearing before the probate court. Several justices of the peace and military officers preempted the governor's punishment by publicly tendering their resignations just prior to being dismissed for passing the banks' notes. The fate of both banks was finally resolved when a group of prominent Boston merchants appealed to Parliament for relief. On 9 April 1741, a bill extending the Bubble Act to the colonies received its third reading and soon became law, making it unlawful for colonials to issue or pass privately issued bank bills and notes.

In 1742, both banks called in their notes and began winding up. The stockholders of each suffered considerable losses. Except for the intervention of the court, Samuel Adams' father might have lost his personal property, lost his malting business, and found himself in jail. As it was, Adams inherited his father's Land Bank debts and barely escaped having his own house seized and sold at auction. One historian has argued that the Land Bank's legacy fanned Adam's radical revolutionary fervor.[20]

Another legacy of the Land Bank scheme was the uneasy alliance of mercantile and agricultural interests behind bank formation that continued throughout the next century. Mercantile interests dominated, but concessions were made to an often vocal majority of farmers and manufacturers clamoring for credit. Some of these early experiments in money and banking—colonial loan offices, land banks, and merchandise (silver) banks— destroyed public trust. For decades thereafter, paper money was looked upon with suspicion. By the end of the revolutionary era, however, public sentiment changed and banks were seen not only as desirable but also as necessary.

The Origins and Growth of New England's System

When the Massachusetts General Court offered a charter to Philadelphia's Bank of North America in 1782, it was believed that Boston needed a bank and that the quickest and least expensive way to get it was to entice the country's sole existing bank to open a new branch.[21] In 1782, Boston's banking and credit needs were met by wealthy merchant-bankers—prominent and established merchants with surplus trading capital who maintained deposits for a few, made loans, and issued drafts payable through similarly prominent men in foreign ports. Although these merchant-bankers filled a clear niche and provided valuable intermediation services, these proprietor-based institutions could provide only limited assistance to a burgeoning mercantile and entrepreneurial class.

The several abortive colonial experiments, as well as recent experiences with quickly depreciated continental currency, made many wary of banks, their promises of increased credit, and their issuance of paper money. To allay these concerns, early bank promoters made every effort to convince legislators that their institutions would provide public benefits, as well as private gains. In placing their petition before the General Court, promoters of the Massachusetts Bank laid out four benefits likely to result from their bank: (1) borrowers would be delivered from the grip of the usurer; (2) the bank would inculcate the habit of meeting debts punctually (something, apparently, that wasn't generally done); (3) it would serve as a safe depository for money; and (4) it would facilitate exchange by providing an expanded and higher quality medium of exchange.[22]

Even as late as 1805, bank promoters felt obligated to justify their schemes in terms of the benefits their banks might afford the surrounding community. In offering a petition to Vermont's legislature in 1803, the petitioners wrote that they were "convinced of the importance and usefulness of banks" and that their benefits would accrue to all citizens.[23] Another contemporary booster attempted to generate support for his bank scheme by arguing that it would provide credit to all, thereby increasing industry and productivity.[24]

Despite promises of furthering the commonweal, public officials often remained skeptical and unconvinced. The 1803 Vermont petitioners got their bill pushed through the house by the slim majority of 93 to 83. The governor and council were even less impressed. They returned the bill to the house with a list of objections, including their belief that the bank would tend to displace an already scarce specie, that it would distract youth from honest industry (notably farming), that it would promote gambling and speculating, and that it would weaken republican government by establishing and promulgating a financial oligarchy.[25] Many believed banks would bring prosperity, but not everyone was convinced, and the thoughtful knew that banks were not a panacea for mercantile woes.

Notwithstanding the reservations of some, the number of New England banks grew quickly and, after 1810, petitioners simply eliminated lofty appeals to the common good. Bank charters were sought and granted for no other purpose than the private gain of the promoters and shareholders. And charters were nowhere granted more liberally than in New England. By 1820, there was already slightly more than $10 in paid-in bank capital per capita. In 1840, it totaled about $27. It declined somewhat in the 1840s as a result of a deep recession and several bank failures, but the 1850s witnessed an explosion in the region's banking sector. Between 1820 and 1860, New England's bank capital grew at an average annual rate of 3.4 percent.

Table 4.1 shows considerable state-to-state variation within New England. With about $10 to $15 in bank money per capita in 1860, Maine, New Hampshire, and Vermont, though only modestly monetized by New England standards, had money per capita ratios similar to those in the South Atlantic states and the old Southwest but far in excess of ratios in the Old Northwest. Connecticut was a highly monetized economy with about $28 in bank money per capita in 1860. Massachusetts and Rhode Island, however, were clear outliers with the second and third most highly monetized economies in the nation in 1860. They ranked similarly in most other years.

New England's highly monetized economies reflect that region's long-standing willingness to exploit the advantages of paper money. In the colonial era, Massachusetts' issues of bills of credit outstripped those of all other states by a wide margin. By 1765, Massachusetts loan offices had in circulation about £168 per capita; Rhode Island, about £32 per capita. By way of comparison, New York's loan office issues peaked at £3.5; Pennsylvania's, at £2.6; and Virginia's, at £1.8.[26]

Although New Englanders' preferences for easy money and ample credit spilled over into the postrevolutionary period, bank promoters faced chal-

Table 4.1 Bank Money per Capita by State and Region, 1820–1860

Region/State	1820	1830	1840	1850	1860
NEW ENGLAND	$7.14	$9.56	$11.36	$15.99	$26.72
Maine	5.54	2.40	3.51	6.33	10.12
New Hampshire	2.23	3.30	5.08	6.59	13.52
Vermont	0.98	3.71	4.33	10.43	14.41
Massachusetts	11.07	16.56	21.18	24.27	40.21
Rhode Island	13.60	17.37	20.71	23.75	35.14
Connecticut	9.09[a]	4.93	9.77	18.66	27.89
MIDDLE ATLANTIC[b]	2.61	7.71	9.08	15.46	22.77
SOUTH ATLANTIC[c]	5.51	4.39	7.26	10.00	11.29
OLD NORTHWEST[d]	0.60	1.41	4.69	4.80	4.95
OLD SOUTHWEST[e]	4.85	3.65	14.98	7.35	13.74

Notes: [a]Bank money figure from 1823; population from 1820. [b]Bank money figure for 1820 for New York, Delaware, and Maryland from 1819, population from 1820. [c]Bank money figure for North Carolina for 1820 from 1819; figure for Georgia for 1820 from 1821. [d]Bank money figure for Ohio for 1820 from 1819. [e]Bank money figure for Tennessee for 1820 from 1821; figure for figure for Louisiana for 1820 from 1819. Regions are defined as follows. Middle Atlantic: New York, New Jersey, Pennsylvania, Delaware, Maryland, and District of Columbia; South Atlantic: Virginia, North Carolina, South Carolina, Georgia, and Florida; Old Northwest: Ohio, Indiana, Illinois, Wisconsin, and Michigan; Old Southwest: Kentucky, Tennessee, Mississippi, Alabama, Louisiana, and Missouri.

Sources: Fenstermaker, Development, appendix B; U.S. Comptroller of the Currency, Annual Report (1876); U.S. Census Office, Compendium, table VIII.

lenges in garnering support for their schemes. Plans for the first bank in Rhode Island began in 1784, but only $30,000 of the proposed $150,000 capital was subscribed, and the project died. It would be another seven years before the Brown family of Providence could garner the support of enough merchants to launch the Providence Bank. Even then, it appeared that John Brown's motivation was not so much to run his own bank (though he wanted to), but to demonstrate to the directors of the First Bank of the United States that the city was capable of supporting a financial institution.

In the seven years between bank schemes, beliefs among Providence's merchants had undergone a transformation. The 1784 scheme lapsed from lack of interest. Brown's bank plan, on the other hand, was wildly popular, the capital oversubscribed, and the bank was easily chartered in 1791. By modern standards, at least, the absence of any significant restrictions on the bank's activities is notable. The only substantive limitation placed on the Providence Bank was that it was to receive and pay out deposits without charge. The only other restriction included in its charter was a clause requiring the directors "to do nothing contrary to the regulations of the stockholders."[27] Such regulatory laxity may have resulted from the legislature's inexperience with banking matters and corporate charters, it may have resulted from a reasoned laissez-faire position, or it may have followed from a postrevolutionary libertarian bent as merchants "had become accustomed to do as they pleased in financial matters and lawful restraint to them was synonymous with despotism."[28] Whatever the wellspring of this laxity, it was not to last.

At the same time that the legislature failed to limit, in any meaningful way, the Providence Bank's scope of activities, it also gave it privileges and powers not granted to most other businesses—among them, limited liability. Bank stockholders were liable only to the amount of their investment. Subsequent bank charters granted shareholders limited liability until 1833, when the charter of the West Greenwich Farmers Bank imposed unlimited liability on its shareholders. Thereafter, most charters did the same.[29]

The historical record does not shed much light on Rhode Island's about-face on shareholder liability. No rash of bank failures had imposed extraordinary losses on bank creditors. The legislature may have sought to slow the rapid increase in the number of banks, or the change may have simply reflected a fundamental shift in the state's political undercurrents.

The second special accommodation given to the Providence Bank was the rule of summary process. Under summary process, whenever a matured debt went unpaid for 10 days, the president of the creditor bank could notify the debtor of the delinquency and, upon taking oath before a court clerk, obtain a writ of execution and attachment against the debtor without the expense and inconvenience of a trial.

The ostensible purpose underlying a bank's summary execution power was to assist it in maintaining liquidity. By forcing bank debtors to meet their obligations in a timely manner, a bank would be able to meet its own contractual obligations. By avoiding delay in recovering debts, a bank was able to convert overdue paper into a quick asset. "Strict punctuality on the part of one," writes Stokes, "could only be maintained by strict punctuality on the part of the other."[30] In 1836, as a result of protests lead by Thomas Dorr (later leader of Dorr's Rebellion), banks were stripped of their summary execution powers. After 1836, banks, like all other creditors, were forced to proceed under the formality of court hearings to execute a lien and take possession of collateral security.[31]

Time and experience brought a host of new regulations. The charters of the earliest banks rarely limited a bank's note issue, lending policies, or other activities. By the 1830s, all had been regulated in various degrees. In 1829, Massachusetts enacted a series of sweeping changes in one stroke. Its single most important objective was to limit the use of stock notes in generating bank capital. The law required all new banks to have 50 percent of their authorized capital paid in specie and in the vault before the bank opened. Loans to shareholders were prohibited until their subscriptions were fully paid in. Loans made against the bank's own stock were limited to 50 percent of the bank's capital.

In addition, note issues were limited to twice the bank's capital. Directors were personally responsible for any excess over the 200 percent limit. Even this brake on note issue failed to satisfy several reformers. One contemporary wrote that the principle upon which this restriction was based was "radically defective" and indicative of an "unsound system" that "ought not be sustained."[32] Some observers were finally recognizing that bank capital was not just so much idle specie lying in a vault.

Some states imposed liquid reserve requirements, but most persisted in limiting note issue to a proportion of capital.[33] Massachusetts, for instance, limited note issue to 125 percent of capital. Rhode Island developed a sliding scale of note issue–to-capital ratios with the smallest banks allowed to issue up to 75 percent of their paid-in capital; the largest, 20 percent. Only in rare instances were these restrictions binding. With the growing importance of deposits among city banks, the largest banks never approached their issue limit. Small country banks simply could not keep their legal maximum in circulation. The law affected only a handful of banks, and those were among the very smallest. Banks with $50,000 or less in paid-in capital faced a legal note issue ratio of 75 percent, but in 1835 they had an average ratio of just 59.6 percent. Banks with capital between $400,000 and $500,000 had a legal circulation ratio of 20 percent, but their actual circulation amounted to just 6.3 percent.[34]

The other development that concerned legislators and fomented new regulations was the growing importance of deposits and the growing number of banks paying interest to attract them. In the early 1830s, Boston banks were paying interest on an average of about 75 percent of their total deposits, or about 20 percent of their total liabilities.[35] This development worried some observers because there was a long-standing belief that it was bad business to borrow money to relend it (that note issues were of essentially the same character apparently escaped them). It was thought that a bank relying on paid-for deposits would lend too freely to generate revenues sufficient to pay for deposit interest.

The Massachusetts General Court prohibited the practice of paying interest on deposits in 1834. At least they thought they did. The law's wording was ambiguous, and some bankers interpreted it to mean that interest could not be paid on *time* deposits but could be paid on *demand* deposits.[36] Some banks responded by paying interest on demand deposits. This resulted in an inversion of the yield curve, paying higher rates on shorter maturity instruments.

Even some modern bank commentators draw sharp distinctions between core deposits (accounts kept largely for transaction motives) and purchased money (principally, large-denomination certificates of deposit used as investment vehicles). Attracting sources of funding outside one's depository constituency makes sense when a bank faces more or larger opportunities than it can profitably finance through the use of core deposits. Moreover, modern banks that more heavily utilize purchased money do not, seemingly, labor under higher average costs.[37] The use of purchased money, then, encourages local development without significantly raising a bank's cost of funds.

On the other hand, the availability of purchased funds encouraged excessive risk taking among many undercapitalized and unprofitable savings and loan banks in the 1980s.[38] The resulting moral hazard problem among insured thrifts increased the magnitude of the losses they suffered and the subsidy to risk taking paid by taxpayers. Even if purchased funds were not used to finance inefficiently risky ventures, changes in interest rates would have more negative effects on banks making heavier use of purchased funds. Sharp increases in interest rates could turn once-profitable investments into losers, and a bank that relied on purchased funds could see its interest spreads shrink or even turn negative.

Concerns over the practice of paying for deposits in antebellum Boston, then, were not baseless. The concern then, as now, was with liquidity risks (the possibility of depositor runs) and solvency risks (the quality of the assets acquired with the paid-for deposits). There is little evidence on the sizes and kinds of interest-bearing deposits offered at Massachusetts (mostly Boston) banks or the assets purchased with these funds. We know, however, that many New England banks went outside their home range to purchase bills of exchange and other commercial paper. Country banks came to Boston's State Street searching for quality paper; Boston's banks bought on New York's Wall Street and some even had agents buying cotton bills in New Orleans' Exchange Alley. Most of these arm's-length transactions paid off, but asymmetric information problems gave these loans an element of risk that troubled many observers.

Buying deposits and traveling for loans involved tradeoffs. If a bank emerged because of the advantages it had in gathering information and monitoring borrowers, it was less costly for the bank to monitor a loan it originated itself than one originated elsewhere.[39] This didn't mean that buying bills of exchange or commercial paper on State Street was unprofitable for country banks. Indeed, purchasing loans originated by other lenders may have led to greater diversification. It may have allowed the bank to increase its scale of operations to efficient size if local loan demand was relatively low.

Whether buying loans originated by another intermediary provided a net benefit depended on the type of loan bought. There are two cases.[40] The first is when sold loans (like commercial paper) do not have the unique property of many bank loans in that they do not require much specialized credit analysis on the part of the originator because the borrower's credit quality is readily observable. The second is when these loans are not fundamentally different from loans held to maturity. Originating banks engage in credit analysis and follow-up monitoring of sold loans just as they would with loans held to maturity. They do so because they want to develop or preserve a reputation as an originator of high-quality loans so that they can sell loans in the future.

Evidence for modern bank loan purchases is consistent with the first hypothesis. That is, loans to firms whose creditworthiness is more easily observed are more likely to be sold.[41] The evidence from antebellum New England is spotty, is largely anecdotal, and offers no clear support for either hypothesis. Some limited evidence, however, is consistent with the former case. Commercial paper brokers, who sold on commission to banks and other investors, tended to deal in first-class paper issued by well-known and highly regarded mercantile houses. In southern markets, most commercial paper was drawn on cotton trading firms located in London, Liverpool, Amsterdam, and Le Havre. The risks were generally small, and this paper offered many banks geographic and industrial diversification of their portfolios without significantly increasing their monitoring costs.

Other evidence suggests that some banks followed questionable strategies. In 1852, Massachusetts bank commissioners noted that some country banks had agents travel the countryside and discount notes on the banks' behalf. The commissioners noted that these discounters were often charged higher rates, and the practice was "frequently attended with loss on account of the ignorance of the true character of the paper."[42]

The combination of agency problems between the bank and its traveling agent, adverse selection as a result of higher than average interest rates, a lack of information on the borrower's project, and the high costs of monitoring resulted in high-risk banking practice. Without direct information on a bank's portfolio and its loan default rate, it is impossible to determine the extent of the risk, but it was likely to have increased the banks' risk exposure. In 1837, the Phoenix Bank of Hartford, Connecticut, wrote off over $15,000 in bad loans extended to borrowers outside its home territory.[43]

Several other Connecticut banks ultimately wrote off many bad loans made in Ohio.[44] What cannot be determined is the extent to which these travelled for loans differed from the homegrown variety. Theory would lead us to believe that information-based agency problems would be magnified, however, and the casualty rates correspondingly greater.

To correct several real and imagined evils, the Maine General Assembly passed a comprehensive banking law in 1831. It was a propitious time for change because the charters of all existing banks, but one, expired that year. Maine's significant enactments mirrored those in other states. The more notable changes included the following: loans secured by the bank's own stock were prohibited only double-name paper was to be discounted, note issues were limited to 150 percent of capital, debts could not exceed twice a bank's capital, nonbanking pursuits were prohibited, real estate holdings were limited; and the circulation of notes less than $1 was prohibited.[45] The law's most interesting feature, however, was that banks had 15 days to meet redemption demands or face an interest penalty of 2 percent per month for notes not redeemed. This last clause was inserted to protect Maine's banks from runs or unexpectedly large redemption calls.

In addition to facing restrictions under general banking acts, like Maine's act of 1831, many banks labored under specific requirements included in their charters. The second bank chartered in Massachusetts was the Union Bank of Boston in 1792. It was designated as the state depository, which could prove lucrative if the state maintained a sizable balance. In return, the Union Bank was required to lend the state up to $100,000 at 5 percent annual interest.[46] Most subsequent bank charters included similar provisions. In effect, the legislature exchanged a bank charter for an open line of credit for the state.

Massachusetts chartered two more banks in 1811, one of which was the State Bank of Boston with an authorized capital of $3 million. Besides the sheer size of the bank, the novelty was that the state reserved the right to subscribe to an additional $1.5 million (making the potential capitalization $4.5 million). Although the state never exercised the option, similar clauses were placed in many subsequent charters; within a few years, the commonwealth owned about one-eighth of the state's banking capital.

There were several reasons that explain why the state might have wanted to own bank stock. One was that it simply allowed the state to share in the bank's profits. Dividends often accrued to the state's general revenues, which reduced the public's tax burden. A second was that, with share ownership, the state retained some sway over the policies of the bank through its ability to appoint one or more directors. The state could thereby limit practices believed to be inimical to the public good. Yet another was that share ownership placed the state among the bank's other shareholders as a favored customer. If the state had forgotten to include a clause in a bank's charter giving it favored status, it could achieve the same result through stock ownership. Finally, bank promoters often found state involvement a necessary condition for raising the capital with which to start a bank. Although the difficulties in raising sufficient capital were overcome with apparent ease throughout New England, Vermont's first bank was state owned and operated.[47]

Other banks were chartered to assist or subsidize one special interest or another. Soon after the first banks opened in port cities, agrarian calls for specialized bank credit grew louder as they found city banks unresponsive to agricultural needs. City banks, argued farmers, were too far removed, too involved in mercantile lending, and too unwilling to accept real estate mortgages as collateral to offer them any advantages. Because Rhode Island's economy centered on overseas trade and because time at sea was unpredictable in the early 1800s, many 30-day loans were repeatedly renewed and looked like the kind of long-term loans desired by farmers. When bankers refused to lend to farmers because agricultural loans matured too slowly, the agrarians' howls of protest appeared "well founded."[48]

Rhode Island responded by chartering the Washington Bank in 1800 and the Rhode Island Union Bank in 1804. The preamble of the chartering act of the latter stated that "a bank in which the agricultural and mercantile interests should be united would be productive of the most beneficial advantages to a state . . . where those interests are so blended together and dependent on each other."[49] Legislators were often uneasy about wholly agricultural banks and they insisted that they diversify into mercantile lending. Although agriculture was deserving of credit, agricultural prices and profits were volatile. By mixing volatile agricultural and stable mercantile lending, legislators thought they were subsidizing agriculture and protecting the stability of the system.

Some legislatures chartered agricultural banks then required them to diversify into mercantile credit; other legislators took the opposite tack. The charter of the Suffolk Bank of Boston, for example, required that it lend one-tenth of its capital to residents of Massachusetts outside Boston who were engaged in agriculture and manufacturing.[50] These loans, moreover, were to be in amounts between $100 and $500 and secured by real estate mortgages. Both strategies had the same goal—getting credit to farmers or manufacturers through the agency of a diversified intermediary. What differed between the two strategies were the relative proportions. The choice between a mercantile bank lending to farmers and an agricultural bank lending to merchants probably depended on the relative strengths of sectoral demands for credit and the relative political clout of each constituency.

Banks were also used to underwrite and finance fashionable projects. Although banks and internal improvement projects were more closely linked in the Old Southwest and Old Northwest, several New England banks were chartered on the condition that they help finance a specific infrastructure project. Rhode Island conditioned its charter of the Blackstone Canal Bank in 1831 on its buying of $150,000 in canal shares.[51] The Connecticut River Banking Company was required to invest $100,000 in improving navigation on the Connecticut River. The City Bank of New Haven was required to subscribe to $100,000 of the capital of the Hampshire and Hampton Canal. The Mystic Bank seemingly got off easy. It was asked to invest only $1,000 in clearing a channel in the Mystic River. When railroads replaced canals as the improvement project of choice, newly chartered banks were asked to assist this new enterprise. The Quinebaug Bank of Connecticut was chartered in 1832 and required to invest one-fifth of its capital (or $100,000) in stock of the Boston, Norwich and New London Railroad Company.

Despite optimism and good intentions, the mixing of banks and infrastructure improvements often proved detrimental to the bank, the infrastructure project, or both. The Derby Fishing Company of Connecticut provides a vivid example. The company was chartered in 1806 to promote cod fishing.[52] Lacking sufficient funds to further its objectives, its charter was amended in 1807 so that it could underwrite marine insurance. President Jefferson's embargo and nonintercourse acts quickly undermined that business. Its charter was further amended in 1809 so that it could enter the banking business. It changed its name to the Derby Bank; the Derby Bank built and operated ships in the Atlantic trade. In 1815, several ships were lost, others were taken by British privateers, and the whole operation, including the bank, collapsed.

Connecticut's legislature learned little from the Derby Bank fiasco. In May 1822, Connecticut chartered the Farmington Canal to run between Farmington and New Haven, but subscriptions lagged. Recognizing an opportunity when the legislature was otherwise indisposed to charter any new banks, a group enticed the legislature to give them a charter for a promise to further their canal project. In return for a perpetual charter, a perpetual exemption from all state taxes, and the right to issue notes to 150 percent of its capital, the bank promised to provide the canal with $100,000 immediately and another $100,000 as future needs demanded. The legislature accepted the offer and chartered the Mechanics Bank of New Haven in 1825. The canal was a financial failure and a costly investment for the bank. In 1839, the bank sold its canal shares for 75 cents each and wrote down its capital by $200,000, a two-fifths reduction.[53]

The fact that banks could fail seems to have taken the region's legislators by surprise, and when it happened, they were unsure how to respond. The Penobscot Bank of Bucksport (then in the Maine district) was the first of Massachusetts' banks to fail. It opened in June 1806 when its subscribers paid in one-half of the authorized $150,000 capital. Within six months, all but $600 of that amount was loaned to stockholders on notes renewable every six months and secured by the bank's own stock. Other loans nearly equaled its capital. By June 1809, the bank had $190,000 in circulation backed by less than $19,000 in specie. In August, its note redemptions were unexpectedly large and, unable to meet the calls, it suspended.[54]

By January 1810, the bank's notes traded at a 30 to 50 percent discount

in Boston and its notes maintained these values only because the bank spo-
radically redeemed a few when it acquired some specie. A state senate committee found that large amounts remained due from stockholders and directors, and the situation was "not in favor of collecting much under the
present discouraging state."[55] Boston's banks held about 44 percent of the
Penobscot Bank's remaining circulation; about 12 percent had already been
sued upon and brought to execution. Despite overwhelming evidence of its
imminent bankruptcy, the senate committee wavered in its recommenda-
tion. "Under these circumstances," they wrote, "it will remain for the Legislature to decide, whether the Directors of this Bank, have managed its
affairs so improperly as to justify the interference of the Government; and
if so, whether it will be better, since the charter will soon expire, to take it
away, or allow it to continue, as it is, *or put it under certain restrictions.*"[56]
In retrospect, the answer seems obvious, but having no previous experience
with bank failure legislators were forced to labor through its intricacies
without much guidance.

Despite its well-deserved reputation for soundness, New England's early
banking experience was not universally good. Like all other regions, it faced
its share of failures and fiascos. Banks were originally formed with few
regulatory restrictions and even less official oversight. As a result, they
largely did whatever they wanted. Their actions often benefited both the
bankers and the public, but in some instances, the outcome was less favorable. Such was to be expected when bankers and legislators were both learning in the classroom of experience. By midcentury, however, both banks
and legislators had learned some unpleasant lessons. Legislatures responded with various impositions and directives while the banks themselves adopted new internal rules, bylaws, and governance structures in
attempts to stem the most egregious practices. That they did so earlier than
other regions is the likely cause of their favorable historiography. Mistakes
and hard-learned lessons were long buried and forgotten in New England
when westerners were just opening their first banks.

Small Banks and Insider Lending

One of the unique features of New England banks was their relatively small
size. Table 4.2 shows that the average New England bank was small compared to those in other regions. In 1820, for example, the average Massachusetts country bank (excluding Boston) had about the same paid-in capital as a Pennsylvania bank (excluding Philadelphia), but only about
one-half as much as a Virginia bank. Rhode Island's banks were smaller yet,
capitalized at about 35 percent of a Massachusetts bank. Little had changed
by 1850; if anything, New England banks had grown smaller relative to
Middle Atlantic and South Atlantic banks.

Several explanations have been put forward for the relatively small size

Table 4.2 Average Bank Size by Capital and Lending in 1820 and 1850;
Selected States (in thousands of dollars)

State	1820		1850	
	Capital	Loans	Capital	Loans
Massachusetts	$374.5	$480.4	$293.5	$494.0
except Boston	176.6	230.8	170.3	281.9
Rhode Island	95.7	103.2	186.0	246.2
except Providence	60.6	72.0	79.5	108.5
New York	na	na	246.8	516.3
except NYC	na	na	126.7	240.1
Pennsylvania	221.8	262.9	340.2	674.6
except Philadelphia	162.6	195.2	246.0	420.7
Virginia[a,b]	351.5	340.0	270.3	504.5
South Carolina[b]	na	na	938.5	1,471.5
Kentucky[b]	na	na	439.4	727.3

Notes: [a]Virginia figures for 1820 from 1822. [b]Figures represent branch averages.

Sources: Massachusetts, "True Abstract," 1820; Pennsylvania, *Senate Journal*, 1820, pp. 180–211; Pennsylvania, *Senate Journal*, vol. 2, 1850, pp. 372–79; Rhode Island, "Abstract," 1820 and 1850; *Virginia, House, Journal* 1821/22, p. 205; Virginia, General Assembly, *House Documents*, 1850; U.S. House, 32d, 1st, *Executive Doc. No. 122*; U.S. Comptroller of the Currency, *Annual Report* (1876); Fenstermaker, *Development*, appendix B; *Albany Argus*, 25 February 1851.

of New England banks. Contemporary observer Nathan Appleton believed that their size resulted from the states' tax schemes.[57] Unlike most states in other regions that taxed bank dividends, New England states tended to tax bank capital. Massachusetts imposed an annual 1 percent assessment on bank capital; Rhode Island imposed a 0.375 percent capital tax.

Appleton argued that such taxes worked to the detriment of large banks. Banks operating on a large capital found it difficult to maintain circulation-to-capital ratios comparable to those of smaller banks. Because contemporaries often believed that profits flowed directly from note issue, the effective tax rate (i.e., the tax per dollar of banknotes in circulation) worked to the detriment of large banks. The "present system of taxation," wrote Appleton, "produced two evils at the same time; it reduced the amount of bank capital . . . and it increase[d] the number of banks."[58] Some historians have accepted this explanation.

The error of this explanation, however, lay in the long-dominant belief that bank profits flowed directly and inexorably from note issue. They did not. Profits flowed from lending whence note issues originated. Most large banks were urban banks and city banks successfully developed deposit bases. Increased deposits gradually supplanted note issues so that effective tax rates on earning assets (the appropriate measure) were considerably lower than Appleton suggested.

Table 4.3 provides evidence of profitability for Massachusetts banks in three selected years. The statistics support two of Appleton's claims; namely, that larger banks had lower circulation-to-capital ratios and higher effective tax rates per dollar of note issue. But loan-to-capital ratios reflect small differences among banks of different sizes, which tended to equalize effective tax rates. The final column of the table reports estimated rates of return on bank equity and shows that profit rates were nearly equal across bank size. Neither small nor large banks were noticeably more profitable, a result that largely accords with modern studies that suggest that economies of scale and scope are quickly dissipated in banking.[59]

Naomi Lamoreaux offers an alternative explanation for the relatively small size of New England banks.[60] She argues that the region's banks were not impersonal financial intermediaries, but the financial arms of extended

Table 4.3 Bank Size, Taxes, and Profitability in Massachusetts; Selected Years

Bank Capital (in thousands of dollars)	Circulation/ Capital (%)	Loans/ Capital (%)	Tax/ Circulation (%)	Tax/ Loans (%)	Return on Equity (%)
A: 1834					
$1,000+	8.6	139.3	11.7	0.7	7.3
$500–1,000	20.5	169.9	4.9	0.6	7.1
$250–500	21.7	135.8	4.6	0.7	6.3
<$250	42.5	154.7	2.4	0.7	7.3
All Banks	24.7	156.2	4.1	0.6	7.2
B: 1846					
$1,000+	26.6	161.3	3.8	0.6	8.2
$500–1,000	42.4	164.6	2.4	0.6	8.3
$250–500	51.1	165.1	2.0	0.6	7.7
<$250	72.0	169.8	1.4	0.6	8.1
All Banks	48.0	165.4	2.1	0.6	8.1
C: 1855					
$1,000+	18.2	159.8	5.5	0.6	8.9
$500–1,000	29.9	167.7	3.3	0.6	8.9
$250–500	52.2	176.8	1.9	0.6	9.5
<$250	65.9	178.9	1.5	0.6	9.4
All Banks	39.4	169.6	2.5	0.6	9.3

Sources: Massachusetts, "True Abstract," 1833, 1834, 1845, 1846; U.S. House, 33d, 2d, *Executive Doc. No. 82;* U.S. House, 34th, 1st, *Executive Doc. No. 102.*

kinship-based mercantile and manufacturing networks. Throughout most of the antebellum era, banks loaned most, or a great deal at least, of their funds to insiders, such as directors, officers, shareholders, or the business partners and relations of directors, officers, and shareholders. Such practices represented the perpetuation of the eighteenth-century custom of pooling capital to finance extended-family enterprises. In the nineteenth century, the practice simply continued under corporate auspices because the corporate form allowed merchants to raise capital in amounts considerably in excess of what the network could raise internally.[61]

Once the familial and kinship nature of the first banks was established, the system perpetuated itself. When merchants learned that the Providence Bank of Rhode Island had been established not for the commonweal but for the private benefit of its founders and a small circle of friends and family, others began clamoring for their own banks.[62] Rhode Island's legislature accommodated them and the state witnessed several periods of accelerated growth in the number of banks. In 1800, Rhode Island had 4 banks; by 1830, it had 46; by 1860, there were 91. And Rhode Island's experience was not atypical: by 1860, Maine had 68 banks; New Hampshire, 51; Vermont, 44; Connecticut, 74; and Massachusetts, 178.

Merchants, farmers, manufacturers, and others excluded from existing banks remedied the situation by forming their own. Contemporaries, in fact, argued that this was the driving force behind new bank formation and their continued small size.[63] In founding a bank, its promoters assured themselves of a steady supply of credit, but because they were closely held familial organizations, they remained small. For those short of capital, the use of stock notes facilitated the formation process. Men with little capital could establish a bank, pay the initial subscription in specie, and meet subsequent calls with stock notes (loans from the bank secured by the bank's own stock). As the bank established itself, dividends paid off some fraction of the stock notes, and the initial promoters could sell some of their shares, pay off the remaining stock notes, and still maintain an insider's advantage in obtaining credit. In effect, the bank's profits "soon turned stock notes into real capital," and the bank's promoters reaped the rewards.[64]

The situation is analogous to recent instances of fortunes generated in the computer industry, where talented entrepreneurs are lured into jobs with inexpensive stock purchase or option plans available to only a few insiders. Once the start-up firm generates profits and establishes itself, the firm goes public and the value of the insiders' options increase markedly. In similar, if somewhat less remarkable, fashion, Lamoreaux and Christopher Glaisek find that the directors of banks chartered during the bank mania of the 1830s increased their taxable wealth at a much faster rate than either the directors of older banks or the taxpaying public generally.[65] The New England system of liberally handing out bank charters to aggressive youngsters promoted the "fortunes of a rising group of entrepreneurs, giving them the financial wherewithal to challenge the hegemony of the [existing] elite."[66]

Despite the proliferation of banks, or perhaps as a result of it, lending practices underwent little fundamental change in the first third of the nineteenth century. Records from the period show that many, if not most, banks loaned predominantly to insiders. Organizers of the Providence Bank of Rhode Island dominated its affairs and absorbed a majority of its loans. On 31 October 1792 (about a year after opening), over one-half of the bank's loans had been granted to the Brown family. A third went to the bank's other directors. By 1798, the Browns and the bank's other directors accounted for about 75 percent of its outstanding discounts.

Even as late as 1840, the insider habit remained strong, particularly in Rhode Island. At the Pawtuxet Bank of Warwick, Rhode Island, 53 percent of the bank's loans went to the bank's president, his business partners, and his family's businesses.[67] Other directors accounted for another 16 percent of the Pawtuxet's loans. At another bank, the obligations of one director and his immediate family amounted to 84 percent of its loans.

Connecticut's bank commissioners uncovered similar instances. One bank with a capital of $100,000 had loaned $30,000 to one person. Another bank capitalized at $80,000 had loaned nearly $50,000 to one individual and $42,000 to another.[68] Given the insider nature of the region's banks, such results were nearly inevitable. Because most bank directors were engaged in outside business dealings, they had credit needs just like any other merchant or manufacturer but could rarely obtain equal quantities at similar rates from other sources. If the insiders' wants were large, Rhode Island's bank commissioners noted in 1836, there would "be little left for others outside the board. And in many instances banks [had] become to a considerable extent mere engines to supply the directors with money."[69]

Lamoreaux argues that the prevalence of insider lending arose from the "general scarcity" of credit in New England's capital-poor economy, and that the scarcity led bank directors to direct a disproportionate share of their bank's funds into the directors' own projects.[70] But Charles Calomiris notes that other regions with relatively less capital were not characterized by such extensive insider lending.[71] According to the 1845 report of New York's bank superintendent, only about 6 percent of loans went to insiders. In Ohio, which limited insider lending, 10 percent in insider loans was considered large and only barely acceptable. Among Kentucky's large branch banks (discussed in chapter 10), insider loans rarely exceeded 5 percent of all loans.

Lamoreaux offers her "general scarcity" argument because, while she does not altogether dismiss information asymmetry problems, she argues that they were less important in antebellum New England than elsewhere. She argues that because most of New England's banks were located in small towns and cities where lenders were familiar with the creditworthiness of most lenders, information problems were secondary.

Although Lamoreaux's thesis is reasonable, she fails to offer a fully adequate explanation of how these insider affairs resolved information problems internal to the firm and why people were seemingly so willing to hold shares in these small insider banks. She notes that bank shares became the darling of widows and orphans because they provided consistent, if unimpressive, dividends. Moreover, New England banks operated on lower leverage ratios (i.e., more equity and less debt) than banks in other regions. This is unusual in that debt is usually thought to protect outsiders, like small shareholders, by limiting the debt issuer's behavior.

A well-known corporate finance result when an owner-manager sells equity claims on a corporation that are identical to his own in that outsiders share, pro rata, the profit stream, is that agency costs generate a divergence between his interests and those of the outside shareholders. If the former owner-manager, now part owner-manager, owns only 50 percent of the stock, he will engage in activities to the point where the marginal utility derived from an expenditure of an additional dollar of the firm's resources generates marginal utility to him of only 50 cents. As the owner-manager's share in the firm diminishes, his fractional claim falls, which will encourage him to appropriate ever larger shares of the firm's resources in the form of perquisites. Recognizing this, outside shareholders are forced to engage in more monitoring to limit this behavior, which reduces the price outsiders would be willing to pay for the firm's equity. "Thus, the wealth costs to the owner of obtaining additional cash in the equity markets rise as fractional ownership falls."[72]

Andrei Shleifer and Robert Vishny argue that large minority shareholders may form a reasonable monitoring device.[73] Because they take a large stake in the firm, these shareholders' returns from monitoring are internalized. Nevertheless, most of the benefits accrue to other shareholders. Monitors will internalize only the gains on their own shares (just as the manager internalizes only the costs of perquisites that he himself pays) so that a suboptimal amount of monitoring occurs.

Lamoreaux notes that such large minority shareholders did, in fact, exist as insurance companies, savings banks, and other nonbank firms took large stakes in banks. Not only did these firms have incentives to monitor, they had the skills and wherewithal to be effective monitors. While large shareholders, either majority or minority, may mitigate some agency problems, they may introduce others. Large shareholders may control the firm to their advantage at the expense of small shareholders, managers, creditors, and employees. If one of the consequences of having large shareholders is an ability to expropriate profits or dissipate capital, it creates a disincentive to invest, which reduces the aggregate volume of external finance.

One solution to the agency problems that arise when the same agents manage and control is to make the set of residual claimants the same as the set of managers. This restriction replaces costly internal and external control devices by aligning the incentives of managers to those of owners by uniting the two groups. In effect, large shareholders (principal owners) become the managers. Firms of this sort are usually called "closed corporations" because access to shares or residual claims is sharply restricted, typically to a small group of individuals intimately connected with the daily operations of the firm. In actual practice, the pure closed corporation is a rarity, but there are many in which shareholders have some special, often nonbusiness, relationship with the managers. They might be family, friends, or partners from unrelated businesses. Agency problems are not unknown in familial relationships, but alternative forms of monitoring and punishments, as well as extrafirm allegiances, may be particularly effective in aligning the interests of owners, including small shareholders, and managers.

Eugene Fama and Michael Jensen argue that a closed corporation is tenable only when the firm is small and noncomplex, engages in a few operations, and requires narrowly specialized resources or knowledge.[74] The closed form is costly in that it forfeits the advantages of specialization in risk bearing and decision making. Familial firms may take too few risks, making them vulnerable to competition during periods of sharp technological advance. They also lead to poorly diversified portfolios.

But New England's family banks alleviated some of these problems by effectively linking the family's diverse economic interests. The family bank was only a part of the kinship group's manufacturing, mercantile, and financial network. Banks were linked directly (through ownership) and indirectly (through interlocking directorates) to textile mills, iron foundries, foreign trade, insurance, canals, and railroads.

Societies organize along either "individualist" or "collectivist" lines.[75] Collectivist societies are characterized by segregated social structures in that each individual socially and economically interacts with members of specific religious, ethnic, or familial groups. In short, members of collectivist societies become intimately involved in the lives of other members while eschewing extensive relations with nonmembers. Individualist societies, on the other hand, are characterized by integrated relations in that social interactions and economic transactions take place between groups without any specific ethnic, religious, or familial allegiances.

New England society was clearly individualist, but it may be instructive to apply Avner Greif's social dichotomy at a micro level. New England's extended kinship networks (banks, brokers, merchants, and manufacturers tied by familial bonds) can be thought of as collectivist organizations operating within an individualist society. Inside collectivist communities, implicit and explicit contracts are enforced through sanctions imposed by informal social and economic institutions (e.g., banishment from or loss of status within the community), whereas individualist societies rely to a much greater extent on third-party arbitration (e.g., the courts) to enforce explicit, even implicit, contracts.

This explains why banks were able to entice individuals, including widows and the guardians of orphans, to invest in bank shares. Although family members within a bank organization could (and some undoubtedly did) act in unison to the detriment of outside shareholders, as long as there were small shareholders who were also members of the collectivist group, large shareholders were forced to restrain excessively self-interested behavior because the costs were indiscriminately imposed on all small shareholders, outsiders and insiders alike. And acting to the detriment of small inside shareholders was sure to elicit an informal sanction. The aim of small inside shareholders, then, was to generate sufficient trust among outsiders to elicit their investment.

Agency problems remained important in New England's small banks. Even small firms are prone to opportunism when ownership and control are separated. The solution in New England was the closely held, familial bank that operated as the financial arm of extended kinship networks. Recognizing their connection with and acting on their allegiance to a large collective group mitigated, but certainly did not eliminate, agency costs.

Concluding Remarks

Two unique characteristics of New England banks were their small size and their insider character. It seems likely that the former resulted from the latter. Being the financial arm of extended kinship networks, many of the region's banks grew no larger than needed by the principal borrowers. Yet, the advantage of the corporate form was that capital, particularly equity capital, could be raised from outside the kinship network. Outsiders invested in these insider networks because they believed that the banks' managers would work in their general interests. In effect, small outside shareholders thought that the internal and external governance structures provided adequate (if not optimal) monitoring of the banks' activities. Internal governance structures provided only one monitoring and governance mechanism. Debt, as previously discussed, provided another.

This naturally leads us to a discussion of a third, and possibly the defining, characteristic of New England's banking system. The Suffolk system arose endogenously as a regionwide banknote clearing mechanism. Although New England banks were less leveraged (proportionately more equity and less debt) than banks in other regions, they relied more on banknotes relative to deposits than banks in other regions. An extensive reliance on banknotes provided a debt-monitoring mechanism that was utilized in all regions. What differentiated New England, however, was that the debt-monitoring mechanism relied more on a hierarchical, centralized structure rather than a market-oriented, decentralized structure exploited in other regions.

5

The Rise and Fall of the Suffolk System

In previous chapters, we discussed the fact that prior to the 1860s, currency in the United States consisted primarily of banknotes—promissory notes issued by banks, redeemable in specie on demand, and used as currency in hand-to-hand transactions. Banknotes were so common, in fact, that in the 1830s they formed the bulk of the circulating media, possibly as much as 70 percent or more.[1] One much-discussed feature of this competitively is-sued currency was that as banknotes traveled from the issuing bank, their value fell. The specie redemption clause insured that banknotes traded at par in the immediate neighborhood of the bank, but because it was costly to return banknotes to their issuers, they traded at different prices in dif-ferent places. Sometimes they traded for as much as 99.9 cents on the dollar. At other times they traded for as little as 20 cents on the dollar. Such dif-ferences in prices could raise the costs of transacting between places, es-pecially if local traders were unfamiliar with a banknote's issuer or the current market price of a particular currency.

Moreover, in the normal course of business, nearly every bank received on deposit notes of other banks. It was not uncommon to take in the notes of several local and a handful of distant banks in a given week or month. Clearing these notes could be as costly, perhaps more so given the greater volume of notes accepted, for the receiving banks as it was for consumers. Reducing clearing costs required the development of a reliable and regular clearing mechanism.

Suppose there were a dozen banks in a compact geographic area that regularly accepted each other's notes. In the absence of some organized and regular clearing mechanism, each bank would have been forced to engage in bilateral clearings with each of its fellows. Lacking an agreement on a time and place to meet and exchange banknotes and other liabilities, these twelve banks would have engaged $[n(n-1)]/2$ or 66 separate bilateral clearings each period. In some places, market-based entrepreneurs known as banknote brokers arose to reduce the number of bilateral clearings. Banks for which it was uneconomical to return another bank's notes directly sold them to banknote brokers, who purchased them at discounts reflecting the costs and risks involved in returning them. While the details of their business practices still elude us, financial historians argue that they bought notes; bundled them; returned them in bulk, realizing economies of scale in redemptions; and earned normal competitive returns.[2]

In other places, banks grew dense enough that it became economical to arrange formal clearing operations at predetermined times and locations. Histories of New York City banking, for example, often relate the story of how the banks' porters arrived at an endogenous solution to carrying specie and banknotes all over the city by agreeing to meet and settle at a single location. This informal agreement gradually evolved into a formal institution—the New York City Bank Clearinghouse Association. Similar institutions evolved in Philadelphia and Baltimore in the 1850s. After the Civil War, most American cities of any consequence had a clearinghouse organization.

For country banks, clearinghouses remained uneconomical throughout the antebellum era. Banks were too dispersed and too small to justify the costs of organizing regular clearings. This meant that most consumers and banks relied on either banknote brokers or direct presentment of banknotes at the issuing banks' counters. The former were economical for small dollar values and distant banks.

In the early 1800s, Boston's banks grew weary of bearing the costs of direct presentment and paying banknote brokers' fees, so they established a unique interbank clearing operation. The Suffolk Bank of Boston became the principal clearing agent for New England. By the mid-1850s, nearly all of New England's banks had joined the so-called Suffolk system, which operated as a regional clearinghouse. After accepting notes of other banks, members forwarded them in bulk to the Suffolk, which then bundled them together and returned them to the issuing bank. The Suffolk system thereby eliminated the need for bilateral clearings. The result was an elimination of banknote discounts so that all of New England became, in effect, a single currency area. Although each bank still issued its own distinct currency, each traded at face value against all others, reducing the costs of long-distance transactions.

Despite the Suffolk system's successes, its members revolted in the mid-1850s. A competitor in the clearing business was chartered in 1855, and opened in 1858. By 1860, the Suffolk had effectively abandoned the business of banknote clearing, ceding the business to the Bank of Mutual Redemption, which was another of New England's banking innovations in that it was the United States' first bankers' bank. It was wholly owned by the region's commercial banks and its principal function was to act as their clearing agent.

This chapter first provides a brief history of the Suffolk system. The second section discusses its monetary and macroeconomic consequences. The following section places the Suffolk's operations within the context of the modern economic theory of networks. The advantage of networks is that they link individuals and reduce the costs of communicating among themselves. The final section employs the insights provided by the economics of networks to explain the system's rapid demise.

The Development of the Suffolk System

By most accounts, Boston circa 1810 was swamped with country banknotes.[3] Because the regional balance of trade favored Boston, country banknotes naturally tended there and displaced city banknotes in daily transactions. As early as 1796, three Boston banks appointed a joint committee to determine how best to deal with the influx of country banknotes. In 1799, Boston's banks jointly agreed to accept country banknotes on deposit in small amounts, with deposits in excess of $400 accepted at a discount of one-half of 1 percent. When this agreement proved ineffective, banks began accepting country banknotes as special deposits so that depositors received banknotes of similar value on withdrawal. Difficulties and the costs of the record keeping needed to enforce this agreement soon overwhelmed any potential benefits, and the plan was quickly abandoned.

After the breakdown of this agreement, some banks continued to accept country banknotes on deposit at various discounts; others refused to accept them at any price. Dealing in country banknotes then devolved to the city's banknote brokers. Even while Boston's banks, merchants, and consumers sold country banknotes to brokers, some country banks entered into agreements with the city's banknote brokers to redeem and recirculate their banknotes. Like many other country banks, the Augusta Bank of Augusta, Maine, entered into an agreement with the brokerage of Wyman & Stone, which agreed to deal in the Augusta Bank's notes at a discount of 1 percent.[4] Of course, the agreement was expected to generate a profit for each party and to keep the Augusta Bank's notes in circulation. The agreement imposed a penalty on Wyman & Stone for every banknote returned to the bank for redemption. Unless note turnover was substantial, the 1 percent margin was too thin to generate a significant profit for Wyman & Stone, so the real source of revenue must have been the interest income from recirculating the Augusta Bank's notes through their own lending.

Such practices infuriated Boston's banks because country banknotes tended to displace their own in daily transactions (largely because it was cheaper to return a Boston banknote for specie) and competition in the loan market kept interest rates down. If the city banks could rid themselves of the agents' competition, they thought, they could increase their own lending and circulation and, thus, profits. In 1803, three Boston banks formed a partnership to decrease the volume of country circulation in Boston. Each contributed to a joint fund of $300,000, which was used to buy up country banknotes at a discount and return them to the issuing banks for specie redemption. They met with so many obstacles, however, that they quickly abandoned the project. One broker employed by the Boston coalition was even brought before a Vermont grand jury on a complaint of the state's attorney general, who believed the broker was guilty of an indictable offense for demanding specie.[5]

A second scheme to reduce the circulation of country banknotes surfaced in 1804 with the charter of the Boston Exchange Office.[6] The Exchange Office was allowed limited and specialized banking privileges, namely, accepting country banknotes on deposit from Boston merchants. Merchants keeping deposits there could borrow from the office with the loans extended in country banknotes. The Exchange Office was enjoined from issuing its own notes, from buying country banknotes at a discount, and from presenting notes at the issuing bank for specie. This project, too, was short lived. It failed in 1809, holding $384 in specie and $152,385 in country banknotes.[7]

The failure of the Boston Exchange Office and the potential profits involved in buying banknotes at discounts ranging from 1 to 6 percent drew the New England Bank of Boston into note brokerage. The New England's strategy was relatively simple and presaged the Suffolk's later actions. The New England agreed to accept the notes of any country bank on deposit at a discount and then redeemed them at par unless the country bank agreed to maintain a deposit with the New England Bank.[8] Country banks maintaining such a deposit were allowed to redeem their notes at the same discount at which the New England had accepted them. The latter profited by using the country bank deposits as the basis for its own lending. Within a short time, the New England's actions drove the average country banknote discount from 3 to 1 percent, but its activities were not generating exceptionally large profits.[9] Nevertheless, the Tremont Bank entered the business in 1814, and competition between the two quickly drove discounts down to one-quarter of 1 percent. The two formed a cartel and, for a few years thereafter, the average country banknote discount remained stable at 1 percent.

The Suffolk Bank was chartered in 1818; by 1819, it entered into country banknote brokerage. Competition between the Suffolk and the New England–Tremont coalition, as well as among several independent note brokers, lowered the discount so that the "business was hardly profitable."[10] Competition in note brokerage reduced the average country banknote discount to about three-eighths of 1 percent by 1824, but as Fritz Redlich argued, the Suffolk's early brokerage activities represented no great "creative achievement."[11] Instead, it was just one manifestation of the competition between the Suffolk and Boston's other banks.

The banks' brokerage activities, in fact, had not brought about the desired effect, namely, reducing the volume of country banknotes in circulation in and around Boston. In 1824, however, two of the Suffolk's directors presented an innovative note redemption scheme to directors of Boston's other banks. The Suffolk and six other Boston banks entered into the agreement and formed a coalition known as the Associated Banks of Boston. They believed that through concerted action, the association could limit country banknote circulation and expand their own.

Under the terms of the association agreement, the Suffolk and its allies contributed a total of $300,000 to a common fund used to buy up country banknotes. Each of the six banks sent all country notes received on deposit to the Suffolk, which acted as their joint redemption agent.[12] Whenever the Suffolk's holdings of a particular country bank's notes reached a predetermined level, an agent was dispatched who presented them at the issuing bank for redemption. As might be expected, country banks responded negatively.

Most country banks viewed the Suffolk's actions as hostile. They sponsored the publication of pamphlets critical of the Suffolk and raised various obstacles to thwart the Suffolk's plan. When the Lincoln Bank of Wiscasett, Maine, was asked to redeem $3,000 of its notes, it first tendered a Boston draft, which the Suffolk's agent refused, asserting his legal right to immediate specie redemption. The Lincoln Bank's cashier then delayed redemption by counting small coins—nothing larger than 25 cents—and closing time was reached before $500 in notes was redeemed.[13]

The Lincoln Bank's strategy was widely copied and still employed as late as the 1850s. Because of these and many other frustrating redemption delays, the Suffolk soon abandoned its speculative business and proposed to replace it with a more organized and regular redemption system. Initially, the Suffolk proposed a variant of the New England Bank's earlier agreement in that it would accept the notes of any country bank at the current market discount if the country bank agreed to maintain a $5,000, permanent, interest-free deposit plus an amount sufficient to redeem the notes received at the Suffolk.[14] The permanent deposit was later set equal to $2,000 or 2 percent of a bank's capital if it was capitalized at more than $100,000, and notes were accepted at par. Country banks who refused to join faced continued and unannounced specie presentations.

Most of the region's banks agreed to the Suffolk's terms and it created a regional clearing system in which nearly all banknotes circulated at par. The Suffolk's significant post-1824 innovation was its implementation of a "net-clearing" system.[15] Instead of "gross clearing," in which banknotes were returned to the issuing bank for specie redemption, net clearings reduced the costs to both the Suffolk and its members because fewer notes were returned for specie, reducing shipping and insurance and, hence, clearing costs.

Net clearing was simple. Each afternoon, notes deposited at the Suffolk by member banks were sorted by issuing bank and bundled, and the dollar value was debited to the issuing bank's account. Notes were shipped back to their issuers, but specie was shipped only when the issuer's Suffolk account fell below an amount believed appropriate by the Suffolk's management. But member banks' accounts were also credited with the dollar value of the notes of other banks forwarded to the Suffolk. Thus, unless a bank was expanding its own issues more quickly than other banks or, perhaps, experienced an unusually high volume of adverse clearings, member banks would not face regular or unexpected specie calls from the Suffolk.

Although Charles Calomiris and Charles Kahn characterize the Suffolk's clearing system as coordination without coercion, it is clear that the Suffolk employed a combination of persuasion, intimidation, and embarrassment of nonmembers to establish and maintain its system.[16] When the Worcester Bank of Massachusetts refused to join, the Suffolk purposely stockpiled about $38,000 of the Worcester's notes (about one-half of its total circulation) and demanded immediate specie redemption.[17] The Worcester, which then had about $39,000 on deposit with the New England Bank of Boston, offered a Boston draft in exchange for its notes. The Suffolk's agent refused, remaining intransigent in his lawful right to specie. The Worcester redeemed $28,000 in specie and offered to redeem the remaining $10,000 in notes the following day at the Suffolk's office. Refusing even this offer, the Suffolk's agent sent for the sheriff and had the Worcester Bank's property attached.

Employing such practices earned the Suffolk few friends among country banks. More surprising, however, was the mixed response the Suffolk got from the region's legislators. Vermont passed a law requiring that state's banks to join or pay an annual tax equal to 1 percent of its capital. Several banks held out and paid the tax until 1850. Maine's legislature responded oppositely. In 1831, it overhauled the state's banking regulations, adding one statute that explicitly protected Maine's banks from the Suffolk's unannounced redemption calls. The law required banks to meet usual redemption calls in specie on demand, but it gave them the right to delay by 15 days any unusual (read Suffolk) redemption call.[18] By 1837, Maine's bank commissioners still attacked the Suffolk's actions and asked whether further legislation was needed to protect the banks.[19] Although some of Maine's bank commissioners grew more tolerant of the Suffolk in the 1840s, some continued to characterize it as "tyranical [sic] and oppressive."[20]

Several of Maine's banks entered into a compact of mutual support and refused to join. They remained opposed to membership because, in their opinion, the Suffolk's plan worked too well. In the Suffolk's absence, Maine banknotes would have sold at a discount outside the immediate vicinity of the issuing bank and would, therefore, have tended to circulate in a smaller circle. With Suffolk clearings and regionwide par redemption, however, their notes tended to travel toward Boston, from whence they were quickly returned.[21] Calomiris and Kahn argue that Maine's nonmember banks found limited markets for their notes.[22] But this may have been a purposeful, perhaps even a profitable, strategy on their part. Suffolk membership, after all, meant more frequent redemptions and reduced circulation periods.

If other states shared Maine's concerns, their fears were soon realized. Within a year of establishing its organized redemption system, the Suffolk redeemed and returned more than $17.4 million in banknotes. Between 1825 and 1831, the Suffolk's business grew rapidly but remained manageable. The following decade, however, witnessed the opening of more than 90 new banks. The Suffolk was quickly swamped with redeemed notes, country banks were often slow in making remittances, and many were seriously overdrawn on their redemption accounts.[23] This forced the Suffolk to revise its overdraft policy, limiting overdrafts to the amount of a bank's permanent deposit. Once its overdraft exceeded this amount, notes were bundled and returned to the issuing bank along with a request to replenish both its redemption and permanent deposit accounts. Altering its policy reduced the Suffolk's risks, but this did not slow the pace of clearings. In 1837, the Suffolk redeemed about $105 million in country banknotes; by 1847, its clearings increased to $165 million; by 1857, $376 million. The increased volume of clearings followed from two factors: more banks and, more distressing to country banks, a notable reduction in the circulation period.

Table 5.1 reports statistics on total and average New England bank circulation, as well as total and average Suffolk redemptions for selected years. Resulting calculations suggest that in 1825, an average New England banknote cleared 1.7 times per annum. By 1835, an average note cleared 4.9 times, a figure consistent with the Connecticut bank commissioners' estimate of 5 times per year.[24] In 1850, notes cleared about 6.9 times, an estimate again largely consistent with the Connecticut commissioners' estimate of 8.6 times.

Even as the velocity of note turnover accelerated, the Suffolk grew increasingly intransigent, refusing even the smallest, short-term accommodation to its members. It also alienated the few friends it had when it began dictating policy without consulting its Boston and Providence agents. In 1855, country banks banded together and obtained a charter for the Bank of Mutual Redemption from the Massachusetts legislature.

The Bank of Mutual Redemption's charter was unique in several respects.[25] First, the bank was strictly a bankers' bank. Its capital was wholly owned by New England's other banks and it replaced the Suffolk as their central clearing agent. Second, the Bank of Mutual Redemption was given sharply limited note issue privileges. It could issue banknotes in value only up to one-half its paid-in capital. Moreover, it could issue only large-denomination banknotes, which were useful for interbank settlements but not for hand-to-hand transactions.

Table 5.1 Note Redemption at the Suffolk Bank and Average Annual Turnover of Banknotes; Selected Years, 1825–1855

Year	Number of Banks	Total Notes in Circulation	Average Circulation per Bank	Total Annual Suffolk Redemption	Average Monthly Redemption	Average Monthly Redemption per Bank	Annual Average Number Clearings
1825	141	$10,068	$71.4	$17,388	$1,449	$10.3	1.73
1835	277	19,540	70.5	95,543	7,962	28.7	4.89
1840	301	16,571	55.1	94,214	7,851	26.1	5.69
1845	268	25,618	95.6	137,000	11,417	42.6	5.35
1850	307	31,710	103.3	220,000	18,333	59.7	6.94
1855	487	47,742	98.0	341,000	28,417	58.4	7.14

Note: Annual clearings = (average monthly redemptions / average circulation)*12. "Making the Little Guy Pay" by Howard Bodenhorn, table 1, *Journal of Economic History* 62:1 (March 2002). Reprinted with permission of Cambridge University Press.

Sources: U.S. Comptroller of the Currency, *Annual Report* (1876); Fenstermaker, *Development*; Root, "New England Bank Currency."

The Bank of Mutual Redemption commenced operations in 1858, and the rules it laid down provide insights into the country banks' principal grievances. Nonshareholding banks were required to maintain a permanent deposit in the same amount required by the Suffolk.[26] For shareholding members, the interest-free permanent deposit was eliminated. In addition, both shareholders and nonshareholders were required to maintain an additional redemption account sufficient on average to meet redemption calls. Unlike the Suffolk, however, the Bank of Mutual Redemption promised to pay 3 percent on such balances.

Except for the elimination of permanent deposits for shareholders and the payment of interest on redemption accounts, the Bank of Mutual Redemption's plan was not substantially different from the Suffolk's. Such seemingly small differences mattered, though. In a short time, nearly one-half of the Suffolk's members defected to the Bank of Mutual Redemption. The Suffolk staged a brief redemption war to punish the defectors and the Mutual Redemption. Its war was followed by an equally brief refusal to engage in any transactions whatsoever with the Mutual Redemption, which was followed by limited and grudging interactions with the interloper. Finally, the Suffolk retrenched and effectively withdrew from the clearing business in 1860.

Arthur Rolnick, Bruce Smith, and Warren Weber argue that the Suffolk's quick and relatively quiet exit from the industry upon the entry of a rival suggests that the redemption and clearing of country banknotes was a natural monopoly,[27] unable to capture economies of scale and scope as a duopolist, the Suffolk retired from the business and focused on its retail banking business. This may be true, though the New York City and Philadelphia experiences, in which a handful of large banks in each city acted as redemption agents, suggest otherwise.[28]

The reasons for the Suffolk's quick exit from the clearing and redemption business are discussed in a later section. Before we turn to the details of the Suffolk system's demise, we will first analyze the system from the viewpoint of modern network theory. Network theory provides invaluable insights into the Suffolk's successes and failures and, ultimately, explains country bank revolt in the late 1850s. Later sections provide a summary of modern network theory and its application to payments systems, like that developed by the Suffolk Bank in the 1820s. Before that, however, we will first turn to a discussion of the monetary and macroeconomic consequences of the Suffolk system.

The Suffolk System's Macroeconomic Consequences

Calomiris and Kahn note that contemporaries and historians alike adopt either of two views concerning the Suffolk system.[29] One perspective they label the "sanguine" view is characterized by the belief that the Suffolk fostered systemic financial stability through its organization of a regionwide note-clearing mechanism. The alternative view they label the "jaundiced" view is characterized by a belief that the Suffolk was an effective rent-seeking device developed by Boston's banks at the expense of the region's country banks. This section explores the applicability of the sanguine view. Later sections that discuss the Suffolk system's demise explore the jaundiced view.

Traditional histories of the Suffolk system portray it as a protocentral bank that exercised a salutary effect on New England's money supply and macroeconomy. Bray Hammond argues that through its clearing operations it became the region's effective central bank. It regulated the extension of bank credit, placed curbs on banks' expansion, supported them in times of trouble, and advised them on what they should and should not do.[30] Redlich offers similar conclusions. He argues that the Suffolk's actions provided a "check" to note issues of country banks.[31] These propositions both conclude (without any real supporting evidence) that the Suffolk was actually deflationary in the sense that New England's money supply was far less than it would have been in its absence.

Hammond's and Redlich's interpretations were more normative than positive. Hammond wanted to provide post–Great Depression historians and bankers with a lesson from history.[32] What was the lesson? That banks were different from other types of businesses. Banks, by their very nature, are quasi-public enterprises that competitive markets fail to regulate effectively. What was needed was a strong governmental organization to regulate any system, and the more centralized the system, the better. The Suffolk, while not an optimal solution, was certainly superior to pure competitive banking. The essence of Hammond's normative argument is revealed most clearly when he writes that the Suffolk "might have practiced an equivocal indulgence toward" country banks, but instead, "it had a puritan conviction of the moral importance of its policy and pursued it with zeal."[33]

Previous conclusions about the Suffolk's effectiveness have typically been supported by calling attention to the fact that its actions eliminated the circulation of banknotes at a discount, but nonpar circulation is efficient in certain circumstances. Recent writers have challenged the traditional interpretation, especially the belief that the Suffolk provided an effective check to country banknote issues.

Recall that the original intent of the Suffolk was to reduce the circulation of country banknotes in Boston so that Boston banks could supply an increased percentage of the local currency. For a very brief period, the Suffolk succeeded. Between 1823 and 1826, Boston banknotes as a percentage of the region's total increased by about 5 points, from 43 to 48 percent.[34] But after 1826, it fell markedly. In 1836, when the Boston percentage fell as low as 36 percent of the regional total, the Suffolk system was nearly scrapped.[35] The Suffolk Bank, however, found its activities profitable—largely a result of the interest-free deposits held by country banks—and maintained them despite its failure to accomplish the goal envisioned at the outset.

The Suffolk did not prove to be an effective regulator of the aggregate volume of bank money in New England. Using Box-Jenkins time-series techniques, J. Van Fenstermaker and John Filer how that the system had "no visible impact upon the [specie] reserve-bank money ratio and no significant impact on the growth of bank money."[36] In fact, the Suffolk system may have generated a perverse result—an overreliance on banknotes, effectively slowing the development of deposit banking. In the Middle Atlantic region, deposit banking grew markedly during the antebellum era. In New England, it developed much more slowly. The Suffolk increased (relative to what may have been) the banknote-deposit ratio by creating incentives for banks to issue banknotes and for consumers to use them.

Some historians, and even some contemporary observers, recognized this phenomenon. As early as 1857, Amasa Walker commented on the possibility that the system might have increased New England's aggregate circulation. By simplifying collections and creating universal par redemption, the system made the notes of all banks "equally current everywhere."[37] Wilfred Lake, too, recognized the system's tendency, noting that it protected the public from overissue by a single bank, but not from overissue by the system as a whole. As a result, the system was "an ineffective regulator of the total volume of bank-note circulation."[38]

Donald Mullineaux offers a provocative economic interpretation of the Suffolk's effects on the region's money supply. Mullineaux argues that antebellum banknote markets functioned like floating exchange rate systems, with each bank's note convertible into specie at a discount determined by transportation costs and the perceived riskiness of the bank's portfolio. If the market was reasonably efficient (recognizing, of course, the limitations of achieving pure efficiency because of the asymmetric information problems discussed in chapter 1), the discount on a particular bank's note provided information to otherwise uninformed traders about the note's quality. If a bank consistently pursued a riskier strategy than others, its notes would trade at higher discounts.

The Suffolk system eliminated banknote discounts and deprived at least some traders of an important piece of economic information. Once the Suffolk established universal par circulation, all notes became perfect substitutes for one another, so that traders and consumers were unable to distinguish between notes of different underlying quality. This may have made at least some consumers worse off because they could not as easily identify and hold notes of banks having the consumer's preferred risk characteristics.

Once the Suffolk system was fully in place, the market was no longer an effective regulator of the system and it devolved to the Suffolk to monitor its member banks. But as Mullineaux makes clear, this became increasingly difficult as the system expanded. In essence, the Suffolk became a franchisor. It created a trademark for banks in good standing and gave a public guarantee, which was never fully accurate, that each member bank's notes were as "good as gold."

The Suffolk faced the problem facing all franchisors, namely, controlling agency costs. Once the franchisor has created a trademark and guaranteed a standard of quality, individual franchisees face strong incentives to cheat on quality because the cheater reaps the benefits of cheating while pushing some of the costs onto all other franchisees.[39] Through its clearing operations, the Suffolk could offer long-term control over individual banks because a single bank expanding its circulation at a faster pace than its counterparts would eventually suffer adverse clearings that would bring it back into line. But if all banks expanded at nearly similar rates, clearings would cancel out. In such cases, only the largest expanders were checked and the slowly rising volume of bank issues was largely unaffected by the Suffolk's actions.

Calomiris and Kahn have countered, in some regards, Mullineaux's interpretation. They argue that the Suffolk represented an interbank cooperative arrangement whose real value became most evident in periods of financial distress. Noting that bank failure rates were markedly lower in New England than in other regions during the turbulent late 1830s and early 1840s, and that the discount on New England banknotes outside the region fell only slightly, Calomiris and Kahn interpret the Suffolk as an administrator of an implicit interbank coinsurance scheme. Members agreed to maintain markets in each other's notes for brief intervals, and what made this coinsurance possible was that all members recognized and acted on explicit rules of behavior, such as the maintenance of redemption accounts and universal par redemption. "These rules," they note, "limited moral hazard and kept banks from free-riding on the risk-sharing benefits" of mutual coinsurance.[40]

Interbank coinsurance was most useful when the default risk of all bank borrowers rose as a result of an unfavorable macroeconomic shock. Asymmetric information problems, however, made it impossible for banknote holders to determine which banks had greater downside risk exposure. Even if the shock was small relative to aggregate bank capital, banknote holders knew that its effects would be unequally distributed and thus might grow skeptical of their bank's solvency. Such uncertainty exposed even solvent banks to panicky note holders and, hence, bank runs.

To be effective in stemming unwarranted bank runs, the implicit coinsurance agreement needed to be credible with both the banks and the public. By linking the separate banks together, coinsurance elicited effort on the banks' behalf to monitor their peers. Bankers were familiar with the business of banking and were therefore in the best position to determine the riskiness of other banks' portfolios, though perhaps still inexactly.

The Suffolk may have made the implicit monitoring agreement more credible.[41] By agreeing to place deposits in another bank, several incentive and insurance problems were solved. First, the banks captured any potential economies of standardization because all agreed to a common standard for one of their products, if not all of their underlying practices. Second, banks showed uninformed depositors that they were sound by allowing informed creditors relatively easy access to their reserves.[42] Third, by agreeing to maintain similar capital and reserve ratios, banks made it easier for their peers to monitor them. And, fourth, membership in the coalition signaled to outsiders a bank's commitment to the coinsurance agreement, so the threat of being expelled from the group acted as a powerful disciplinary mechanism.

As appealing as Calomiris and Kahn's approach is to laissez-faire proponents, the Suffolk system may not have been as effective as it seems at first blush. With respect to the disciplinary effect of expulsion from the system, the Suffolk rarely made use of this option and, it seems, used it very late when it used it at all. In March 1840, the Suffolk expelled seven poorly operated and nearly bankrupt Maine banks from the system.[43] By the time it took this action, however, banknote brokers had already recognized trouble and priced these banks' liabilities appropriately. Discounts on six of the seven expelled banks' notes had already reached 100 percent (i.e., brokers refused to buy them at any price) as far away as Philadelphia by the preceding January.[44] We should, therefore, be careful not to exaggerate the Suffolk's monitoring abilities and its actual coinsurance actions, though the potential for these procedures was there.

Smith and Weber develop a formal model that casts additional doubt on the Suffolk's potential to affect New England's macroeconomy.[45] They show that a Suffolk-type bank can eliminate some problems arising in a private money regime, but it is not a cure-all. In fact, bank runs and financial panics can occur even in the presence of a central clearing agent. Moreover, interest rates and inflation rates oscillate and the operation of a Suffolk-like agent can actually magnify rather than dampen these effects.

Although Smith and Weber do not offer a formal test of their theory, they do show that much of the historical record is consistent with the predictions of their model. They argue that the Suffolk was welfare enhancing in that its operations reduced country bank holdings of unproductive specie reserves. Massachusetts banks consistently held lower specie reserves than Pennsylvania banks. Nevertheless, they also show that note circulation was more volatile in Massachusetts than in Pennsylvania. This is consistent with the model's prediction that a Suffolk-like clearing agent may not significantly reduce volatility.[46] Further, the presence of a Suffolk-like bank does not imply a lesser probability of endogenously induced shocks, nor does it reduce the probability or consequences of financial panics.[47] Again, the historical record is consistent with the model's predictions. Although New

England experienced fewer bank failures than other regions during the panics of 1837, 1839, and 1857, interest rates in Boston rose just as markedly as rates in other U.S. cities.[48]

Thus, we are left with an equivocal view of the Suffolk's macroeconomic consequences. Contemporaries, historians, and economists all recognize the likelihood that the Suffolk system improved banking practice in some regards. It made the notes of the region's banks widely acceptable and freed resources for alternative employments. In this regard, the Suffolk was welfare enhancing. But it is gross overstatement to argue, as Hammond does, that the Suffolk was "the central bank of New England" if the term is used in its modern sense.[49]

It is not clear that the Suffolk effectively reined in aggregate note issues. In fact, it may have actually encouraged expansion and slowed the use of deposits relative to banknotes. Moreover, it is not clear that the relevant macroeconomic time series followed a different path than those of other regions. More information is needed on regional prices before definitive conclusions can be drawn, but existing series do not show a markedly different time path in New England compared to other regions. Interest rates, too, followed similar paths in Boston, New York, and Philadelphia. There is no compelling evidence that the Suffolk's actions smoothed interest rates, prices, or money supplies. Hugh Rockoff is probably correct, then, when he warns against aggressively pursuing the symbolism of the Suffolk as a protocentral bank.[50]

Despite its inability to live up to its earlier billing, the Suffolk did represent an effective payments system network that facilitated interbank clearing. The next section analyzes the Suffolk from that perspective. The final section then builds on the insights provided by a network perspective to explain why the Suffolk system collapsed so quickly and so completely in the late 1850s.

Payments System Networks

Envision a number of economic agents who wish to communicate or interact with one another. In the absence of a network, communication is necessarily bilateral in nature; that is, each agent interacts with others directly. Moreover, if there are k such agents and each communicates with all other $k - 1$ agents, the group will establish $[k(k - 1)]/2$ distinct connections.

Suppose, instead, that a network forms so members can communicate through a central node rather than bilaterally. Some agents may join the network; some may not. The establishment of the network does not alter the optimal aggregate volume of interactions. Even after the network is in place, an individual will still interact with the same agents (ceteris paribus) regardless of whether they subscribe to the network. But the benefit of network membership is the resource savings of routing at least some communications through the jointly operated and maintained network. In addition, network membership often generates aggregate benefits greater than the sum of the private benefits.

Networks are composed of links and nodes, and the analysis of a network is typically carried out under the assumption that these links and nodes are combined to produce a marketable good or service. Nicholas Economides labels this feature "network compatibility" and argues that a necessary precondition for networks is the ability to combine links and nodes in economically meaningful ways.[51] Everyday examples of networks are telephone systems, railroads, automated teller machine (ATM) systems, and airlines.

Suppose we have a basic "star" network, like that shown in figure 5.1, with a central switch S and spokes radiating out to nodes a, b, c, d, and so on. If connections operate in both directions—that is, from b to S to c (call this bSc), as well as from c to S to b (cSb)—we have what is commonly referred to as a two-way network.[52] There are several important features of two-way networks. First, all components are complementary, so any two of them can be combined or connected to form a composite good, such as bSc. Second, the components are complementary even though they are very similar goods. Third, seemingly similar goods such as bSc and cSb are distinct and are not interchangeable. Fourth, composite goods that share common components (such as bSc and dSc) are not close substitutes. Fifth, proper network operation requires compatible components, which may require the adoption of certain technical standards.

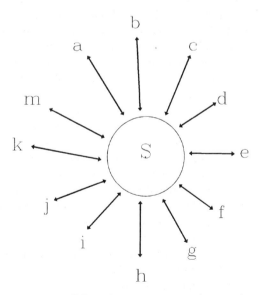

Figure 5.1 A Star Network: Suffolk at the Center; Respondent Banks on the Periphery.

The most important feature of any network, however, is the presence of network effects or externalities, which have two essential elements. The first is that the benefit to an individual user increases with the number of distinct nodes or locations connected to the network. Garth Saloner and Andrea Shepard label this the "accessibility" effect.[53] Classic examples are telephone networks with geographically dispersed connection points (e.g., phones in hotel rooms and pay phones in bus terminals) and retail distribution in which the value of a commonly consumed good increases with the number of retail outlets carrying the good. The second element, the "production-scale" effect, is the source of network externalities for subscribers to a particular network. In effect, the value of subscribing to a network increases with the number of potential communicants (recall MCI's "Friends and Family" discount plan).

The production-scale effect generates externalities for existing members by increasing the size of an existing network. In a simple star network, the externality is direct. If there are n existing network nodes, there are $n(n - 1)$ potential composite goods. An additional node (i.e., node $n + 1$) provides direct external benefits to all existing customers by adding $2n$ potential new goods by providing a complementary link to all existing nodes. For a telephone system, the more subscribers, the more people a given individual can communicate with. For an airline operating a simple hub and spoke network (a basic star), the addition of a single new destination doubles the number of possible connections for passengers.

Two problems arising from the presence of this externality, however, is the possibility that the network good will be underproduced and mispriced. As long as the network is strictly internal, its organizer faces an incentive to include an optimal number of nodes because the network externality is internalized.[54] If, on the other hand, the network is composed of several autonomous firms or individuals, the network may be suboptimally small. Adding another member to an existing network benefits all existing members, but if the existing members do not offer a subsidy to some potential subscribers, they will not participate.[55]

Joint provision of the network good and shared benefits implies common costs for the subscribers, and sharing the fixed costs among users becomes a nontrivial problem.[56] Common costs are those costs that cannot be explicitly attributed to a single user.[57] For example, the cost of providing a telephone connection is common to both the initiator and the receiver of the call, but it cannot be attributed to either separately. Common costs take many forms, such as the laying of infrastructure in a communications network, physically transporting goods from one place to another, or record keeping. In addition, many common costs are fixed relative to the volume of traffic on the network (a switching station) and cannot be allocated to a single item passing through the network.

Common costs, then, make it impossible to identify an individual subscriber's share of the network's total costs. It follows that determining the efficient price is difficult. For most goods, efficiency requires that consumers pay marginal cost. If the price is set below marginal cost, they will overutilize the good; if the price is set above marginal cost, they will underutilize it. For network goods, however, a situation in which the standard price equals marginal cost may not lead to the efficient output. Some subscribers must pay more than marginal cost or the network provider will not recover the common fixed costs. The fundamental pricing questions are: Which subscribers pay more than marginal cost? And how are those costs distributed among the subscribers?

Answers require a recognition of the network effects—that one subscriber's participation in the network provides benefits to all other subscribers who might communicate with him. Recognizing that these benefits are external to the individual subscriber but internal to the network means that it is optimal to shift some members' connection costs on to other subscribers. Generally, such cost shifting takes place so that individuals who place a low personal value on network participation but who also bring large external benefits to other members pay a smaller share of the common costs. If the external benefits of a particular individual's membership are large enough, it might even be efficient for that subscriber to pay less than marginal cost.

Jeffrey Lacker, Jeffrey Walker, and John Weinberg developed the following example.[58] Consider an existing network to which the marginal cost of adding a new member is C_n. Suppose that this individual's subscription to the network would provide benefits to existing subscribers of B_n and that the marginal costs and benefits to the potential new subscriber are C_i and B_i. It is efficient for this individual to subscribe if

$$B_n + B_i > C_n + C_i$$

The network operator must also charge the new subscriber a start-up price, p. He will subscribe as long as $B_i > C_i + p$, and the network operator will offer a subscription as long as $B_n + p > C_n$. Thus, any price that satisfies

$$B_i - C_i > p > C_n - B_n$$

will result in efficient subscriptions. That is, the net private benefits to an additional subscriber must exceed the cost of subscribing even while that cost exceeds the aggregate net costs to current subscribers of including the additional subscriber in the network.

It follows from the above, as well, that if $B_i - C_i < C_n$, the network should charge the new member a price lower than the network's marginal cost of inclusion because the value of membership to the individual is low, but inclusion in the network creates substantial external benefits that accrue to other members. In effect, existing members will be asked to subsidize this individual's entry into the network if the external benefits he generates exceed the costs of connecting him. Similarly, the network operator should charge a potential subscriber a price greater than marginal cost if $B_i - C_i >$

C_n because the individual's private net benefits of membership are high and the price should reflect his willingness to pay. It is efficient for both the low-personal-value and the high-personal-value user to join the system because of the external benefits membership entails. Each, however, should pay a different price even if they are similar in other respects.

Dominique Henriet and Herve Moulin's network model provides an analogous pricing rule.[59] They show that networks can employ a "private-cost" pricing rule (charging each subscriber the cost of connection to the network), an "external-cost" pricing rule (charging each subscriber a fraction of all other subscribers? connection costs), or any convex combination of these two. All such pricing schemes involve some cross subsidization, with the exact pricing mechanism determining the direction, extent, and efficiency of the cross subsidization.

Suppose there are rural and urban subscribers and the cost of connecting urban subscribers is strictly less than the cost of connecting rural subscribers. If most network traffic is rural to urban, Henriet and Moulin show that optimality requires that urban subscribers pay everyone's connection costs and rural subscribers connect for free.[60] A more realistic situation, of course, is that urban subscribers pay membership fees greater than their connection costs and rural subscribers pay less. Thus, subscribers who place a high individual value on connecting to the network subsidize the connections of those who place a low personal value on connecting. Cross subsidization is inevitable if the network operators desire universal participation.

A basic communication network model is easily extended to a payments system network. James McAndrews and Weinberg argue that clearing and settlement functions involving financial institutions separated by time and distance are network services.[61] Instead of viewing the Suffolk system as a protocentral bank intent on controlling the region's money supply (as some historians, such as Hammond and Redlich, do), it may be more useful to view it as a private supplier of a clearing and settlement network established and operated to generate profits.[62] Furthermore, an organization involved in the clearing and settlement of payments generates network externalities.

One of the principal functions of banks is their provision of the means of payment. Banknotes and demand deposits will become an important means of payment only if a reliable method for clearing, settlement, and redemption arises.[63] As New England's agricultural economy developed, exchange increasingly involved transactions separated by time and space, meaning that the location at which trade occurred differed from the location at which the means of payment was issued. In such a case, settlement required communication between places. The Second Bank of the United States engaged in some limited gross clearing and settlement operations but never emerged as a national or regional clearinghouse for bank liabilities. The Suffolk Bank, on the other hand, became New England's principal banknote clearinghouse in the first half of the nineteenth century.

With little or no branch banking, correspondent relationships were used to clear banknotes when the issuing bank was distant from the receiving bank.[64] If both banks had a common correspondent, the collection and clearing of banknotes proceeded at a significantly lower cost than if redemption required personal presentment or even redemption by mail.[65] Any two banks sharing a common correspondent formed a network, however rudimentary. We can easily generalize this to several country banks sharing the same city correspondent if they regularly accepted each other's notes or their notes regularly traveled in a particular direction in the course of trade.

Which banks would voluntarily join such a network? Clearly, the value of belonging to a settlement and clearing network depended on the frequency with which the bank received notes issued by distant banks. Consider the problem faced by a bank receiving on deposit the notes of a distant bank with which it had few dealings. The receiving bank could send an agent to present the banknotes to the issuing bank or it could send them through the post, but this could be risky if specie were shipped in return. If both banks were members of the same network, however, the receiving bank forwarded the issuing bank's note to a common correspondent for clearing and collection. The receiving bank had its correspondent account credited; the issuing bank's account was debited and its notes were returned.

Clearing and settlement did not require that every country bank have the same correspondent. New York and Philadelphia witnessed the development of competitive clearing operations in which a handful of city banks performed overlapping clearing and settlement functions.[66] If one country bank remitted the notes of another with whom it did not share a city correspondent, clearings required a second level of interbank cooperation. The city bank receiving the notes of a nonrespondent country bank simply cleared those notes with its correspondent. Such roundabout methods may have sacrificed some economies of scale in network clearings, but the costs were still less than simple bilateral exchange.[67]

Correspondent networks generated two sources of resource savings. First, direct redemption or presentment costs (either travel or post and insurance) were avoided. Second, there were savings arising from economies of scale in the transport of banknotes. The marginal cost of clearing and placing an additional banknote in a bundle of banknotes already destined for the issuing bank was practically nil and certainly smaller than the cost of sending it separately. At the same time, a correspondent may have been able to exploit economies of scale in clearing and settlement functions. In the presence of significant fixed network costs, the average costs of providing clearing services fell rapidly as the network expanded.[68] Moreover, establishment of networks may have fostered long-term interbank relationships and lowered interbank monitoring costs.[69]

In a payments system network, the value of communicating between two points depended on the volume of transactions between those points. Bankers in Bangor, Maine, valued a network that included members in Newport, Rhode Island, or Pittsfield, Massachusetts, only if a significant volume of trade and transactions took place between Bangor and Newport or Bangor and Pittsfield. Each endpoint or network node was differently valued by each member. An efficient network included only those endpoints for which the total value of participation (private and external benefits) exceeded the resource costs of participation.[70] That is, if banknotes issued by the Agricultural Bank of Pittsfield, Massachusetts, rarely ended up in the hands of any of the three New Bedford banks, and vice versa, the private and external benefits were potentially small relative to the costs of connecting the Agricultural Bank. The Agricultural Bank, then, may not have voluntarily participated.

It follows that the value to a given bank of subscribing to a payments system network depended on the network's existing subscribers. Generally, agents in one location placed a high value on network membership if the network connected it to a large number of agents with which it regularly interacted. Efficient pricing forced banks to recognize and react appropriately to the network externalities involved. In a network made up of members with different valuations, seemingly similar subscribers should have paid different prices for similar services.[71] The questions addressed below are: What prices did the Suffolk charge for connecting to its network? And did these prices generally accord with efficient network pricing? That many of the Suffolk system's participants were always unhappy and on the verge of revolt suggests that it may not have priced its services properly.

The Collapse of the Suffolk System

The principal network benefit accruing to New England's consumers from the Suffolk system was the accessibility effect. Banknote holders were better off the larger and more geographically inclusive the network because a larger network increased the likelihood that any banknote received in the course of trade would be "current," that is, it would exchange at par. This is similar to the ATM networks described by Saloner and Shepard in which ATM users are better off the larger the ATM network because a more geographically expansive network lowers the cost of obtaining currency.[72]

An analog in the Suffolk era was interbank correspondent relationships in which banks agreed to accept each other's notes at par, which effectively extended the area across which a bank's notes retained their currency. The larger and wider the network, holding all else constant, the more convenient it was for consumers to use a given bank's notes. The more convenient the use of its notes, the greater the demand for them and, under fairly general cost and demand conditions, the greater the bank's profits.

Because of differences in location, consumer spending habits, and the bank's own lending patterns, each bank's optimal correspondent network was a different size. A remote bank with few customers who traded outside the immediate neighborhood of the bank would be unlikely to enter into a correspondent agreement because its customers' demands (hence, its own) for such services would have been small. On the other hand, more centrally located banks had a greater derived demand for correspondent redemption agreements, which is why clearinghouses formed in the 1850s in New York, Philadelphia, and Baltimore.[73] Under clearinghouse agreements, each bank sent a representative to an agreed-upon location where each presented notes to the other. Doing so avoided the costly duplication of exchanges that occurred under bilateral exchange. Moreover, banks generally considered clearinghouse presentations as equivalent to presentations at the bank's own counter because notes were cleared at par.

Establishment of clearinghouses in sparsely populated rural areas was uneconomical. Instead, each bank engaged in irregular clearings with banks in their own vicinity. Notes drawn on distant banks were probably rarely seen and were either redeemed by post, forwarded to a note broker, or simply recirculated. As country banks grew, as their customers' spending habits changed, as their customers' trading circles widened, and as the banks' notes circulated over an ever expanding area, the banks' demand for inclusion in a correspondent-redemption network increased. As the payment technology diffused throughout New England and more people were brought into the monetary economy, the more valuable it became for even remote banks to join a redemption network. The network would have naturally expanded as the relative costs of subscribing to the network fell. A reasonable expectation, then, is that banks expecting to use the network more often or to a greater extent would join first. In antebellum New England, these were banks whose customers were engaged in more extensive dealings with the center than with the periphery. A naturally evolving correspondent network would begin small and expand out from the center.

Pre-Suffolk clearing arrangements in New England invariably imposed some of the expenses of clearing and collection on urban banks. Such costs included postage, record keeping, and presentation. If clearing and redemption services were supplied competitively, the discount on banknotes provided an upper bound to the resource cost (including a risk component) of banknote collections. It was not unusual for interregional banknote discounts to exceed 10 percent, sometimes even 20 percent. Intraregional banknote discounts, however, were usually small, often as little as one-eighth of 1 percent, though they could reach 1 or 2 percent on occasion.

In the pre-Suffolk period, city banks bore these costs. The New England–Tremont coalition accepted country banknotes at small discounts and then returned them to the issuing banks, bearing the redemption and presentment costs for those banks opting not to join its proto-Suffolk arrangement. Early on, the Suffolk adopted a similar policy, and the discount was generally sufficient to cover the bank's costs.[74] Occasionally, however, the Suffolk or one of the other Boston banks suffered losses if a bank failed before its notes were returned. Moreover, many country banks refused to enter into redemption arrangements. In other words, an endogenous clearing and collection system was expanding more slowly than city banks preferred. The Suffolk's 1824 plan accelerated the process.

Contemporary complaints about nonpar banknote exchange were not necessarily complaints about the inefficiency of the system or the total costs associated with banknote redemptions. Rather, they were complaints by city banks about the distribution of these costs. Under certain circumstances, nonpar banknote exchange was efficient. A banknote discount was the price paid by a collecting bank to a broker to avoid the cost of direct presentment. Using the notation developed in the previous section, we can analyze nonnetwork clearings in the following manner. Let the current banknote discount be $d = -p$. There were costs (C_i) to the issuing bank of direct redemption (interest costs of specie reserves), as well as costs (C_n) to city banks of redeeming the notes (record-keeping and presentment costs). In the absence of a collection network, the internal and external benefits of participating in a nonpar, broker-based redemption system were practically nil, so the terms B_i and B_n were effectively zero.

Nonpar banknote circulation was efficient if

$$C_i < d < -C_n$$

That is, as long as the banknote discount was less than the costs to city banks of direct presentment, nonpar circulation of country banknotes was efficient. Note, as well, that an efficient discount might exceed the cost of presentment to the issuing bank. The latter condition surely infuriated collecting (mostly city) banks. Thus, nonpar circulation imposed costs on Boston's banks, which felt aggrieved at having to bear those costs. The early nineteenth-century history of Boston banking included a continual search for a mechanism to shift more of these costs on to the country banks, something the Suffolk finally accomplished.

The Suffolk charged neither explicit network subscription fees nor network usage charges. Instead, it required its members to maintain a deposit that could be separated into two distinct components. Each member was required to maintain a permanent deposit equal to 2 percent of its paid-in capital; banks with less than $100,000 in capital deposited the $2,000 minimum. In addition, each member was required to maintain a redemption account sufficient to redeem its clearings. The Suffolk loaned the deposited funds at market rates to offset the network's operating costs.

Although balances in the redemption accounts were regularly drawn down, the Suffolk demanded that they were large enough, on average, to cover ordinary clearings. When the redemption account was exhausted, the Suffolk returned the member's notes and asked it to replenish its account. Doing so imposed costs on member banks because remitters of funds typically paid commission fees of one-half of 1 percent for Boston drafts. The Suffolk offered some members overdraft privileges, which, Smith and Weber argue, constituted an offsetting subsidy. But by the late 1830s, the Suffolk offered overdrafts only grudgingly and rebuffed banks that abused the privilege.[75]

Not all of the network's costs were indirectly paid by country banks. Boston banks were also expected to maintain permanent deposits. In 1824, this deposit was set at $30,000 regardless of the bank's size.[76] In 1833, it was lowered to $15,000; it was further reduced to $10,000 in 1834 and finally reduced to $5,000 in 1835. Its members, therefore, were required to keep substantial deposits with the Suffolk, though the Boston banks' share fell markedly both absolutely and relative to their capital and to the country banks' deposits.

Given the cross subsidization inherent in a network, the issue at hand is how the Suffolk distributed the network's costs across its members. The two principal costs of Suffolk membership were the interest foregone from keeping a specie deposit with the Suffolk and the interest that could have been gained from financing additional lending. The interest cost of the permanent deposit was a clear loss to the subscribing bank because it lost the use of these funds regardless of the Suffolk's effect on banknote circulation and redemption patterns.

Calculating the interest and other costs associated with the redemption account is less straightforward. Member banks lost some interest income if the redemption account exceeded the specie reserves it would have held in their own vaults in the Suffolk's absence. It is generally accepted that the Suffolk increased redemptions or note turnover, so that in its absence, country banks may have expected fewer or slower redemptions. For simplicity, it is assumed that the Suffolk doubled note turnover. Thus, the interest cost of the redemption account is calculated as one-half the average weekly redemption balance times the market interest rate. Finally, country banks, unlike Boston banks, had to pay commissions on drafts to replenish their redemption accounts. It is assumed that they tendered weekly drafts.[77]

Table 5.2 provides two estimates of the cost of membership as a percentage of paid-in capital for four size classes of country banks and two classes of Boston banks. One set of estimates, marked (1), reports only the interest cost of the permanent deposit, which represents a lower-bound estimate of the cost of Suffolk membership. The other set of estimates, marked (2), includes estimates of the interest cost of the permanent deposit, the redemption account, and the commission charges associated with keeping the redemption account current. The second estimates provide an upper bound to the costs of Suffolk membership.

Two features are immediately evident. First, the lower-bound estimates for 1827 imply that city banks paid proportionately more (as a percent of capital) of the Suffolk's network costs than country banks. Half-million-dollar Boston banks, in fact, paid the highest proportionate connection charge, equal to about one-half of 1 percent of paid-in capital. The upper-bound estimates, on the other hand, show that country banks paid a higher

Table 5.2 Suffolk Membership Costs by Bank Size and Location;
Selected Years, 1827–1855

	1827 (%)		1835 (%)		1845 (%)		1855 (%)	
Bank Size	(1)	(2)	(1)	(2)	(1)	(2)	(1)	(2)
Country Banks								
<$100,000	0.29	0.64	0.32	1.67	0.22	1.81	0.33	2.65
$100,000	0.14	0.76	0.16	2.06	0.12	2.52	0.18	3.06
$200,000	0.14	0.55	0.16	1.12	0.12	1.99	0.18	2.70
$300,000	0.14	0.31	0.16	0.68	0.12	1.34	0.18	2.53
Boston Banks								
$500,000	0.42	0.48	0.08	0.17	0.06	0.19	0.09	0.30
$1 million	0.21	0.26	0.04	0.08	0.03	0.10	0.05	0.18

Notes: See text for description of calculations. Detailed appendix available from author on request. From "Making the Little Guy Pay" by Howard Bodenhorn, table 2, *Journal of Economic History* (forthcoming). Reprinted with permission of Cambridge University Press.

Sources: Massachusetts, "True Abstract," 1827, 1835, 1845, 1855; Rhode Island, "Abstract," 1827, 1835, 1845, 1855.

proportionate fee, generally between one-third and three-quarters of 1 percent of paid-in capital, though the differences between country banks and city banks are not substantial.

After 1835, and the substantial reduction in the Boston banks' permanent deposits, country banks paid an even greater, and ever increasing, share of the system's costs. By 1855, the lower-bound cost estimates show that a country bank with $100,000 capital paid twice as much as a percentage of capital as a $500,000 Boston bank. The smallest country banks paid nearly four times as much. The upper-bound estimates show that the country banks' costs were proportionately even larger. With membership costs to country banks approaching 2.5 to 3 percent of paid-in capital, it was not surprising that open revolt broke out in 1855 with the chartering of the Bank of Mutual Redemption. It is also apparent why the Boston banks fought so hard to keep the Suffolk system intact. While a country bank might pay an annual membership price equal to 2 percent of its capital, Boston's banks paid less than one-third of 1 percent. The Suffolk effectively pushed the costs of clearing and collection on to country banks, and more so (as a percentage of capital) the smaller the bank.

Recall that efficient network pricing involves cross subsidization in which high net benefit subscribers subsidize the participation of low-net-benefit users. Boston banks were high-individual-, but low-external-benefit subscribers, as were those country banks whose customers engaged in extensive trade with the center. The external benefit generated by the participation of a Boston bank was relatively low because it was not significantly more costly to redeem a Boston banknote at the Suffolk than it was to walk across State Street and tender it directly to the issuing bank. The low-individual-, but high-external-, benefit subscribers were remote country banks with relatively few interactions with the center and with relatively high direct presentation costs.

Efficient pricing in the Suffolk network, therefore, would have enticed a remote member to subscribe by waiving a connection fee (the permanent deposit) and possibly even its usage fee (the redemption account). But connecting remote country banks imposed costs on the network provider, costs it should have recovered from high-individual-benefit users (Boston banks) by charging them connection and usage fees in excess of the incremental costs they imposed on the network provider. Instead, the Suffolk effectively reversed the efficient cross subsidization pricing scheme. Large city banks paid a proportionately small share of the network's costs, even while country banks paid a proportionately large share. Moreover, by reducing the permanent deposit required of Boston banks beginning in 1833, the Suffolk pushed even more of the costs on to low-individual- and high-external-benefit users.

Viewed from a network perspective, the Suffolk's method of allocating the common costs takes on a perverse aspect. With little to gain from participating in the network, small rural banks were reluctant to join, which reduced the usefulness of the Suffolk as a payments system network. Because the Suffolk mispriced its services, it could not elicit voluntary membership, but it recognized that the system would be effective only if it attained nearly universal participation. If country banks failed to join of their own volition, how did the Suffolk attract members?

Instead of efficient prices, the Suffolk used threats, intimidation, and coercion. Almost all commentators on the Suffolk have portrayed it from the outset as unpopular with most of its members. Its activities were viewed as a war against country banks waged by a "Holy Alliance" of Boston banks. The Suffolk employed a very effective device against country banks reluctant to join—an organized, highly focused bank run. If a bank, like the previously discussed Worcester Bank, refused to join, the Suffolk purposively collected a large volume of its outstanding circulation that it presented without warning. Few banks could meet such large calls on such short notice, and the Suffolk typically asked the local sheriff to attach the bank's property, notified the state's bank commissioners that it had refused to redeem its notes (an offense that could be punished by charter revocation), and publicly sued the bank as a bankrupt. Most country banks, not surprisingly, relented and joined the system rather than risk further embarrassment, charter revocation, or another Suffolk attack.

There were clearly instances in which the Suffolk employed these tactics when others may have worked. It continually received applications for reduced permanent deposits or for interest-bearing accounts. The bank curtly rebuffed every such application, saying that no preferences would be granted to any member. In the summer of 1852, for example, the South Royalton Bank of Vermont inquired into making an arrangement with the Suffolk on better-than-standard terms. The Suffolk refused and notified the bank that unless it made immediate arrangements for the redemption of its notes, the Suffolk would send back $10,000 for redemption. An agent was later sent to South Royalton, but the bank had the Suffolk's agent arrested and filed a preemptive civil suit against the Suffolk. Apparently, the Suffolk responded by punishing some of the South Royalton's allies in Vermont, because "at the request of the other banks in Vermont the difficulties were finally adjusted, [with] the South Royalton Bank acceding to the usual terms," but not before the South Royalton pushed its case all the way to the Vermont Supreme Court[78]

By hiring agents to travel to country banks and redeem their notes at par, the Suffolk was largely acting outside normal banking practice. It was likely that the costs of such redemption raids exceeded the costs of nonpar acceptance of country banknotes. If it were otherwise, private clearing operations elsewhere would have pursued the Suffolk's strategy. To the best of our knowledge, none did, which explains why no Suffolk-like system appeared elsewhere. A pale shadow of the system was created in New York in the 1840s, but it was imposed by legislative fiat and allowed competitively supplied clearing and collection arrangements, as well as nonpar circulation of country banknotes. A system of voluntary clearing arose in Pennsylvania at about the same time the Suffolk appeared, but it had neither universal participation nor universal par circulation of country banknotes.

The Suffolk's actions against banks unwilling to join its network foreshadowed actions by the Federal Reserve system in the late 1910s when it engaged in similar practices in an attempt to establish nearly universal par check collection.[79] Federal Reserve members were required by law to accept checks at par. Nonmembers could choose to join the network or not. From the Federal Reserve's perspective, adoption of par check collection was infuriatingly slow. To expand participation, several Reserve banks collected checks of nonpar banks and presented them in bulk at the banks' counters where they were legally obligated to pay par. As a result, the number of participating nonmember banks quickly increased from about 10,000 to about 19,000. By the end of 1920, only about 1,700 nonpar banks remained.

Opposition to the Federal Reserve's actions, like opposition to the Suffolk a century earlier, was fierce. Some banks refused to join and sued. Several cases eventually reached the U.S. Supreme Court. The Court found in the nonpar banks' favor. Reserve banks could no longer accumulate checks of nonpar banks and coerce them into participating in the presentation network. The Court also determined that country banks could pay in drafts on urban correspondents rather than lawful money. Subsequently, the Federal Reserve Board ordered the Reserve banks to desist. Not surprisingly, country banks withdrew from the par collection network so that, by 1928, the nonparticipating banks numbered 4,000. It was not until the 1980s that nonpar collection finally disappeared entirely.[80]

In the Suffolk's heyday, only Maine allowed its banks to resist the Suffolk's organized bank runs. By allowing its banks a 15-day grace period to meet unusual (read Suffolk) redemption calls, Maine's legislators effectively bypassed the twin requirements of immediate redemption and redemption in lawful money, just as the U.S. Supreme Court did a century later. A 15-day grace period provided Maine's banks with the opportunity to draw on funds in Boston to meet the call. Other states, like Vermont, were less willing to make concessions to its banks. Vermont even encouraged participation by placing a special tax on nonmembers. That the Suffolk's network connection fees were too high is seen by the fact that several of Vermont's banks opted to pay the tax. Thus, the Suffolk used methods inconsistent with the formation of an efficient, voluntary network. They used their power, with the assistance and encouragement of the other Boston banks, to shift the common costs of collecting banknotes from city to country banks. It is not surprising, then, that most of the Suffolk's country correspondents abandoned it for a competitor at the first opportunity.

Concluding Remarks

The Suffolk had two principal motivations in establishing its regionwide clearing and collection network. First, the circulation of banknotes at a discount imposed presentment costs on Boston's banks, which the Suffolk system aimed to avoid. Such costs, however, do not necessarily imply payments system inefficiency. Under certain, fairly unrestrictive conditions, nonpar circulation is efficient. Second, contemporary complaints about the costs of nonpar circulation of banknotes were not necessarily complaints about the aggregate costs of nonpar circulation. It is important to note that most, and the most vociferous, complaints originated among city banks. Switching from nonpar to par circulation of banknotes did not reduce the costs of note collection, it restructured them, shifting most of the costs of note collection and redemption from city to country banks. With par redemption in Boston, city banks paid a relatively small share of the common network costs while country banks paid a relatively large share. This was a reversal of the situation in which country banknotes exchanged at a discount, and it effectively inverted efficient network pricing rules.

There were a number of methods that might have been employed by the Suffolk to elicit membership of institutions providing large external benefits. It could have waived the permanent deposit requirement for some banks; it could have paid below-market interest rates on the permanent deposit; and it could have paid an above-market rate on the deposit of some members, effectively subsidizing their membership by charging them a negative membership fee. Clearly, it could subsidize only a few such banks, but there were surely instances, perhaps among Maine banks, in which this would have made more sense than a recurrent redemption war.

Such pricing strategies recognize that remote country banks—those banks with the largest banknote discounts and the highest presentation costs in a freely operating banknote market—would have paid little to join. The same pricing rule would have charged higher fees to Boston's banks. But because the Boston banks were searching for a method of reducing their clearing, collection, and redemption costs, the Suffolk could not impose such prices and maintain the support of its Boston allies. Faced with an intractable pricing problem, the Suffolk opted for a second-best solution. What it could not accomplish through an appropriate set of prices, it accomplished through coercion. And because it was unlikely to coerce its Boston neighbors through organized bank runs, it was forced to threaten and intimidate country banks.

The fundamental flaw in the Suffolk's plan, as Weinberg and Henriet and Moulin make clear, is that its network operator did not respect the ability of its participants to form a competing network. Some members of any network will almost inevitably generate large external benefits for others, and those members may need to receive a share of the net benefits that appears inordinately large relative to the price they pay. Unless the network operator makes this concession, it faces the risk that its members will defect and form a competing network that recognizes the externalities and prices them accordingly. The Suffolk failed to set appropriate prices and its members, particularly those whose participation generated the largest external benefits (namely, country banks), established a competing network whose prices better reflected the external effects inherent in any network.

6

Middle Atlantic

Conservatism and Experimentation

State banking systems in some regions were so fundamentally similar that treating them as a group a priori is logical. The New England banking system is a good example. With the establishment of the Suffolk system, the region's banks grew ever more similar as the antebellum era wore on. True, Connecticut banks more often dealt with banks in New York City than those in Boston, but they adopted similar practices and operated under similar philosophies, broadly defined. Even the annual reports of the region's banks looked alike, indicating an acceptance of similar accounting practices, which facilitated interbank and interstate comparisons.

State systems in other regions are not so easily combined for analysis. On the surface, the Middle Atlantic's principal systems—those of New York, Pennsylvania, and Maryland—appear markedly different. Bray Hammond writes of New York's banking policy that it was "always more hospitable to the new and experimental" but quick to eliminate any policy that proved impracticable.[1] New York's two principal innovations—bank liability insurance and free banking—were radical ideas, ones that shaped state and federal bank policy for the next century or more. They will be discussed in detail in chapters 7 and 8.

Even while New York was experimenting with its banking system, Pennsylvania and Maryland, two early leaders, grew ever more conservative. Adopting conservative stances toward financial innovation gained these states the admiration of banking historians who, like Hammond and Fritz Redlich, like to draw ethical implications from a banking system's credit policies. As they see it, liberal credit too often coincided with loose business morals. Albert Gallatin praises Philadelphia's banks for having "sound capital" that was "cautiously administered."[2] Of course, no bank should be criticized for a sound administration, but systems that fail to adapt often fail in other regards, as Pennsylvania's banks sometimes did. What about Maryland? Alfred Bryan writes that very little was developed in Maryland that was new. Of course, this meant that it avoided some "disastrous experimentation," but it also meant that it did not follow the "lead of more progressive States . . . in the adoption of new ideas."[3] In other words, by the end of the era, Maryland was left behind.

Resisting new structures or straitjacketing existing banks did not, therefore, always translate into sound banking policy. As we shall see below, Pennsylvania and Maryland adopted excessively conservative policies following banking collapses largely brought on by their states' own flawed policies. This represents another of the fundamental differences between New York and Pennsylvania and Maryland. New York not only allowed for financial innovation, but it also stayed out of the banks' way in some important respects. This is not to say that New York was the exemplar, as we shall see in later chapters, but it did avoid some costly errors.

Nevertheless, there is some underlying logic in analyzing the state banking systems of the Middle Atlantic region as a group. Despite the absence of surface commonalities, there are several deeper ones. First, each state was forced to grapple with the issue of how best to meet the credit needs of its citizens. Each was forced to select between a number of competing models for its initial bank. Each was then forced to develop a strategy for expanding the system once a model was formulated. Second, the region's three principal cities—New York, Philadelphia, and Baltimore—were leading commercial and financial centers in the early 1800s. Each city's merchants, politicians, and boosters devised various schemes to maintain or enhance its existing commercial or industrial advantage or to steal another's away. Canals, turnpikes, railroads, river and harbor improvements, and a host of other infrastructure projects were all designed to divert trade with the interior to one city and away from another. Although it was not a zero-sum game, it was often seen as such by contemporaries, and each state's banks were brought, sometimes unwillingly, into the process. In most cases, projects like the Erie Canal and the Cumberland Road were proposed, planned, and underwritten by the state. Almost invariably, however, the state's banks were asked for financial assistance. A few banks benefited from their involvement, but many did not, particularly when the infrastructure scheme soured. An enlightening approach to a study of this region's banking systems, then, is how they responded to and recovered from their involvement in the region's infrastructure projects. But first we will examine the establishment of the region's first banks and the politics surrounding them.

Rocky Beginnings: The First Banks in the Birthplace of American Commercial Banking

As in New England before the chartering of its first banks, the credit needs of the Middle Atlantic's merchants, artisans, and farmers were met by merchant-bankers, men with temporarily idle capital who loaned it to others, usually at short term. Merchant banking never disappeared, of course, but commercial banks took center stage because they received special legislative sanction and because they supplied the media of exchange. Because merchant bankers could not form limited liability partnerships nor issue their own currency, they slipped into the shadows of antebellum finance. As a result, comparatively little is known about the extent or the practices of private bankers despite a renewed interest in recent years.[4]

Although it was an important source of credit throughout history, merchant banking was incapable of meeting the demands of a credit-hungry and specie-starved merchant class. As early as 1685, Thomas Budd published *Good Order Established in Pennsylvania*, wherein he proposed the establishment of an incorporated bank that would attract hoarded specie as bank reserves that could then be put to use for the benefit of all. Budd's proposal would have capped the bank's interest rates at the rather odd figure of 8.1 percent, perhaps reflecting the current state of the money market. Further, all promissory notes and bills of exchange purchased by the bank were to be entered into a ledger available for public inspection. A similar register of mortgaged real estate and structures was also to be made available for public inspection.[5]

The latter two features of Budd's proposal show that he recognized that bank portfolios are opaque. By opening up the discount and collateral ledgers for public inspection, he was providing a mechanism whereby some bank creditors could become informed monitors. Inspired by Budd's plan, a group of Philadelphia merchants petitioned the provincial governor for a charter, but they were rebuffed. The provincial governor believed that the current stock of specie, supplemented by sterling bills of exchange that circulated like money, "fully served the public needs."[6]

Whether bills of exchange or colonial bills of credit actually met the needs of merchants is debatable, but it seems that they constituted the bulk of the circulating media for the next century. Various difficulties of relying on such a currency, particularly its inelasticity, promoted persistent complaints. It was not until 1763, however, that the next legitimate bank proposal surfaced.

Robert Morris encouraged the scheme forwarded by some of Philadelphia's prominent merchants to establish a commercial bank. Negotiations were entered into with the Privy Council, but the proposal was not well received either at home or in Britain.[7] Earlier colonial experiments with land banks had disaffected British merchants, mostly because the colonial scrip quickly depreciated against sterling. Some colonists objected, too, because they believed that the benefits generated by the bank would be confined to a relatively small group. These critics were voicing a sentiment that was to be repeated time and again during the next 50 years and more, namely, that this bank would grant a small group of already wealthy men a virtual monopoly in money lending.

Britain's Currency Act of 1765, which restricted the further issuance of colonial bills of credit, eliminated any hope among the North American colonists that they would be allowed to form their own bank. It was not until they broke from the mother country that a bank scheme stood any chance of success whatsoever. The American Revolution delivered the opportunity, but monetary conditions were decidedly unfavorable to specie-based commercial banking. Wartime contingencies and sheer necessity, however, set the stage for the nation's first commercial bank.

Although Morris had been a moving force in the 1763 bank proposal, his real legacy was established in the founding of the Bank of North America. Soon after his appointment as superintendent of finance for the Continental Congress in February 1781, Morris received a letter from Alexander Hamilton outlining a plan for a national bank. Hamilton envisioned an institution modeled after the Bank of England: a large bank with a capital of $3 million to be operated in close alliance with the revolutionary government. Morris appreciated the idea of a national bank, but he pictured a smaller, more easily established and funded institution.

Morris laid his plan before the Continental Congress on 17 May 1781. The bank, to be called the Bank of North America, was to operate on a specie capital of $400,000. It was to be semiautonomous, with the superintendent of finance having no direct control over the bank or the appointment of its twelve directors. The bank was required to report to the superintendent on a daily basis, however, and the superintendent reserved the right to inspect its books and investigate its activities.[8] The bank's notes were payable on demand in specie and receivable for all duties and taxes in every colony. To calm public fears that its issues would depreciate as rapidly as the continental issues, the bank's notes were to be accepted at their specie equivalent in all official transactions.

Morris defended the plan on several grounds. Extensive issues of continental currency had driven specie into hoards and, Morris argued, a specie-paying bank would draw it out. In doing so, the bank could replace an unsound with a sound currency and ultimately integrate the separate colonies with a uniform national currency. Morris recognized the symbolic importance of a common currency for his fledgling nation, but he surely overestimated the extent of the bank's potential circulation. Finally, and perhaps most important, the bank pledged to assist the struggling government with its embarrassed finances.

By December 1781, $85,000 of the bank's capital was paid in and its promoters petitioned Congress for a charter. On 31 December, after considerable debate and hand-wringing about the right of Congress to charter corporations, the bank received a perpetual charter. It was not until 7 January 1781, more than two months after Lord Cornwallis surrendered at Yorktown, that the bank originally organized to facilitate wartime finance opened for business.

The bank's early days were unpropitious. Shortly after opening, Morris, as superintendent of finance, was forced to borrow sums far in excess of the government's capital subscription and deposit. Public mistrust about any sort of government-issued paper currency lingered, so the bank's notes did not readily circulate. Army contractors, in particular, promptly returned the bank's notes for specie that, when combined with other government demands, dwindled the bank's specie reserves. Morris's vision of a unified, single-valued, and sound currency was never fully realized because the bank's notes circulated in New England at discounts up to 10 to 15 percent against specie.[9]

Its early difficulties notwithstanding, the Bank of North America prospered. It returned to its shareholders 8.75 percent in dividends in 1782, 14.5 percent in 1783, and 13.5 percent in 1784. The bank's political fortunes, however, did not mirror its economic fortunes. The pattern of initial public distrust, limited success as the business elite made use of its services, resentment voiced by excluded outsiders, followed finally by grudging acceptance and expansion of the industry was first experienced by the Bank of North America and then repeated in nearly every other state.

Given lingering concerns about the legitimacy of its Continental charter, the Bank of North America's directors sought a Pennsylvania charter, a strategy that ultimately created as many problems as it resolved. The bank was widely resented and quickly became a political flash point. The closed nature of the bank's ownership and directorships raised the hackles of many, particularly Quaker merchants, who felt excluded from the bank's accommodations and its profits. Constant demands for more credit and complaints about its niggardly ways compelled the bank's directors to offer additional shares. Its original shares had a par value of $400, but they had quickly risen in value, so the directors proposed selling the new shares at $500 each. To placate its critics, existing shareholders were prohibited from subscribing to the new shares, even though buyers of new shares were given the same status and voting rights as old shareholders.[10]

Evidently, this olive branch failed to appease disfranchised merchants, who proposed their own bank. When 700 shares were subscribed, its promoters petitioned the legislature for a charter. The proposal was warmly received in Lancaster (then the state capital). When the legislature refused to meet with a committee sent by the Bank of North America, the old bank proposed offering 1,000 new shares at the original $400 price. Apparently satisfied with this compromise, the Quaker merchants withdrew their petition and readily bought up the new shares in the old bank.

Popular opinion turned decidedly against the bank when it openly op-posed the emission of state bills of credit. By March 1785, less than three years after having received its Pennsylvania charter, antipathy toward the bank's hard money stance grew so strong that several legislative petitions sought a charter revocation. A legislative committee, whose charge was to determine the bank's compatibility with "the public safety and the equality which ought ever to prevail between individuals of a republic," inquired into accusations made against the bank.[11] Many people believed that banks, as large corporations endowed with perpetual lives and rights unavailable to proprietors and partnerships, were ignominious to a democratic ideal. This was the opening salvo in a half-century-long battle pitting those who viewed banks as indispensable engines of growth against those who saw them as usurpers of the powers inhered to the republican populace.

A voluminous pamphlet literature appeared along with numerous leg-islative petitions on each side. Charges against the bank were numerous, including usury, favoritism, interference with the state's right to issue bills of credit (the constitutional ban was not yet in effect), refusal to lend at long term, refusal to lend to farmers and mechanics, and "miscellaneous mis-chiefs," the most egregious of which may have been its insistence on the punctual repayment of debts.[12] Most of these same charges were to resurface in the chartering and rechartering debates surrounding the First and Second Banks of the United States, as well as hundreds of state-chartered banks throughout the antebellum era.

Public sentiment was decidedly antibank and when the legislature con-vened in August 1785, the bank question remained at the fore and the bank's president traveled to Lancaster to defend his institution. His pleas fell on deaf ears and a bill revoking the Bank of North America's charter was passed in September 1785. The actions taken by Pennsylvania's legislature im-pressed on the bank's directors that even its congressional charter might not be unassailable, so they received a charter from Delaware and contemplated relocating to Wilmington. Bills rescinding the charter revocation were de-feated in two 1786 legislative sessions, but the charter was restored in 1787. The new charter, however, was considerably more restrictive than its orig-inal one. The bank's term was limited to 14 years, its total assets could not exceed $2 million, it could not hold real estate, and it was prohibited from dealing in any merchandise other than bullion.[13]

Similar acts were played out in both New York and Baltimore. The suc-cess of the Bank of North America enticed a group of New Yorkers to or-ganize their own bank. The first such proposal, supported by Chancellor Livingston, was a land bank that was to be called the Bank of the State of New York. The proposed institution was to have a capital of $750,000 di-vided into shares of $1,000 each, two-thirds of which could be paid with mortgages, so the bank was conceived as an institution run by, and probably for, the state's wealthy landed class.[14] As a concession to political realities and to counter charges of creating an aristocratic organization, the governor was ceded the right to appoint two of six directors.

Opposition to the proposal, especially among the city's merchants, was intense. It was argued that such a bank would provide little assistance to the city's merchants; that an institution with such a large capital and so little specie would not engender public confidence; that in time of financial crisis the bank would not be in a position to offer relief (though reasons were not spelled out); that such a bank would further entrench a landed aristocracy (itself repugnant to the republican ideal); and that landed security, as so many failed colonial experiments had amply demonstrated, was an inappropriate basis for a bank of issue. Alexander Hamilton threw himself into an assault on the proposed bank, largely because he disagreed with Livingston, who "had taken so many pains with the country members, that they all began to be persuaded that the land bank was the true philosopher's stone that was to turn all their rocks and trees into gold."[15]

The truth was that Hamilton opposed the land bank scheme because he had his own bank in mind. His bank was to have a paid-in capital of $500,000 divided into 1,000 shares. When one-half that amount was subscribed and paid in, the subscribers were to elect directors, a president, and a cashier. Its shares were quickly subscribed. On 15 March 1784, the bank was officially organized, adopting bylaws written by Hamilton.[16]

Directors were elected who sat Alexander McDougall as its first president and William Seton as its first cashier. Seton was immediately sent to Philadelphia to study the operations of the Bank of North America. He arrived, however, during the charter revocation brouhaha and found the bank in chaos. The charter revocation instituted a brief bank run, one large enough that the bank stopped discounting until matters settled. Seton nonetheless remained in Philadelphia, learning the Bank of North America's accounting and business practices. The Bank of New York opened promptly after his return to New York in early June 1784.

Hamilton, McDougall, and Seton quickly faced their own crisis. Long-festering animosities developed during the merchants? attack on the land bank proposal were now turned toward Hamilton's bank. In November 1784, McDougall petitioned New York's legislature for a charter, something the incorporators thought would be easily obtained. Their sanguine expectations were soon dashed. A chartering act introduced in 1785 was defeated, largely due to opposition from up-country legislators still seeking vengeance for having their own plan quashed.

Without a charter, the Bank of New York's subscribers faced unlimited liability and lost the legal right to issue notes. Some subscribers backed out; others reduced their subscriptions because they worried about the potential liability. One subscriber informed the bank's directors that "unless it can obtain a charter, I cannot consider myself under any obligation to pay in my subscription."[17] Although the lack of a charter exposed its shareholders to the risks of making good on the bank's debts to the extent of their personal estates, the bank continued. And it was reasonably successful, paying 6 to 7 percent dividends, which were consistent with dividends paid by later banks but fell well short of the 14 percent regularly paid by the Bank of North America when it held a monopoly in the Philadelphia market. Two more failed attempts to obtain a charter occurred in 1789 and 1790. Finally, in 1791, the Bank of New York received the state's imprimatur.

Baltimore's history parallels, in some regards, New York's. The first bank proposal surfaced in 1782, when James McHenry introduced a chartering bill in the Maryland senate. The bill passed the senate but failed in the house. A second proposal surfaced two years later, when a group proposed the Bank of Maryland with a capital of $300,000 divided into $400 shares. If the state recognized the bank's notes and accepted them in payment of taxes, the organizers were willing to submit their bank to regular legislative examination. One hundred and fifty shares were subscribed within ten days.[18]

The proposal sparked a debate that ultimately pitted mercantile and agricultural interests against one another. Merchants favored the Bank of Maryland proposal because it promised credit and an increased circulating medium, both of which were in short supply in Baltimore. Tobacco warehouse receipts constituted an important part of Baltimore's circulating medium. In some instances, like large wholesale transactions, these receipts were handy. In other instances, typically small retail transactions, they were not. Moreover, warehouse receipts suffered two critical disadvantages. First, the supply was inelastic, depending largely on the weather and the tobacco crop. Second, the supply was highly seasonal. Tobacco receipts abounded in late fall as the crop came to market, but they grew increasingly scarce through the winter and nearly disappeared in late summer just prior to the next crop coming to market. Sterling bills also circulated, but they tended to be drawn in large and odd denominations, which limited their usefulness as currency.

Farmers, landowners, and other agricultural interests opposed the Bank of Maryland plan because they feared that a specie-reserve bank would draw specie out of circulation and into the bank's vaults, further compounding the already inconvenient currency shortage. They, of course, failed to recognize that a fractional reserve banking system would actually expand the money supply, but few early Americans truly understood this feature of banking. And bankers were not particularly willing to educate them. In a now-famous letter from Thomas Willing, first president of the Bank of North America, to the directors of the Bank of Massachusetts, Willing wrote that the "world is apt to suppose a greater mystery in this sort of business than there really is. Perhaps it is right that they should do so and wonder on."[19] In addition, farmers feared being forced to pay tribute, not to a landed aristocracy, but to a mercantile one. This fear grew when it was publicly revealed that the bank's 300 subscribed shares were held by only 17 people. Once again, the charter passed the senate but was tabled in the house.[20]

It was six years before another bank bill reached the Maryland legislature. Unlike its predecessor, this proposal was delivered to the legislature with little fanfare. Perhaps because its promoters had witnessed previous failures when the merits of a bank plan were debated in public, this group quietly delivered a bill and purposively avoided public debate. This bank, too, was to be called the Bank of Maryland and would have a capital of $300,000. Adopting the low-key strategy proved successful. The chartering act moved easily through both houses and subscription books opened on 10 December 1790. In less than two weeks, more than two-thirds of the bank's capital was subscribed.

Competition and Cooperation Come to the City

Despite political difficulties and open opposition from various factions, each of the region's principal port cities had at least one bank by 1800. More important, the inauspicious beginnings of the first banks did not give way to more reassuring starts for later-chartered banks. Not only did second and third banks need to overcome the objections of legislative factions, but they also had to deal with first movers, who rarely received a newcomer that threatened their established monopoly with good humor. More often than not, upstarts received nothing but hard terms from existing banks. On occasion, open warfare broke out, generally initiated by an existing bank sending a delegation to the legislature to testify about the ill effects of allowing an entrant. If that strategy failed, existing banks often responded by refusing to receive the newcomer's notes, by refusing credit to the new bank's supporters, or by initiating a redemption war meant to embarrass the upstart. Such actions rarely accomplished more than making later cooperation more difficult.

When the Bank of Pennsylvania opened in Philadelphia, relations with the Bank of North America and the main office of the Bank of the United States were publicly amicable. The two existing banks readily agreed to accept the new bank's notes and to engage in daily clearings. Over the next few years, in fact, the three banks formed several joint committees to coordinate policy. Anna Schwartz attributed the Bank of Pennsylvania's relatively warm welcome to the fact that it was specifically chartered as the state's fiscal agent. In addition, the Bank of North America had already had its charter revoked once,[21] and its directors didn't want to place it at risk again by giving the state's darling a hard time.

Although the Bank of Pennsylvania received a pleasant enough welcome, it was not so generous to subsequent entrants. When the Philadelphia Bank opened in 1804, the Bank of North America and the Bank of the United

States again quickly came to terms with the new bank, agreeing to mutual acceptance of each other's notes and daily clearings. The Bank of Pennsylvania's response was openly aggressive. It vigorously lobbied against its charter, going so far as to offer a bonus of as much as $400,000 to the legislature if it rejected the charter. When that ploy failed and the Philadelphia Bank received its charter, the Bank of Pennsylvania refused to deal with it. The old bank refused to accept the new bank's notes or to include it in joint committees. The Philadelphia Bank quickly (and smartly) responded by collecting Bank of Pennsylvania notes and returning them for specie. The Bank of Pennsylvania soon found its policy untenable because the Philadelphia Bank was draining its reserves. Because the Bank of Pennsylvania refused to accept the Philadelphia Bank's notes, it had no choice but to pay out specie. Eventually, the old bank recognized the futility of its nonintercourse policy and the two banks established an uneasy truce, agreeing to daily settlements.

Nicholas Wainwright attributed the Bank of Pennsylvania's aggressive stance to social factors.[22] The Philadelphia Bank, like its predecessors, was founded by successful merchants. Unlike the directors and shareholders of the existing banks, however, the principals behind the Philadelphia Bank were young upstarts, largely Jeffersonian in political leanings and not welcome in Federalist circles. Nothing reflected these men's Republican attitudes as obviously as their eagerness to invite the middling sorts into the ranks of bank shareholding. While the Bank of North America and the Pennsylvania Bank issued their shares with $400 par values (with market prices often well above $500), the Philadelphia Bank's capital was divided into $100 shares. More important, the new bank promised to lend to individuals ignored by existing banks. The Philadelphia Bank granted loans at longer nominal terms and accepted collateral rather than demanding two good endorsers, which made credit more available to mechanics and tradesmen. To existing bankers, "the whole program smacked of Jeffersonianism," which unnerved the old Federalist elite.[23]

While social concerns, like fears of growing republicanism, undoubtedly motivated some of the existing banks' actions, economic considerations were surely as important. Existing banks feared that entrants would do little more than deplete their reserves and limit their ability to extend credit. In effect, bankers believed that both the supply of specie and the demand for credit were static and the arrival of a new supplier implied a finer division of the existing pie. The hard terms given to newcomers were also attempts to maintain a monopoly or protect a fragile (implicit or explicit) oligopoly agreement.

Incumbent bankers had good reason to resist and resent entry. Evidence from later in the antebellum era, in fact, shows that entry increased interbank rivalry, manifested by a greater churning about of market shares.[24] Marked and repeated changes in market shares in oligopoly markets generally indicate less-effective coalitions, and a decline in profits. While the evidence is inconclusive because other factors did not remain constant, it appears that entry reduced the Bank of North America's profitability. In the quinquennium 1795–1799, when the bank had only one local competitor, it paid an average annual dividend of 11.8 percent of capital. In the 1800–1804 period, when it had two competitors, its average annual dividend declined to 9.6 percent. In 1805–1809, with three competitors, dividends fell to 9.0 percent.[25] Thus, the threat of increased competition was the likely motivating force behind an incumbent bank's hard treatment of actual and potential entrants.

As combustible as the mixture of banking and politics could be in Philadelphia, it was no match for New York's experience. In few other places did existing banks go to the same lengths to quash entry. Not surprisingly, New Yorkers employed all sorts of schemes to obtain charters and compete with incumbents.

Alexander Hamilton, who had employed his influence to defeat the land bank scheme of 1784, used his influence as U.S. secretary of the treasury to defeat a similar plan in 1791. The proposed bank was designed to promote and partially underwrite the building of canals and the development of the state's increasingly market-oriented agricultural sector. The plan was placed before a legislative committee from which it never reemerged. Voicing the opinion of shareholders in the Bank of New York, Hamilton asserted that the addition of another bank would be "a dangerous tumor in your political and commercial economy."[26]

With Hamilton's Bank of New York earning substantial profits (paying about 14 percent in dividends after its early struggles) and facing only limited competition from a branch of the Bank of the United States, several plans for new banks surfaced between 1784 and 1799. Each new plan was defeated in the legislature. It was Hamilton's nemesis, Aaron Burr, who finally succeeded in securing a charter, albeit through an artful ruse.

The Bank of New York was widely seen as an openly Federalist institution that focused on mercantile lending and catered almost exclusively to the city's leading Federalist merchants. Burr, a prominent Republican, wanted to establish a second bank that would cater to the city's neglected Republican merchants and mechanics. But the legislature, still under control of the Federalists, refused to charter a rival for the Bank of New York. Burr believed that the establishment of a new bank would succeed only if he disguised his group's real intentions.

In 1799, an opportunity presented itself. With a rapidly increasing population stressing Manhattan's wells, the city's already inadequate water supply was deteriorating. In 1798, a yellow fever epidemic erupted and the speed with which it spread was blamed on the meager supply of fresh water. Fever reappeared in 1799 and swept through the city with even more virulence than that of the previous time. The arrival of annual epidemics alarmed city and state officials and convinced them that a plentiful supply of fresh water was required. Such conditions made the passage of a bill chartering a water company easy.[27]

Burr jumped at the opportunity. His group received a charter for the Manhattan Company, which was to supply the city with fresh water. Not knowing what the capital requirements of such an undertaking might be, the legislature allowed the company a $2 million capital. Burr was instrumental in having a clause inserted in the charter providing that any capital not immediately required to finance the water project could be "employed in the purchase of public or other stocks, or in any other moneyed transactions or operations not inconsistent with the laws and constitution of the State of New York."[28] Shortly after receiving its charter, Burr's waterworks company announced its intention to employ $500,000 of its capital in a bank. The Manhattan Company did, in fact, construct waterworks consisting of about 20 miles of bored logs that supplied about 1,400 homes with water piped from wells in what is now midtown Manhattan. It operated these waterworks until the mid-1840s, at which time it turned its attention to banking alone.

Generations of historians have argued that Burr's scheme succeeded because New York's legislators failed to recognize the ramifications of charter clauses allowing nonbanking companies to engage in financial transactions. In 1848, a writer in *Bankers' Magazine* claimed that it was "certain . . . that an immense majority of the legislature did not entertain the least suspicion that the charter contained a grant of banking powers."[29] Leonard Helderman, too, argues that the legislature was sloppy in its use of such ambiguous language, and Robert Chaddock suggests that the legislature was "duped."[30] Robert Wright makes a slightly different argument.[31] Noting that Burr pushed the bill through in the final days of a busy legislative session, Wright believes that many legislators did not have time to read the bill carefully and others had no time to read it at all. Wright also argues that Hamilton encouraged Burr's plan, hoping that the spread of banking would reduce hostility to it, and then claimed foul only after the deed was done to discountenance Burr politically. However, it seems unlikely that Hamilton would encourage a competitor. Few monopolists invite competition.

It is difficult to accept the notion that not even a single legislator was shrewd enough to appreciate the implications of the charter clause. In fact, the company's charter was passed over the objection of the state's chief justice, who reviewed all legislation prior to final enactment and recognized that the clause gave the Manhattan Company a very wide latitude, including the right to engage in various branches of trade.

Such mistakes were repeated too often to have resulted from legislative oversight, laxity, or incompetence. It is more likely that when public opinion opposed additional bank charters, surreptitious methods were resorted to so that legislators could charter banks and then claim to have been duped. If the Manhattan Company experience had indeed been the result of carelessness, it is difficult to explain why subsequent legislatures repeated the error over and over without learning anything. The New York Manufacturing Company (1812) became the Phoenix Bank, the Aqueduct Association (1818) became the Green County Bank, the New York Chemical Manufacturing Company (1824) became the Chemical Bank, and the Dry Dock Company (1825) became the Dry Dock Bank when each was chartered with similarly open-ended clauses.[32] Such a pattern of serial carelessness implies either utter and nearly incomprehensible incompetence or political shrewdness and opportunism. It was likely that legislators resorted to cloaking a bank in a nonbank charter when the demand for banking services increased, but chartering a single-purpose financial institution would have alienated an important or vocal constituency.

Whether they came by their charters directly or surreptitiously, the number of city banks grew. By 1850, New York had 40 banks; Philadelphia, 15; and Baltimore, 10. All of these banks circulated banknotes and had depositors who drew checks. Being in close proximity to one another, they received large volumes of banknotes and checks drawn on other banks. In March 1842, the Mechanics Bank of Philadelphia (capital of $1.4 million) reported holding $18,280 in notes of the Girard Bank; $9,168 of the Bank of Penn Township; $2,113 of the Manufacturers and Mechanics Bank; $1,474 of the Moyamensing Bank; $2,503 of seven other Philadelphia banks; and $14,511 in notes issued by country banks in Pennsylvania, Maryland, Delaware, and New Jersey.[33] Chapter 5 discussed alternative clearing mechanisms for country banknotes. What was needed was some method to facilitate regular collections between city banks. The method that endogenously arose was the bank clearinghouse.

Up to the late 1840s, New York City banks allowed clearings to accumulate during the week and settlements were made on Fridays. Margaret Myers characterizes the typical Friday afternoon as bedlam.[34] Porters weighed down with bags or valises filled with banknotes, checks, and gold dashed from one bank to the next to settle accounts. Paying tellers (tellers in charge of the bank's specie) spent the day waiting for porters to appear, at which time checks and banknotes and specie were exchanged.

Growth in the number of banks in the late 1840s and early 1850s made the continuance of this practice impractical. After a series of discussions, a plan for a clearinghouse association was settled on in October 1853. Under the clearinghouse system, banks cleared daily instead of weekly. Porters were sent to a central place where clearings were presented and settlements were made simultaneously. Net clearings and record keeping quickly replaced the inefficient and cumbersome methods of gross clearing. In August 1854, five of the city's largest banks jointly contributed $1 million to a common fund and issued large-denomination clearinghouse certificates to be used only in interbank settlements. Some time later, the American Exchange

Bank assumed responsibility for the certificates, and by 1857, it held inter-bank deposits of about $6.5 million and cleared about $20 million on a typical day.

Clearinghouses facilitated banknote clearings, but their real advantage lay in the clearing of claims drawn against demand deposits, or checks. Because there were market makers in banknotes (banknote brokers), the market was capable of revealing information about banks and the price mechanism allocated resources.[35] The increased use of demand deposits in the late antebellum era presented a different challenge. Whereas a banknote was a claim against a single, easily monitored issuer, a check was a dual claim in that it was a claim against a specific party keeping an account at a specific bank. When a merchant accepted a check, he needed to determine three things: (1) whether the individual had sufficient funds in the bank, (2) whether the individual's bank would meet the specie call, and (3) whether the merchant's bank would accept and pay the check at par.[36] Condition (1), particularly, meant that markets for dual claims were very thin because it was simply uneconomical for brokers to gather information about the creditworthiness of every depositor in every bank. Moreover, the check contract guaranteed par exchange so that different prices reflecting different bank and depositor quality did not develop. Because outside markets never developed in checks and acceptors demanded quick clearings, banks were forced to develop an organization that internalized the function that markets failed to provide.

The clearinghouse's potential became fully evident during the panic of 1857. Bank reserves citywide began declining in early August. With the collapse of the Ohio Life and Trust Company, the drain accelerated and commercial paper rates rose sharply as the money market tightened. The typical response by banks in similar circumstances was to contract their loans to protect their own reserves. But such actions were self-defeating when all banks followed this course in unison. It only worsened the effects of the panic as money markets tightened. Under the direction of the clearinghouse, however, New York banks agreed to expand their loans proportionately so that additional clearings would cancel without threatening any particular bank's reserves. This generated about $5 million in additional credit. Although this concerted action was insufficient to stem the panic, it nevertheless represented a marked break from past practice.[37]

Panics generally occurred because an exogenous macroeconomic shock reduced the value of bank portfolios, but not all banks were equally affected because each held a unique portfolio. Depositors, however, were not in a position to distinguish between low- and high-risk banks, so all banks were prone to a run. Clearinghouses might mitigate this effect through their joint production of confidence.

Clearinghouses produced confidence in a number of ways. First, they used a number of screening mechanisms to assure bank quality. Most clearinghouses imposed an admission standard, often in the form of minimum

capital requirements. They also imposed admission fees and reserve requirements and periodically audited members.[38] Members who failed to
meet the clearinghouses' standards were fined. Members who repeatedly
departed from accepted practice were expelled, like the Mechanics Bank in
September 1857. Expulsion sent a unequivocal negative signal to the public
about the expelled bank's viability. Expulsion was an effective enforcement
threat.

Second, the clearinghouses' strength arose because banks were in the
best position to value the portfolios of other banks. The valuation advantage
was manifested in the issuance of clearinghouse certificates. A bank in immediate need of currency could rediscount assets with the clearinghouse,
which gave the bank large-denomination clearinghouse certificates. The certificates were used in clearings with other banks, which freed currency that
could be used to pay depositors. What made the clearinghouse certificates
valuable, apart from the rediscounted collateral, was that they represented
a joint liability of all clearinghouse members.[39] Rediscounting and issuing
certificates, then, represented a joint insurance guarantee. If a member bank
failed while holding clearinghouse certificates, remaining members shared
the loss. But the real intention of the joint insurance guarantee, of course,
was not to pay out, but to mollify the public by signaling a member's joint
soundness and thus turn aside a run *before* it developed so that the insurer
would never be asked to pay out.

In the course of a half century, city banking had evolved markedly. At
the beginning of the 1800s, incumbent banks fought vicious fights to protect
their monopoly or existing oligopoly positions. When incumbents were unable to ward off entry, entrants typically found nothing but hard treatment.
Purposive collection of banknotes and redemption wars were common.
Such battles often resulted in long periods of bad feelings and mutual distrust. Once it was recognized that initial monopoly positions were politically untenable, especially in the Jacksonian economy of the 1830s and
1840s, existing banks made room for entrants. Entry was never welcomed,
of course, but banks learned that it was more productive to work together
than at odds. One manifestation of that recognition was the endogenous
formation of clearinghouse associations. New York saw the emergence of
the nation's first clearinghouse in 1853. By the end of the decade, the idea
had spread to Philadelphia and Baltimore. Competition was increasingly
tempered by cooperation.

Banking Comes to the Countryside

In the previous section, we saw that legislators often felt compelled to make
credit available, by way of banks, to important and vocal constituencies.
Farmers proved to be just such an important and vocal constituency to
whom state legislatures responded in remarkably similar ways throughout

the Middle Atlantic region. By 1804, Maryland had chartered only two banks, both located in Baltimore, that catered to city merchants. Farmers argued that agricultural regions had not yet received their due. To provide credit to this previously ignored constituency, the Farmers Bank of Maryland was organized in August 1804 and opened for business without a charter.[40] The bank's principal office, located in Annapolis, served two purposes. One was to attract merchants to the city so that it could compete with Baltimore as the state's principal entrepot. The second was to diversify the bank's portfolio by dealing with these merchants.

The bank's second branch was located in Easton, where it served farmers and merchants who wanted to replace Alexandria, Virginia, as the regional destination of export-bound agricultural goods. A third branch was located in Frederick, and it loaned to farmers and a few local merchants. The state's two existing banks worked diligently against the Farmers Bank's charter, claiming that none of its locations merited banking facilities. Despite their objections, the Farmers Bank received its charter in 1805.

The Farmers Bank's influence on Maryland banking went beyond its intent to cater to farmers and others unserved by existing banks. Its decision to open for business as a partnership and then obtain a charter produced imitators. In the next decade, it became common for hopeful bankers to form private partnerships and open for business before securing a charter. Up to 1812, no previously organized bank was denied a charter. In addition, Maryland law required that a newly organized bank's subscription books be opened in all counties in the state. Banks previously operating as a partnership were exempt from this requirement. The original partners could subscribe to as many shares as they desired. By following a strategy of first forming a partnership and then obtaining a charter, the organizers were assured as much control over the bank as they preferred. Moreover, organizing as private partnerships did not place these firms at a substantial competitive disadvantage relative to chartered banks. Maryland law was unusually lenient in that it recognized the common law right to issue small-denomination, payable-on-demand promissory notes (banknotes, for all intents and purposes), albeit with unlimited liability of the issuers, until 1842. Thus, unlike other states, Maryland placed few obstacles in the path of private bankers.

Following the formation of several banking partnerships between 1805 and 1812 the state passed a law forbidding them. The new law notwithstanding, the City Bank of Baltimore was organized as a private partnership in 1812 to the "great alarm" of state authorities.[41] Despite its blatant disregard for the law, the City Bank eventually received a charter and there is no evidence that any of the penalties spelled out in the 1812 statute were ever imposed. The City Bank was, however, the last bank chartered for the Baltimore market until 1835. Between 1812 and 1835, Maryland chartered 19 country banks that catered mostly to farmers and small-town merchants.

As a group, these banks were unsuccessful. Six closed by the end of 1821; six others never raised enough capital to organize.[42]

Such instances rarely calmed the agricultural sector's vehement demands for more banks and more credit or the number of proposals to supply them. Maryland incorporated the Real Estate Bank of Frederick in 1835 and the Real Estate Bank of Baltimore the following year. These banks' capital was to consist of unencumbered mortgages transferred to the banks. The banks were then to raise specie by issuing and selling 6 percent bonds with mortgages serving as the underlying collateral. Each person conveying a deed was a shareholder with a share proportionate to the value of his mortgage and remained responsible to make up any deficiency between the market and face values of the mortgage. Both banks were designed on a model used extensively in the southern United States and discussed in greater detail in chapter 10. Neither bank's promoters were able to generate sufficient interest in their plans to bring them to fruition. Given fluctuations in the real estate market, landowners were probably wary of the liability implications of having to make up any deficiency between face and market values. A sharp drop in the price of land (which represented most landowners' principal asset) would induce a call for additional security or cash. A call would probably also occur in the face of sharply rising interest rates, which would generate even larger discrepancies between face and market values.

Even in the face of country bank closings and the inability of chartered banks to attract capital, Maryland's farmers continued to complain about the persistent lack of credit, arguing that Baltimore's merchants received disproportionate preferences. Whether these were ultimately complaints about a legitimate lack of financial institutions serving the agricultural community, or whether the complaints reflect interest rates or collateral requirements that farmers were unwilling or unable to meet, remains unresolved. Alfred Bryan sympathized with the farmers and even suggested that the lack of agricultural credit slowed the development of the state's agricultural regions.[43] While a fully convincing reckoning demands additional research, the fact that Maryland adopted a liberal attitude toward country and private banking suggests that features of Maryland's economy other than its banking system slowed its development.

Farmers were not the only occupational group demanding what they thought was their fair share of bank credit. Artisans, mechanics, and manufacturers were as vocal as farmers in their credit demands, and most states responded in various degrees. In 1807, Pennsylvania chartered the Farmers and Mechanics Bank of Philadelphia. The unusual feature of this bank's charter was that it was designed specifically to promote agriculture and manufacturing. No officer was allowed to hold stock in any other corporation or hold any elected or bureaucratic office.[44] The presumption underlying these restrictions was that those who already held corporate stock or held elected office were of higher socioeconomic status than farmers and artisans and thus had alternative sources of credit. Moreover, the bank was required to lend an amount equal to 10 percent of its $1.25 million capital to farmers secured by mortgages at an interest rate not to exceed 6 percent. The charter required that most of its directors be farmers, mechanics, and manufacturers rather than merchants, and its original board of directors included a saddler, farmer, paper manufacturer, currier, bookseller, watchmaker, hatter, iron manufacturer, attorney, and two merchants.

The idea to charter banks to serve the credit needs of particular occupations and sectors quickly caught on. The Mechanics Bank of New York City (1810) required that at least seven of its thirteen directors be active members of that city's General Society of Mechanics and Tradesmen and that at least four directors be actively engaged in their artisanal occupation.[45] The Mechanics Bank of Philadelphia (1824) established similar requirements of its directors as did the Farmers and Mechanics Bank of Pittsburgh (1814). The charter of the Mechanics Bank of Baltimore (1806) also required that nine of fifteen directors be mechanics or manufacturers, but the requirement was apparently not met because its charter was later amended with a strict definition of a mechanic.

Other groups in other places were favored with similar institutions. Pennsylvania, for example, chartered the Agricultural and Manufacturing Bank of Carlisle (1814), the Farmers Bank of Lancaster (1814), the Miners Bank of Pottsville (1828), the Lumbermans Bank of Warren (1834), and the Farmers and Drovers Bank of Waynesburg (1835).[46] Two Maryland examples were the Farmers and Mechanics Bank of Frederick (1826) and the Farmers and Millers Bank of Hagerstown (1836). New Jersey had the Farmers and Mechanics of Rahway (1828), the Mechanics Bank of Newark (1831), and the Manufacturers Bank of Bellville (1834). Not unexpectedly, New York carried this trend further than most states. If a bank's name actually indicated its primary constituency, New York City had narrowly specialized institutions, including the Leather Manufacturers Bank, the Butchers and Drovers Bank, the Corn Exchange, the Grocers, and the Shoe and Leather Bank.

It is not clear how diligently or for how long these specialized banks catered to their ostensible clientele. In 1834, the lending policies of the Farmers and Mechanics Bank of Philadelphia were reviewed by the bank's discount committee. At that time, the bank's discounts for which renewals would almost certainly be sought amounted to $657,174. Long-term loans on bonds and mortgages amounted to another $185,000. These locked-in loans tied up nearly two-thirds of the bank's capital and 40 percent of its aggregate lending. The committee reported that such loans discouraged "active business from keeping accounts because they cannot be accommodated in cashing their business notes, and it is from this class of customers that the Bank receives much of its deposits and circulation which are the principal means of the Bank's profits."[47] They recommended that the bank reduce its lending on long-term notes and other loans prone to repeated renewals. If it followed the committee's recommendations, the volume of credit extended to farmers was likely to decline, thus moving away from the bank's original charge.

Of more concern, at least to modern economists if not contemporary bankers and commentators, was the limited ability of some of these banks to diversify. If these banks actually served the specific clientele implied by their names, they were unlikely to hold loans of various maturities and originating in different sectors, which made them vulnerable to both idiosyncratic (bank-specific or portfolio-specific) and systematic (general macroeconomic) risk. If, for example, the demand for lumber or domestic manufactures declined, banks catering to lumber cutters and merchants or manufacturers would be much more likely to experience significant losses than well-diversified banks holding portfolios of mercantile, manufacturing, and agricultural loans. It is not surprising then that the Lumbermans Bank of Warren, Pennsylvania, failed within five years (1835–1839), that the Mechanics Bank of Patterson, New Jersey, had an even briefer existence (1832–1834), and that both failed during periods of pronounced macroeconomic volatility.

Of course, many of these banks lived long and healthy lives; some thrived into the late nineteenth and twentieth centuries. The Leather Manufacturers Bank of New York City operated for 30 years (1832–1862). The Butchers and Drovers Bank survived for 23 years (1830–1853). The Corn Exchange Bank nearly merged with the National City Bank in 1929.[48] The Miners Bank of Pottsville, Pennsylvania, founded in 1828, was still in operation as late as 1976 as the Miners National Bank. What separated these banks from their shorter-lived brethren was some combination of good fortune, good management, and, perhaps, more or better opportunities to diversify their portfolios. New York City banks had easy access to commercial paper, and the Miners Bank could diversify by lending to extraction companies, farmers, and local merchants. Given the active coal market, spurred by the canal craze that lowered transportation costs and speeded movement, the bank could hold a diversified portfolio that turned over regularly.

Pennsylvania's real and significant concession to the credit demands of its farmers came in 1814. By 1803, Pennsylvania had chartered only four banks, all of which were located in Philadelphia. With no banks in the hinterlands, Philadelphia's banks served the eastern half of the state. Financial services in the western half were supplied by Pittsburgh merchants and a handful of exchange brokers and private bankers. Both the Bank of Pennsylvania and the Philadelphia Bank were given the right to establish branches.[49] By 1813, the former had established branches in Lancaster, Easton, and Pittsburgh. By 1809, the latter had branches in Washington, Harrisburg, Columbia, and Wilkes-Barre.

In 1810, even with these branches, the sentiment that the state still had too few banks prevailed. Entrepreneurs, seeing an opportunity, took matters into their own hands. The Bank of Pittsburgh, a competitor to the Bank of

Pennsylvania's branch, opened in 1810 without a charter, as had the Bank of Northern Liberties, located in the far northern suburbs of Philadelphia.[50] To protect the chartered banks' favored position, the legislature passed an act forbidding unincorporated companies from banking. Both the Pittsburgh and Northern Liberties banks immediately requested charters, but both were denied. The Bank of Northern Liberties, in apparent defiance of the law, continued. The Bank of Pittsburgh changed its name to the Pittsburgh Manufacturing Company and carried out its banking operations behind the false front. And these were not the only unchartered, hence illegal, private banks extending credit and issuing notes.

The organization of these unauthorized banks demonstrated a growing demand for credit in the hinterlands, a demand that the branches of the two Philadelphia-based banks were unable or unwilling to meet. The Lancaster branch of the Bank of Pennsylvania, for example, was described as operating in a "rather small way" until 1840, when it closed.[51] Branches of the Philadelphia Bank never met the expectations of those working and living nearby. The parent board demanded that its country branches discount only mercantile paper, and each was allocated limited capital—$100,000 for the Wilkes-Barre branch, for example. Moreover, once the parent board discovered that there wasn't much good commercial paper in small-town Pennsylvania, it quickly abandoned its branching experiment. By 1818, both banks had closed most of their branches and spent the next decade collecting on nonperforming loans. As late as 1829, the Pennsylvania Bank still carried $154,800 of loans made at its branches in Easton, Lancaster, Pittsburgh, Reading, and Snow Hill, of which it expected to eventually have to write off more than $45,000.

The expiration of the charter of the First Bank of the United States in 1811 led to what has been widely described as a bank mania in several states. Pennsylvania was one. During the 1812/13 legislative session, Pennsylvania's legislature passed a bill, by a majority of one in both the house and the senate, chartering 25 new banks.[52] The governor vetoed it. In the next session, a more expansive bill, chartering 41 banks with a combined capital of $17 million, was passed. It too was vetoed, but support for this bill was strong enough that the veto was overridden.

The chartering act, known as the Omnibus Banking Act of 1814, divided the state into 27 banking districts and allocated at least one bank to each. Philadelphia city was allocated three new bank charters; Lancaster County, five; Dauphin County, two; Cumberland County, two; and Franklin County, two. It is unclear how many of these banks represented de novo establishments and how many were already operating banks (like the Pittsburgh Manufacturing Company and the Bank of Northern Liberties) that were legitimized. With names like the Marietta and Susquehanna Trading Company and the Lancaster Trading Company, it is likely that some of these institutions had followed the Bank of Pittsburgh's ploy of assuming banking practices while hiding behind a nonbank title. In other cases, the Philadelphia Bank and the Bank of Pennsylvania divested themselves of their branches by selling them to local investors who received charters through the Omnibus Banking Act.

The act was sweeping. In authorizing the 41 banks, the act identified the cities or towns in which they would be located, provided the names under which they would operate, determined the number and par value of shares, set maximum loan interest rates and minimum banknote denominations; and limited their indebtedness. In order to fill the commonwealth's coffers, the act also required that each bank declare annual dividends on which they had to pay a 6 percent tax. Failure to declare dividends was grounds for charter revocation; three charters were eventually revoked for failure to pay dividends and taxes. It is unlikely that the provision created undue pressure on banks to declare dividends. When profits did not justify dividends, banks sometimes met the letter, if not the spirit, of the law by declaring one cent per share dividends.

More troubling than the dividend requirement were the portfolio restrictions imposed by the act. The law required each bank to loan 20 percent of its capital to farmers, mechanics, and manufacturers at maturities up to one year.[53] No more than 20 percent of its capital could be invested in loans originating outside that bank's home district. In addition, no more than 20 percent of the bank's capital could be invested in corporate or government securities.[54] Finally, the act required banks to loan to the commonwealth, at the commonwealth's discretion, at a rate not to exceed 5 percent per annum.

The onerous restrictions, particularly those that dictated portfolio allocations, placated some credit-hungry constituents, but those same restrictions did not bode well for many of these banks. At least six of the new banks were located where the Philadelphia banks' branches had proved disappointments. The act certainly lacked universal praise. One editorialist, writing in the *Connecticut Courant*, argued that:

> the continual multiplication of banks and manufacturing institutions with the privilege of issuing bills of credit, is a subject of just alarm to the community. The power of creating these monied institutions is exercised by the State legislatures, which appear to be governed by local views, without any general regard to the state of trade. . . . The creation of forty-one banking institutions in Pennsylvania at a single stroke is the most bold and inconsiderate step ever taken on this subject—and shows manifestly how little competent popular assemblies are to manage the concerns of commerce.[55]

Philadelphian and contemporary economist Condy Raguet was also critical of the law. Unlike some writers and most bank boosters, Raguet recognized that the establishment of a bank did not guarantee commercial and financial expansion in the neighborhood of the bank. Basic fundamentals, like those discussed in chapter 1, were necessary prerequisites for economic growth and legitimate financial development.

Later experience showed that the legislature was overly optimistic and probably too much influenced by political rather than commercial motives. Of the 41 banks authorized by the Omnibus Banking Act, 39 organized. The financial crisis of 1819 brought many to their knees. By the beginning of 1822, 17 had failed. Although the lack of extant data (like that found in account books and discount ledgers) makes firm conclusions problematic, it appears that the panic brought economic realities to the fore. Rates of return to total shareholder equity (paid-in capital and retained earnings) of 18 continuing banks averaged 5.75 percent in 1820 and 5.37 percent in 1821.[56] Rates of return for 8 banks that failed averaged 3.26 percent in 1820 and −0.04 percent in 1821.

It is impossible to determine whether the low rates of return earned by failing banks resulted from incompetent management, poorly performing loans, overly sanguine expectations, or simple misfortune, but it is likely that all played a part. The experience of one continuing bank is informative and possibly indicative of early nineteenth-century country banking practice.[57] By 1823, the books of the Farmers Bank of Bucks County were so poorly maintained that the bank's directors needed outside assistance to put them in order.[58] The president of the Farmers Bank asked Nicholas Biddle, president of the Second Bank of the United States, for help. Biddle dispatched Caleb P. Iddings, an accountant with considerable banking experience, to assist the bank's directors in reconstructing its books.

Iddings' instructions helped save the Farmers Bank, but recovery was slow. The bank earned 7.27 percent on equity in 1820, but its earnings slipped to −4.76 percent in 1821, 1.28 percent in 1822, and 2.57 percent in 1823, for a four-year average of just 1.59 percent. Following Iddings' intercession, the bank's returns improved in the next half decade to an average 3.56 percent. It was not until 1829 that the bank's return exceeded 6.00 percent.[59] Several factors, including a general macroeconomic recovery following the recession of the early 1820s, certainly assisted the bank's recovery, but the adoption of good bookkeeping practices, allowing more informed managerial decisions, almost surely helped, too.

The experience of the Farmers Bank demonstrated one of the more serious side effects created by a sudden growth in the banking sector, and one probably not contemplated by the legislature when it chartered 41 new banks. In chapter 2, we discussed the fact that bank tellers, clerks, cashiers, directors, and presidents tended to advance through the ranks, apprentice style, as they gained experience and demonstrated their competence. The sudden appearance of 41 banks (many of which appeared de novo) surely forced hurriedly organized banks to employ relatively inexperienced men as clerks, cashiers, and presidents. Such practices inevitably led to shabbily kept ledgers and a multitude of honest mistakes.

J. S. Gibbons argued that the rapid increase in the number of New York City banks in the 1850s had a similar effect. As the number of banks expanded, tellers were made cashiers and bookkeepers were made tellers, and mistakes "became so common, and were occasionally so large as to be quite serious."[60] This occurred in populous, commercially oriented New York City in the mid-1850s. Imagine the relative dearth of banking know-how in Carlisle or Gettysburg, Pennsylvania, in 1814. When viewed this way, the historians' traditional interpretation is cast in a different light. Hammond, Redlich, F. Cyril James, and a host of other banking historians all quote Thomas Willing, first president of the Bank of North America, at great length. In a letter addressed to the directors of the Bank of Massachusetts, he wrote:

> When the bank was first opened here, the Business was as much a novelty to us, who undertook the management of it, as it can possibly be to you. It was a pathless wilderness, ground but little known on this side of the Atlantic. . . . In this situation, we adopted the only safe method to avoid confusion. Educated as merchants, we resolved to pursue the road we were best acquainted with. We established our books on a simple mercantile plan, and this mode, pointed out by experience alone, has carried us through so far without a material loss, or even a mistake of any consequence.[61]

It is interesting that these historians hold Willing in high regard, but it is probably because his ignorance of good banking practice did not result in his bank's failure. Placed in similar circumstances, others were not so fortunate. It seems likely that mistakes resulting from inexperience were too often interpreted as fraud and moral turpitude. The outcome may have been largely the same—bank failure and public losses—but causes should be considered more carefully before characters are attacked and laid to waste. Failed bankers, by and large, were decent, well-intentioned men whose endeavors, no matter how hard they worked at them, were unlikely to succeed. Small businesses fail at incredible rates even in modern times. There is no reason to think that it would have been any different in the nineteenth century. The quick coming and going of most small businesses, with the remarkable success of a very few, was the essence of the process of creative destruction made famous by Joseph Schumpeter.[62] Banking, whether in the country or in the city, was no different.

Banks and the Internal Improvement Craze

Poor administration doomed more than a few banks to failure. Fraud doomed a few more. Neither, however, was as potentially devastating to the banking sector as sectional and state rivalries. Throughout most of the late colonial and early federal periods, Philadelphia was considered the first city of North America. It was North America's largest city, it had served as the capital for the revolutionary government, and, with the establishment of the Bank of the United States in 1791, it had firmly established itself as the financial center of the continent.

Its long-held preeminence notwithstanding, some of the city's more forward-looking citizens recognized that its continuation was not guaranteed. Other cities, such as Boston, New York, even Norfolk and Charleston, were blessed with superior natural harbors and, being situated on rivers that reached farther inland than the Delaware, were better positioned to profit from the flow of goods into and out of the hinterlands. Even the Susquehanna River, mostly in Pennsylvania, opened into the Chesapeake Bay, making Baltimore a more cost-effective link to most of the Pennsylvania upcountry than Philadelphia. Ensuring Philadelphia's continued preeminence, therefore, meant building connections between it and upstate hinterlands. Its attempts to construct these links proved mostly futile, very nearly driving the state itself and most of its banks into bankruptcy.

As early as the 1760s, many Philadelphians realized that a far-ranging internal improvement system was critical to Philadelphia's continued success. Iron foundries in Lancaster found overland transportation to Philadelphia prohibitively expensive. The total cost of iron plus transportation exceeded the Philadelphia price of imported iron. Founders soon discovered that iron could be shipped down the Susquehanna River to Baltimore, where it could compete with imports.[63] With the deplorable state of upcountry roads, more and more of the staples, foodstuffs, and lumber produced in the rich Susquehanna River valley found its way to Baltimore.

In 1787, sectional rivalries were so strong that Thomas Paine argued that the willingness of Pennsylvanians to trade with Baltimore rather than Philadelphia merchants smacked of treason.[64] More practical-minded men recognized that something more than accusations of treason and appeals to patriotism was needed to alter natural trade patterns. The American Philosophical Society funded a commercial survey of the Susquehanna valley in 1769. Unless something was done to alter developing trading patterns, the surveyors said, Baltimore would receive three-fourths of Pennsylvania's upcountry produce. Philadelphia's merchants and upcountry citizens alike began clamoring for more and better roads into the interior.

During the 1770s and 1780s, pleas made to the Pennsylvania legislature for internal improvements fell on deaf ears. Other than appropriating a small sum for improving navigation on the Susquehanna River, little was done. It was not until the 1790s that Pennsylvania embarked on any internal improvements in earnest. The principal concern remained connecting the fertile Susquehanna valley with Philadelphia. Work was begun on canals designed to connect the Delaware River with the Chesapeake Bay, as well as the Schuylkill and Delaware Rivers just north of the city. Because there was no reasonable water route connecting the Lancaster region with the city, the Lancaster Turnpike was built to bring south-central Pennsylvania into Philadelphia's commercial orbit.

Philadelphia's attempts to stem the natural flow of produce and the decline of its commercial prominence generated few results. In 1796, Philadelphia exported more than $17 million in produce, which represented about 25 percent of the national total and 25 percent more than New York City, the nearest rival. The year 1796, however, represented Philadelphia's apogee. New York quickly replaced it as the nation's leading export city. In 1821, Philadelphia's exports were only about half as much as New York's. With its loss of station, Philadelphia's ardor for internal improvements waned as well. Technical difficulties, mismanagement, and financial losses dimmed the city's fascination with turnpikes and canals. Although a few city boosters kept the debate alive, Pennsylvania eschewed additional infrastructure investments until the unexpected success of the Erie Canal "aroused all America."[65]

Construction of the Erie Canal revived interest for internal improvements everywhere. Moreover, it forced merchants to reflect on the importance of improving ties with the rapidly expanding hinterlands. Not only was the backcountry a growing source of export business, but it was also an increasing market for manufactured goods. The opening of the Erie Canal roused Pennsylvanians, and Philadelphia merchants grew concerned that they would lose even more of their relatively diminishing business to their northern rivals. In 1818, Samuel Breck expressed a widely held opinion when he wrote that "rivals in the north and south are about to deprive us of our trade. We must defeat their efforts. . . . We shall behold storehouses and commercial streets lining the banks of the Schuylkill."[66] A society for internal improvements was founded in Philadelphia, and members were sent to Britain to study canal building and management, as well as to investigate the feasibility of railroads. In the meantime, both Philadelphia and Baltimore developed projects to establish their supremacy in the Susquehanna valley. The Chesapeake and Delaware Canal and the Union Canal projects were revived in Pennsylvania. Maryland sponsored work on the Chesapeake and Ohio Canal and the Cumberland Road.

Plans for achieving supremacy in the Susquehanna region paled in comparison to designs on the far western trade. In 1826, Pennsylvania entered into what George Rogers Taylor labeled a "canal-building orgy."[67] The backbone of the state's canal system was the Pennsylvania Main Line Canal. The narrow Union Canal already connected Philadelphia with the Susquehanna River, so the Main Line pushed westward from Columbia along the Susquehanna and Juniata Rivers to Holidaysburg at the base of the Allegheny Mountains. From there, the famous Portage Rail Road, which consisted of a series of cable cars designed to carry canal barges up and over the highest mountains, connected the eastern leg of the canal with the western section, which followed the Conemaugh and Allegheny Rivers to Pittsburgh.

The Main Line Canal opened along its entire length in 1834, but despite moving considerable tonnage, the state's topography determined that it was not cost effective, which limited its ability to compete with the Erie Canal. The Main Line stretched 395 miles, included 174 locks (compared to 84 on the Erie), reached 2,200 feet above sea level at its highest point, and cost more than $10 million to complete.[68] The Portage Rail Road became a bottleneck, the excessive number of locks slowed traffic, and shifting cargo into smaller barges at Columbia for shipment to Philadelphia along the narrow Union Canal created delays and increased costs. Ultimately, the economic boom envisioned by Philadelphia's merchants never materialized. Philadelphia's flour exports remained flat between 1830 and 1845 and much below typical colonial era volumes.

The Chesapeake and Delaware Canal shared the increased Susquehanna River traffic with Maryland's Susquehanna and Tidewater Canal so that both were barely economically viable. The Union Canal was unable to handle the proposed volume of traffic, and a parallel railroad siphoned off much of its traffic in any event. In the end, the Main Line Canal never really threatened the Erie Canal's dominance in the western trade.

With one or two exceptions, the state's canals proved unprofitable. More than $65 million was spent on their construction; by 1840, the state's debt ballooned to $36 million and the financial depression of the early 1840s made additional borrowing infeasible. By 1841, the treasurer could not even meet interest payments on the state's outstanding bond debt. Some called for repudiation, but the legislature called on the state's banks to bail out the treasury.[69]

Pennsylvania was not alone in its practice of including clauses in charters that required banks to lend to the state, but it made more use of them than others. During the canal mania of the 1830s, these clauses were regularly invoked and very nearly abused. In 1830, the Bank of Pennsylvania's charter was renewed while the legislature was seeking financial assistance for its canal building. The extent to which the bank was asked to underwrite the state's project is clearly seen in the bank's rechartering act, titled "An Act to authorize a loan to defray the expenses of the Pennsylvania Canal and Railroad, and to continue for a further time . . . the Pennsylvania Bank."[70] The rechartering act required the bank to lend up to $4 million to the state at 5.5 percent annual interest. Extant records do not allow for a delineation of borrowers to determine how much the state actually borrowed, but it undoubtedly reduced the bank's ability to extend consumer credit. Moreover, it locked in a large fraction of the bank's portfolio. The bank became effectively less diversified and more vulnerable to systemic macroeconomic shocks.

Pennsylvania's 1841 legislation represented a nadir in the commonwealth's financial policy. The treasury suspended cash interest payments on its bonds and did not resume them until February 1845. In the interim, the market price of 5 percent, $100 par coupon bonds fell as low as $40.[71] The treasury paid interest in scrip that sold in Philadelphia at about 50 cents on the dollar.

Finally, it called on the state's banks to maintain whatever credit it had remaining. Like banks throughout the country, Pennsylvania's banks suspended specie payments during the autumn panic of 1839. Suspension was grounds for charter revocation, but the state legislature was willing to overlook the suspension if the banks conceded to what can only be labeled legislative extortion. The hastily formed Relief Act of 1841 authorized the state to borrow $3.1 million, payable in five years, paying 5 percent annually.[72] Every bank was eligible to subscribe to the loan up to 1.75 percent of its paid-in capital. Bond subscriptions were paid in clearly identified, small-denomination notes of the subscribing bank, called relief notes, which were redeemable not in specie but in state bonds.

As long as these notes circulated, the state paid the issuing bank 1 percent interest. If the notes were presented for redemption, the redeemer was given a certificate for an equivalent amount of the state loan, a liability that the *issuing bank* ultimately assumed. Banknotes issued according to this law were receivable for all debts due to the commonwealth and could be reissued by the state treasury. Banks complying with these terms were exempted from all penalties and forfeitures arising from suspension. Any bank refusing to subscribe to the loan had 40 days to resume specie payments or have its charter revoked. The governor vetoed the bill, but the legislature was able to override it and the bill became law on 4 May 1841. The state effectively monetized about one-tenth of its debt, even while it pushed most of the redemption risks onto the state's banks.

Most state banks relented, largely so they could avoid resuming specie payments, but eight Philadelphia banks refused to buy into the loan.[73] The directors of the Bank of North America expressed concerns because the plan was vague and indefinite. The North America's contribution would have amounted to $175,000, and its directors saw little hope for anything but complete loss. If it had participated, the bank's burden would have taken either of two forms: the bank would have held the 5 percent loan to maturity, which meant tying up one-fifth of its capital for at least five years; or the bank would have had to assume of a debt of indefinite duration (i.e., until the relief notes came in for redemption). Moreover, the bank doubted the constitutionality of the act and the willingness of the legislature to maintain it if it became politically unpopular. If it did, in fact, become unpopular, which seemed likely, it also seemed likely that the relief notes, rather than the state loan, would eventually be redeemed in specie.

Facing these uncertainties, and having what they believed were adequate specie reserves, the eight Philadelphia banks decided to resume specie payments. These banks' concerns about the state's plan were realized. Relief notes, not surprisingly, were unpopular. Having state bonds as security was not an attractive feature, given that the state had already failed to meet interest payments on part of its existing debt. Furthermore, after two years of suspension, the public was growing increasingly impatient with the suspended banks. By the beginning of 1842, the legislature itself was pushing banks to promptly resume business despite their promise of at least partial suspension until 1845. Less than one year after passage of the five-year

Relief Act, the legislature passed a new act requiring immediate and total resumption of specie payments, without making any provision for the payment of the state's debts and the retirement of the relief notes.

Philadelphia's banks had not become encumbered with relief notes and state loans, so they quickly resumed payments. Most country banks that had accepted the terms of the Relief Act still had not resumed a year later. It was not until the legislature replenished the treasury and redeemed some of the banks' relief note issues that these banks resumed payments. Moreover, it was not until the mid- to late 1840s "that confidence and credit were in any degree restored to the mercantile and financial world."[74]

Not only did the relief issues undermine confidence in Pennsylvania's banks, but they also undermined those banks' ability to extend credit, issue notes, and generally engage in banking activities. Table 6.1 reports statistics on two types of banks: those that issued relief notes, with notes still outstanding in November 1844; and those that either opted not to issue relief notes or had redeemed their relief issues by November 1844.[75] Recall that the relief issues had been suspended in 1842, so the banks with outstanding issues in November 1844 were likely to have been the largest issuers of relief notes.

Statistics in table 6.1 show that some country banks issued considerable quantities of relief notes. A handful issued amounts equal to nearly 25 percent of their paid-in capital. A handful of others had notes outstanding equal to 10 percent or more of their capital. What effect did these issues, and the assumption of a debt paying 5 percent interest with no effective maturity, have on the banks' activities? Columns 3 and 4 report each bank's total assets in November 1844 and November 1849; column 5 reports the average annual growth rate of each bank's assets. It is readily seen that banks with relief note liabilities in late 1844 experienced much slower growth rates than those banks that either issued no relief notes or quickly redeemed them. Overall, banks with outstanding relief notes in 1844 grew at an average annual rate of just 1.8 percent in the next half decade. Banks without the burden of relief notes grew at a considerably more rapid average rate of 6.2 percent per annum.

Clearly, there were a host of contributing factors to the differential patterns of growth outlined in table 6.1. Changing trade routes, changes in the underlying quality of regional borrowers, changes in systematic risk of a region's borrowers, and changes wrought by the panic of 1839 and the recession of the early 1840s all contributed to a bank's growth opportunities. Nationally, recovery was well under way by late 1844, so the difference in asset growth between these two groups was surely affected by, if not driven by, the (non)assumption of an open-ended, expensive, and unpopular liability. If that debt limited some banks' credit-creating ability, the state's actions hindered not only financial but also broader economic development.

Events in Maryland during the internal improvement craze of the first quarter of the nineteenth century mirrored those in Pennsylvania. Besides

Table 6.1 Growth in Assets of Pennsylvania Country Banks Issuing Notes under Provisions of the Relief Act of 4 May 1841

Bank	Issues as Percent of Capital (%)	Total Assets 1844 ($)	Total Assets 1849 ($)	Average Annual Growth (%)
A. Banks with Relief Note Issues Still Outstanding in November 1844				
Columbia Bank & Bridge	5.8	492,483	600,408	4.0
Bank of Germantown	1.7	315,568	421,894	5.8
Bank of Delaware County	2.8	386,756	427,186	2.0
Bank of Chester County	0.6	727,058	728,732	0.0
Bank of Chambersburg	21.7	491,475	505,133	0.5
Bank of Gettysburg	22.3	360,505	332,863	−1.6
Wyoming Bank	24.4	211,660	192,026	−1.9
Farmers Bank of Bucks	0.3	217,857	230,484	1.1
York Bank	25.0	570,224	626,811	1.9
Lebanon Bank	17.7	243,189	285,733	3.2
Monongahela Bank	22.1	358,524	448,436	4.5
Farmers Bank of Reading	17.0	785,860	803,370	0.4
Miners Bank	14.5	602,476	709,425	3.3
B. Banks without Relief Note Issues Outstanding in November 1844				
Doylestown Bank	na	180,515	208,851	2.9
Easton Bank	**	924,069	1,225,234	5.6
Bank of Montgomery	na	573,749	747,226	5.3
Lancaster Bank	na	851,818	1,744,991	14.3
Lancaster County Bank	**	232,094	498,191	15.3
Harrisburg Bank	**	684,255	816,640	3.5
Bank of Middletown	na	291,798	456,856	9.0
Bank of Northumberland	na	336,671	599,403	11.5
Honesdale Bank	na	136,236	614,425	30.1
West Branch Bank	**	284,882	330,996	3.0
Bank of Pittsburgh	na	2,174,131	2,474,858	2.6
Exchange Bank	na	1,531,603	1,565,007	0.4
Merchants & Manufacturers	na	1,084,947	1,291,404	3.5
Farmers & Drovers	na	268,870	433,615	9.6
Franklin Bank	na	296,568	405,747	6.3

Notes: "na" implies not available or not applicable. **Signifies that the bank issued relief notes but had redeemed them all by November 1844. Some of the na banks may have issued relief notes, but these issues were not reported in annual bank reports.

Source: Pennsylvania, *Senate Journal* (1842–1845, 1850).

its early canal ventures, Maryland got caught up in extensive road and turn-pike building programs in the 1810s. One of the more ambitious projects was a road designed to connect Baltimore with Cumberland to the west. During several legislative sessions dealing with the road issue, it was sug-gested that because charters gave banks special privileges, banks should be taxed to support road construction.[76] These proposals were defeated, but the feeling lingered that banks should be doing more to support Maryland's rivalry with its northern neighbors.

In 1813, a bill was introduced into Maryland's legislature that would have extended the charters of Baltimore's banks to 1835 if they agreed to an open-ended contingency to underwrite the road's completion and a one-time school tax payment. Not surprisingly, the banks lobbied against the original bill, which was defeated. They proposed a modified bill, one that included all of the state's banks, not just Baltimore's. It proposed a reduced school tax and exempted the banks from any new taxes for the duration of their charters. Finally, it forbade the chartering of any new banks located in Baltimore until 1835, which effectively protected the existing oligopoly from entrants. The amended bill was passed.

Ultimately, bank involvement in the Cumberland Road ended disas-trously. The banks agreed to it because they expected the turnpike to be profitable. But the road never met expectations. Between 1816 and 1822, Baltimore's banks subscribed 56,000 shares of the road at $20 per share. The project did not pay any dividends until 1830, and these never exceeded 3 percent. By 1841, the dividends declined and shares traded at $2 to $3 per share. Banks with an aggregate $8 million paid-in capital suffered a $1 million loss.

As in Pennsylvania, the state's interference in bank portfolios had det-rimental effects on Maryland's banks and credit markets. In the mid-1840s, the Farmers & Merchants Bank of Baltimore wrote off its losses (many of them attributable to its investment in the Cumberland Road), which reduced its capital by 20 percent. The Franklin Bank of Baltimore was forced to write down its capital by 40 percent, and the Union Bank of Baltimore reduced its capital from $1.84 million in 1842 to $923,850 in 1845, a reduction of nearly 50 percent. The assets of each, particularly their loans, diminished proportionately.

Concluding Remarks

Chapter 1 reported evidence from antebellum America supporting Raymond Goldsmith's proposition that there was a "rough parallelism" between fi-nancial development and economic growth.[77] The evidence even provides modest support for the proposition that financial development leads eco-nomic development. Pennsylvania's and Maryland's legislators can be forgiven for embroiling their states' banks in infrastructure projects because they thought that the banks could assist these endeavors in a common objective, namely, economic growth. Ultimately, however, the legislators were wrong and may have done more to slow economic growth than they might have ever imagined. Some have argued that even though the Cumberland Road or the Main Line Canal never generated a private return sufficient to repay their investors, once a road was built or a canal was dug, it was there for all to use. In other words, such projects created significant external benefits that promoted growth and encouraged economic development. There is no denying that infrastructure and public goods often do. There is also no denying that public goods should be supplied by governments, financed through either general taxation or targeted user fees. Few economists argue that public goods should be supplied by private firms when those firms are unlikely to profit from them.

It was unfortunate for many of these banks that the public often viewed them as pseudopublic institutions, as much a part of the commercial infrastructure as any turnpike, road, or canal. It followed, therefore, that one infrastructure project should support another. What these people forgot was that bankers, if they were any good at what they did, specialized in assessing the creditworthiness of borrowers and the likelihood that their endeavors might succeed. If banks in Philadelphia, Baltimore, Pittsburgh, or Gettysburg did not invest in a turnpike or canal of their own volition, it must have been because they saw better investment opportunities elsewhere. That is, they were exercising their judgment that the Main Line Canal and the Cumberland Road projects were unlikely to repay their investors their opportunity costs.

To the extent that states interfered in the banks' investment choices, they imposed costs on society in that resources were directed away from more-deserving projects to less-deserving ones. Doing so reduced output not only in the short term, but in the long term as well. In the short term, resources were directed from manufacturing or mercantile concerns to turnpikes and canals. In the longer term, losses arising from these poor investments were written off, reducing the banks' ability to extend credit and promote growth and development. Thus, Pennsylvania's and Maryland's ill-founded attempts to emulate or compete with New York proved untenable and quite possibly counterproductive, over a potentially long horizon.

Pennsylvania responded to the banking problems that grew out of the panic of 1839; the depression of the early 1840s; the spectacular failure of the Bank of the United States of Pennsylvania in 1842, which took down two of Philadelphia's other banks; the collapse of the state's bond credit rating; and the failure of several country banks by withholding new bank charters. Having been burned largely through its own actions, the legislature preferred to blame the financial sector, hence the moratorium on new bank charters. New York, different from Pennsylvania in so many regards, chose two alternative strategies. Instead of weakening and then limiting its banking sector, it fell upon two plans designed to strengthen and expand the system. The first, known as the Safety Fund System, is the topic of chapter 7. The second, free banking, is discussed in chapter 8. One largely achieved its expected result; the other didn't. Nonetheless, both were remarkable specimens of bank policy that influence U.S. bank policy to the present.

7

New York's Safety Fund System

America's First Bank Insurance Experiment

Economists and regulators justify bank liability insurance on the grounds that banks are unique among capitalist institutions. They are the channel through which capital is financed, and they represent a particularly important channel for young, small firms that find it uneconomic to borrow in arm's-length markets. Banks also provide most of the media of exchange in the form of banknotes and deposits. Finally, banks operate the payments system. They engage in a host of clearing operations (like those discussed in chapter 5) that reduce the costs of transacting for nonfinancial firms and consumers. Furthermore, banks hold highly idiosyncratic, hard-to-value portfolios. Thus, negative macroeconomic shocks present special problems for banks, and any macroeconomic shock that threatens banks also threatens the vitality of the overall economy. The convergence of these features provides an intellectual basis for governmental oversight and regulation of banks and protection of their creditors.[1]

Banks in the antebellum era were especially vulnerable to macroeconomic shocks. Most early U.S. financial panics began as small disturbances relative to aggregate bank capital, but the opaque nature of bank portfolios made it difficult for note holders and depositors to distinguish between banks likely to suffer substantial losses and those likely to pass through the storm relatively unscathed. The result was that all banks faced runs. Lacking a mechanism allowing them to act in unison (such as the New York clearinghouse discussed in chapter 6), banks responded by suspending convertibility of their liabilities into specie. Systemwide suspensions occurred during the panic of 1819 and the depression of the early 1820s, during the panics of 1837 and 1839 (lasting through 1842), and during the panic and recession of the late 1850s.

Such suspensions further eroded the public's confidence in the banking system. In the worst cases, liabilities of suspended banks became virtually worthless, hence they were useless as media of exchange.[2] Uninformed noteholders became unwilling to accept banknotes because they feared that they were being sold lemons by informed insiders. Sometimes at the depths of a panic, even informed creditors, such as other banks and banknote brokers, refused to accept notes or checks drawn on other (solvent) banks. Given the distrust that arose during a panic, disintermediation was inevitable.

Disintermediation forced banks to adopt more-conservative lending and issuance policies that accelerated the downward spiral of macroeconomic activity. Explications of this so-called debt-deflation problem date back at least to Irving Fisher's 1933 statement that Ben Bernanke and Mark Gertler, and others, had extended and formalized.[3] They argue that panic-induced disintermediation affects real economic activity by restricting the flow of financial services to borrowers without access to nonbank credit. As the panic progresses, borrowers' balance sheets deteriorate and their collateral loses value, both of which reduce their capacity to borrow. Moreover, the deterioration of their balance sheets implies fewer internal resources available for direct financing of investment. Both features—higher borrowing costs and declining internal resources—choke off investment.

If a mechanism could be found that mitigated this effect, the likelihood and intensity of systemic bank runs might be reduced. Relative, long-run macroeconomic stability would follow. One such possible mechanism was bank liability insurance. If an outside agency guaranteed the value of bank liabilities, especially in the face of exogenous macroeconomic shocks, uninformed creditors could rest assured that insiders were not systematically dumping bad notes. Banknotes, and deposits, for that matter, could continue as the principal media of exchange, and the damage wrought by a debt-deflation problem might be avoided.

A number of banking problems, including bank suspension and failure, during the recession of the early 1820s prompted New York to develop a new financial system. Its cornerstone was the Safety Fund, a widely recognized precursor to modern deposit insurance like that provided by the Federal Deposit Insurance Corporation (FDIC) since 1934. The Safety Fund insured bank creditors (notably noteholders and depositors) from losses due to bank failures and represented a bona fide attempt to insulate the payments systems from the worst effects of macroeconomic shocks. Ultimately, it failed to insulate the financial sector from exogenous shocks as a rash of bank failures following the panic of 1839 exposed the system's weaknesses. It also failed to insulate the macroeconomy from weaknesses in the financial sector.

The bank failures of the early 1840s were not a *direct* result of the Safety Fund system. Peter Temin showed that they were the result of contractionary policies pursued by the Bank of England.[4] Its actions induced specie outflows, reduced U.S. bank reserves, drove up nominal interest rates, and generated an unexpectedly sharp deflation. The latter two effects produced Fisher's debt-deflation argument. With bank debtors unable to repay increasingly expensive bank debts, most banks became illiquid and many became insolvent. Banks contracted, which further drove up interest rates and drove down prices.

The Safety Fund's failure, as Charles Calomiris notes, was not directly traceable to the Bank of England's contractionary policy, however.[5] Aggregate banking capital was large relative to the initial negative shock, so the state's system might have passed through the initial stages of the panic in better shape than it did. The system's bankruptcy resulted from the convergence of a number of factors that undermined the system's integrity. In addition to the classic insurance problems of moral hazard and adverse selection, the system labored under the combined weight of ineffectual supervision, mispriced insurance premia, a limited ability to impose emergency assessments, and fraud.

The Safety Fund Act and the Evolution of the System

Following the expiration of the charter of the Bank of the United States in 1811, New York chartered 23 new banks, which more than doubled the state's banking capital. The partisan politics and legislative logrolling involved in the chartering process, however, soured the assembly's taste for granting new charters. The party in power typically made the distribution of bank charters "part of the spoils of political victory."[6] Fittingly, Robert Chaddock characterized New York's banking experience as one of "reckless banking and speculation."[7] The governor's assessment was even less flattering. Despite a demonstrated demand for increased banking services, he cautioned against the chartering of any more banks because the rash of recent charters had brought about the "banishment of metallic money, the loss of commercial confidence, the exhibition of fictitious capital, the increase of civil prosecutions, the multiplication of crimes, the injurious enhancement of prices, and the dangerous extension of credit."[8] To scapegoat banks for nearly every social evil was more a political than an economic statement; nevertheless, it had significant economic ramifications. If bank credit mattered to development and entrepreneurship, any refusal to augment the aggregate amount of bank capital in the face of *legitimately* increased demand raised interest rates, made credit relatively more scarce, and ultimately slowed growth.

Following the panic of 1819, Governor DeWitt Clinton called on New York's legislature to reform the state's banking system. It was not until 1827, though, that any significant changes were enacted. The 1827 legislative session received 19 applications for new charters along with 23 petitions for

renewals of existing charters. The governor warned against such rapid expansion without first adopting a new regulatory structure. The legislature
offered several revisions, the more important of which were requiring that
banks pay dividends from profits instead of drawing on capital, limiting of
debts to three times paid-in capital, impositing double liability on shareholders, limiting director borrowing to one-third of a bank's paid-in capital,
prohibiting banknotes less than $1, and prohibiting a bank's own officers
and directors from purchasing its notes at a discount.[9] The law also imposed
a watered-down form of summary judgment. If a bank failed, it was assumed
to be guilty of fraud until it proved itself innocent. Despite the sweeping
revisions to the state's banking code, the legislature chose not to charter any
new banks. Some of the petitioners for new banks withdrew their requests
in the face of the new regulations, and most existing banks tried to escape
the restrictions by insisting that their original charters be reinstated without
modification. With memories of the panic of 1819, the depression of the
early 1820s, and several bank failures still fresh in their minds, the legislature refused to charter or recharter banks that refused to accept the new
regulations.

With the legislature refusing to grant new or renewed charters except on
the terms of the 1827 act, and with of existing banks refusing to accept the
conditions, the state's banking system was moving toward crisis. In 1828,
New York had 48 banks, but the charters of 31 were due to expire between
1829 and 1832.[10] All 31 applied for charter renewals in 1828. None succeeded in obtaining the constitutionally mandated two-thirds majority in
either house. In 1829, all but 2 of the previously unsuccessful renewal applicants tried again. In addition, 37 petitions for new charters were received
by the legislature. Both the legislature and the new governor, Martin Van
Buren, recognized that the time to strike was at hand and sought out genuine reform proposals.

Several proposals were brought forward. One suggested a slight modification of the existing system that required bonus payments from successful
applicants to fund the state treasury. Van Buren argued that this system was
"condemned by experience" and that it inevitably led to logrolling and bribery; it even promoted at least one fistfight on the assembly floor.[11] Another
proposal suggested allowing the existing charters to lapse, requiring those
banks to close, and replacing them with a state-owned, multiple-branch
bank modeled after those chartered in several southern states.[12] A third
proposal put forward by a Syracuse lawyer, Joshua Forman, was the one
that captured Van Buren's imagination.

Forman's plan was original. It included a mutual guaranty (or coinsurance) provision, it required banks to invest their capital in high-grade government bonds, and it directed banks to engage in strict real-bills lending.
Forman's idea originated in the practices of Hong merchants of Canton.
Even though the Hong operated independently, the price of a right to engage
in foreign trade was that each was made liable for the debts of all others.[13]

Forman argued that legislative charters placed New York banks in a similar position in that they were given an exclusive right to issue currency and thus should be made jointly accountable for aggregate banknote circulation. Finally, his plan required banks to submit to regular examinations to ensure that they were abiding by the other regulations.

The first two components of Forman's plan satisfied Van Buren's demand that bank creditors should be insulated from bank failures, and Forman's plan held the state's banks individually (bond security) and severally (co-insurance) liable for losses from failure. The discussion in chapter 3 showed that the real-bills provision was naive, but it reflected Forman's belief that losses due to bank failure paled in significance to the harm done by the mismanagement of solvent banks.[14]

New York's legislature adopted the coinsurance and examination portions of Forman's proposal. They left the bond-secured note issue idea to find favor in the 1838 Free Banking Act. They ignored the real-bills provision. Popularly called the Safety Fund, the insurance system imposed six annual assessments of one-half of 1 percent of each bank's paid-in capital. If a failure depleted the Fund's reserves, the state comptroller, who administered the fund, was required to make emergency assessments not exceeding one-half of 1 percent per year until it was fully restored to 3 percent of aggregate bank capital. Bank creditors (a group not clearly defined, though the legislature surely had note holders in mind) were insured in full and, in the event of failure, were to be reimbursed by the fund. All banks receiving a new or renewed charter were required to join the fund.

Opposition to several clauses in the sweeping 1827 banking act was widespread, and the Safety Fund amended them. Foremost among the changes was the elimination of double liability for shareholders, which had become a particular sticking point in several charter renewals. During legislative debates, it was regularly argued that double liability requirements drove men of capital and integrity from banking. Of course, there is no evidence that this was true. Most other states imposed double liability; some imposed triple liability; still others, like Rhode Island, imposed unlimited liability. Virginia, for example, was a double liability state, and its bank shareholders were generally regarded as men of character, pillars of the mercantile and planter communities.

Van Buren recommended the coinsurance plan as a compromise. His advisors argued that it obviated the need for personal liability.[15] In this arrangement, Van Buren believed he was getting greater protections for bank creditors. Double liability ultimately provided little protection to note holders, and it never effectively protected the payments system. Collections from share holders were slow, meaning that note holders and depositors were repaid only after a substantial lag. Assessments, too, were difficult to collect.[16] Van Buren played his hand well, ceding double liability but receiving significantly tightened restrictions in return. The Safety Fund Act reduced note issues from 250 to 200 percent of paid-in capital; aggregate assets were reduced from 300 to 250 percent of capital.[17] The latter restriction was important because it limited the fund's potential exposure as a bank guarantor.

To ensure that banks complied with the restrictions, the act provided for the creation of a three-member bank commission with one member appointed by the governor and two elected by the banks themselves. The commissioners' primary duty was to perform a quarterly inspection and audit of each bank. Each bank forwarded a quarterly balance sheet, and then the bank commissioners visited the bank, inspected its books, and questioned its officers under oath. If they found evidence of fraud or any charter violation, the Safety Fund Act required them to immediately seek a court-ordered injunction. The commissioners were also instructed to seek injunctions against insolvent institutions. If the bankruptcy court agreed that the bank was insolvent, the state comptroller appointed a receiver to wind up the bank's affairs. Before 1840, this option was exercised only once, when the commission sought an injunction against a bank in 1831.[18]

The legislature that enacted the Safety Fund also rechartered 16 banks and chartered 11 new banks subject to its terms. New York City banks withdrew their rechartering petitions when it became clear that their charters would be renewed only if they became Safety Fund members. City banks viewed the fund as a mechanism through which they would be subsidizing country banks. City bank circulation averaged about one-third paid-in capital; country bank circulation was typically 150 percent and more. Thus, city banks argued that circulation rather than capital was the appropriate assessment base. Using capital as the assessment base overtaxed city banks and undertaxed country banks.

Although the act was represented as a guaranty for note holders only, it was loosely worded so that it insured all bank creditors, including depositors. Because city banks held more deposits than country banks, assessments based on capital did not represent a significant tax on city banks and a subsidy to country banks. Despite their reservations, when the city banks realized that their charters would not be renewed unless they joined the Safety Fund, they relented.

The decade following passage of the act witnessed rapid growth in New York's banking sector. The combined capital of the 27 original fund banks amounted to less than $8 million. By 1837, 90 banks operated on a combined capital in excess of $32 million and total assets in excess of $82 million, and more than 86 percent of all demand liabilities issued by banks was insured.[19] Such rapid growth in the system was both a source of pride and a point of concern for the fund's commissioners. As early as 1832, they noted that specie reserves were below their historical levels.[20] In five years, the aggregate reserve ratio had fallen to less than 14 percent of banknotes and deposits, less than half the ratio for Pennsylvania's banks.

The next five years brought additional growth and maturation of the system. Between 1832 and 1836, loans and discounts increased 182 percent; bank capital increased 141 percent. Moreover, by 1836, banks were loaned in aggregate nearly to the extent allowed by law. The aggregate loan-capital ratio, capped at 250 percent, then stood at 235 percent.[21]

It was not so much the growth in lending per se that concerned New York bank commissioners, but the growth in mortgage lending. In the course of their quarterly inspection tour, the inspectors uncovered a marked growth in loans financing land speculation in western New York.[22] Remarkably, the commissioners argued that the banks, although complicit in the speculation (as they labeled it), were blameless as to its extent. Their report highlighted the risks inherent in mortgage-based lending, but they did nothing to limit it and suggested no legislative course of action to stem it.

One of the many shortcomings of the Safety Fund Act was the limited powers granted to the bank commissioners. While they could seek injunctions against fraudulent or insolvent banks, they had no real authority over banks pursuing excessively risky strategies or even those that may have been insolvent had their portfolios been accurately marked to market. Other than moral suasion, the commissioners had no effective, controlling legal authority. It is notable that they chose not to employ their power of persuasion. They advised greater caution and more prudent strategies, even while they implicitly condoned the banks' high-risk practices by noting the potentially large profits earned in mortgage lending. What is most telling is the commissioners' sentiment that questions concerning the judiciousness of mortgage lending lay outside the scope of their competencies, even their investigations.

Later in 1836, a special legislative committee appointed to investigate allegations of bank fraud noted several other concerns. The committee wrote that some banks had "over-reached the bounds of prudence";[23] others had engaged in acts that may have observed the letter but not the spirit of the law. Still, none had obviously impaired its equity. Because the Safety Fund Act gave them the power to seek an injunction only if a bank's capital had been impaired by one-half, both the commissioners and the special committee considered their hands tied.

It soon became evident that the committee's assessment that none of the banks had seriously impaired its capital was in error. In an ironic twist, in the very month that the committee submitted its report to the assembly, three Buffalo banks were adjudged insolvent. Injunctions were granted, and the banks' operations were suspended.

A shortcoming in the original act was immediately exposed. Creditors could recover from the fund only after a bank's assets were liquidated and found insufficient. In the interim, note holders suffered losses as the notes of closed banks depreciated. Notes of the Bank of Buffalo exchanged in February 1837 at a 1 percent discount. In late April and early May, banknote brokers listed them as "no sale," or at a 100 percent discount.[24]

Legislators hurriedly passed an amending act that instructed the state comptroller to restore the value of the failed banks' notes. He instructed Erie Canal authorities and local tax collectors to accept these banks' notes at par. Between May and June, the canal and treasury took in about $65,000. The comptroller's action restored public confidence in the notes. In July, the Bank of Buffalo's notes traded at a 5 percent discount. They returned to par in August. Before the court initiated bankruptcy proceedings, however, all three Buffalo banks found enough specie to buy their notes from the comptroller. He ordered the injunctions lifted, and the banks reopened.[25]

It was not until February 1840, with the failure of the Commercial Bank of Buffalo, that the first call was made on the fund. A second occurred in December 1840. The fund promptly met these demands, but its reserves were depleted by one-half.[26] In September 1841, the Commercial Bank of New York City failed, which further depleted the unreplenished fund. Although it then had reserves of more than $360,000, the comptroller reported that only about $60,000 of that was available to redeem the notes of another failing bank. He noted that the 1829 act earmarked one-third of the fund's reserves for the reimbursement of general creditors other than note holders. When the Bank of Buffalo closed in November 1841 with a circulation rumored in excess of $290,000, the comptroller reported that he lacked the authority to redeem its notes.

Within weeks, a fifth bank, with a circulation of about $140,000, failed. The comptroller immediately issued a call for the first emergency assessment of one-half of 1 percent of each remaining bank's capital. This increased the fund's reserves only by about $162,000, or less than the amount needed to redeem even the notes of the Bank of Buffalo. By the end of 1842, another six banks failed. The fund itself was bankrupted.

Table 7.1 reports the calls made on the fund by the 11 failures. Between February 1840 and September 1842, the fund's obligations amounted to $2.5 million. More than one-half that amount arose from the failure of the three Buffalo banks enjoined in 1837 and allowed to reopen.

In response to the increasingly apparent inadequacies of the 1829 Safety Fund Act, the 1842 legislative session passed several amending acts. An April amendment changed the nature of the fund's obligation; it would thereafter guarantee only banknotes. Depositors and other creditors would no longer be insured. This finally corrected an oversight in the 1827 act. Debates surrounding the original bill demonstrate that most legislators believed that the fund's purpose was the exclusive protection of note holders. The original act's wording, however, made the fund liable for the entirety of a failed bank's debts, exclusive of capital. The amendment reflected a widely held opinion that note holders required additional protections because depositors "selected" their banks, but note holders typically did not.[27] Depositor claims were subordinated to those of note holders.

A second amendment enacted in 1842 was the requirement that creditors be repaid in the order in which injunctions were issued. This benefited creditors of early failing banks at the expense of creditors of later failing banks. Note holders and other creditors suffered losses as later failing banks' notes depreciated and depositors' funds were tied up for years in bank res-

Table 7.1 Payments Required from Safety Fund to Reimburse Creditors of Failed Banks (thousands of dollars)

Failed Bank	Date of Failure	Circulation Reported Prior to Failure ($)	Actual Note Redemptions ($)	Payments of Other Debts ($)	Receipts from Asset Sales ($)	Balance Paid by Safety Fund ($)
City Bank of Buffalo	2/1840	$268.9	$317.1	$0	$100.0	$217.1
Wayne County Bank	12/1840	144.3	113.1	16.1	0	129.2
Commercial Bank of New York City	9/1841	121.4	139.8	146.1	7.2	278.8
Bank of Buffalo	11/1841	195.8	435.5	149.2	0	584.8
Commercial Bank of Buffalo	11/1841	246.7	186.9	424.5	5.0	606.4
Commercial Bank of Oswego	12/1841	216.1	163.2	78.4	2.4	239.1
Watervliet Bank	3/1842	114.5	134.1	77.5	13.3	198.3
Clinton County Bank	4/1842	167.8	71.9	156.3	0	228.2
Lafayette Bank	2/1842	71.6	0	0	0	0
Bank of Lyons	9/1842	80.8	52.9	40.1	3.8	89.0
Oswego Bank	10/1842	94.5	0	0	0	0

Sources: Root, "New York Bank Currency," p. 295; Chaddock, Safety Fund Banking System, p. 332. From "Zombie Banks and the Demise of New York's Safety Fund," by Howard Bodenhorn. Eastern Economic Journal, no. 1 (Winter 1996), table 1, p. 25. Reprinted with permission of Eastern Economic Association.

olutions. The assets of nine banks making claims against the fund amounted to more than $6 million. By 1845, only about $1 million had been collected by the court-appointed administrators. Delays resulted from the poor quality of the failed banks' assets and the comptroller's unwillingness to write them off. In one case, the comptroller sent his own agent to an auction of a bank's assets to purchase any assets selling for less than fair market value.[28] The agent bought assets with a face value of $470,000 for just $16,900.

Delayed resolutions and banknote depreciations cost note holders an estimated $350,000.[29] To mitigate these losses, the legislature enticed still-solvent banks to make advance contributions to the fund. Banks forwarding the notes of failed Safety Fund banks in anticipation of future supplementary assessments earned 7 percent interest. Sixty-four banks forwarded a total of $477,000 in failed banknotes to the comptroller. This provision constituted an exception to the previous redeem-in-order provision, and it was reversed in May 1843. An injunction was issued against the comptroller that required that he wind up the first four failures before reimbursing creditors of later failing banks through any method.[30]

In 1845, the legislature finally acknowledged that future contributions to the fund would not provide the wherewithal to resolve all the failed banks for another decade. It gave the comptroller the authority to issue 6 percent bonds, guaranteed by future contributions to the fund, to accelerate the pace of bank resolutions. Proceeds from the bond sales were used to redeem only the notes of failed banks, and about $1 million in bonds was eventually issued. To limit future calls on the fund, double liability was reimposed in 1846. It was not until 1866, however, that the fund met the last of its obligations and the system was officially discontinued.

Assessing the Safety Fund

Even while New York City was emerging as the financial center of North America, Safety Fund banks were overwhelmingly located in small-town New York. A handful opened in New York City, but between 1829 and 1836, places like Auburn, Binghamton, Cooperstown, Ithaca, Little Falls, Odgensburg, Poughkeepsie, Utica, and Waterloo were the real beneficiaries of the Safety Fund. Many of these banks established themselves near the newly opened Erie Canal; others opened in towns located on Lake Ontario, the St. Lawrence River, and Lake Champlain to exploit opportunities to finance some part of the rapidly expanding waterborne trade in agricultural goods and a booming real estate market.

While profitable opportunities for bankers were manifold in these once out-of-the-way places, especially if they held a local monopoly, one potentially negative consequence was the limited opportunity for effective portfolio diversification.[31] Legitimate manufacturing, even on a modest scale, remained a score of years or more away in most of these towns, but artisan and merchant paper was available. Still, agriculture underlay almost every transaction in upstate New York so that even portfolios that appeared diversified remained heavily reliant on agriculture. In addition, the small, remote, and isolated nature of these banks made interbank coordination and cooperation difficult. Understanding how each of these represents a threat to banks requires an appreciation for the subtle ways in which the mercantile, agricultural, and financial sectors were linked and how they reacted to macroeconomic shocks.

Despite New York City's relative economic maturation, agriculture remained the state's principal employer. Up to 1850, the distribution of New York's labor force was not much different from the national average. In 1820, about 71.4 percent of all Americans worked on a farm; in New York, 66.3 percent did.[32] In 1840, the national average exceeded New York's agricultural employment share by about 7 percentage points. In 1850, however, New York's transformation was becoming increasingly evident as only about 42.2 percent of New Yorkers worked on a farm, compared to 59.7 percent of all Americans.

When the Safety Fund was established, New York remained tied to agriculture. In fact, New York's per capita income was only about 84 percent of the national average.[33] Again, it was not until 1850 that per capita income in the Empire State exceeded the national average.

Thus, in the 1820s, 1830s, and 1840s, shocks to agricultural prices were likely to reverberate throughout New York's economy. A significant price decline invariably meant lower farm incomes given the inelasticity of short-run supply. Such a shock was likely to rattle the state's financial system as well. Sharp and unexpected price declines made bank creditors jittery anyway, and negative agricultural price shocks markedly increased farm debt burdens. Because banks were heavily involved in agricultural lending, both directly to farmers themselves and indirectly through merchants who transformed bank credit into consumer credit, the volume of nonperforming loans increased even while they experienced reserve drains.[34]

In the late 1830s, these events converged. Between 1830 and 1837, the general price level increased in all but two years, with an average annual increase of 2.93 percent. Farm prices followed a similar pattern with increases in all but two years, but they rose at an annual rate of 4.64 percent.[35] Farmers responded to the increase in relative prices by expanding output, financed at least in part with bank debt. In 1836, New York bank commissioners noted an increase in mortgage lending among the state's country banks, and while it is not possible to separate agricultural from other lending, the increase in bank credit is unmistakable. Between 1830 and 1837, per capita bank credit increased from $6.61 to $35.11, an annual average increase of 20.86 percent.[36]

The customary autumn pressure in 1837 was compounded by the Bank of England's contractionary policy, and the exuberant economy received its first jolt. During 1838, the general price level fell 4.45 percent, agricultural prices declined just 2.41 percent, but bank credit contracted by 28.50 percent. During 1839, prices and bank credit rebounded, but in 1840, the downturn quickened. The general price level declined 16.46 percent, farm prices fell 27.90 percent; and per capita bank credit contracted 28.30 percent. Fisher's debt-deflation cycle was spiraling downward and the U.S. economy fell into one of the deepest recessions of the nineteenth century, probably the deepest of the first half of the century. It was 1845 before per capita bank credit returned to levels seen in 1835, and it was 1853 before farm prices returned to their 1836 peak.

Throughout the nation, banks failed in unprecedented numbers and all were forced to suspend payments in 1839 to halt a severe reserve drain. The stage was set for a test of the Safety Fund system. While it could deal with the first few failures and protect the payments system, it was not in a position to deal with a systemic bank panic, and its shortcomings were quickly revealed. The remainder of this chapter documents the fund's successes and shortcomings.

Provisions for Bank Oversight and Supervision

As previously noted, government oversight and regulation of banks is motivated by twin concerns of protecting individual bank creditors from loss and protecting the payments system from macroeconomic shocks. Both concerns originate in the belief that most bank creditors cannot or will not effectively protect themselves from loss. Research by Douglas Diamond and Philip Dybvig, as well as Mathias Dewatripont and Jean Tirole, among others, begins from the premise that small bank creditors (note holders and depositors) can neither identify nor control bank risks because of the opaque nature of bank portfolios and free-riding problems.[37] Under this approach, government supervision remedies a market failure by gathering, processing, and acting on information unavailable to small creditors. The premise is that regulators can observe inside and often confidential information *and* that regulators, because of training or experience, are better evaluators of such information.

To be effective, any supervisory system must be capable of accurately assessing bank conditions and be given the power to discipline banks whose activities substantively diverge from accepted or safe practice.[38] In other words, the regulatory structure must create incentives for the supervisory agency to perform legitimate audits and then to prosecute regulatory violations through appropriate disciplinary channels.

New York's legislators clearly recognized that the success of their bank liability insurance program depended on an effective supervisory mechanism. Indeed, the original 1829 act included 12 sections outlining the selection and duties of the system's commissioners. It provided for three commissioners—one appointed by the governor and two elected by the bankers themselves. Each commissioner served a two-year term and was eligible for reelection or reappointment. A commissioner could be removed from office at any time by the governor for failure to perform his duties.

It was the responsibility of the commissioners to examine every bank once each quarter, and the law allowed for individual commissioners to visit and examine a bank. Their charge was broad and sweeping. Section 15 of the act instructed the commissioners to thoroughly inspect each bank's operations, including a detailed examination of all "books, papers, notes, bonds, and other evidences of debt"; to compare the state of the bank with the quarterly statements of condition submitted to the legislature; to count the specie on hand; and "to make such other inquiries as may be necessary to ascertain the actual conditions of the said corporations, and their ability to fulfill all the engagements made by them."[39]

In addition, commissioners were required to take sworn testimony from the bank's officers and any other agents of the bank believed to have information relevant to the commissioners' investigations. The only restriction was a clause requiring the commissioners to protect the confidentiality of the bank's borrowers; they could disclose information about individual bank debtors or creditors only in a court hearing.

If an investigation found that a bank was insolvent, that it lost one-half of its paid-in capital (which may or may not imply insolvency), that it suspended specie payments for more than 90 days, that its officers refused to give testimony under oath, that it failed to remit an insurance premium, or that it violated any other charter requirement, the commissioner was required to seek an injunction immediately suspending the bank's operation. The chancery court appointed a receiver who worked with an agent of the state comptroller's office in liquidating the bank and reimbursing creditors.

The Safety Fund's commissioners proved insufficient to the task given to them. One sure difficulty was the potentially overwhelming effort expected of them. Three commissioners, acting without assistance, were required to examine each bank four times per year. The operation of 30 banks implied 10 examinations per quarter for each commissioner, assuming they worked independently. Such a schedule allowed for thorough investigations. A commissioner could spend as much as a week at each bank, poring over its books, taking sworn testimony, and engaging in informal discussions with its officers. A conscientious commissioner could depart confident that he had taken a bank's pulse.

By 1835, there were nearly 90 banks, which implied 30 examinations per commissioner per quarter. Given the realities of upstate travel, this afforded little time to spend at each bank, probably no more than a day or two, and fewer opportunities to uncover even mildly troublesome bank actions, let alone a serious infraction or problem that the bank's officers wished to conceal. Thus, the quality of bank examination surely deteriorated as the system expanded, not because the commissioners grew complacent or neglectful, but because they were overworked and the legislature made no allowance to increase the number of examiners in the face of an escalating workload.

In 1843, after the Safety Fund was effectively bankrupted, Governor Bouck mused on the state of the fund in his annual address to the assembly. It was "quite evident," he said, "that the appointment of the Commissioners has not answered all the valuable ends which were anticipated from the measure."[40] While Governor Bouck implicitly questioned the commissioners' competence and integrity, the real shortcoming was the limited disciplinary powers given to the commissioners. They could seek an injunction and halt a bank's operations only if it was demonstrably insolvent or engaged in clearly illegal activities.

There were, therefore, a host of activities that threatened a bank's solvency or that skirted the edges of legality that the commissioners had no authority to punish or curtail. The case of the Wayne County Bank is telling in this regard. In their 1841 report to the assembly concerning the failure of this bank, the commissioners stated:

> During the greater part of [its history], the bank had a reputation of being managed in such a way as to produce large profits for its shareholders, although it appears that soon after its establishment [in 1830], the improper practices sometimes adopted, with a view to these profits, were the frequent subject of complaint and reprehension on the part of many who had dealings with it.[41]

The long-standing complaints revolved around practices that barely met the letter, and certainly not the spirit, of the state's usury laws. Even if the practice had been uncovered earlier, the commissioners claimed that they could not have sought an injunction because the actions were not unequivocally illegal.

Despite their failure to uncover this practice earlier, the examining commissioner had determined that the bank was in serious trouble at least seven months before it was closed. In May 1840, the commissioners found the bank "grossly mismanaged" and likely to suffer substantial losses on its loan portfolio.[42] To allay the commissioners' concerns, the Wayne County Bank's directors replaced the cashier. His replacement did not know the exact amount of bad paper held by the bank, but he assured the commissioners that the expected losses would not require a writing down of the capital stock by more than $25,000. The examining commissioner believed that the bank was on the verge of failure, but without proof that it had in fact lost one-half of its capital, he could do nothing.

At the next examination in September 1840, after lengthy questioning of the cashier and other officers, the commissioners concluded that the bank was recovering but still troubled. Following the December examination, however, the examining commissioner had no choice but to obtain an injunction. In the end, the bank's losses paid by the Safety Fund amounted to $130,000. Its assets were unrecoverable.

Even good faith examinations and conscientious regulators were unable to deter risky banking practices if commissioners were not given the authority to halt practices that placed the Safety Fund at risk. Additionally, the workload itself nearly insured that regulatory mistakes were made, irrespective of the commissioners' abilities and willingness to perform their tasks.

Effects of Fund Insurance on Outside Monitoring

While one group of economists argues that bank liability insurance represents a cornerstone of a stable banking system, another argues that it often reduces incentives among market agents to engage in socially beneficial monitoring. In their study of modern U.S. banks, Mark Flannery and Sorin Sorescu find evidence that deposit insurance compromises private incentives to assign risk premia to bank debt.[43] That is, institutional bank investors generally evaluate individual bank risks accurately, but they do so only when they believe that their principal is at risk. By eliminating most of the risk from bank-issued debt, government insurance mutes monitoring incentives.[44]

Other researchers have also found evidence that questions the presumption that small creditors do not have the inclination or resources to accurately assess bank risks in a timely manner. Edward Kane finds that depositors could distinguish between different kinds of banks during the run on thrifts insured by the Ohio Deposit Guaranty Fund in the 1980s.[45] Not only can small depositors distinguish between banks during a run, they can distinguish and discipline risky banks at other times. Sangkyun Park and Stavros Peristiani argue that risky banks find it difficult to attract deposits even though they promise higher interest rates. They also find that the effect is not as pronounced among insured as among uninsured depositors, but it exists. Interestingly, Lawrence Goldberg and Sylvia Hudgins show that depositors identified risky banks as much as 48 months prior to failure because banks that eventually failed witnessed marked declines in deposits two to four years prior to failure.[46] From this evidence, Park and Peristiani conclude that "depositors in general are potentially effective monitors" and that bank liability insurance mitigates their effectiveness by muting their incentives to monitor.[47]

Thus, two questions arise: Did individuals and institutions in antebellum America monitor banks? And did the Safety Fund mute the incentives to monitor New York banks?

Articles by Calomiris and Charles Kahn, as well as Kahn and William Roberds, develop models of the role of demandable debt (banknotes and checkable deposits) in eliciting effective bank monitoring. Calomiris and

Kahn's model suggests that the issuance of demandable debt, combined with a first-come, first-served constraint, will prompt efficacious monitoring.[48] Although monitors bear all of the costs of their monitoring activity, nonmonitors cannot free ride because monitors will be first in the cashing-out queue when a bank approaches insolvency. Monitors are (indirectly) compensated through their recovery of the full face value of their claims. Nonmonitors accept later places in the queue and may receive only fractional returns. Despite the potential for less than 100 percent recovery, the system provides monitors with incentives to close insolvent banks before their net worth is dissipated.

Kahn and Roberds extend this result by investigating the conditions under which banknotes dominate checks, or vice versa, as transactions media.[49] They argue that the choice reflects a fundamental tradeoff between liquidity and monitoring. Banknotes are highly liquid (they circulate freely), while checks are redeemed after a single transaction. Checks continually verify a bank's ability to meet its contractual obligations; banknotes, on the other hand, provide verification only infrequently. Moreover, there are costs associated with the early or quick redemption of banknotes because this forces the bank to prematurely liquidate its portfolio. Within such an environment, they show that banknotes dominate if the bank can credibly guarantee both the redemption value of its notes and the composition of its portfolio. With incomplete contracting (banks do not contract for a particular portfolio), the optimality of checks or banknotes depends on the cost of early banknote redemption. With high early redemption costs, checks dominate. With intermediate redemption costs, the threat of early redemption acts as an effective check on bank risk taking, so banknotes dominate, even though they may circulate at a discount.

As Kahn and Roberds note, their conclusions depend, as do Calomiris and Kahn's, on the presumption that outside agents can and do gather, process, and act on information about a bank's risk taking. A spate of recent research into early American banknote markets supports that presumption.

Gary Gorton provides compelling evidence that outside agents were effective monitors.[50] Gorton constructs a sample of banks issuing notes for the first time between 1838 and 1860. We have previously seen that banknotes were priced by banknote brokers, so resolving the issue of whether these brokers could provide effective monitoring depends on the time-series trajectory of the price of banknotes issued by these start-up banks.

Gorton uses this banknote pricing data to test the twin hypotheses that: (1) debt issued by new firms will be more heavily discounted than debt of seasoned firms even if the two firms' financial structures are otherwise identical, and the discount will decline as market participants observe defaults; and (2) prior to the establishment of a reputation, new firms will be more intensely monitored. He finds that the data are consistent with the hypotheses. Banknotes of young banks were discounted more heavily than older banks. This price discrepancy creates incentives for more intense monitoring of young banks as agents attempt to arbitrage on any differences between market prices and fundamental values. As banknotes are redeemed by monitors, the price-value gap disappears.

An alternative approach is to investigate reputation deterioration.[51] That is, instead of looking at reduction in banknote discounts as young banks establish reputations for soundness, it may be informative to investigate the extent and timing of declines in banknote prices as banks neared failure. Using a sample of banks that failed in the 1840s and an event study methodology, Howard Bodenhorn finds that discounts on notes of eventually failing banks declined gradually about 24 months prior to failure and declined sharply about 12 months prior to failure. About 8 months before closing, the notes of these banks had fallen, on average, to about one-half of their face value.

It seems clear, then, that market participants were capable of monitoring antebellum banks when they faced incentives to do so. What remains to be seen is whether Safety Fund insurance muted this incentive and reduced monitoring by banknote brokers.

To test the effects of insurance on banknote pricing, comparable samples of 25 country banks were drawn from New York and Pennsylvania. Discounts on banknotes in the Philadelphia market were collected from *Bicknell's Counterfeit Detector, Banknote Reporter, and General Price Current* between the first quarter of 1835 and the second quarter of 1841. Table 7.2 reports the mean quarterly discounts and the coefficients of variation for New York and Pennsylvania banks. Comparisons of means reveals that the notes of banks sold for similar prices, even though New York banks were farther away and the costs of physically returning their notes would have been greater. The notes of more-remote New York Safety Fund banks sold at marginally lower discounts in many periods; this provides a simple measure of the value of the insurance to the Safety Fund banks. By reducing the risk of loss attached to a bank's notes, the insurance effectively raised the price of the bank's debt, which increased the bank's overall value.

The coefficients of variation provide a metric that reflects the operation of the market and the ability of market agents to observe and price bank risk. In a well-functioning market, assets with different expected future values (arising from differences in productivity, return, or risk) should sell for different prices. That is, holding the nominal return of a loan constant (say 6 percent), the one with the higher default probability should fetch a lower price. The same should apply to banknotes. Holding the effective return constant (illiquidity and depreciation features), a note issued by a riskier bank should exchange at a lower price than a note issued by a bank holding less-risky assets. A well-functioning market, then, should produce a variety of prices reflected in a positive and, perhaps, substantial variance.

One way to judge whether a market was pricing assets with different risk-return characteristics separately (not necessarily efficiently, though) is through a comparison of the coefficient of variation of prices. Recall, in this

Table 7.2 Average Discounts and the Coefficient of Variation on
Banknotes in New York and Pennsylvania, 1835–1841

| | New York | | Pennsylvania | |
| | Average Banknote Discount | Coefficient of Variation | Average Banknote Discount | Coefficient of Variation |
Year Quarter				
1835				
I	1.16	0.10	1.92	4.58
II	0.95	0.11	1.11	3.95
III	1.00	0.00	1.12	3.92
IV	1.00	0.00	0.94	3.76
1836				
I	1.00	0.00	0.92	3.73
II	1.35	0.17	1.01	3.31
III	1.15	0.16	0.93	3.59
IV	1.35	0.17	1.10	3.15
1837				
I	1.70	0.27	1.11	3.02
II	1.41	0.10	1.05	1.93
III	0.00	—	0.63	2.82
IV	0.00	—	0.39	1.90
1838				
I	0.00	—	1.26	4.02
II	0.00	—	0.42	1.85
III	0.60	0.38	1.71	4.91
IV	0.93	0.19	1.73	4.87
1839				
I	0.95	0.16	1.81	4.65
II	1.00	0.00	1.97	4.33
III	1.25	0.00	2.10	4.01
IV	−3.53	−0.27	0.56	1.99
1840				
I	−2.00	0.00	0.45	1.94
II	−2.00	0.00	0.46	1.98
III	−2.00	0.00	0.29	2.08
IV	0.50	0.00	0.35	1.92
1841				
I	0.00	—	0.59	3.06
II	−2.00	0.00	0.30	2.29
III	−1.50	0.00	NA	NA
IV	−1.00	0.00	NA	NA

case, that the standard of deviation is a measure of the dispersion of discounts around the mean. The standard deviation, however, is an absolute measure of dispersion; that is, it does not take into account differences in the underlying means of two or more samples. The coefficient of variation (the standard deviation divided by the mean) accounts for differences in the mean. It is, in fact, a relative measure of the dispersion as a proportion of the mean.

Statistics reported in table 7.2 show that there was very little dispersion in the prices of Safety Fund banknotes. What dispersion there was, in fact, was driven by small differences in the prices of notes issued by banks in Albany and Troy compared to those issued by more-remote banks. Typically, Albany and Troy banknotes exchanged at about one-half the discount of other banks. If the four Albany and Troy banks were excluded from the sample, the standard deviation collapses to zero in nearly every period.

Note by way of comparison that the coefficient of variation for the discount on notes issued by Pennsylvania's banks was 45 times as great as that for Safety Fund banks in March 1835. In June 1836, the Pennsylvania coefficient of variation was 20 times higher. In other months, it was infinitely higher.

What conclusion can be drawn from this basic evidence? It appears that specialists who otherwise spent their time analyzing and pricing bank risk stopped once the Safety Fund promised to protect note holders from losses. In the absence of a blanket insurance guarantee, uniform prices (a constant standard deviation and coefficient of variation) would imply nearly uniform portfolios or, at least, portfolios with similar risk-return structures. Without detailed evidence on the loan portfolios of each bank, we will never determine the true underlying portfolios, but it seems highly improbable that 25 randomly selected Safety Fund banks all held comparable, very low-risk portfolios while 25 randomly selected Pennsylvania banks held markedly different, relatively high-risk portfolios. Banks almost certainly fell into different risk classes, but the insurance guarantee muted the incentives of market agents to ascertain each bank's riskiness and price its notes appropriately. Pennsylvania banknotes, on the other hand, carried no such guarantee and the market priced notes reflecting their estimates of the expected value of a bank's portfolio.

In a number of articles, Calomiris has argued that the most-effective monitors of banks are other banks.[52] Clearly, they are favorably positioned to evaluate opaque assets because they are in the same business. Additionally, one bank is often a creditor of several other banks through interbank deposits and holdings of others' notes, which creates incentives to monitor to protect itself. Perhaps the best incentive to monitor, however, is making banks responsible for each other through a coinsurance scheme. A true coinsurance scheme would have required still-solvent banks to fully reimburse creditors of failed banks. That is, the 80-odd remaining Safety Fund

banks in 1841 would have had to fully reimburse the failing banks' creditors.

Calomiris argues that this contingent liability would have motivated low-
risk Safety Fund banks to uncover, expose, and punish high-risk practices
by other banks. Instead, the Safety Fund Act limited the contingent liability
to additional assessments of no more than one-half of 1 percent per annum.
This future contingent liability discounted to the present, even with a substantial probability factor, represented a relatively small contingency. The
terms of the act, then, effectively reduced incentives to monitor by individual and institutional bank creditors. This would have been of limited concern had the fund established an effective supervisory and regulatory structure. But it did not, so the fund was left without a credible monitor.

Insurance Premia and Bank Risk Taking

Studies of the savings and loan crisis of the 1980s focused attention on the
perverse incentive effects created by mispriced deposit insurance.[53] Specifically, underpriced insurance encourages excessive risk taking. If the insurance premia do not accurately reflect the inherent risks of a bank's portfolio,
the insurer effectively bears a portion of the default risk of every bank
loan.[54] Because banks now share the risks with the insurer, their expected
risk-adjusted rate of return to their portfolio exceeds what it would be without the insurance subsidy. Higher rates of return induce banks to engage in
additional lending. The net effect is that the banks? loan-to-capital ratio
increases, as does the riskiness of the overall portfolio. In turn, the probability of a call on the insurer increases because of the twin effects of a
reduced owner-contributed equity buffer and a larger volume of nonperforming loans. Unless the insurer uses its regulatory and supervisory powers to impose capital requirements and other sorts of portfolio restrictions,
the subsidy can grow quite large.

Furthermore, the subsidy takes two forms. On one hand, the subsidy
increases the risk-adjusted return on any particular loan, thereby increasing
the expected return on the overall portfolio. On the other hand, the subsidy
accrues to the bank in the form of lower funding costs. In the absence of
insurance, bank creditors (primarily note holders and depositors) demand
compensation for bearing the increased expected costs of default reflected
in the bank's riskier loan portfolio. Liability insurance obviates most of this
payment as long as creditors believe that the insurer will reimburse them
quickly when the portfolio sours. Again, unless the insurer's premia reflect
this risk, the bank is paying less on its liabilities than it otherwise would.
These reduced funding costs reflect the operation of the subsidy.

Research into the pricing policies of the FDIC has produced no clear
consensus on whether modern deposit insurance underprices (subsidizes)
or overprices (taxes) bank liabilities. Modern evidence suggests that the tax
or subsidy, if either exists, is small on average.[55] It seems likely, as well,

that the average subsidy to Safety Fund members was relatively small. One estimate calculates the Safety Fund's average annual assessment on total insured obligations at about 0.24 percent.[56] This is approximately equal to the FDIC's assessment rates between 1991 and 1994, but it is well above its long-run historical average assessment of about 0.04 percent and 100 times the FDIC's 1996 average assessment rate of 0.0024 percent.[57]

Recall, however, the complaints of New York City banks about the funding basis of the fund, namely, the use of capital instead of circulation or some other basis for the assessment. The city banks' complaints, ultimately, may not have been so much about the absolute level of the insurance premia as it was about their distribution. Even if the Safety Fund's premia were actuarially fair on average (something that requires demonstration), the flat premium schedule provided high-risk banks with a subsidy while low-risk banks were taxed.

Although city banks were just as capable of pursuing high-risk strategies as isolated rural banks, close proximity to one another and easier observation of one another's discounting practices would quickly expose a city risk taker. The same was not necessarily true of country banks whose portfolios were rarely observed, even indirectly, by fellow bankers. Moreover, after the first six years of a bank's life, its insurance premium fell to zero, at least until a failure necessitated an emergency assessment. While a zero premium may be actuarially sound for low-risk banks, it seems likely that a flat-rate zero premium provided a substantial subsidy to high-risk, perhaps even moderate-risk, banks.[58]

The evidence in the preceding two sections also suggests that the Safety Fund provided a substantial subsidy to its high-risk members. One way to mitigate the incentive effects of the subsidy is to impose portfolio regulations and then provide a supervisory mechanism capable of enforcing them. The Safety Fund Act attempted to restrict particularly egregious risk taking by restricting the size of its members' portfolios—recall that total loans could not exceed 250 percent of capital. But it did nothing to restrict the composition of its members' portfolios. Moreover, the act provided for cursory supervision, at best, in that its examiners were overworked and not given power to halt especially risky practices until the bank's net worth was depleted by half.

Recall, as well, that the subsidy reduced independent monitoring (at least until it became clear that the fund would not reimburse creditors in a timely manner), reflected in smaller and less-variable banknote discounts. The Safety Fund's subsidy became manifest in the banks' low funding costs. Normally, a high-risk bank would have faced difficulties circulating its notes (i.e., its notes would have fetched a lower price in the market), but the insurance guarantee very nearly generated a single price for all notes regardless of risk. Differences in note prices were driven almost entirely by physical redemption costs instead of risk characteristics.

How did the risk-inducing incentives of the Safety Fund manifest themselves? Without detailed information on representative samples of insured and uninsured bank portfolios that includes both ex ante and ex post risk measures, the question may never be answered satisfactorily. There remain, however, a number of potentially suggestive measures. One straightforward possibility is the loan-capital ratio. The higher the ratio, the less owner-contributed equity available to serve as a buffer for the insurer in the event of bank failure. In 1834, the aggregate loan-capital ratio for New York banks was 2.08, which was substantially larger than the 1.21 ratio in Connecticut and the 1.85 ratio in Pennsylvania.[59] By 1837, New York's ratio had increased to 2.14, Connecticut's to 1.51, and Pennsylvania's to 1.88. It was not until year-end 1840, following the initial Safety Fund failures, that the New York ratio fell to 1.43, or the same as Pennsylvania's 1.44, but remained well in excess of Connecticut's 1.18. New York banks were more leveraged than banks in neighboring states, which suggests that its banks were exploiting an effective insurance subsidy.

A second potentially informative measure of risk taking may be the ratio of real estate holdings to total loans. Recall that in both 1832 and 1836, the Safety Fund's commissioners expressed a growing concern with some banks' real estate speculations. In hindsight, we know that these loans were risky because the collapse in land prices in the late 1830s prompted several bank failures. Of course, some mortgage loans may have presented low risks ex ante but proved otherwise ex post. The commissioners' concerns suggest that many were high risks ex ante.

Comparisons are drawn with difficulty because of spotty reporting in many states, but Rhode Island provides one point of comparison. In the early 1830s, banks in both New York and Rhode Island reported aggregate real estate holdings representing about 2.5 percent of total loans.[60] In the late 1830s, however, the two states' experiences diverged markedly. While real estate holdings among Rhode Island's banks remained relatively constant at just under 2.0 percent of total loans through 1840, they began rising in 1836 in New York and reached nearly 6.0 percent in 1840.

The numbers are even more telling for a handful of Safety Fund failures. At the Bank of Buffalo and the Commercial Bank of Buffalo, for example, real estate holdings increased nearly tenfold between 1835 and 1840. At the City Bank of Buffalo and the Watervliet Bank, they increased sixfold.[61] These data, suggestive as they may be, are highly imperfect. The decision to foreclose may have been endogenous, responding differentially at different points in the business cycle and to the amount of real estate already assumed by the bank. As the economy turned down, some bank managers may have become more forgiving about delinquent payments and allowed mortgagors to hold onto their land if they made even token payments. Moreover, as banks accumulated more unsalable property, they may have become less likely to foreclose. Still, the fact that some banks foreclosed and assumed control of real estate equal in value to about one-half of their paid-in capital suggests that high-return, high-risk strategies were subsidized in part by the insurer.

The risk-taking incentives created by underpriced deposit insurance are magnified when previous losses have impaired a bank's capital to such an extent that pursuing excessively risky, long-shot strategies does not present much downside risk to either managers or stockholders. Because the benefits accrue to the bank's principals while any losses accrue to the insurer if the long shot pays off, the bank will typically pursue the gamble. Kane labels these banks "zombies" because they enjoy an "unnatural life-in-death experience, in that if they had not been insured, the firm's creditors would have taken control from the stockholders once it had become clear that their enterprise's net worth was exhausted."[62] Zombie banks avoid the finality of economic death through the black magic of blanket insurance guarantees.

Banks are thus allowed to engage in these high-risk practices because market discipline is lacking. Insulated from downside risks themselves, banknote holders and depositors remain willing to accept banks' liabilities, more so because these zombie banks often fund their high-risk redemption strategies by offering above-market rates on their liabilities. Complicating this situation, very often, is a regulatory authority or political authority reluctant to publicly expose the extent of the problem and close troubled institutions. By failing to act in the place of market agents and close bankrupted institutions, the supervisory body magnifies the insurer's loss as zombie banks' failed long-shot liabilities pile up.

Kane labels this lack of will of the supervisory body "regulatory forbearance," which he defines as a repeated pattern of leniency on the part of the insurer toward insolvent or nearly insolvent banks.[63] When looking at practices of Safety fund banks and the Fund's commissioners, it is no easy task to delimit regulatory forbearance from the effects of excessive workloads, limited information, ineffectual regulatory powers, and simple error. There are three cases, however, that suggest regulatory forbearance.

Recall that three Buffalo banks suspended in 1837, but the state comptroller allowed them to buy back their notes and resume operations. Not surprisingly, these three banks attracted the commissioners' attention, and they were mentioned by name as a point of concern in the final paragraph of the commissioners' January 1838 annual report to the legislature. No mention was made in either their 1839 or their 1840 annual report, however.

The extant evidence indicates a pattern of high-risk investment strategies, bordering on outright fraud, in each bank's last months. Of the City Bank of Buffalo's $400,000 loan portfolio, the receiver considered nearly one-half uncollectible just weeks after assuming control of its assets. Another $100,000 or more was considered doubtful. The bank's directors owed the final $100,000, which the receiver considered a total loss.[64] The bank held $225,000 in real estate, and the receiver estimated its market value at

$150,000. Although the bank was closed in February 1840, the receiver was convinced that not only was it insolvent at least six months earlier, but its net worth shortfall in November 1839 amounted to $200,000. Once liquidation began, the receiver estimated the shortfall at $350,000. It eventually amounted to $217,000. This bank had not lost one-half of its paid-in capital, it lost one and one-half times its capital (see table 7.1). A diligent examination would have been unlikely to miss such losses.

Similar questions arise about the commissioners' handling of the deteriorating conditions of the Bank of Buffalo and the Commercial Bank of Buffalo. The assets of the Bank of Buffalo were completely uncollectible and only $5,000 of the Commercial Bank's assets was realized. Eventually, the Safety Fund paid $1.2 million to these banks' creditors; these were banks that in 1840 had a reported $1.4 million in combined assets. Moreover, Buffalo's banks either misrepresented their total circulation or played last-minute, go-for-broke games that never paid off. In its July 1840 statement of condition, for example, the Bank of Buffalo reported a circulation of $196,000. The Safety Fund ultimately redeemed $435,500 in its notes.

While there is no direct evidence that the bank commissioners allowed broken institutions to continue (i.e., that they practiced regulatory forbearance), indirect evidence leads to that conclusion. First, even the most overworked examiner could not have missed the remarkably low quality of these three banks' portfolios. More to the point, however, were a number of articles and editorials appearing in the *Albany Argus* following the failures. One editorial insisted that the City Bank of Buffalo "went into operation in a lame and crippled condition" and that it remained so throughout its brief four-year existence.[65] It was also reported that the state comptroller was aware of its (near) insolvent condition, but instead of calling for its closure, he tried to shore it up by making it a depository for Erie Canal receipts. When it failed, it owed the canal authorities $80,000.

The *Albany Argus* later revealed that state officials had deposited a combined $340,000—mostly canal receipts—in the three banks. It argued that these banks had been made state depositories not because of their financial solidity but because of their promoters' political connections in Albany. Even commissioners and examiners with the best of intentions would have found it difficult to push against the wind and close a bank with strong political connections. Moreover, the commissioners may have chosen not to seek an injunction against a bank politically allied with the governor because he could remove any commissioner at will for misconduct—a word subject to broad interpretation.

A fundamental shortcoming of the Safety Fund was that its insurance premia were mispriced. Flat rates effectively taxed low-risk banks and subsidized high-risk banks. That subsidy became especially pronounced once a bank suffered some initial losses and sought out even riskier loans, which promised higher returns if the gamble paid off but probably had low expected payoffs. Combined with a supervisory body not given the time or

the tools to halt practices that placed the insurer at risk, it was nearly inevitable that the fund would be bankrupted by a few spectacular failures.

The Note Holder Preference Amendment of 1842

New York's response to the combination of mispriced insurance and ineffectual supervision did not include changes to the pricing system or improvements to the supervisory and regulatory structure. Rather, lawmakers
responded by lessening potential liability by reducing the scope of the guarantee. In 1842, the New York General Assembly passed a law amending the
wording of the original act so that only note holders were insured. All other
creditors, including depositors, only held subordinated debt.

The likely effect of this amendment can be analyzed with a model developed by William Osterberg and James Thomson that investigates the potential effects of depositor preference now practiced by the FDIC.[66] Their
model implies that in the absence of note holder preference, underpricing
by the Safety Fund increased the claims of deposits relative to total liabilities. Moreover, the size of this effect was positively related to the fund's
pricing error. The more underpriced the insurance, the larger the percentage
of deposits for which the insurer may have ultimately been liable.

Osterberg and Thomson also show that the value of a bank's debt (in
terms of payment priority) affected a bank's net value only through the net
tax or subsidy of the insurance.[67] If the insurance was efficiently priced,
meaning that the premium equaled the expected value of the guarantee, the
structure of a bank's liabilities had no effect on its market valuation. If, on
the other hand, the insurance was underpriced (as it almost certainly was
for many banks), the structure of the bank's liabilities mattered. With underpriced insurance, a bank could reorder its portfolio away from subordinated debt, which becomes increasingly expensive as the bank's riskiness
increases, toward debt covered by the insurance guarantee, which would
increase the bank's market value.

Note holder preference subordinated the claims of depositors and other
creditors to note holders and the insurer. Thus, the 1842 law made deposits
more akin to subordinated debt.[68] Under certain conditions discussed by
Osterberg and Thomson, deposits and other general credit acted as equity-
like claims because depositors and other creditors became residual claimants. The overall effect of note holder preferences, however, was that they
unambiguously reduced the value of depositor claims.

New York's assembly was correct in contending that a noteholder preference effectively provided the insurer with a senior claim on the bank's
assets, which reduced the probability that an insurer would be called on to
reimburse note holders for losses. Nevertheless, banknote insurance still
provided a subsidy to the bank equal to the difference between the premium
and the expected cost of the guarantee. Just as a sweeping insurance guar-

antee increased the value of the bank and increased the bankruptcy threshold (i.e., the loss of shareholder equity required to induce creditors to close the bank), note holder preference still increased the market value of an insured bank's debt, though not by as much.

Changing the insurance status of creditors mitigated the effect of the subsidy provided by underpriced insurance, but it may also have altered banks' relative mix of circulation and deposits, which endogenized the insurance problem. Depositors and other creditors were likely to respond to changed insurance status by demanding higher interest rates to compensate them for the greater risks attached to a subordinated claim. As uninsured funds grew more expensive, banks were likely to shift their debt portfolios toward low-cost insured claims. A greater reliance on banknotes countered the insurer's attempt to limit its exposure and little reduced a troubled bank's ability to attract funds.

A second potential endogenous effect may have been that uninsured creditors effectively shortened the maturity of their debt. Such a response increased the probability of bank runs, not by noteholders, but by uninsured claimants. The result was that even mildly distressed banks opted not to issue much uninsured debt. This had two important implications.[69] First, it reduced the insurer's buffer, exposing it to still-substantial claims. Second, the unwillingness of uninsured depositors to renew debts in troubled banks could trigger a full-blown liquidity crisis. Not surprisingly, it was large and unexpected deposit withdrawals that drove the panic of 1857.[70] The note holder preference law failed to protect an increasingly important element of the payments system.

Banks may have avoided both of these effects by offering collateral to uninsured creditors, effectively placing the debts held by uninsured creditors higher in the pecking order than insured note holders and the insurer itself. Such a strategic maneuver by risk-taking banks increased the insurer's risk exposure, diminished the value of debt held by insured note holders, and further diminished the value of debt held by uninsured, noncollateralized creditors, which may have made them even more likely to provoke a liquidity crisis. Again, because there were few opportunities to collateralize deposits, while corresponding banks and other institutional creditors could and would demand collateral, it is not particularly surprising that the panic of 1857 was driven by panicky depositors withdrawing en masse.

Bank Exit and Adverse Selection

While the Safety Fund labored under the stress of mispriced insurance guarantees and ineffectual supervision and regulation, the principal cause of its eventual collapse was an indirect result of the shifting political terrain in the mid- to late 1830s. The legacy of the Albany Regency's political favoritism in bank chartering remained a palpable force in New York politics for decades even after the Regency faded. Franchises were granted to political allies, which produced not only partisan, but poorly managed, banks.[71] In the mid-1820s, attempts were made to repeal statutes restraining private, unincorporated banking, which would have created an alternative to and posed a competitive threat to Regency-granted local monopolies. These initiatives were defeated by slim margins and the laissez-faire sentiment remained a potent and growing force in the state's political philosophy and banking policy.

The laissez-faire sentiment that arose in the mid-1820s ultimately manifested itself in free banking. Spearheaded in Michigan, but originating in New York, free banking promised to resolve two perceived shortcomings in current policy: (1) protection of note holders from loss, and (2) the lack of naturally arising competition in local bank markets. The free banking alternative revolved around the last of the recommendations made by Joshua Forman in 1827 but rejected in the 1829 Safety Fund Act, namely, bond-secured note issue. Free banking allowed bankers to tender federal or state bonds with a state regulatory body, which acted as a de facto insurance guarantee for the bank's circulating banknotes. Banks opting for free bank "charters" were excused from Safety fund membership. As the expected costs of remaining in the Fund increased, more and more banks shifted from Safety Fund to free bank charters so that only the riskiest banks remained in the insurance system.

The adverse selection problem eventually became so potent and problematic that the state refused to renew the charters of even longtime Safety Fund members. The number of members dwindled, as banks switched to free banking charters, until the fund was officially closed in 1866 when the charter of the last remaining Safety Fund member expired.

Concluding Remarks

No one historical episode can provide a definitive answer to the question of whether government-sponsored bank liability insurance is socially beneficial in developing, price-sensitive economies. Case studies can, however, provide valuable insights. This study of the Safety Fund system demonstrates, as Calomiris notes, that "adverse selection and moral hazard are more than theoretical constructs; deposit insurance systems that failed to deal effectively with these problems were undone by them."[72] In this, unfortunately, the Safety Fund proved rather than countered the rule. When alternatives to insurance membership exist, low-risk banks will exit the system, leaving only high-risk banks behind. The adverse selection problem worsens until the expected payments by the insurer far outweigh its reserves. A negative shock to the financial sector quickly exposes the insurer's net worth shortfall. Moreover, without effective safeguards against excessive risk taking, high-risk banks free ride on the premia paid by low-risk banks.

Adverse selection and moral hazard ultimately undid the Safety Fund, but they were assisted by ineffectual supervision, ineffective to nonexistent portfolio restrictions, everything from marginally legal activities to outright fraud, and some politically motivated regulatory forbearance. The mixture was combustible, and it led to the Safety Fund's failure. Furthermore, the 1842 law designed to limit future calls on the fund may have done little more than induce a reordering of bank liability structures, which exposed the financial sector to greater systemic risks of bank runs than before.

If bank liability insurance was to be truly effective, it had to do more than protect the solvency of the system's members and the insurer itself; it had to protect the payments system from economy-wide liquidity crises. An insurer with small reserves, a limited ability to solicit emergency contributions from members, and an unwillingness to insure all media of exchange would not prevent bank runs. To be an effective guarantor, an insurer needed a substantial reserve and the ability to borrow against its future income stream to inject needed liquidity into a system in the early stages of a crisis to stem a full-blown bank run.[73]

In this regard, an insurer should not be confused with a lender of last resort. It was not the insurer's charge to rediscount at penalty rates or to manipulate reserves or interest rates. Those are tasks best left to a central bank. It was the insurer's responsibility, however, to step in after the first bank failure and resolve it quickly. Delays in winding up a bank magnified creditors' losses and encouraged distrust. Through timely reimbursements of note holders and depositors, the insurer could reestablish confidence in the system and the safety of the bank's liabilities. For a multitude of reasons, the Safety Fund was unable to do these things. The state lacked the political will to do them.

8

Free Banking

The Populist Revolt Takes Root in New York

Although the Safety Fund was not bankrupted until 1842, it was abandoned as New York's principal banking system in 1838 and replaced with free banking. Free banking may not have caused the fund's demise, but it surely hastened it. Because free banking represented an alternative regulatory formula that protected note holders without the implicit subsidization of high-risk banks, low-risk banks opted out of the Safety Fund System and reorganized as free banks. This adverse selection problem left the insurer with many high-risk and few low-risk clients. The insurer's contingent liabilities effectively increased, but raising its premiums would only have encouraged the exit of the lowest remaining risks, further worsening its contingent position.

Thus, the Safety Fund reigned for just nine years. Free banking enjoyed a much longer life, lasting from 1838 through 1865, perhaps longer if we consider that the national banking system established during the Civil War extended free banking to a national scale. Before jumping too far ahead in the story, however, it is notable that, though events would ultimately reveal the Safety Fund's weaknesses, free banking was put in place before the rash of failures between 1838 and 1842. By 1838, a few troubled fund banks had received assistance, but neither the fund nor note holders suffered a significant loss. Free banking, then, must have held some unique appeal. It turns out that contemporaries found free banking appealing on both economic and political grounds.

Economists and regulators typically justify bank liability insurance on the grounds that banks are unique institutions. They channel capital to borrowers with highly idiosyncratic investment opportunities, mostly small firms unable to borrow in arm's-length markets, and they operate the payments system, facilitating real transactions by lowering the costs of clearing financial assets and liabilities. Because banks hold opaque portfolios, they are particularly vulnerable to changing expectations about economic activity so that even small macroeconomic shocks can and do reverberate through financial markets.

Uninformed (or misinformed) bank creditors, notably depositors and note holders, sometimes lose confidence in bank-issued liabilities and rush to cash them in. When a large number of bank creditors simultaneously cash out, a banking panic ensues. Unable to distinguish between solvent and insolvent banks, uninformed creditors grow increasingly unwilling to accept or hold the liabilities of any bank, fearing that informed insiders are unloading lemons on uninformed outsiders. In the worst cases, trust between informed agents (mostly other banks) breaks down and bank-issued currency becomes less useful as a medium of exchange. The breakdown in the payments system increases the cost of transacting and real activity slows.

As discussed in the preceding chapter, one mechanism for mitigating the transmission of negative shocks to the financial sector and the payments system is bank liability insurance. A credible guarantee from an outside insurer insulates the payments system from exogenous macroeconomic shocks. Assured of the value of bank-supplied money, people continue to accept bank liabilities as payments and the system operates smoothly.

Contemporary commentators and legislators debated several alternatives to bank liability insurance, including the popular free banking. Free banking's distinguishing characteristic was bond-secured note issue. Banks were required to deposit 100 percent backing for their notes in either government bonds or mortgages on improved, unencumbered property. The collateral was taken in by New York's state comptroller, who held it in trust and distributed accrued interest to the banks as long as they remained in business.

In effect, free banking offered an alternative guaranty mechanism to the Safety Fund that eliminated the state's implicit contingent liability. By restricting note issues to the value of collateral security, the value of the notes was guaranteed, note holders were protected from bank failures, and the payments system was insulated from macroeconomic shocks.

When banks issued their own notes, the primary concern for everyone involved (i.e., banks, customers, regulators, and the public) was how to enforce the contractual redemption promise. As long as banks issued notes in quantities consistent with reasonable and conservative expectations about regular redemptions, the legal issue was simply one of contract enforcement. When bank issues exceeded any real expectation of redeeming them, the issue was fraud.[1] Robert King notes that most early American bank regulation grew out of the view that bank failure was inherently fraudulent.[2] Not surprisingly, most regulations aimed to eliminate fraud. To the extent that such regulations accomplished their objectives, they could have more far-reaching consequences. When combined with the intermediary function, even commonplace fraud in the banking industry could generate disastrous macroeconomic consequences. Milton Friedman, for example, writes that:

> the pervasive nature of the monetary nexus means that the failure of an issuer to fulfill his promises to pay has important effects on persons other than either the issuer or those who entered into a contract with him in the first instance or those who hold his promises. One failure triggers others, and . . . [these] third-party effects give special urgency to the prevention of fraud in respect of promises to pay a monetary commodity and the enforcement of such contracts.[3]

In other words, the failure of one fraudulent bank could become contagious, radiating out into a wave of failures. Even if contagion did not ensue, public concerns with the lemons problem may have sharply reduced the use of bank-supplied currency, which reduced the efficacy of the payments system, as well as the banks' intermediary abilities.

Note guaranty promised a way out. First, by requiring bankers to deposit assets equal to the value of note issues, opportunities for profitable fraud were eliminated. If a bank breached the specie redemption obligation, the comptroller closed the bank, sold the collateral bonds, and redeemed the remaining circulation from the proceeds. Second, free banking helped insulate the real economy from financial shocks. Bond collateral was designed to reduce uninformed note holder fears that informed insiders would dump low-value notes so that the payments system would not collapse if a few banks failed. Free banking was a potential solution to the intertwined problems of fraud and bank runs.

Despite much optimism about the workings of free banking and its ability to curb fraud, stem runs, and protect the payments system, it was unlikely to succeed. Protecting the payments system within an antebellum context meant maintaining confidence in the value of banknotes, which implied keeping banknotes convertible into specie on demand. Most discussions about free banking focused not on convertibility but on ultimate security. That is, it guaranteed repayment, but not necessarily quick repayment. Harry Miller argues that most contemporaries failed to make the intellectual distinction between continuous convertibility and ultimate security.[4] Some may not have made such distinctions, but many did. The original Free Banking Act of 1838 included a reserve requirement that was later repealed. The inclusion of a reserve requirement clause suggests that at least some contemporaries distinguished between the two, but they inexplicably abandoned convertibility safeguards without necessarily improving the security guarantees. As such, free banking was an unlikely protector of the payments system if reimbursing creditors of failed banks proceeded slowly, especially if a number of banks failed in rapid succession.

This chapter reviews the political and social forces that made free banking an attractive alternative to traditional chartering in New York. It then provides an assessment of free banking in terms of its effects on both the financial industry and the wider economy. Although free banking was no cure-all, it provided reasonable protection from note holder losses and made the industry more competitive, which enhanced consumer welfare. On the other hand, free banking generated an inelastic currency (relative to chartered bank issues) and a general underissue of notes. The latter effect may not have significantly lowered consumer welfare, however, because it may have prompted the development of deposit banking. The current chapter focuses on New York's free banking experience. Other states' experiences, particularly in the South and West, are discussed in chapter 10.

The Political and Social Origins of Free Banking

As noted in previous chapters, political and social attitudes toward banking differed from those held about most other industries. Banking stood as a notable exception to the general sense that entry into most industries and occupations should be free and unfettered.[5] British colonial law forbade the formation of most banks in the North American colonies; after the Revolution, New York, like all other states, adopted formal legislative chartering procedures. Charters granted bank incorporators the right to issue notes, discount promissory notes and bills of exchange, and accept deposits. Most charters also required a minimum contribution of owner equity and often restricted note issues to a multiple (often three) of paid-in capital.

Chartering implied monopoly or oligopoly, which made charters valuable. Recognizing this, legislatures typically demanded side payments in return for charters. Monopolies were valuable, however, only to the extent that they were protected from interlopers.[6] New York's Federalist legislature provided the necessary protection with an 1804 restraining act. The act explicitly forbade the formation of note-issuing unchartered banks.[7] The law was strengthened in 1813 and again in 1818. The latter act even forbade unchartered companies or individuals from taking in deposits. To make the law self-enforcing, there was a bounty of $500 for the conviction of unchartered bankers, and promissory notes discounted by such bankers were null and void.

Because banking monopolies were valuable, chartering gave rise to real and perceived abuses both at the legislative stage and in the subsequent distribution of stock. In the 1790s, only Federalist-dominated banks were chartered to support and promote Federalist commercial interests.[8] After the War of 1812, the Federalists were discredited for not having supported the Republican war. Yet, in New York, a rift developed within the Republican Party itself over the banking question. One faction, led by Martin Van Buren (a powerful legislative leader), advocated continued strict legislative control over banking. The opposition, led by DeWitt Clinton (internal improvement champion and one-time presidential candidate) advocated greater freedom. Van Buren's faction carried the day by forming an alliance with the state's bankers. Bank charters continued to be allocated on a highly political basis. Between 1815 and 1819, Van Buren emerged as a potent force, largely because the political distribution of bank charters welded "an alliance of factions into a disciplined party."[9]

The 1810s marked the emergence of a new attitude toward banks. Early American legislatures only incorporated firms that provided some sort of public service. As such, banks were held in much the same regard as churches, schools, bridges, turnpikes, libraries, and fire brigades.[10] In the early nineteenth century, specific public (governmental and nonprofit) organizations and private (for-profit) companies were incorporated because they were viewed as infrastructure—things that promoted the common welfare. Corporations were chartered to provide services that enhanced everyone's utility even if not everyone directly consumed the corporation's services. Economists say that such things generate large positive externalities and deserve governmental support and encouragement, even subsidies.

By the 1810s, the list of companies thought deserving of governmental support was growing (out of control, perhaps, but growing nonetheless). By this time, banks were known entities and profitable. Legislators exploited the public's willingness to invest in banks to accomplish other goals when it suited the legislature's purposes. In 1812, the legislature chartered the New York Manufacturing Company to produce iron and brass wire. Fearing that such a new business might not attract sufficient investment, the legislature granted it banking powers. Thus, the Phoenix Bank was born. The same methods were employed in 1824 to underwrite the New York Chemical Manufacturing Company and its subsidiary, Chemical Bank.

Dissatisfaction with Albany's bank allocation strategy emerged as early as the late 1810s. Van Buren's Regency was faced with a fundamental choice: it could continue to restrict banking to a limited number of chartered corporations, or it could throw the business open to any entrepreneur with the willingness to invest a substantial capital in the business. Van Buren opted for the former because his experience told him that a few close allies could be more easily managed and would better serve the party's interests.[11] Regency control was exerted in two ways. First, by maintaining the chartering process, the party guaranteed that new banks would promote republicanism. Second, the Republican Party maintained continued allegiance through its promise to restrict entry and protect the incumbents' entrenched position and profits.

Still, Van Buren was savvy enough to recognize that continued popular support demanded sating the public's desire to buy and own bank shares. In 1814, the legislature dropped its long-standing requirement that new banks hand over shares to the state treasury in return for charters. This freed shares for public sale. By 1820, the clamor for bank shares had grown and the state met it not by chartering more banks but by selling off most of its

$1 million in accumulated shares. The sale reduced New York's revenues from dividends from more than $300,000 in 1820 to less than $25,000 in 1821. The sale was successful in meeting the public cry for bank shares, however. Most people wanting to hold bank stocks purchased them.

In 1821, New York's rewritten constitution required a two-thirds majority for the passage of any corporate charter. One potential effect of this requirement was the further protection of existing banks' favored positions. By reducing the odds of obtaining a charter, incumbents were given greater pricing latitude than if they faced potential entry. The professed purpose of the two-thirds requirement was to eliminate, or at least mitigate, the bribery and scandals associated with a politicized chartering process. It was unsuccessful. Sponsors of the Chemical Bank engaged in extensive bribery, after which the flood gates of reform calls broke open.[12] Entrepreneurs argued against chartering and demanded that the business become more open. Agrarians, too, grew increasingly disenchanted with the politics of bank chartering. The two-thirds clause had little effect other than raising the ante in securing a charter.

A. C. Flagg, one-time comptroller of New York, recalled that after 1815, committees of merchants, bankers, and manufacturers from New York City made regular pilgrimages to Albany to impress on legislators the need to open banking to greater competition.[13] Several such delegations were led by former U.S. Secretary of the Treasury Albert Gallatin. Like all others, they were sent away, informed that repealing the restraining acts would spell disaster.

Despite repeated legislative rebuffs, pressure to repeal the acts grew. In 1824, the senate banking committee recommended that nonbank associations discount commercial paper and circulate notes of equal value. As long as they accepted only investment-grade paper, the issues were secured and the public was insulated from loss.[14] In 1825, a bill was introduced to repeal selected parts of the restraining acts so that unincorporated firms could receive deposits and issue notes, provided that they deposited some form of collateral security. Support for this idea came from rural areas in need of credit but not economically advanced enough to support a stand-alone bank. Public loss would be avoided through the deposit of the (unspecified) security and unlimited liability. The bill failed when the president of the state senate cast the deciding vote against it. The measure was reintroduced in the 1826 session and it, too, was narrowly defeated.

Debate over banking reform in New York turned on two issues. First, the restraining acts effectively prohibited all forms of private banking. The 1820s witnessed the coalescence of a strain of commercial thought that advocated unfettered freedom in all pursuits, banking included. Writing in 1826, Thomas Cooper argued that bank charters were unconstitutional because they deprived citizens of the basic right to pursue a calling and conferred "exclusive privileges on another class, upon motives and pretenses often fraudulent, seldom excusable, never justifiable."[15]

By the mid-1830s, Cooper's argument was a commonplace. Early American economists, like Henry Carey and Richard Hildreth, made similar claims.[16] By 1836, New York's own comptroller championed repeal in an anonymous article published in the Democrat-controlled *Albany Argus*.[17] By making private banks offices of discount and deposit only, the noteholding public would be protected from fraud and bank failure. It made no sense, Flagg argued, to restrain private capitalists willing to invest $50,000 or more in a banking enterprise. Fritz Redlich scorns contemporary appeals to natural rights and commercial liberty, writing that "in becoming the possession of the common man, the noble ideas of the Lockes, Humes, and Rousseaus had become debased and were passed about like small coins in the market."[18] But Redlich reads all such arguments skeptically. To him, the debate was manipulated by the rhetoric of debtors and speculators whose only hope of success was cheap credit.[19] Neither Carey nor Hildreth nor Gallatin were easy-money, pro-debtor men willing to align themselves with petty speculators. These were thoughtful men who believed that certain and specific natural liberties had been wrongfully infringed and that the reinstitution thereof would advance the general welfare.

The populist position eventually won out. In his annual message to the legislature in January 1837, Governor Marcy of New York called for a partial repeal of the private bank restraining acts. Noting the success of European private banking, Marcy argued that there was no reason the model could not be transferred to New York. He even anticipated the establishment of offices of European banking houses in the United States. The next day, a senate committee forwarded a bill allowing individuals and partners the right to operate banks of deposit and discount, without the right of note issue. To keep the two separate, directors and officers in incorporated banks were barred from taking any interest in a private bank. With only minor amendments, the bill passed the senate by a vote of 25-0 and the assembly by 96-0.[20]

The second issue on which the banking reform debate turned was how to secure additional note issues. Several early proposals suggested that new banks secure their issues with good securities without specifying exactly what that security might be. Both Miller and Redlich attribute free banking's ultimate adoption to the suggestions of John MacVickar, who combined Adam Smith's free-entry position with David Ricardo's proposal to protect bank creditors from loss by asking them to hold government securities equal to the value of their note liabilities.[21] In his 1827 pamphlet, MacVickar argued that a system of investing bank capital in government securities would guarantee the value of banknotes and protect against note holder losses. MacVickar may have been the first to publish the idea of bond collateral, but the notion was either already in the air or so attractive that it gained rapid acceptance. Within a year or two, related notions were put forth by Philadelphia economist Condy Raguet; Connecticut banker Isaac Bronson; English Ricardian John Ramsey McCulloch; Joshua Forman, who had included a bond-collateral clause in his original 1828 Safety Fund proposal and who may have been influenced in this regard by James Alexander Hamilton, Forman's friend and advisor to Van Buren; and Eleazor Lord, founder and president of the Manhattan Fire Insurance Company.[22] Although their plans differed in the details, they all began from the premise that banking could be freed from the chartering process if banknotes were secured by something more concrete than the too-easily breached specie redemption obligation.

These advocates of free banking were all about the same age, so their opinions probably grew out of common experiences and influences. Two elements of that shared experience were the corruption involved in chartering and the bank war. Defeat of the Second Bank's rechartering petition implied an influx of new banks because the state banking sector needed to expand to meet credit needs. Long experience with graft and corruption did not sit well with Jacksonian populists. Free banking offered a purer, more egalitarian alternative.

Free banking was also an unanticipated outcome of the bank war. Jacksonians whipped up a frenzy against not only the Second Bank, but also the preferences given to all corporations, a powerful sentiment that eventually spun out of the Democrats' control. Restraining acts protected corporations from competition, which flew in the face of Jacksonian ideals. Before 1804, banking functions could be assumed by anyone. Chartered and private banks alike retained the common law privilege to discount promissory notes and bills of exchange, to take in deposits, and even to issue evidences of debt. A fundamental difference, of course, was that incorporated banks operated with limited liability whereas private bankers assumed unlimited liability. To the extent that the state wished to encourage banking, it could offer corporate limited liability. The 1804 law, however, had superseded the individual's right to engage in a legitimate business. It was the Democrats' aim to reestablish it.

To the Equal Rights Party, often called Loco-Focos (to whom free banking is often mistakenly attributed), the issue was not so clear-cut.[23] Although the Loco-Focos opposed the privilege and corruption associated with corporate banking, repeal of the restraining laws represented a dilemma. If they supported the restraints, they aligned themselves with favoritism and elitism. If they opposed the restraints, they stood with liberal Democrats who wanted banking thrown open to all. Equal Righters wanted neither. They took the antimonopoly, antipaper rhetoric of the bank war literally and championed the elimination of all banks—chartered, free, private, and otherwise. The existing New York statute most attuned to the Equal Righters' stance was the state constitutional requirement that every act creating, altering, or rechartering a corporation pass with a two-thirds majority. The law mostly affected banks and, because two-thirds majorities were rare, strict observance of this constitutional requirement would gradually eliminate banks. Few new banks would be chartered and most existing banks would pass away—like the Second Bank—when their recharter bids failed. To enemies of corporate privilege, this was how it should be—corporations were antithetical to the common law and their influence should be diminished to the fullest extent possible. To Equal Righters, the fact that the restraining laws insulated incumbent banks from competition was disagreeable, but it represented the lesser of two evils—better to have a few and shrinking number of privileged banks than a state overrun with paper-issuing private banks. Thus, free banking actually represented the least preferred outcome for the Loco-Focos.

A narrow, newly elected Whig majority quickly rejected the Regency's Safety Fund mutual insurance model for one involving collateral security. Because the bill's supporters could not garner a two-thirds majority, the resulting banks could not be called corporations, so they were labeled "associations." To reinforce the fine distinction, the law designated their issues "circulating notes" rather than "banknotes." In fact, banks that relinquished their charters to reorganize as free banks reported both types in their quarterly reports until they fully redeemed all banknotes authorized by and issued under the terms of their Safety Fund charters. Also reinforcing the distinction was the requirement that suits brought by or against them be instituted in the name of the association's president rather than the association. Although they may not have been de jure corporations, free banks were de facto corporations; this finding was appealed and reversed several times between 1838 and 1864, but it was one that accorded with any common sense notion of a corporation.[24] They had perpetual lives independent of their owners, had no upper limit on capitalization, had a $100,000 minimum capitalization, and could be owned by one or more persons. To insulate them from the politics surrounding the existing banks, the state's bank commissioners were given no supervisory authority over the free banks.

Thus, New York's free banking experiment was born. It was a tree with four distinct taproots. First, the rise of a radical free-market or laissez-faire populism in the 1830s. Second, the antiprivilege rhetoric stirred up by the Jacksonians' attack on Biddle's bank that bloomed into a deeper and broader rhetoric against all forms of corporate privilege. Third, a general demand for more credit among people who found it uneconomical to obtain it from existing sources. These may have been the speculators and other poor credit risks highlighted in traditional tales, but they were also Whigs, political independents, and others shut out from credit at historically Republican banks. Fourth, and not least (but the one most often ignored in traditional assessments), the general belief that banking and financial deepening promoted, or at least supported, economic growth. To the extent that this was the case, as it almost certainly was, anything that promoted additional intermediation improved aggregate economic welfare.

Free Banking in Practice

As previously noted, free banking's defining features were free entry and collateralized note issue. These were fine generalizations in the abstract, but making them operational demanded delineations and delimitations. Free entry did not imply that anyone could start a bank, despite Bray Hammond's oft-quoted assertion that it became nearly as easy to become a banker as a bricklayer.[25] The 1838 act imposed a $100,000 minimum capital requirement, which was later reduced to $50,000, for free bank proprietorships called "individual" banks. Few bricklayers could raise these sums alone when average annual incomes rarely exceeded $700 to $1,000.

Free bankers were required to register with the state comptroller and provide an "association" name, a list of officers, and maximum life. In regard to the last, optimism ran high. All but four of the first fifty applicants requested a charter life of at least 100 years. Fourteen sought a life of 400 years; two, 1,000 years; and one, 4,050 years.[26] In addition, they were required to surrender security to the comptroller, who had the authority to declare the bank closed, sell the collateral security, and advertise for the redemption of all remaining circulation if the bank refused to redeem even a single banknote.

New York's free banks came in two types. The first secured its notes with government bonds and its circulating notes (which were printed by the state comptroller's office, which also retained possession of the engraved plates) carried the inscription "Secured by Public Stocks." The second type secured its notes with a combination of government bonds and real estate mortgages. Banks selecting the second option tendered mortgages on improved, unencumbered real estate, bearing at least 6 percent interest and worth less than one-half the value of the property exclusive of any structures. Banks could guarantee a maximum of one-half of their note issues with mortgages, and these banks' notes carried the inscription "Secured by Public Stocks and Real Estate." There was no mechanism by which a bank was required to proffer additional security if the market value of collateral bonds or mortgages fell below the market value of the bank's circulating notes.[27]

In December 1841, 43 free banks with a total capital in excess of $10.7 million had surrendered about $2.3 million in mortgages and $4.5 million in government bonds.[28] It was not mandatory that all of a bank's paid-in capital be invested in security, just a fraction equal to the value of circulating notes. By December 1849, there were 111 operating free banks with $16.8 million in paid-in capital that secured their notes with $10.6 million in government debt and just $1.9 million in mortgages.[29] In December 1859, 274 free banks with an aggregate paid-in capital of $100.6 million secured their note issues with $26.5 million in bonds and $7.6 million in mortgages.[30]

Changes in the relative proportion of bonds and mortgages were driven in part by changes in the relative prices of bonds and mortgages. Price data for bonds are scarce, however, and mortgages prices are altogether unrecoverable short of compiling county-level records. Figure 8.1 plots the percentage of bonds relative to total security held by New York banks at selected call dates between 1843 and 1859. It also plots the price of a representative collateral bond, the U.S. 6 percent bond that matured in 1862. For the most part, the use of bonds as collateral and bond prices moved in opposite directions. Falling bond prices in the mid-1840s encouraged banks to guarantee a greater percentage of their circulating notes with government bonds. Between 1847 and 1853, the situation reversed, with rising bond prices associated with declining percentages of bond collateral. The mid-1850s saw a break in the negative relationship, but they moved in opposite directions again in the closing years of the decade.

Bond prices alone, do not explain all aspects of the banks' bond-mortgage mix. There were sharp differences in the relative use of mortgages between city and country banks and between the proprietorship or "individual" banks and joint-stock or "association" banks. In December 1852, for example, government bonds accounted for 99.5 percent of the note collateral tendered by 33 New York City and Brooklyn free banks, 78.7 percent of the collateral used by individual banks, and 68.1 percent of the collateral used by country joint-stock banks.[31] Only one New York City bank proffered mortgage collateral to the state comptroller, and it gave only $26,000 in

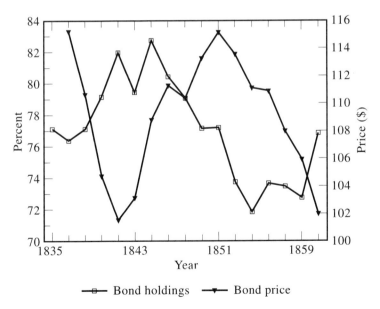

Figure 8.1 Bond Holdings as a Percentage of Note Collateral and Bond Prices. Sources: New York, *Assembly, Documents* (1848–1861).

mortgages. Among country banks, 25 individual banks (42.4 percent) used only bond security, whereas only 16 joint-stock banks (18.8 percent) relied solely on bonds.

These marked differences may have been driven by the city banks' easier access to bond markets, but that seems unlikely given the nature of inter-bank relationships and the ubiquity of brokerage firms ready to arbitrage on any sort of profitable financial transaction. If modern real estate markets provide any clues, it may have been that city property mortgages were expensive relative to country mortgages, so city banks found bonds more economic. On the other hand, the greater scale of city banking ($1 million paid-in capital, on average) compared to country banking ($131,000) and the different types of lending may have militated against mortgage security among city bankers. Moreover, local country bank customers were likely to know the type of property a bank used as collateral, thereby relieving a transparency and information asymmetry problem that city banks could not so easily resolve. In fact, several New York City banks held mortgages but did not use them as collateral security. In December 1859, the American Exchange Bank of New York held $263,377 in mortgages but secured its note issues with $459,000 in New York 6 percent bonds, Illinois 6 percents, and U.S. 5 percent. Similarly, the Metropolitan Bank held $51,000 in mortgages but its issues were secured by $300,000 in New York 5 percent and 6 percent.[32]

Individually owned free banks remain the curious case. Although most were country banks typically located in small towns, mortgages accounted for a considerably smaller share of their collateral security than that used by joint-stock associations. Individual banks, like country joint-stock banks, should have been capable of mitigating a potential information asymmetry problem, but they apparently did not uncover equally reliable mechanisms. Given the smaller capitalization of these proprietorship banks, the lack of internal checks, and more sophisticated governance structures, the public may have been wary of holding notes of individual banks until they established a reputation. It is notable in this regard that the annual reports of the superintendent of banks published the names of each individual banker, his residence, the names and residences of any silent partners, and sometimes the names of their principal New York City correspondents. No similar information was regularly published for joint-stock banks. In publishing this information, the superintendent's office, founded in 1851, may have partly allayed concerns with the quality of these banks' notes, allowing them access to lower-cost collateral. In the late 1840s, individual banks typically collateralized 90 percent or more of their circulating notes with bonds. After 1851, this proportion steadily declined so that by 1857, individual banks tendered 60 percent or less of their collateral security in government bonds.

As previously noted, the Free Banking Act insulated the free banks from Regency politics by giving oversight responsibilities to the state comptroller instead of the Safety Fund bank commissioners. His office held the collateral bonds, had plates engraved, collected and published unaudited quarterly balance sheets, collected and distributed coupon payments on collateral bonds and interest on mortgages, and supervised the liquidation of closed banks. By 1851, these tasks overwhelmed the comptroller and the responsibilities were transferred to the newly established superintendent of banks.

How did free banking work in practice? Suppose a number of partners came together and formed the Thistle Bank. With their pooled funds, they purchased $75,000 in government bonds and $25,000 in mortgages on real property. These were handed over to the comptroller, who printed $100,000 in circulating notes and gave them to the partners. With the proceeds, they then went out and purchased $20,000 in specie held as reserves supporting the note issue and extended $80,000 in loans. The Thistle Bank's (highly stylized) balance sheet then took the following form:

Thistle Bank Balance Sheet #1

Assets		Liabilities	
Mortgages	$25,000	Notes	$100,000
Bonds	75,000		
Specie	20,000		
Loans	80,000	Equity	100,000
Totals	$200,000		$200,000

The balance sheet shows why free banking was so popular. Free banks were highly leveraged organizations. Investors turned $100,000 in earning assets (the equity capital) into about $180,000 in earning assets. Recall that free banks, as long as they met their redemption calls and remained in business, received the coupon payments on the bonds they handed over to the comptroller, as well as the accrued interest on any mortgages. The current yield on bonds averaged about 5.0 to 5.5 percent, depending on the coupon, the issuer, and the maturity; most mortgages paid the legal maximum of 7 percent, yielding a weighted average return (assuming the proportions given in the balance sheet) of about 5.3 percent. Moreover, the bank earned up to the legal maximum of 7.0 percent on the loan portfolio. Without the free banking mechanism, the investors could have invested their $100,000 and earned about $5,300 annually (exclusive of capital gains and losses). Free banking made it possible to invest the same $100,000 and earn as much as $10,900. Not every free bank did this well, of course, but it was not uncommon for them to pay 8 percent dividends annually and still add to their retained earnings account.

The free bank could do better yet if it developed a substantial deposit business due to a sufficient gap between loan yields (risk adjusted) and deposit rates. Suppose the Thistle Bank attracted $20,000 in deposits by promising an average annual 2 percent return on deposit balances. The balance sheet produced below reflects the Thistle's new position if it held a 20 percent reserve against deposit balances and circulating notes. The Thistle Bank added $4,000 to its specie reserves and loaned $16,000 at up to the 7 percent legal limit. If everything else remained unchanged, the bank became more leveraged and, in doing so, increased its revenues from $10,900 to $11,700. The result was an effective yield on investment for the bank's shareholders of 11.7 percent, as opposed to the 5.5 percent or so that could have been earned by simply holding government securities or the 7 percent maximum paid by mortgages or short-term commercial paper. Leverage was profitable and free banking allowed greater opportunities to exploit it.

Thistle Bank Balance Sheet #2

Assets		Liabilities	
Mortgages	$25,000	Notes	$100,000
Bonds	75,000	Deposits	20,000
Specie	24,000		
Loans	96,000	Equity	100,000
Totals	$220,000		$220,000

Though profitable, leverage did not come without costs. Highly leveraged institutions failed, especially those that tried to operate on thin specie margins or those that overextended themselves and in the process accumulated excessively risky portfolios. Hammond reports that of the first 80 free banks in New York, fewer than 60 survived the first three years.[33] While a 25 percent failure rate was just cause for concern, the timing of free banking was unfortunate in that the law passed as the economy was slipping into a deep recession.

High failure rates also prompted changes in the law. Recall that the principal provisions of the original 1838 act were: (1) $100,000 minimum capital, (2) a 12.5 percent required specie reserve against note issues, (3) notes redeemable on demand, (4) notes secured by eligible state bonds and New York mortgages on improved, unencumbered real estate; and (5) shareholders were given corporate or limited liability.

An amending act in 1840 changed several features of the original act. It eliminated the 12.5 percent reserve requirement. It also eliminated the eligibility of state bonds other than New York's. More important, however, was the change in the rate at which the state accepted collateral bonds. Under the original act, any bond declared acceptable by the comptroller was accepted as the equivalent of a 5 percent bond; that is, a 6 percent bond was accepted for collateral at five-sixths of its value. In addition, the original act provided that no bond would be accepted above par value. In 1840, this condition was changed so that bonds selling below par were accepted at the lesser of par or market value.[34]

The last significant amendments to the free banking law were incorporated into New York's 1846 constitution. One provision extended stockholder liability (effective 1 January 1850) so that shareholders were doubly liable. This meant that shareholders in a failed bank stood liable up to the amount of their initial investment. Someone holding $5,000 in shares of a failed bank lost the $5,000, plus his property could be attached to an equal amount to indemnify note holders and other creditors. In a misguided effort to protect the payments system, the state constitution also made note holders preferred creditors by giving them first lien on a failed bank's assets. While this protected note holders from ultimate loss, giving them preferred status gave depositors subordinated claims, making them more likely to initiate a run in the face of a negative shock to bank portfolios. The panic of 1857, in fact, was a depositor panic, not a note holder panic.

Although New York's Free Banking Act was imperfect in the sense that all contracts are imperfect, it served New York well in many regards (as discussed below). Many banks were short lived and closed while owing creditors, but the law generated more successes than failures. Hammond noted that contemporary observers were often of two minds about free banking. At one time, Thomas Wren Ward of Boston wrote that the law promoted fraud and speculation and that there was little "danger from the establishment of *good* banks under" it.[35] Yet, when the Bank of Commerce of New York City was organizing some time later, Ward became an enthusiastic supporter. In correspondence with the Baring Bank in England, Ward extolled the integrity of the bank's promoters, saying that it would be under the "management of able and experienced and prudent men" who would run it "upon old fashioned principles."[36] He advised the Barings to take up $100,000 of the bank's stock and become its London correspondent. Ward himself intended to take up as much as $40,000 of its stock on his own account.

The following sections discuss several aspects of free banking, assessing its successes and its shortcomings. In doing so, we will see why some contemporaries ardently supported free banking and why some doubters, like Ward, eventually embraced it.

Issues in Free Banking

Since Hugh Rockoff's initial reexamination of free banking, several writers have offered new and revisionist interpretations of the system's successes and shortcomings. Nearly every aspect of the system, from entry and exit to profitability to the elasticity of note issue, has come under the scrutiny of financial historians. This section synthesizes many of the existing findings and offers a few novel interpretations.

Entry and the Allocation of Bank Capital

If free banking is judged solely on the grounds of encouraging additional banking, the law was an unquestioned success. Entry was thrown open to all those willing to make the minimum capital investment, purchase the requisite collateral, and lodge it with the comptroller. Within 20 months of the Free Banking Act's passage, the comptroller was notified of 134 bank formations. Not all of these schemes succeeded in attracting enough capital to organize, but the number of banks doubled between 1838 and 1841. Fifty banks opened within a few months, and 120 opened within two years.[37]

Standard interpretations focus on chartering requirements as barriers to entry. Once the chartering requirement was eliminated, new banks flooded in and provided long-demanded banking services to previously unserved and underserved sectors and regions. Although this argument certainly has some merit, freedom of entry alone does not explain the flood tide of joint-stock bank formation in the post-1838, and especially the post-1850, period. Recall that New York's assembly repealed the 1815 private banking restraining laws in 1837, yet there was not a similarly notable influx of private banking in New York. Private banks, with no mandated minimum capital, bond-collateral, or reserve requirement, were formed, but not in such large numbers as to attract the attention of contemporaries or historians. Yet, bank associations, with all of these restrictions and more, were formed in large numbers.

What was the special attraction of joint-stock banking? The note issue privilege was part of it, at least until deposit banking became a viable alternative. But Jack Carr and G. Frank Mathewson argue that the unlimited liability inherent in private banking created entry barriers.[38] They argue that anything other than strictly limited liability creates barriers to entry. In effect, unlimited liability has a detrimental effect on the price of shares (partnership or joint-stock) of unlimited liability relative to limited liability firms. A mandated and invariant risk-sharing arrangement may have deviated from that which freely contracting parties may voluntarily arrive at, which implied a suboptimal number of small private banks. Where free banking associations could freely contract for additional liability, private bankers could not contract away unlimited liability. Double liability imposed in 1846 may have made free banking less-attractive, but Carr and Mathewson argue that it is not immediately clear that double liability represented a significantly less efficient risk-sharing arrangement than single liability. One avenue for future research would be to investigate differences in the share prices of firms with different liability arrangements to see if one type of share (single, double, or unlimited) commanded a premium.

Kenneth Ng recently challenged the long-held view that free banking laws represented a significant break from chartering systems by throwing banking open to entry.[39] He notes that the enactment of free banking laws in several states, including Massachusetts, Vermont, Georgia, Alabama, and

Florida, resulted in few entrants. Furthermore, he argues that aggregate bank assets in free banking states did not grow significantly faster, on average, than aggregate bank assets in traditional chartering states. Ng provides two possible interpretations. First, free banking exchanged one set of effective entry barriers under chartered banking for a different set of entry barriers under free banking. Second, interstate competition to retain or attract financial capital induced traditional chartering states to liberalize their chartering systems so that banking grew at similar rates independent of chartering procedures.

The postbellum dual banking system (i.e., national and state banks operating side by side) created regulatory competition to attract charters. Similar interstate competition may have occurred in antebellum America. It is easy to envision Rhode Island liberally offering charters to bankers who were refused charters in other New England states. This may explain the deep monetization of Rhode Island's economy, with more than $20 in per capita bank money in 1840 compared to less than $10 in Connecticut and New York and less than $5 in Maine, New Hampshire, and Vermont.[40] Rhode Island may have been a corporate haven in the antebellum period, much as Delaware is in the modern era. Furthermore, Richard Sylla argues that chartered banking in New England, especially Massachusetts and Rhode Island, became de facto free banking with the growing liberalization of chartering in those states.[41]

Ng's provocative and revisionist conclusions have not gone unchallenged. Andrew Economopoulos and Heather O'Neill disaggregated the free banking series and tested for differences in bank capital accumulation in free and chartering states. They developed a model in which changes in actual bank capital respond elastically, but less than perfectly, to changes in desired bank capital. In testing the model, they find that shortfalls of actual to desired bank capital were reduced by about 50 percent in one year in free banking states. By comparison, shortfalls in chartering states were reduced by the same amount only after about five years.[42] Moreover, there seems to have been a short-run liberalization in chartering states in response to free banking laws, but such liberal chartering policies were not sustained throughout the decade of the 1850s. Economopoulos and O'Neill conclude that some states responded by passing free banking acts of their own, some states responded by allowing increased capitalization of existing banks, and still others responded by maintaining average capitalization but allowing more banks. Such interstate responses meant that Ng was unable to isolate notably larger increases in entry in free banking states relative to chartering states because the chartering activities of non–free banking states were endogenous to changes in the law in free banking states.

Using a standard model of entry taken from the modern industrial organization literature, I also challenge Ng's interpretation. I show that conservative chartering systems significantly reduced entry relative to liberal chartering and free banking states.[43] After controlling for such things as average market profitability, market growth, financial depth, and the business cycle, entry into Pennsylvania and Baltimore (two of the more conservative chartering states) was significantly lower than entry into Rhode Island (the most liberal chartering state). Entry into New York banking, on the other hand, was not significantly different from that into Rhode Island. Such results also call into question Ng's comparison of entry into chartering and free banking states because chartering states adopted different policy stances. Some chartering states mimicked free banking states by denying few, if any, charter applications; others, like Pennsylvania, went through extended periods when nearly every bank charter was rejected.

A fundamental issue concerning free banking, and one related to entry, is whether and to what extent it improved the allocation of bank capital. There is no unequivocal method of determining whether one allocation is more efficient than another, however. One way is simply to look at the geographic distribution of banks under chartered and free banking. If free banking was more responsive to credit demands, the distribution of free banks may have been substantially different from that of chartered banks that were thought to be responsive as much to political as to financial demands. Figure 8.2 presents a type of Lorenz Curve that shows that the geographic distribution of free banks was not markedly different from the

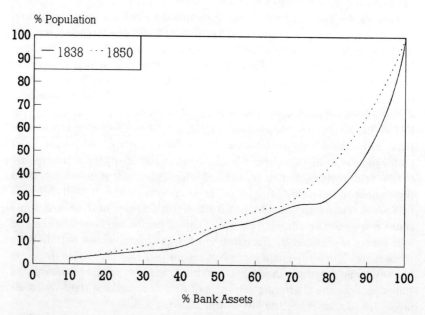

Figure 8.2 Lorenz Curves for Bank Assets and Population in New York in 1838 and 1850. Sources: U.S. Census Office, *Compendium*; New York, *Assembly Doc. No. 71* (1838); *Albany Argus*, 25 Nov. 1850.

distribution of chartered banks in New York. Low-population counties attracted small proportions of the state's banking capital. Urban and commercial centers, such as New York City and Albany, attracted the lion's share of the state's banks whether they were allocated through a political chartering process or by market forces. Although chartering may have been politically motivated, it did not imply an obviously inefficient allocation of bank capital. Because it is based on existing bank assets, however, figure 8.2 does not capture differences in the size of the banking sector or its relative competitiveness under the two regimes. Just because most bank assets were located in well-populated commercial centers does not imply that an appropriate number of banks existed.

A second approach to determine whether free banking improved the allocation of bank capital, and one more in tune with economic reasoning, is to compare rates of return to bank capital. Economic theory, indeed, suggests that rates of return are good indicators of efficient allocation as long as there is no considerable divergence between private and social returns. Rockoff finds evidence of lower bank profits in New York City banks relative to those in Philadelphia and other cities in chartering states in the early 1850s.[44] There is little evidence, and that which exists is equivocal, about free banking's effects on country bank profits. In 1832, New York banks paid dividends (a proxy for profitability) equal to 7.3 percent of paid-in capital, which exceeded dividend rates paid by Massachusetts banks (5.8 percent) and Virginia's banks (5.5 percent) but were about the same as Pennsylvania's (7.4 percent).[45] In 1842, by which time 46 free banks were operating in New York, the average dividend yield for New York banks had fallen to 6.6 percent. While this represents a reduction from the 7.3 percent yield distributed a decade earlier, it still exceeded dividend payouts in Virginia (4.3 percent) and Pennsylvania (5.4 percent).[46]

More evidence is needed before satisfactory conclusions about free banking's effects on bank profitability can be drawn. Yet, New York banks' relatively high dividend yields in the early 1840s may have signified desirable financial resilience rather than undesirable market power. In 1842, the U.S. economy was experiencing the early stages of recovery from the depression years, so the ability of New York banks to pay dividends may have been a sign of relative stability. Resolving the issue of free banking's effects on bank profitability still demands additional research, but Rockoff's original interpretation that free banking increased competitiveness and reduced profits still seems warranted.

The driving force behind the lower bank profits in New York was free banking and its encouragement of actual and potential entry. In a study of six major antebellum banking markets, Bodenhorn finds that lagged entry and free banking increased bank mobility, measured as year-to-year changes in firm rank.[47] The attractiveness of this formulation is that it likely captures the effects of potential entry—a critical element in standard models of firm behavior that Ng's, as well as Economopoulos and O'Neill's formulations fail to capture. Passage of free banking laws may have increased competitive behavior, independent of actual entry, by increasing the number of potential entrants and the probability of entry for a given excess of bank profits over economic returns offered in alternative employments.

The available evidence, then, is generally consistent with the economist's prior expectation that lifting entry restrictions encourages entry, reduces profits, and stimulates competition between incumbent firms, as well as actual and potential entrants. In this regard, free banking achieved at least some of what its advocates desired. By relieving potential bankers of the onus of navigating sometimes treacherous political waters, free banking created entrepreneurial opportunities for financiers and eliminated monopoly or oligopoly rents. As Sylla demonstrated for a different case, free bank entry could be and probably was associated with monopolistic or imperfect, rather than perfect, competition. While firm conclusions about the relative efficiencies between different market structures demand calculations of the areas of Harberger triangles, there is a general sense that imperfectly competitive structures result in smaller reductions in consumer welfare than oligopolistic or monopolistic markets.

Wildcatting

One issue that arises during discussions of free banking is whether the wrong type of entry took place. That is, did free banking encourage fraud and destabilizing arbitrage on the public's asymmetric information about bank portfolios? In contemporary usage, such fraud or arbitrage was associated with "wildcat" banks. Such banks earned this moniker because they were ostensibly located in remote locations where wildcats, instead of note holders seeking redemption, predominated.

Despite the multitude of tales of wildcat banks, there is no generally agreed-on definition of a wildcat. Traditional histories characterized them as fraudulent banks located in out-of-the-way places. Rockoff does not offer a definition in the strict sense but argues that they were short-lived institutions that arbitraged on differences between par and market values of their collateral security (to be explained shortly). Arthur Rolnick and Warren Weber argue that a wildcat bank needed to meet all or most of the following five conditions: (1) it remained in business for only a few months; (2) it closed imposing losses on its note holders; (3) it arbitraged on a substantial difference between the par and market values of collateral bonds; (4) it issued more notes than it could ever expect to redeem; and (5) it was located in a remote location.[48]

Suppose that the price of a bond declared eligible as collateral depreciated so that a banker obtained $100,000 in circulating notes for an investment of $85,000 in bonds with a par (or face) value of $100,000. In such cases, a wildcat banker could readily exploit an arbitrage opportunity. In return for an $85,000 expenditure, the banker received $100,000 in notes that represented general purchasing power. An obvious profit opportunity existed. The banker purchased $100,000 in assets and absconded with the $15,000 difference.

Bankers exploiting this par-market differential had to be selective in their asset choice, however. As Rolnick and Weber correctly note, bankruptcy courts took possession of a closed bank's assets to satisfy the creditors' demands. Successfully managing the arbitrage thus demanded that the banker neither extend loans to the general public nor purchase relatively immobile assets, such as land, livestock, and so forth. Rolnick and Weber suggest that one easy path to success was to make bad loans to relatives and, presumably, these relatives would transfer some of the wealth back to the banker.[49] While this plan might ultimately prove successful, court-appointed liquidators could be determined and unrelenting and could harass a bank's delinquent debtors for years. A simpler way to perpetrate the fraud was for the banker to simply step back into the financial market and purchase $100,000 in corporate equities or government bonds, readily transferable and easily concealed assets, and slip away with enough of a head start to make it impracticable for bank creditors and court officers to track him down.

How much wildcatting actually took place? Traditional interpretations argue that it was common, but they tend to rely on anecdotes and indirect evidence to support their hypotheses. Redlich and Hammond believe it occurred but do not offer details. Redlich argues that New York escaped the worst consequences of it when the legislature rejected a clause in the original legislative bill that would have allowed the acceptance of U.S. and New York securities at 90 percent of their market value.[50] But, in his view, mortgage collateral very nearly caused what market valuation avoided.

Rolnick and Weber are considerably more optimistic about free banking's record. According to their estimates, less than 4 percent of New York banks qualified as wildcats in that they closed within a few months of opening and imposed losses on note holders. The actual number may be lower yet because the combination of rapid failure and an inability to redeem all notes could have followed from poor management that was not overtly fraudulent. Rockoff, too, offers a generally sanguine interpretation. As he notes, framers of free banking laws walked a tightrope. If they allowed a large-enough gap between the market price of bonds and the price at which the banking authorities accepted them as collateral, they risked wildcat banking. If they narrowed the gap somewhat, they could produce a stable free banking system. But if they accepted bonds at rates considerably below the current market price, free banking may have proved abortive.[51]

Recent research by Gary Gorton utilizes information on the prices of banknotes to assess the likelihood and extent of wildcat banking. If banknote markets were efficient, in the sense that participants consistently, accurately, and rationally priced notes, wildcat bankers would have been

quickly exposed and closed before they inflicted much harm on note holders. Estimating a variant of the well-known Black-Scholes option pricing
model, Gorton shows that free banking was not associated with greater risks,
defined as higher volatility of prices of notes.[52] Gorton argues that this finding supports claims that wildcat banking was uncommon. What made it
relatively uncommon, in part, was the fact that market participants disciplined banks by pricing factors that affected banknote risk and by continually exercising the contractual redemption guarantee. Banks that took excessive risks saw the price of their notes fall, all the way to zero in the limit.
Moreover, the redemption clause allowed note holders to run banks that
held excessively risky portfolios.

Wildcatting, although not unheard of, was probably rare. Less than 5
percent of free bank failures in New York met two parts of Rolnick and
Weber's definition of a wildcat: a very short life and an inability to redeem
all of its notes at par. If it were possible to gather information about the
other three elements of their definition for these banks, we would undoubtedly discover that very few were true wildcats. Because most of these potential wildcats failed in the first three years of free banking in New York,
during one of the most severe economic downturns of the nineteenth
century, it is likely that some of them were simply unfortunate enough to
enter at the wrong time. Business success is rarely serendipitous—it usually
results from insight, foresight, and hard work—but business failure sometimes is.

Bank Failures and Consumer Losses

If wildcatting was neither widespread nor the principal cause of free bank
failures, what was? And how large were the losses borne by creditors of
failed free banks?

With the possible exception of a handful of modern free banking advocates, most economists accept the proposition that bank failures involve
potentially sizable externalities. If markets were complete and information
perfect and symmetric, the failure of one or more banks would be of little
consequence. Failed banks would be subject to the same bankruptcy laws
and procedures as any other business. The banks' remaining assets would
be turned over to a court-appointed trustee responsible for dividing them
among the creditors while respecting voluntarily contracted-for priorities
and subordinations. Liquidators would determine the creditors' pro rata
shares, and that would be that.

For most nonfinancial businesses, liquidation procedures may not be
quite that simple, but they need not have economy-wide ramifications either. Bank failures, of course, may be very different. If markets were complete and information symmetric, there would be no need for banks in the
first place. Recall, banks arise because there are investors who cannot sell
private securities in arm's-length markets. Moreover, bank failures appear

after substantial, and usually unexpected, downward revaluations of bank portfolios. Such revaluations typically arise because of fresh doubts cast on the solvency of a particular class of borrower, which are, therefore, transferred onto a particular class of bank.[53]

Modern information-based theories of financial intermediation have produced banking panics in models in which the observation of some intrinsically irrelevant event (sometimes called a sunspot) generates an unwarranted run, or in which the observation of a shock to some macroeconomic variable correlated with the value of bank portfolios triggers a panic because depositors have imperfect and asymmetric information about specific bank portfolios.[54] Rolnick and Weber label the first type "extrinsic uncertainty" models. In these models, people randomly and inexplicably change their preferences for bank-supplied currency.[55] In an antebellum context, extrinsic uncertainty panics occurred when people decided to switch from banknotes (or deposits) to specie, which led to reserve drains and the eventual closing of many banks, even some with positive net worth. Because banks operate with fractional reserves, some note holders suffered losses, the expectation of which leads to contagious runs and widespread bank failures.

The alternative explanation of bank failures is the related notion of "intrinsic uncertainty." Intrinsic uncertainty models depend on a shock that affects bank creditors with asymmetric information. Under intrinsic uncertainty explanations, a local macroeconomic shock causes the value of some banks' assets to fall below the market value of its liabilities (i.e., its net worth becomes negative). Informed creditors cash out. Under full information, withdrawals are not indiscriminant. Creditors will force the closure of insolvent banks. Without full information, however, ill-informed creditors observe the closing of insolvent institutions and, being unable to discriminate between solvent and insolvent banks, engage in systematic and indiscriminant withdrawals. Such "runs" cause the closing of good and bad banks and quickly spread outside the locality of the shock.

A much-discussed recent example of intrinsic uncertainty is the less developed country (LDC), or Mexican crisis, of the 1980s. All banks with LDC exposure experienced downward revaluations, even though some were but little exposed while others had substantial exposure. Charles Goodhart argues that widespread runs were avoided because a strong central bank made a credible commitment to maintain liquidity and a deposit insurer stood ready to protect the payments system.[56] In the antebellum era, there was no central bank (in the modern sense of the term) and we have seen that bank insurance, when it existed at all, was barely credible. Thus, it is not surprising that small shocks, such as the Bank of England raising its discount rate, abnormally large price shocks, or the failure of one or two notable trading firms led to rapid disintermediation, bank failures, and suspension of specie payments.

Before we can determine whether New York's free bank failures resulted from extrinsic or intrinsic uncertainties, we first need some evidence on the time pattern of bank failures. Good data are unavailable for the 1838 to 1841 period, but it is known that three banks failed in early 1840, and another twelve banks failed between November 1840 and September 1841.[57] Most of these closings imposed significant losses on note holders and other creditors. In 1842, the first year for which data become available, six banks failed with loss rates of 4 percent of outstanding notes. After 1842, bank failures became rare and loss rates were small. The loss rate was to 0.2 percent in 1844 and rose to 0.4 percent during the mild recession of 1848; thereafter, it never exceeded 0.1 percent. Gerald Dwyer notes that a loss rate of less than 0.1 percent due to bank failure was probably less than the losses arising from lost and inadvertently destroyed notes.[58]

King attributes bank failures to the recession of 1837–1842 and note holder losses to the details of the bond-collateral requirement.[59] The original 1838 act allowed banks to tender bonds from any state. The economic downturn drove several states into arrears on their debts; others repudiated their debts altogether. Such actions drove the market value of many states' debts down sharply and note holders bore an atypically large share of those losses in the early 1840s. In May 1840, the free banking law was amended so that only New York (and later U.S.) bonds remained eligible collateral. Because New York debt was considered investment grade, New York's free banking system performed admirably and banks, hence their note holders, were generally insulated from one type of negative macroeconomic shock.

Lawrence H. White, as well as Rolnick and Weber, extends King's explanation, arguing that the inherent term-structure risk of bond-backed note issue caused free bank failures.[60] Bond-collateral requirements forced banks to hold unbalanced portfolios, top-heavy with bonds, that exposed them to the risks of declining bond prices. Banks were placed at risk because the price of state bonds typically declined during economic downturns, while the notes collateralized by those bonds remained redeemable at par. If bond prices fell enough, some banks became insolvent because their net worth turned negative. Rolnick and Weber collected monthly price data for several state bonds and compared these data to the time pattern of bank failures. They found that 25 New York free banks failed during periods of falling bond prices; 20 of those failed between January 1841 and April 1842, a period of sharp economic decline. Only 9 banks failed during periods of rising bond prices, and 3 of those failed between May 1842 and April 1844. As such, the latter failures may be rightly attributed to the previous period of sharply declining prices as well. They simply hung on long enough to fail in a recovery.

Based on these findings, Rolnick and Weber conclude that most free bank failures were the result of falling bond prices.[61] Their interpretation has not gone unchallenged. Gorton, for example, notes that the failures of free banks subject to the bond-collateral requirement were highly correlated with the failures of chartered banks that were not subject to the law and that held very few bonds in their portfolios.[62] Banks failed during periods of disintermediation when the price of all bank assets, not just bonds, was declining. Rockoff follows up on this criticism when he argues that although "the notion that falling asset prices is not strictly a tautology, it is hard to imagine a case of massive bank failures in which falling asset prices did not play a role."[63] The interesting issue, he notes, is understanding why asset prices fell when they did and the role administrative policies, legal restrictions, and banking practices played in the failures.

One contributory administrative policy was the legislature's demand that banks publish quarterly balance sheets and annual lists of collateral bonds. Such transparency surely increased day-to-day confidence in the financial system. At the same time, it made it more fragile and more vulnerable to asset price shocks.[64] Now people knew which states' bonds each bank held as collateral. If the price of Arkansas bonds declined, holders of notes issued by banks that had tendered Arkansas bonds rushed to cash out. There was no need for creditors of banks collateralized with New York or U.S. or even Illinois bonds to follow suit unless, of course, those bonds' prices fell similarly.

That bank failures, while occurring in clusters, did not become contagious is consistent with this observation. Rolnick and Weber, as well as Iftekhar Hasan and Dwyer, note the apparent lack of contagion effects with free bank failures.[65] Part of the explanation undoubtedly lies with the requirement that banks publish the value of all collateral bonds. Part also lies with the ability of banks to hold different bond portfolios. Transparency was enhanced because people could quickly mark a fraction of each bank's portfolio to market. The cost of increased transparency was that banks were unable to conceal their exposure, which increased the possibility of a run in the event of asset price declines. The benefit of making several different bonds eligible was that (to maintain the contagion metaphor) it quarantined sick patients and slowed or even stopped the transmission of the disease. In one sense, then, New York may have improved the system by eliminating the eligibility of high-risk, mostly western, state bonds. But it may have simultaneously exposed its banks to greater risk by limiting them to New York securities. New York's banking system remained sound only as long as New York's finances remained sound as well.

Hasan and Dwyer offer a related criticism of Rolnick and Weber's declining asset price theory of free bank failures. Whereas Rolnick and Weber assume that bond price movements were exogenous events, Hasan and Dwyer argue that bond price declines were likely to have been endogenous. By the late antebellum period, banks held substantial amounts, in some cases a majority, of a state's bonds, so any shock that decreased the public's demand for bank-issued currency (whether intrinsic or extrinsic) triggered a bond price decline. To meet increased redemption claims, banks liquidated earning assets to bolster specie reserves. Bonds were typically their most readily marketable asset, so a significant reordering of the public's specie-banknote preferences could prompt a massive bond sell-off that would push down prices, causing further deterioration in the banks' net worth. Hasan and Dwyer conclude that declining bond prices were endogenous parts of bank runs, not causal exogenous events.[66]

Finally, Rockoff argues that previous writers underestimate the effects of the full and continuous banknote convertibility requirement as an important underlying source of instability in both free and chartered banking systems.[67] A seemingly equitable requirement that every bank meet its obligations without exception at every moment meant that any small change in the demand for specie could completely disrupt the entire banking system. Under New York's free banking law, if a single note holder's redemption demand went unsatisfied, the comptroller was left no choice but to close the bank, sell its collateral assets, and redeem all its remaining notes from the proceeds. It was little wonder that banking systems proved unstable in the face of small aggregate shocks.

Ultimately, the cause of free bank failures has not yet been resolved. Although wildcatting was surely less of a factor than nineteenth-century commentators and early twentieth-century historians believed, Rockoff contends that Rolnick and Weber went overboard in their attempt to debunk the myth. Rockoff notes, "Trying to compare a theory that bank failures [were] caused by falling asset prices with a theory that they were caused by wildcat banking is unsatisfactory because it compares different levels of analysis."[68] A bank did not have to close because its net worth fell below zero for a time. Banks, as Gorton and Michael Haupert rightly note, maintained an unreported asset, labeled "goodwill" in modern usage, that reflected the banks' value as a continuing concern.[69] As long as a bank met normal redemption calls, its book-value net worth could be negative while its market-value net worth was still positive. What differentiated such a bank from a wildcat bank was that the latter was a shell company without reputational capital. There was no reason for a firm to continue when its reported liabilities exceeded its reported assets. Firms with valuable reputational capital, including banks, had a reason and an economic justification for continuing. "The explanation proposed by Rolnick and Weber, then, is not a truism that applies to all banks at all times. It applies to wildcat banks precisely because they were dubious operations to begin with."[70]

A Free Banking Note-Issue Paradox?

Many writers contend that free banking represented a nearly perfect arbitrage opportunity. Free bankers purchased government bonds, received notes in return, extended loans, and profited from the substantial gap in the cost of funds and the market loan rate. Efficient markets, however, rarely allow profitable arbitrage opportunities to persist for long. As long as the arbitrage possibility offered any marginally positive return, new or existing banks should have purchased more bonds and issued more notes. Early students of the National Banking Era (1863–1913) uncovered what is now called the "note-issue paradox," namely, that national banks failed to expand note issue despite the apparent profitability of doing so.[71] Several generations of bank historians have refined the early profit measures and offered their own explanations for why national banks failed to exploit seemingly profitable arbitrage opportunities. Because the National Banking Act was modeled closely after New York's Free Banking Act, similar note issue incentives were likely to have operated in New York, too. Did they?

Bodenhorn and Haupert believe they did.[72] Combining information on bond prices and bank issues, they find that, like national banks in the postbellum period, free banks in antebellum New York underissued banknotes in the sense that additional issues would have generated pure arbitrage profits. Depending on the exact collateral bond used, rates of return to note issue ranged from a low of 8.4 percent on New York 5 percent bonds in 1853 to potential returns in excess of 500 percent on New York 6 percent bonds in 1847, 1856, and 1857. Between 1844 and 1860, rates of return averaged 25 to 35 percent. Clearly, such rates of return should have induced entry and elicited marginal note issues. That they did not requires explanation, and Phillip Cagan and Anna Schwartz's insistence that bankers acted irrationally simply does not square with evidence that they acted rationally in most other regards.[73]

In their explanations of the national bank note-issue paradox, Bruce Champ and Michael Kuehlwein focus on two features of bond-secured note issue that concerned bankers who intermediated long-term assets into short-term liabilities.[74] One was the variability of note redemptions; the other was the variability of bond prices. If a bank experienced a sharp, unexpected increase in note redemptions, it would be forced to raise specie, and the quickest way of doing so was to sell some fraction of its collateral bond holdings. Because such unexpected redemption demands often coincided with periods of falling bond prices, divestiture of collateral bonds held the potential for significant capital losses. Bankers thus had to recognize that holding-period returns could be negative at times and factor that into any calculation of the profitability of marginal note issues. Indeed, adjusting profit calculations for potential holding-period losses substantially reduces the expected profitability of free bank note issue, and returns are negative in some years.[75] Still, profit rates in most years exceeded 20 percent, so the risks of declining bond prices do not fully explain the free bankers' reluctance to issue additional notes.

Spurgeon Bell's and Goodhart's explanations for the failure of national banks to increase their note issues hinge on the bankers' fears that the note issue privilege could have been revoked.[76] The bankers reasoned that what Congress gave, Congress could take away, and there were several periods when they questioned Congress's commitment to the status quo. Cagan and Schwartz dismiss the bankers' fears as ex ante irrational because they proved to be so ex post. The bankers' right to issue notes was, in fact, suspended in 1935, so their fears were conceived with large forecast errors but were not entirely ill founded.

Fears over the revocation of their note-issue privilege surely weighed on New York's free bankers. Hammond writes eloquently about the court battles over the constitutional standing of state banknotes. In *Briscoe v. Bank of Kentucky*, the U.S. Supreme Court argued that note-issuing banks chartered by the various states did not violate the constitutional prohibition on state-issued bills of credit even if the state was the bank's lone shareholder.[77] Hammond notes that the *Briscoe* decision was unlikely to allay banker concerns because it was "about as weak and timid" as any decision the Court ever handed down and its very timidity left the door open for a future court to modify or overturn it.[78] Justice Story, in fact, wrote a blistering dissent to Justice McLean's majority opinion, arguing that banknote issues were "subject always to the controls of Congress, whose powers extend to the entire regulation of the currency of the country."[79] Congress exercised that power in 1865 and 1866 when it placed prohibitive taxes on state banknote issues; the act was found constitutional by the Court when it determined that in exercising its control over the nation's currency, Congress was within the scope of its powers to authorize the circulation of some banknotes and prohibit the circulation of others.[80]

New York's free banks were concerned not only with Congress and the federal courts but also with the state legislature and New York's courts. Ronald Seavoy provides a detailed account of the legal quagmire surrounding passage of New York's Free Banking act.[81] In brief, the legislature that passed the act attempted an end run on the state's constitution that required a two-thirds majority of both houses for a corporate charter. Moreover, the constitution forbade the establishment of an indefinite number of corporations in a single chartering act. Each corporation required its own chartering act. The 1838 legislature avoided these provisions by designating free banks "associations" rather than "corporations," though it was clear that they were de facto, if not de jure, corporations. At issue was the state courts' willingness to legitimize this technicality. It was possible, even probable, that an anti-Whig, anti-bank court sympathetic to Jackson, Van Buren, and the Democrats would declare free banks de facto corporations, hence unconstitutional.

Not unexpectedly, within a year, the state court of appeals was asked to determine the free banks' legal status. The court determined that the banks were corporations, but it demurred on their constitutional standing.[82] Like the *Briscoe* case, the New York court handed down a timid decision. The justices did their best to avoid judgment on an explosive political issue, and they were harshly criticized in the contemporary business press for having failed to resolve such a fundamental issue.[83] Within the next two years, a number of related cases worked their way through New York's court system, and the courts handed down some rather convoluted decisions. In one, the state's Court of Errors (then its highest court) found that the banks may not have been constitutional *in fact*, but they were constitutional *in intent*, whatever that meant.[84] Later cases determined that free banks were not corporations within the "meaning of the constitution" but were within the "meaning of the tax law."[85] Similar cases arose throughout free banking's tenure, leaving the banks in legal limbo. As late as 1857, the state's banking superintendent informed the assembly that free banks were of "doubtful legality,"[86] a situation that the legislature should rectify.

New York's free banks then faced the very real possibility that not only their note issue privilege but also their very existence could be revoked or radically modified if the legislature grew disenchanted with the system. Again, because such concerns proved misplaced ex post does not imply that they were unreasonable ex ante. Recall that free banking was instituted when the legislature became unhappy with the Safety Fund, which in 1838 had not yet revealed its shortcomings. Both Redlich and Carter Golembe discuss New York's banking history as a policy of experimentation.[87] If bankers viewed free banking as the most recent, potentially short-lived experiment, it was not necessarily irrational for bankers not to exploit every arbitrage opportunity. These were not arbitrage positions that were closed out quickly (with the exception of wildcatting). They were profitable only to the extent that bankers were willing to take long-term positions that exposed them to the risk that the note-issue privilege might be modified or revoked. Modification or revocation of the privilege may have meant wholesale liquidation of bonds whose values were, in part at least, determined by the issue privilege attached to them.

While shortsightedness, holding-period risk, term-structure risk, and legal uncertainties all factored in to a banker's decision not to exploit marginally profitable arbitrage opportunities, there may have been a more compelling reason for the reluctance to issue more notes. Bodenhorn and Haupert find that, at the margin, it was more profitable for banks to use deposits instead of notes.[88] Although banks could fund their loan portfolio with banknotes and earn a pure note-issue profit generally in excess of 15 percent, they could finance their loan portfolio with lodged deposits and earn marginal returns generally in excess of 25 percent.

The issue is whether this finding accords with the available empirical evidence. That is, did banks actually cultivate deposit usage and use low-cost deposits rather than high-cost, high-risk notes to finance their lending operations? Between 1845 and 1860, the value of loans increased from about $60 million to more than $200 million (a 233 percent increase). Over the same period, the value of deposits increased from $26 million to $110 million (323 percent), while note issues expanded from $18 million to $28 million (55 percent). Thus, marginal note issues were profitable and banks did, in fact, arbitrage on them. But marginal deposits were marginally *more* profitable and banks, especially city banks, encouraged their use relative to note issues. In the late antebellum era, deposits grew at about five times the rate of notes largely because implicit rates of return to additional deposits were about twice the rate of return to note arbitrage. New York's free bankers were not irrational, shortsighted individuals who failed to exploit available arbitrage opportunities. Instead, they rationally exploited the more profitable opportunity to the extent that increased loan demand allowed.

Seasonal Inelasticity of Note Issues

White and George Selgin argue that free banking's bond-collateral provision "proved to be far from innocuous." The preceding discussion has proved them correct in several regards. Bonds exposed banks to at least some maturity risks, liquidity risks, and solvency risks not borne by banks free to issue notes without the collateral requirement. While free banks bore some of the costs of bond-secured note issue, the public bore some as well. As White and Selgin note, the collateral restriction made the supply of currency "notoriously inelastic" and thereby contributed to banking panics.[89]

At the macroeconomic level, bond-secured note issue made the currency less elastic than note issues secured by reserves and other assets subject to a banker's discretion. Buying bonds, depositing them with the state comptroller, waiting for additional notes to be printed, and then getting them into circulation could be a tediously slow enterprise. By the time the first three steps were complete, the demand for additional credit may have passed and the bank incurred an expense to no benefit. In the same way, it was cumbersome and costly to retire notes, retrieve the bonds, and sell them in the face of declining loan demand.[90] Free banks, therefore, were likely to reach the point at which the marginal cost of an additional loan exceeded the marginal benefit earlier than a chartered bank that did not operate under similar collateral requirements.

The actual and potential inelasticities of bond-secured note issue did not escape the attention of contemporaries. Lord, in his treatise advocating free banking, wrongly argued that in elastic currencies were desirable and that free banking would, in fact, make the currency inelastic.[91] Furthermore, in 1852, Maryland's legislature considered adoption of a New York–style free banking law. Ultimately, it was rejected on several grounds, one of the more important being that collateralized note issues were less elastic than note issues of traditional chartered banks. Banking's response to the demands of industry would be "slow and unnatural. This was the direct opposite of the object desired."[92]

Free banking indeed generated an inelastic currency. Although the market for New York and U.S. bonds was relatively thick, the collateral requirement obstructed quick responses to unexpected shifts in the demand for currency. Moreover, it is well established that national bank currency demonstrated an undesirable seasonal inelasticity that reinforced autumn money-market pressures and contributed to banking panics.

The traditional autumn panic took the following path. Farmers needed currency to move their harvest to market, [93] Bound by bond-collateral requirements, country banks could not convert deposits into notes, so farmers took reserve currency instead. In response to declining reserves, country banks drew on their reserves at banks in Chicago, St, Louis, Minneapolis, Philadelphia, New York, and elsewhere. City reserve banks experienced similar reserve drains and began calling overnight and other short-term loans. Even presently unaffected country banks, afraid of being locked out if they hesitated, tried to realize their reserves. Banks, from the largest bank in New York City to the smallest in Cazenovia, experienced reserve losses; interest rates rose markedly; and some banks failed. White notes that it would be interesting to know the extent to which this problem appeared during the free banking era.

Just like national bankers, free bankers forced to accommodate changing seasonal demands for currency would have had to make substantial concurrent late summer or early autumn outlays on state debt, which surely would have driven up the price, making the arbitrage opportunity less attractive in the aggregate. Moreover, sizable concurrent sales in slack demand periods would have driven down the price of state debt, imposing capital losses on banks. As such, we would expect free bank note issues to demonstrate less seasonal variation than note issues of chartered banks. Figure 8.3, in fact, shows that free bank issues were not wholly acyclical, but they were less seasonally responsive than chartered bank issues. Such

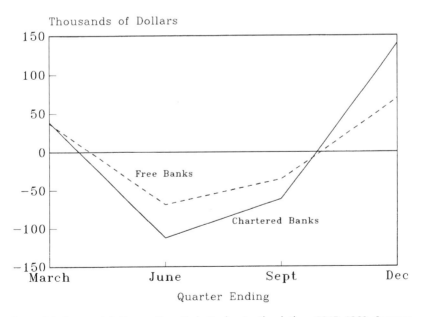

Figure 8.3 Seasonal Patterns: New York Banknote Circulation, 1845–1860. Sources: *Albany Argus*, 1845–1853; New York, *Assembly Documents* (1845–1861).

a pattern could signify two separate ill effects of free banking. Not only were free banks less able to respond to increasing demand for currency, which resulted in money-marketpressure and financial stringency in the autumn, but they may have faced incentives to keep too many notes in circulation in the spring and summer. Allan Bogue reported this telling adage about lending in agricultural communities: "June loans and June bugs no good."[94]

Free bankers were forced to balance the incremental foregone profits of not meeting peak note demand in the autumn against the incremental opportunity cost of holding piles of redeemed notes in the slack season. The result was that their aggregate note issues were more likely to reflect average annual demand rather than the peaks and troughs of a highly seasonal cycle. Chartered banks, on the other hand, were not constrained by the bond-collateral requirement, and their note issues displayed a more marked seasonal pattern.

Because New York had its own sort of dual banking system (i.e., free banks and chartered banks operating simultaneously), the seasonal effects may have been less pronounced than they were under the postbellum national banking system. With state banknotes taxed out of existence, the country was forced to rely on national banknotes that, like free bank notes, were made inelastic by the bond-collateral requirement. Antebellum America did not escape the repeated autumnal pressure in the money market as the few extant interest rate series demonstrate, but they were less pronounced before the war than after. Having chartered banks that could respond more quickly to changing money demands dampened the seasonal cycle and partly insulated the banking sector from recurring stringency and panic.

Assessments

To most historians, the lessons of free banking were clear. Banking, left to its own devices, was inherently unstable. Unless banks were closely supervised, banking and financial markets degenerated into chaos, causing substantial losses to the public, and eventually slowed real economic activity. Cagan bluntly asserts that the "nation could not so easily have achieved its rapid industrial and commercial expansion during the second half of the nineteenth century with the fragmented currency it had in the first half."[95] Free banking made an already bad situation worse.

The past score of years has witnessed a resurgent interest in free banking among financial and monetary historians. For the most part, they have investigated whether free banking actually increased macroeconomic and financial fragility. The importance of this issue comes to the fore when we recognize that a substantial externality exists in banking markets. Because banks operate with fractional reserves and hold opaque portfolios, they are vulnerable to runs as depositor confidence erodes. If depositors and note holders suspect that a bank or group of related banks cannot meet their obligations, the first-come, first-served withdrawal rule creates incentives to be at the head of the queue. An externality exists if depositors, after observing the failure of one bank, run other banks without knowing whether the conditions surrounding the first bank's failure apply to others. The externality becomes sizable if a run on one bank becomes contagious and spreads to banks that do not resemble the first in any real way.

Evidence presented by Rolnick and Weber, as well as Hasan and Dwyer, and interpretations by Rockoff suggest that free banking, at least as practiced in New York, was not prone to runs. We simply do not have enough information about the failures occurring in the 1838–1841 period to draw solid conclusions. Between 1842 and late 1857, no systemic run arose, and the suspension of payments in 1857 was driven by nervous depositors, not note holders. In that one regard, free banking was not a source of inherent instability.

Nevertheless, it must be remembered that regulation (in whatever form) can be a stabilizing influence in one set of circumstances and a destabilizing influence in another. George Benston notes that regulation affects bank stability in four principal ways: (1) it can create undiversified bank portfolios; (2) it can diminish profitability; (3) it can alter incentives among bank owners and managers to take or avoid risks; and (4) it may affect incentives to monitor, which may influence fraud and mismanagement.[96] Consider free banking's effect on each in turn.

Because bank managers cannot predict the future accurately, they should hold diversified portfolios. Bank regulation, however, often impairs many banks' ability to diversify. One prominent and much-discussed limitation was the prohibition of branch banking. New York did not allow its free banks to branch (only two chartered banks had branches), which meant that banks located in small, rural towns were potentially overinvested in the agricultural sector. Even when they loaned to local merchants and manufacturers, merchant and artisan income was usually dependent on agricultural outcomes. A second and more relevant way in which regulation limits diversification is through restrictions placed on allowable asset and liability mixes. Free banking placed heavy restrictions on bank portfolios by requiring them to hold substantial amounts of government debt. Chartered banks, by comparison, held very little. Such requirements made free bank portfolios top heavy and exposed free banks to interest rate, term-structure, and holding-period risks. This requirement distorted asset mixes and made banks especially vulnerable to disintermediation when interest rates rose.

Restrictions on free bank portfolios, as well as existing usury laws, reduced free bank profitability. Although the balance sheet analysis above showed that free banks exploited leverage opportunities to generate attractive rates of return, few banks fully exploited every opportunity. Moreover, rising prices of government debt driven by the increased demand reduced profitability. Although more research needs to be done before firm conclusions can be reached, dividend payments by free banks (5.7 percent) were substantially lower than those paid by chartered banks (6.8 percent) in 1842.[97] Many factors influenced bank profitability, but the bond-security requirement surely inhibited profitability in manifold ways.

Free banking's effects on risk taking were equivocal a priori. By asking bankers to invest most of their capital in relatively safe government bonds, contemporaries believed that note holders were insulated from excessive risk taking. To the extent that collateral bonds retained their value, this was true. But it may have placed other bank creditors at even greater risk. With banks earning low returns on bonds, some faced incentives to invest large parts of their portfolio in relatively high-risk projects that promised greater expected returns. As such, other creditors, notably depositors, were placed at greater risk of loss. This effect may be partly reflected in lower profits among free banks. Recognizing that they were at greater risk of loss, depositors demanded a risk premium in return, which raised the cost of funds and lowered profits. On the other hand, students of the U.S. thrift crisis of the 1980s have argued that one of the best deterrents to inefficiently excessive risk taking is owner-contributed equity. When bank owners have more of their own funds at stake, they are more likely to balance expected returns and expected losses at the margin and, thus, provide more-efficient intermediary services. During the thrift crisis, small, undercapitalized institutions were more likely to fail.[98] Again, more research needs to be done, but New York's individual banks (with a $50,000 minimum capital requirement) were seemingly more likely to close than joint-stock banks (with a $100,000 requirement). By requiring most free banks to operate with substantial owner-contributed capital, New York's law may have mitigated some risk-taking incentives.

Finally, monitoring should aim to eliminate fraud and reduce excessive risk taking. Unlike the Safety Fund system, which created a board of auditors and demanded regular inspections, free banking imposed no such requirement. In fact, free banks were insulated from any interference by the Safety Fund's inspectors and were required simply to provide unaudited quarterly balance sheets to the state comptroller or the superintendent of banking after 1851. As New York's bank regulators learned during the Safety Fund collapse, fraud is difficult to detect before (even during) the fact because perpetrators know they are engaged in illegal behavior and will falsify records and otherwise cover their tracks. A second problem is that any asset is prone to fraud (as wildcatting shows), so portfolio limitations are no guarantee against fraud. Free bankers may not have been subject to formal audits and direct oversight; however, they were subject to market-based monitoring that Gorton and Bodenhorn show to be quite effective.[99] New York's legislators may have opted for market monitoring. By publishing balance sheets and requiring all country banks to establish a formal correspondent relationship with a city bank, legislators facilitated monitoring, but there is no evidence in the legislative record that this was their intent.

Concluding Remarks

Traditional assessments of free banking are highly critical. Redlich spills much ink in criticizing free banking as the product of naive, have-not egalitarians who desired easy money and cheap credit.[100] Moreover, securing note issues with bonds and mortgages represented a return to what he sees as an ill-conceived and long-discredited mercantilist belief that fixed assets, like land, could be coined. Redlich, in some sense, misinterprets the bond and mortgage collateral requirements, limited as he is by his misplaced, strict real-bills perspective. Free banking notions, broadly interpreted, enjoyed a twentieth-century revival from Irving Fisher and Friedman, who advocate 100 percent reserve banking to modern free banking theorists, those influenced by F.A. Hayek's monograph who advocate free competition in everything associated with money, from the competitive establishment of units of account to the supply of the media of exchange.[101] None of the modern proposals can be labeled, however broadly, mercantilist, nor should the antebellum ones.

A second common criticism, one offered by Redlich, Hammond, and others, is that opportunistic legislators adopted a populist rhetoric to exploit laissez-faire sentiments to their own advantage. Bank promoters saw profit opportunities in the public's demand for bank shares and legislators went along to siphon as much of this capital as possible.[102] A third criticism, voiced most powerfully by Hammond, is that free banking's real objective was to advance states' rights and undermine federal regulatory power in all fields of endeavor.[103] As he notes, the vocabulary used in defense of free banking was decidedly antifederal and anti-Hamilton. Hammond sees free banking as a final defeat of Jefferson over Hamilton, though Hamilton would have recognized the defeat more readily than Jefferson would have recognized the victory. To Hammond, the results of this "Jacksonian revolution were obvious in monetary inflation, in speculation, in wasted labor, in business failures, in abandonment of an efficient means of credit control [a strong central bank], and in corruption of a sound monetary system."[104]

Modern assessments are more generous. Richard Sylla argues that it was not surprising that a sudden extension of freedom would be followed by a period of sometimes painful adjustment.[105] A rapid influx of banks was followed by a period of industrial shakeout in which some failures and closings reflected the pushing out of less-efficient banks. In other circumstances, the desire to operate a bank was not matched by an ability to do so. In yet other cases, some bankers were simply unlucky enough to open just before the onset of the midcentury's deepest recession. Ultimately, most entrants remained in business for extended periods, providing valuable intermediary services to their customers and the general public. Moreover, free banking allowed for rapid entrepreneurial responses to geographic and sectoral changes in the demands for financial services. Such responses meant that the financial sector could achieve its potential influence on the pace and pattern of economic growth and development.[106]

Free banking was no panacea, however. Regulations specific to free banks, as well as those applicable to all banks, generated a host of potential inefficiencies. Bond-security requirements may have led to underissuing and almost surely created an inelastic currency. Moreover, bond-security requirements may have pushed bankers to adopt excessively risky lending practices to counter the low returns generated by their bond portfolio. On the other hand, free banking created certain transparencies that facilitated market-based monitoring and required bankers to make substantial equity investments. The latter may have mitigated excessive risk taking, resulting in relatively few free bank failures after the bumpy start.

Free banking's real long-term influence may not be found in its influence on banking per se, but rather in its influence on corporations more generally. Sylla argues that the two aspects of New York's free banking law—free entry and bond-secured note issue—that are typically held up as imaginative advances really were not.[107] Sir James Steuart and Adam Smith advocated free entry; Ricardo proposed bond-secured note issue. What was original about free banking was *free incorporation*. New York's free banking law made incorporation a routine administrative function rather than a legislative function. Although it was not the first general incorporation statute, it was one of the more important early ones. It clearly defined the boundaries within which a firm organizing under its provisions could operate. It was, as one contemporary judge argued, "an invention of modern times" [108] and modern import. In the long run, general incorporation banking laws established bureaucratic administrative units to supervise and regulate bank activities. As such, free banking represented the beginning of what Jonathan Hughes labeled a "governmental habit"[109] that mushroomed in the subsequent century.

9

Banking in the South and West

Banks and the Commonweal

Banking policy in the South and West followed two contradictory paths. One favored competition and freedom from government interference. The other favored a strong central role for the state, up to and including full government ownership of banks. Attitudes varied partly by political party, but they were also influenced by region, historical experience, and the current state of the economy.[1] Both Whigs and Democrats, at different times and places and for very different reasons, favored a central role for government. Democrats favored intervention to mitigate the banks' perceived tendency toward income inequality. Whigs, in the Federalist tradition, envisioned a state taking an activist role in economic growth.

Throughout the antebellum era, competing parties, whether Alexander Hamilton's Federalists and Thomas Jefferson's Republicans or Henry Clay's Whigs and Andrew Jackson's Democrats, weighed in on the bank question. Political debate in Virginia, though not always typical, illuminates fundamental differences. One side followed John Taylor of Caroline, a Jeffersonian who abhorred banking because he believed that paper money was a financial trick sanctioned by special privilege that subverted the political process. The opposition believed that financial development was a prerequisite for economic development and advocated a strong, powerful, and influential bank like the Bank of the United States. Virginians reached a barely stable compromise in the form of two partly state-owned banks closely modeled after it.

Rapid economic growth in the early 1830s strained the fragile coalition. Rapid economic decline in the late 1830s rended it. Between 1837 and 1842, Whigs controlled the legislature. The editor of the influential, Democratic Richmond *Enquirer*, Thomas Ritchie, aligned himself so closely with the Whig position that hard-money Democrats nearly formed an alternative party newspaper. In regard to banking policy, Ritchie's position nearly mirrored that of William Rives, editor of the competing Richmond *Whig*, who denounced the hard-money Democratic position, which called for revoking the charters of all banks suspending specie payments. Ritchie openly opposed the official Democratic Party position when he supported two pending acts. One legitimized specie suspension and the other provided for the issuance of small-denomination ($1 and $2) banknotes. When a legislative committee considered a free banking proposal, both Ritchie and Rives opposed it as a northern mania.

Virginia's Democrats splintered on the suspension question and disintegrated on the small-note question.[2] Small-denomination notes were vital in a specie-short but heavily commercialized economy like Virginia's. More Democrats eventually voted for the small-note bill than for the suspension bill. Whatever Democratic support there was for banks depended on banks retaining a strict commercial focus and agreeing to stringent regulations. Although there were a few radical hard-money Democrats in the assembly, Democrats were overwhelmingly moderate on the bank question, possibly because the president of the Bank of Virginia was an influential Democrat who, not surprisingly, considered the radical hard money stance untenable.

Virginia's 1837 general banking law, which did not embrace free banking but rationalized state law so that all existing banks were subject to the same rules and regulations, included several important concessions to Democrats, including a ban on notes less than $10. To the Democrats, victory in the small-note battle represented a pivotal first step on the way to the elimination of all notes. Radical Democrats, however, never represented a real threat to Virginia's banks. Without the income accruing to the state from its bank investments, other elements of the egalitarian impulse would have gone unfunded. Additionally, Virginia's banks were widely regarded as among the best in the nation. Ultimately, Virginia's Democrats were unable to form an effective antibank coalition to undo the existing structure.

Virginia's political leadership chose not to impose fundamental changes on the state's financial system once a system was put in place. Stability mattered, and Virginians respected that. The intersection of politics and economics produced substantially different outcomes in other places. Banking policy in Florida, Arkansas, Mississippi, and Louisiana swung, pendulum-like, between rapid expansion and equally rapid contraction, between liberal chartering and state ownership, and between free banking and outright prohibition.

Although political and economic tensions between urban merchants and rural farmers played out everywhere, they were especially pronounced in the southern and western United States. Farmers viewed banks as flexible suppliers of money and credit. Credit was important because it was advanced against agricultural goods in process, mostly cotton and tobacco. One Alabama planter, however, noted the uneasy connection between farming and banking: "What a glorious business planting is, for we always hope the next crop will bring us out."[3] What planters wanted out of was debt. On the other hand, merchants wanted reliable sources of credit and a stable price level. Merchants argued, in real-bills style, that banks should supply credit, not capital. Although real-bills theory may have partly motivated such statements, they were mostly inspired by a pragmatic belief that agricultural lending froze a bank's assets and made the money supply prone to rapid overexpansion. Neither was good for business.

Determined by the political process, banking policy alternately reflected these opposing worldviews. States adopted first one approach, then the other. Louisiana provides a telling example.[4] In the 1830s, Louisiana liberally chartered banks and encouraged agricultural investment by selling its own bonds to capitalize so-called plantation banks that mixed commercial and mortgage lending (see chapter 10). When these banks suffered large losses between 1837 and 1842, losses that the state bore as a contingent liability, the state placed sharp restrictions on lending practices. In 1843, the legislature reordered the bank supervisory board, which tried to liquidate the still-solvent Union Bank (a mixed mortgage-commercial lender). In 1845, a new state constitution forbade the chartering or rechartering of any bank. Finally, an 1848 act prohibited the chartering of any firm engaged in factorage, brokerage, or an exchange business of any kind.

Within a short time, the effects of the state's restrictions and prohibitions manifested themselves in higher interest rates, reduced intermediation, and a redirection of commerce from New Orleans to other ports. Louisiana responded with a free banking act. Its act was more restrictive than those of most other states in many regards, and it discouraged mixed mortgage-commercial lending. Policy swung back again in 1854 when the act was amended so that banks could help finance the state's two large railroad projects—the New Orleans and the Jackson and Great Northern—as well as some smaller ones. In Louisiana, the pendulum swung first in one direction, then in the other, and then back again, all in less than 25 years. Similar patterns emerged in such dissimilar places as Ohio and Arkansas, Florida and Wisconsin, and Mississippi and Michigan.

In his survey of American commercial banking, Paul Trescott argues that legislators found it difficult to reconcile their responsibilities toward credit availability with their responsibilities toward monetary stability.[5] Maintaining public confidence in money and the payments system required continual specie convertibility. Accomplishing this typically involved restrictions on bank credit. Restrictions on credit, however, led to unsatisfied loan demands among politically powerful constituencies, which produced changes in banking policy that emphasized credit expansion and risked monetary disturbance. When the disturbances occurred, banking policy switched back. Southern and western legislators were forced to grapple with the unique demands of urban merchants and artisans, as well as rural planters and farmers. They also faced atypical demands for the finance of internal improvements in recently settled regions. The combination provided the South and West with challenges not faced in the Northeast and produced banking systems that differed in both style and substance from northern banks. While some aspects of northern banking, such as free banking, were copied in the South and West, other features arose independently or were adapted to such an extent that they little resembled their northern genesis.

Banking and Agriculture in the South and West

Contemporary southerners saw a direct correlation between banking and economic growth. Although several of Virginia's prominent political leaders opposed banking, especially state-sponsored, state-chartered banking, on the grounds that it violated Revolution-era republican ideals by creating a financial oligarchy, popular sentiment overcame political philosophy. In 1791, about $2 million in produce was shipped from Maryland ports; Virginia's exports totaled about $3 million.[6] Within a decade, Maryland's exports increased to $12 million but Virginia's increased to just $4 million. Contemporaries did not attribute Maryland's rapid growth solely to its banks, but they did believe that credit was partly responsible. The time had come for Virginia to enter the age of banking.

Legislative debate on a bank charter invited a legion of merchants and planters in every small town along the James River to make a case for why they deserved a bank. Although the legislature accepted the legitimacy of the credit demands, they were convinced that few such places would support a bank. Torn between competing interest groups—merchants and planters clamoring for credit and Jeffersonian Republicans opposed to any grant of corporate privilege—the legislature chartered a bank they thought capable of meeting legitimate credit demands while allaying the worst fears of its critics. The Bank of Virginia (1804) was a compromise, a model later copied throughout the southern and western United States.

With the exception of the Manhattan Company, the Bank of North America, and the Bank of Pennsylvania, the $1.5 million Bank of Virginia was substantially larger than most banks.[7] The state subscribed one-fifth of its shares with the right to appoint one-fifth of its directors so that it could simultaneously profit from it and exercise a measure of control over it. Having mollified concerns over unfettered corporate privilege, legislators met the widely scattered credit needs by establishing five branches. Moreover, if residents of any town owned 300 or more shares in the bank, they could request an agency that would dispatch loan requests to the nearest branch.[8] Virginia successfully negotiated competing viewpoints and established a bank that influenced southern banking for the next 60 years.

The Bank of Virginia model was widely emulated, but the South was not populated solely by banks of its kind. In fact, the southern and western United States produced a patchwork quilt of banking structures that took on one of three types identified by Bray Hammond (prohibition, monopoly, and laissez-faire) or a fourth emphasized by Larry Schweikart (a partly or wholly state-owned bank operating alongside one or more privately owned banks).[9] Their differences were shaped, in part, by distinctive geographic, commercial, and agricultural conditions. The credit needs of black belt cotton farmers differed from those of coastal merchants; planters' needs differed from those of family farmers. Because the decentralized Federalist polity allowed endless opportunities for emulation and adaptation, each state modified its banking structures to local needs and expectations.

As the discussion of the South's and West's myriad banking structures proceeds, one thing should be kept in mind: the impetus for banking was economic growth. "Credit," wrote Thomas Govan, "was essential to the commercial agriculture that was the basis of the economy of . . . the South, prior to the Civil War."[10] Southerners grew rice, tobacco, cotton, and sugar cane for sale in far-removed markets, and moving goods to market required credit. They needed credit to purchase land. They needed credit to purchase slaves. They needed credit to finance land improvements. They needed credit to buy clothes and food for themselves and their slaves. They needed credit to pay for seed and fertilizer and tools for working their crops. In short, credit was as much the lifeblood of southern agriculture as it was of eastern manufacturing and widespread mercantile activities.

Planters and farmers alike were fully aware of their dependence on credit. An anonymous writer in the Macon *Georgia Messenger* wrote that "without them [banks], one half of our national wealth would never have existed. Without them, the wilds of the South and Southwest would not have been cultivated, as they are now, for a century to come."[11] The same themes were repeated in the Old Northwest. In 1837, Ohio's governor wrote that "credit has given us one of the most enterprising and active set of businessmen that have lived in any age or any country . . . credit has bought our land, made our canals, improved our rivers, opened our roads, built our cities, cleared our fields, founded our churches, erected our schools and colleges."[12] Contemporary Americans shared a belief, which modern studies support, that banks and credit were important and responsible for a significant fraction of the economic growth experienced in the early stages of development.[13]

Despite the dependence of commercial agriculture on credit and contrary to several historical interpretations, southern banks were *not* "expressly organized to loan on real estate."[14] Except for a few wealthy planters, most agriculturalists had little interaction with banks short of using and holding banknotes. Most southern banks focused on mercantile lending. In South Carolina, for instance, the charters of almost all of the state's banks allowed, even encouraged, the establishment of rural branches. Few banks opened them. Instead, they financed exports moving through Charleston. Schweikart contends that the banks' reluctance to deal with farmers created a rural-urban, planter-merchant rivalry that helped define state politics and prompted the establishment of the Bank of the State of South Carolina in 1812, designed to provide longer-term mortgage credit.[15] By 1835, even this institution had turned to financing merchants and manufacturers. The bank held almost $2 million in commercial bills and notes and only about $600,000 in mortgages.[16] Available evidence for most other banks suggest a similar reluctance to engage in direct mortgage-based, agricultural lending.

Just because banks preferred not to deal directly with farmers did not mean that farmers and planters were cut off from credit. It did mean, however, that they got it indirectly. Farmers and planters relied on local merchants and produce factors for credit, marketing, and provisioning services. Factors bought and forwarded goods to planters, saving them the expense of traveling to purchase supplies and marketing their crops. Factors had standing agreements with a New Orleans cotton broker who received and marketed all of the cotton forwarded by the upriver factor. Once the factor accumulated the output of several planters, he drew a bill of exchange at a local bank payable by the New Orleans broker at a New Orleans bank. The local bank purchased the bill, charging about 6 percent plus a 1 to 2 percent exchange fee, which provided the factor with the funds to transport the cotton to New Orleans. After the New Orleans broker sold the cotton, he took up the bill of exchange that the local bank had forwarded to a New Orleans correspondent for collection. After honoring the bill and deducting his own commission (usually about 2 or 3 percent), the New Orleans broker deposited the remaining proceeds in the factor's account in a New Orleans bank. The factor then drew a sight bill at his local bank on his New Orleans account. After deducting his expenses and commissions, the factor then credited the planters' accounts. "The factor was the factotum of our business life," wrote one contemporary southerner, "our commission merchant, our banker, our bookkeeper, our advisor, our collector and disburser, who honored our checks and paid our bills."[17]

The factor stood at the heart of southern commerce and finance, where agricultural produce, largely cotton, served as the basis of an immense credit system.[18] Although it was the farmers' property and produce that secured the credit, it was the factor who organized, directed, and allocated it. Banks extended credit to factors; factors then extended it to farmers and planters. It was not only at harvest time that factors provided credit to them. Planters often needed funds long before they had any cotton to sell, and factors provided it. Factors procured and forwarded provisions, implements, and other supplies secured by advances on crops not yet harvested. The costs of such supplies, as well as shipping costs, interest costs, and the factor's commission, were debited to the planter's account and settled when the crop was sold.

Credit relations and institutions in the Old Northwest differed from those in the South in degree rather than in kind. When the State Bank of Indiana was chartered in 1817, about 90 percent of the state's labor force was engaged in agriculture; however, as Logan Esary noted, the bank's president believed that farmers furnished very little direct business for banks.[19] Instead, he turned to traders at Vincennes who moved produce to market. The bank loaned money to traders who bought produce from local farmers and shipped it to New Orleans. After the produce was sold, the trader deposited the money in an account to the credit of the State Bank in Vincennes.

As such, the State Bank had little to do with long-term agricultural credit. Instead, the bank indirectly met the farmers' short- and medium-term credit needs in much the same way that southern banks worked through factors to meet the planters' short- and medium-term credit needs. Although the State Bank failed during the depression of the early 1820s, its successor, the State Bank of Indiana, chartered in 1834, operated on the same principles. Samuel Merrill, the new bank's first president, informed its directors that the state had established a *bank* and not a *loan office*.[20] In Merrill's eyes, the bank's mission was to directly accommodate mercantile rather than agricultural pursuits. Farmers were expected to obtain their mortgages elsewhere.

As well as the factorage system worked, it was not immune from criticism. Historians have correctly noted that some planters were chronically indebted to factors. They never fully paid off their annual debts, so their indebtedness compounded. Similar to the debt-peonage debate surrounding Reconstruction-era sharecropping and provisioning merchants, historians such as Morton Rothstein and Robert Roeder claim that the factorage system retarded rather than promoted economic growth because it reduced planter income and involved significant deadweight losses.[21] Once a factor had a planter locked into debt, he exploited his monopoly position by adding excessive factorage costs and charged interest rates 1 to 2 percent greater than banks. Rothstein and Roeder argue that factors monopolized the cotton trade and forced indebted planters to inefficiently overspecialize in cotton and cash crop production. In addition, the factorage system concentrated capital in a few large, urban, commercial centers, which inhibited the growth of smaller towns that could have improved their commercial facilities, promoted manufacturing, generated a larger domestic market, and encouraged industrial diversification. While there is evidence that too little manufacturing developed in the South, it is probably unfair given evidence presented in chapter 3 to lay the blame at the feet of the region's bankers.[22]

A second criticism is that the system simply pretended to abide by real-bills precepts in lending short term to factors when it was little more than an elaborately disguised land bank system. Chapter 3 provides a rebuttal to the real-bills doctrine in general, but modern economic theory that links formal and informal credit markets provides a specific rebuttal for this instance.[23]

Suppose there are two types of lenders—formal (banks) and informal (small-town merchants or factors)—who may either compete for the same business, (say, loans to farmers and planters) or complement each other's lending activities. Because the market was reasonably competitive, both types of lenders faced similar lending rates, all else being equal. But everything else was not equal. A fundamental difference between banks and factors resided in three key determinants of lending rates: transaction costs, risk premia, and the opportunity cost of funds. If factors held a comparative advantage in evaluating and pricing one or more of these determinants, they held a comparative advantage in lending to farmers and rightly intermediated between banks and farmers.

In the antebellum South, it was more profitable for bankers and factors to complement one another's actions than to compete. Banks loaned to factors at relatively low costs because, in so doing, they economized on information costs, gathering and analyzing information on a relatively small number of factors and merchants. Factors and merchants, on the other hand, were in a better position to gather and process information about the credit histories and economic prospects of only those planters with whom they repeatedly contracted. Charles Nisbit argues that smaller, less-formal lenders (such as factors) had intimate knowledge of their clients.[24] Factors knew the size of the planters' farms; which crops, and in what proportions, each planter planted; how many animals and slaves a planter owned; and each planter's recent production, debts, and entrepreneurial skills. Because the local money lender (i.e., the factor) had a long-standing relationship with a bank, much like the local relationship between a farmer and the factor, banks exploited their comparative advantage in mobilizing large blocs of funds while factors exploited their comparative advantage in gathering information (which reduced transaction costs) and evaluating it (lowering risk premia). The result was that total interest costs to planters were lower and the total volume of credit was greater than if they had dealt directly with banks.

Persistent complaints about the factorage system arose from two sources. First, as middlemen, factors exploited farmers. Such criticisms are common among those who fail to recognize that middlemen generally provide valuable services. Acting as middlemen, factors provided bankers with better information than bankers could have obtained through similar expenditures, which lowered effective interest costs and increased credit availability. Moreover, by offering his own note to the bank instead of the planter's the factor insulated the banker from delinquencies and defaults, which reduced risk premia. Through the intermediation of factors, bankers actually indirectly financed more long-term loans to planters than they would have otherwise. It was the factor's risk-pooling activities that enabled the entire process.[25]

The second largely unfounded basis of complaint was that factors monopolized bank accommodation. A factor's credit was the equivalent of modern trade credit (i.e., loans between firms used to finance inventories and goods in process). As such, factor lending was a redistributive mechanism between firms and substituted for direct bank loans. The factorage system may have reduced the incidence of credit rationing. Although planters paid marginally higher rates to factors than banks charged, it is likely that planters were (and would have been in the factors' absence) sharply rationed at current lending rates.

The South and West, then, developed a complex financial hierarchy of formal and informal, regional and local lenders that mobilized and allocated funds. The success of these regions' financial institutions was the result of the specific forms they took. George Starnes is not alone in contending that the adoption of the Virginia-style banking structure in other places promoted economic growth and encouraged financial stability.[26] The details of the southern system have been ably described elsewhere, but its success lay in the fact that it established a large, well-capitalized mother branch and a rationalized branch network. Some branches tapped local reservoirs of capital, while others distributed it. Such practices diffused the bank's notes, monetized the economy, and fostered trust in the institution.

Despite the banks' large capitals and extensive branching networks, the efficient allocation of loanable funds fell largely on the shoulders of factors and traders. "Through his endorsements and acceptances," writes Harold Woodman, "the factor was able to open credit resources all over the world to the planter."[27] Many factors' endorsements were known throughout the world and bankers everywhere stood ready to discount them. They obtained credit from northern, as well as southern, banks, Dutch and French banking houses, and English cotton traders. Factors increased the volume of credit available to planters far beyond what was mobilized locally.

Although the South and West lagged behind the North in industrial development, the regions' bankers were financial sophisticates. Financial and credit structures in the South and West were as developed as anything observed in the North. Southern and western banks and their agents developed a complex financial network that spanned the entire Atlantic economy. It is, therefore, incorrect to view these two regions as two disconnected financial regions. Each was designed to accomplish specific geographic, political, and economic goals. Yet, all were pulled into a national financial network that directed capital throughout the North Atlantic economy.

Banks and Internal Improvements

Not only did contemporaries expect banks to indirectly promote economic growth, but they also expected them to invest in and otherwise underwrite tangible public investments associated with economic development. Like banks in other regions, those in the South and West were drawn into a host of internal improvement programs. Canal building proceeded in three distinct waves. The first wave ended in 1828 with the completion of New York's Erie Canal and Pennsylvania's Main Line.[28] The second wave, which peaked in 1840, saw the development of southern and western systems, principally the Ohio and Erie Canal in Ohio and the James and Kanawha

Canal in Virginia. Ending in 1855, the third wave completed the system by constructing smaller lines that fed into the main lines. Aggregate state expenditures during all three phases amounted to about $188 million. About three-quarters of that $188 million was supplied by state treasuries, and although each state's experience was different, banks directly or indirectly supplied a substantial fraction of the remainder.

After 1810, Virginia embarked on a system of public works and internal improvements. The Farmers Bank's (1812) charter and the Bank of Virginia's (1814) recharter extracted bonus payments earmarked for internal improvements.[29] New York's and Pennsylvania's canal building frightened Virginia's legislators, who feared that completion of the canals would siphon off a considerable volume of Virginia's western trade. To formulate a coherent, competitive response, the legislature formed a coalition called the President and Directors of Public Works in 1816, made up of the governor, the state treasurer, the attorney general, and ten members selected by the legislature. To fund the agency, the state turned over all shares of existing canals, turnpikes, and banks owned by the state, which provided the agency with $1.5 million in shares that generated an annual dividend income of about $115,000.

Because $115,000 was insufficient to underwrite any meaningful project, additional revenue sources were needed and the state quickly found one. Both of Virginia's chartered banks were located east of the Allegheny Mountains, but several small, note-issuing private banks had sprung up in the western half of the state. Because they operated in western Virginia, they had not interfered with the chartered banks' privileges and had gone largely unnoticed. When the state extracted chartering bonuses from the Bank of Virginia and the Farmers Bank, it realized it had overlooked an untapped revenue source. In February 1816, the uncharted western banks were prohibited from issuing notes and given a year to wind up their affairs. In January 1817, two new banks were created—the Northwestern Bank based in Wheeling and the Bank of the Valley based in Winchester. In return for their charters, each bank supplied the public works board with 15 percent of their shares.[30] In time, these banks became as sound as any in the state, but the demand for gratis shares surely increased the costs of establishing these banks in a region that, in another time, may have been subsidized rather than taxed.

The Erie Canal's early success spurred Virginia into action. Rechartered again in 1825, the Farmers Bank paid a $50,000 bonus to the public works board. In 1832, the James River and Kanawha Company was granted the authority to push from Richmond to the Ohio River by either canal or railroad. The state subscribed 25,000 canal shares and authorized the banks to buy up to 5,000.[31] The banks demurred. To encourage bank investment, the state authorized them to increase their capital equal to their investment in canal stock. Only the Bank of Virginia did so. The others argued either that the canal stocks were too risky or that canal investments would force a reduction in commercial lending.

Between 1830 and 1837, Virginia became deeply involved in several other internal improvement projects that placed the treasury under constant strain. Once again, the state turned to the banks for support. An 1837 general banking law created a common regulatory structure for all banks that had operated under slightly different charter provisions. One clause in the 1837 act gave the state the right to appoint four of nine directors at each bank's central office and three of seven directors at each branch. Such restrictions surely reflected Democratic demands for government oversight, but Starnes argues that egalitarian rhetoric veiled the real intent, which was that state-appointed directors would direct bank funds to internal improvement companies.[32] Additionally, a one-half of 1 percent tax on bank capital was earmarked to support improvements.

By 1837, the James and Kanawha Canal was not producing any significant revenue, and Virginia's tax revenues were barely able to meet the interest payments on the state's debt.[33] The financial downturn of the late 1830s only worsened the state's finances, and by the mid-1840s, the treasury was unable to meet its obligations. In December 1837, it borrowed $200,000 from the banks to meet its interest payments. Still in search of additional revenue, the state imposed an additional tax on bank shares, except for those owned by the state, of one-eighth of 1 percent. The following year, taxes on bank shares were increased by another one-quarter of 1 percent. Even as late as 1853, the state's finances remained so poor that it borrowed $350,000 to cover its budget deficit.[34] In 1855, the state's deficit increased to $385,000. Finally, in 1856, the legislature decided to sell its bank shares and use the proceeds to extinguish a substantial share of its bonded debt. In doing so, the state relinquished its right to appoint directors and directly control bank operations.

By the 1850s, the relationship between the state and its banks had, in a way, come full circle. The state had subsidized and otherwise offered support to the banks in their formative years when capital was not easily mobilized and agglomerated, and the public was suspicious of or unknowledgeable about banks and their credit and monetary activities. Once banks established themselves and became trusted, they returned the favor in the 1840s by supporting the state's impaired credit. By the 1850s, the state and its banks were able to extricate themselves from their mutual entanglements. Virginia even went so far as to pass a free banking act of sorts (see chapter 10).

Like their northeastern counterparts, southeastern merchants understood the economic importance of cultivating commercial ties with western farmers, which demanded improved transportation. While New York, Pennsylvania, Maryland, and Virginia turned first to canals and only later to railroads, South Carolina immediately turned to the railroad. In 1818, the state embarked on an ambitious transportation infrastructure campaign that centered on a rail line connecting Charleston and Hamburg. By locating the terminus of the railroad in Hamburg, on the Augusta River, it diverted exportable produce that had formerly flowed downriver to Savannah. This short-line railroad proved so successful that plans to connect Charleston with the far western interior were quickly put forward.

Construction of the Charleston-Hamburg line was funded through the sale of $800,000 in state bonds sold by the Bank of the State of South Carolina and secured with the bank's capital. In 1821, the bank established a sinking fund into which profits were diverted to meet interest payments on the bonds, as well as their eventual retirement.[35] Between 1822 and 1826, the state issued an additional $750,000 in bonds, which were also handed over to the bank. The early days of the Bank of the State of South Carolina demonstrate the myriad, sometimes competing, demands placed on banks. Originally designed as a mortgage lender intended to finance plantation agriculture, the state quickly saddled it with $1.7 million in bonded debt. By 1830, the bank was punctually paying out $90,000 annually in interest on these debts, yet a legislative committee produced a critical report. Criticized for not generating enough profits to meet interest payments, add to the sinking fund, and still hand money over to the state treasury, the bank altered its lending policies.[36] It no longer renewed mortgage loans at maturity as a matter of course and it greatly expanded its commercial lending business because commercial lending provided higher returns. Although more profitable, this policy shift, not surprisingly, provoked criticism from planters.

The success of the Charleston-Hamburg Railroad encouraged South Carolina to embark on one of the most ambitious improvement programs of the decade. It chartered the Louisville, Cincinnati and Charleston Railroad, designed to connect the Carolina coast with the vast agricultural regions surrounding the Ohio River Valley and rival the Erie Canal. South Carolina subscribed for $1 million of its stock and ordered the Bank of the State to pay for it from the state's share of the federal surplus distributed in 1836. Schweikart calls the project "one of the great might have beens" of the era.[37] The project was troubled nearly from the outset. By the end of the decade, its troubles were manifold: the railroad's visionary president, Robert Y. Hayne, died unexpectedly in 1839; the politically powerful and influential John C. Calhoun resigned from the board of directors in a dispute over the railroad's proposed route through the mountains; continuing disputes surrounded the railroad's merger with Tennessee's Hiwasse Railroad; Kentucky refused to charter the line and join the system; and the financial depression that persisted through the early 1840s hindered completion.

In an effort to bolster stock subscriptions, the railroad requested and received permission to engraft a banking subsidiary, known as the South Western Rail Road Bank, onto the company's transportation operations. Though it was designed to assist the railroad, the banking subsidiary retained its autonomy to ensure proper banking procedures. Each holder of a $100 railroad share was eligible to subscribe to one $50 bank share, with the shares perpetually linked. A transfer of a bank share required the transfer of a rail share and vice versa.[38] The bank could not call for subscription installments before an equal amount was paid on railroad stock. The bank's capital could not exceed $6 million until the tracks reached Tennessee, $9 million prior to its reaching Kentucky's southern border, or $12 million before reaching Lexington, Kentucky. South Carolina demonstrated its commitment to sound banking by creating separate boards of directors. Moreover, the bank was *not* responsible for the railroad's debts, but the railroad was liable for the bank's debts. The South Western Rail Road Bank operated out of Charleston, but the charter allowed it to establish branches throughout the state. Branches could be established in Tennessee and Kentucky, too, if those states approved.

The railroad floundered through the 1850s. When the Civil War interrupted construction, over $1.5 million had been spent tunneling through the mountains and the line was still hundreds of miles short of the Ohio River. The South Western Rail Road Bank, on the other hand, flourished. It was a widely respected, conservatively run bank and one of the very few antebellum southern banks to survive the Civil War.[39]

South Carolina had apparently taken a lesson from northern systems in combining transportation infrastructure construction and banking. Recall that Pennsylvania chartered mixed companies such as the New Hope Bank and Bridge Company and the Columbia Bank and Bridge Company. When subscriptions for the bridge companies languished, the state gave the construction companies banking privileges. As such, they loaned (mostly to themselves) and circulated notes to finance construction. Ultimately, these were among Pennsylvania's least esteemed banks.[40] South Carolina adopted the practice and upped the ante. With a $6 million capital, the South Western Rail Road Bank was several orders of magnitude larger than Pennsylvania's $150,000 Columbia bridge bank. As such, the former could have quickly become a real nuisance and a serious political and economic liability. South Carolina averted trouble by separating control, yet it linked ownership so that each subsidiary faced incentives to cooperate rather than compete.

Louisiana did not follow South Carolina's lead in its separation of banking and improvement companies, and its outcome was nearly opposite. Although New Orleans' export trade increased throughout the antebellum era, and its export trade was rivaled only by New York, city and state politicians believed that they, too, had to embark on extensive infrastructure projects or lose out to rival cities. Like other states, Louisiana turned to its banks, chartering several that assisted, organized, and supervised the construction of one infrastructure project or another. The first one was the New Orleans Canal and Banking Company (1831). With a $4 million aggregate capital, the bank invested $1 million in the construction of a canal linking the Mississippi River in central New Orleans with Lake Ponchartrain. Another $1.3 million of its capital was divided among four rural branches, with at least two-thirds of that amount used for mortgage lending.[41] The Canal Bank, as it was popularly called, was to be all things to all borrowers: general contractor, mortgage lender, commercial lender, and canal financier. It was a lot to ask of one bank, no matter how large.

Despite its scattered focus, the Canal Bank thrived, which encouraged Louisiana's legislators to develop others in a similar mold. The Exchange and Banking Company (1835) spent $616,775 building the St. Charles Hotel, which it subsequently operated.[42] The New Orleans Gas Light and Banking Company (1835) constructed, operated, and maintained a system of gas streetlights in New Orleans and five other towns in which it operated a branch. The New Orleans Improvement and Banking Company (1836) constructed the St. Louis Hotel. And like South Carolina, Louisiana expected its banks to bring the state into the railroad age. The New Orleans Carrollton Railroad and Banking Company (1835) and the Atchafalaya Railroad and Banking Company (1836) were joint railroad-banking companies.[43]

With the exception of the Canal Bank, which itself closed its four rural branches in 1846, all of Louisiana's improvement banks failed in the 1840s. Clearly, these banks failed to conform to the dominant view that banking was sound only when it remained focused on short-term commercial lending, and historians who accept that underpinning argue that the collapse of the system was largely the inevitable outcome of poor choices.[44] George Green disagrees.[45] Although these banks faced challenges peculiar to their missions, failed in the turbulent 1840s, and relinquished their charters, they were not inherently unsound. More than anything else, they were chartered at an unfortunate time, just prior to the panics of 1837 and 1839. "Given enough capital," Green writes, "and enough time to enlarge its deposits and its note circulation, it [an improvement bank] could acquire sufficient liquid assets (e.g., commercial loans) to balance its portfolio and survive financial pressures, as the success of the Canal Bank amply demonstrates."[46] Indeed, the Canal Bank rivaled the largest, soundest, and most respected banks of its day. It developed a substantial deposit base, maintained correspondent relationships with banks outside the state and the region, and became heavily involved in the domestic and foreign exchange business. Its notes passed currency up and down the Mississippi River. That it also constructed and managed a canal was an added benefit.

Critical of the practice of integrating banks and infrastructure projects, one contemporary observer argued that America's westward expansion was financed through a systematic program of "bank-ruptcy." While most improvement banks failed and many were ill conceived, the real measure of their success depended on whether the long-term social benefits of the financed infrastructure outweighed the costs of the bank's eventual failure. No estimates of the costs of bank failure exist for the antebellum era, but one estimate for the National Banking Era (1863–1913) places the direct costs of failure at 5.6 percent of failing banks' liabilities.[47] Indirect costs effectively tripled that amount. Assuming that failure costs were similar in the antebellum era and assuming that the typical improvement bank issued about $3 million in liabilities exclusive of capital, the direct and indirect costs of a failure amounted to about $500,000. Assume further that the bank financed a $1 million infrastructure project and then failed 10 years afterward. Under these fairly general assumptions, the social costs of bank failure just offset the social benefits of the infrastructure project if the project yielded an 11 percent social rate of return and the bank produced no social benefits outside financing the project. Given that Albert Fishlow, based on conservative estimates, finds that the social rate of return to canals exceeded 50 percent, the net costs of an improvement bank's failure were relatively small, though they were surely significant to those unfortunate enough to be one of a failing bank's uncompensated creditors. Even the Ohio Canal, a notorious financial failure, yielded a 10 percent social rate of return.[48] If this canal was responsible for a bank's failure, society broke even on the exchange. It got a canal and lost a bank of about equal social value.

Although improvement banking did not conform to the dominant contemporary banking theory, improvement banks proved popular because they yielded a significant social benefit and contributed to the continued geographic expansion and economic growth even after they closed their doors. An improved transportation infrastructure encouraged the exploitation of regional comparative advantages by reducing the costs of trade. Nowhere was this more important than in the Old Northwest. In 1833, Ohio completed 400 miles of canals connecting the Ohio River with Lake Erie.[49] In the same year, construction began on an extended network that, by 1847, created a system with more than 800 miles of interconnected canals. Carter Golembe estimates that during the late 1830s and early 1840s, Indiana, Ohio, Illinois, and Michigan spent more than $40 million on various internal improvement projects.[50] In one way or another, those states' banks contributed about $8.6 million, or 22 percent, of that amount. A decidedly negative consequence of entangling banks in such projects was that many banks failed.

While generations of historians have roundly criticized banking policies that mixed banking and infrastructure financing, Golembe is more forgiving. Bankers, he argues, were not ignorant of good banking practice. They were fully cognizant of the risk involved in enterprises pursuing multiple objectives, and it was a risk they willingly accepted for one very good reason. They were "assisting aggressive, enterprising men to transform, at a very rapid rate, a primitive agricultural economy into one which was more modern and highly productive."[51] That a few banks were sacrificed on the altar of progress was acceptable to most contemporaries, if not most historians.

The social benefits of bank-financed canals and related projects were pronounced; these improvements aided farmers in the region in achieving their market objectives. Between 1835 and 1860, western and southern wheat flour exports increased from 0.4 million to 5.0 million barrels. The difference between the New York and the Cincinnati prices fell from $1.29 per barrel in 1831 to just $0.63 in 1860.[52] Although the Old Northwest would have eventually achieved its economic potential, banks played a vital role in accelerating the process. Mixed bank-infrastructure enterprises facilitated trade by making markets in bills of exchange. They financed settlement and land development by buying mortgages. They underwrote improvements and infrastructure by directly investing in or lending to turnpike, canal, and railroad companies. And because much of this capital was provided when states were foreclosed from alternative sources, like bond issues, the banks' importance should not be underestimated.[53]

Banks and the Commonwealth Ideal

Besides the heavy use of banks in underwriting infrastructure in the South and West, massive state involvement was a second defining characteristic of banking outside the northeastern United States. This is not to imply that northeastern states did not involve themselves in the operations of, or take ownership positions in, their banks. They did. But state ownership was relatively modest in the Northeast. At its peak, Pennsylvania owned more than $1 million in bank shares, most of which represented its stake in the Bank of Pennsylvania, the state's fiscal agent modeled after the First Bank of the United States. Fiscal crisis in the 1830s elicited the state's divestment of most of its holdings. Massachusetts, similarly, owned about $1 million in various bank shares in 1812, an amount that represented about one-eighth of the state's aggregate bank capital. But Massachusetts, too, divested most of its shares following the War of 1812 to pay off its war-related debts. The histories of most other New England and Middle Atlantic states follow a similar trajectory.

States in the South and West took a much greater interest in their banks. There were wholly owned state banks in South Carolina, Alabama, Arkansas, Kentucky, Tennessee, and Illinois. Virginia owned one-fifth of the Bank of Virginia and the Farmers' Bank of Virginia, and it took a significant stake in three other large branch banks. Kentucky owned the Bank of Kentucky (1806) and the Bank of the Commonwealth of Kentucky (1820), yet it also chartered and took up $2 million of the (second) Bank of Kentucky's (1834) $5 million capital. The state subscribed to lesser amounts in the Louisville Bank (1833) and the Northern Bank of Kentucky (1835). Similarly, Indiana, Louisiana, Missouri, and several other states subsidized substantial fractions of their banks' capitals.

States took up bank shares for a number of reasons. New England states purchased bank shares because banking was well established and profitable.[54] Shares were considered safe and dividend revenue replaced taxes, in whole or in part. Pennsylvania modeled the Bank of Pennsylvania after the

First Bank of the United States and expected it to act as the state's fiscal agent and revenue generator. The state took a stake so that it could exercise some control over the bank's policies, mainly through the appointment of directors. States in the South and West had these plus an additional motive. Although these states expected their investments in banks to generate revenue, reduce tax burdens, and allow them some measure of control, state involvement ultimately encouraged private investment. State participation usually implied a large, well-capitalized institution carrying an implicit governmental contingent liability. Such banks proved to be low-cost mechanisms for pooling scattered pockets of savings.

In Virginia, for example, a number of small towns (even Richmond was small compared to Boston or Baltimore) had sprung up along the state's rivers and local merchants clamored for credit. Few of these towns were large enough to justify a stand-alone bank and none could provide enough capital to build one capable of quieting critics. The state stepped in and subsidized a branch network. By supplying one-fifth of the Bank of Virginia's capital, the state increased the bank's scale and scope and increased public confidence in the institution by retaining some control.[55] The state treasurer voted the state's 3,000 shares and the treasurer himself was made an ex officio member of the board.

Indiana's example provides an instructive study of state-bank synergies and how a state could underwrite a bank later labeled the "best in the West."[56] Indiana chartered the State Bank in 1834, but there was not enough private capital to take up the public's quota of the bank's $50 par shares. To stimulate subscriptions, the state asked subscribers to pay only $18.75 on each share and the state loaned the remaining $31.25 to subscribers on deeds of mortgage worth at least twice the value of the state's advance.[57] Subscribers agreed to pay 6 percent annual interest, and both interest and principal were repaid from the bank's dividends. To fund its advances to subscribers, Indiana sold 5 percent bonds in London, which were taken up at a premium, reducing the state's interest costs. Secured by the state's share in the bank and the mortgages given by subscribers, the bonds matured in 25 years. Because the bank's average dividends exceeded 6 percent, stockholders were free of the state lien by 1850 and the state retired the bonds before maturity. State intervention produced a highly regarded institution that provided Hoosiers with a stable currency and adequate credit facilities for two decades. The bank liquidated in 1855, not because it had outlived its usefulness, but because the state opted for free banking instead.

To those unfamiliar with antebellum America's polity and economy, the extent of state involvement in banking may come as a surprise. The era is often portrayed as one of rugged individualism and rampant laissez-faire. G. S. Callender long ago noted the error of such interpretations, a finding supported by any number of subsequent studies.[58]

None other than Thomas Jefferson, champion of the yeoman farmer, called for a rationalized transportation network and had Albert Gallatin lay out a plan for a national network of canals and roads to be subsidized by the federal government. By 1806, work on the National Road was under way. Work was halted prior to completion, however, by executive veto. A federal bank later fell victim to executive vetos too. When the federal government failed to provide something, states usually stepped in. In the 1810s, states stepped in to clear rivers and harbors, build lighthouses, underwrite turnpikes, and subsidize and otherwise encourage canals, bridges, and railroads.

Modern economists argue that navigable rivers, passable roads, and harbors cleared of obstructions are classic public goods (i.e., goods that combine nonexcludability and nonrivalrous consumption) that markets provide in inefficiently small quantities. Turnpikes, bridges, canals, and railroads are not pure public goods, but they often involve sizable positive externalities that admit the possibility of subsidization in many cases. With the possible exception of a central bank, few modern economists consider banks and other financial intermediaries elements of a transaction infrastructure deserving of direct government financing, much less partial subsidization. Early Americans believed otherwise. In the South and West, particularly, state subsidization of banking predated involvement in other elements of the basic infrastructure. The heavily subsidized Bank of Virginia was founded in 1804, the wholly state-owned Bank of Kentucky was organized in 1806, and the Bank of the State of Tennessee was formed in 1811.

Contemporaries clearly accepted banks as basic infrastructure. Some banking historians, such as Fritz Redlich, claim that state involvement and subsidization arose because outdated and mistaken mercantilist precepts prevailed in the commercially unsophisticated West. In short, critics argue that westerners, wanting of hard currency, simply attempted to "coin their land." The dispute, then, turns on whether we can identify any substantive externality generated by early western banks. That is, did the social returns to banks exceed the private returns? Measuring private and social costs is difficult enough even with good data from the late twentieth century; it is especially troublesome for the early nineteenth-century West because records and documents are few. Nevertheless, a good case can be made for bank-generated externalities.

A potentially significant externality was the banks' influence on the nature of capital.[59] In many developing economies (nineteenth-century America included), wealth took the form of inventories of foodstuffs, livestock, land, and land improvements. In financially underdeveloped countries, such inventories represented the only reasonably liquid and divisible asset that offered some protection from price and output shocks. Such inventories, while individually rational, were costly to both the individual and society because storage and spoilage costs were high. Moreover, hoarding prevented resources from moving to more productive employments.

Early banks were important because they encouraged households to release inventories of productive goods in exchange for financial or paper
claims to those assets. In the earliest phases of development, this exchange
of real for financial assets centered around the simplest of financial instruments—the banknote. By monetizing the local economy, early banks coaxed
productive resources from hoards, facilitated trade, and hastened development. The fundamental changes wrought by the banknote can be seen in
the reaction of Kentuckians to the receipt of their first banknotes:

> They were handled with care and admired for the fine pictures upon
> them. If an old farmer got hold of one of them he showed it to his
> wife and children and enjoyed their wonder and admiration. It was
> laid away between the leaves of the family Bible, and kept smooth
> and nice until a pressure, not to be borne, extorted it for debt, or it
> went for something that had to be bought.[60]

Thus, banknotes performed their dual role as medium of exchange and store
of value.

The use of banknotes in these functions represented an elemental shift
in the nature of economic activity that promoted economic development.
Before banknotes, currency on the American frontier consisted of a ragtag
mixture of foreign and domestic coins (usually highly worn and heavily
depreciated), land warrants, tobacco warehouse receipts, and even animal
pelts. Such nonstandard currencies increased the costs of transacting over
what they were with easily exchanged, conveniently denominated, paper
banknotes. Banks, then, provided a good that reduced transaction costs,
which provided benefits to everyone engaged in economic transactions
whether they dealt directly with the bank or not. A bank received interest
from borrowers who circulated the notes, so the bank was compensated for
its services, but the marginal borrower paid a rate equal to the opportunity
cost of the bank's funds, which compensated the bank only for its lending
services. The bank received no such direct compensation for the transaction
services its notes provided. At an even more basic level, banknotes helped
establish market prices and the price level itself can be seen as a type of
public good. The ability to quote prices in terms of a widely accepted de-
nominator facilitated trade.

Moreover, the banknote was nonneutral in that it reinforced an incipient
commercial ethos. Banknotes inculcated a habit to exchange financial for
real assets. While this habit came to full flower in the post–Civil War era,
the increased familiarity with one paper asset animated the demand for
others, such as stocks, bonds, and commercial paper. As an increasing share
of household wealth took the form of financial rather than real assets, investors and entrepreneurs were provided with a greater quantity of productive resources earlier than they would have been without banknotes.
Clearly, if western states had not subsidized banking, banks would have

eventually appeared on their own. But one of the hallmarks of America is its youthful impatience. Such eagerness sometimes resulted in hasty and precipitate action, but it just as often created wealth.

A second economic justification for state-owned banks in the American West is provided by Alexander Gerschenkron, who observes a recurrent pattern of expanding the role of the state among late-developing economies attempting to catch up to early developers.[61] Moreover, both he and Joseph Schumpeter contend that financial development was a prerequisite for wider economic development.[62] Financial institutions arose first and redirected capital from existing economic agents to innovative entrepreneurs. Their view is labeled the "supply-leading" hypothesis, strong versions of which hold that the establishment of financial institutions must predate modern industrial advance. A fundamental shortcoming of the traditional supply-leading hypothesis is its narrowness. It is based on a model of German universal banking and, thus, not widely applicable to many other countries' emergent banking sectors.

There is general acceptance of the competing "demand-following" hypothesis, which holds that finance follows enterprise. Henrietta Larson, for instance, argues that early American bankers were passive intermediaries, between highly risk-averse savers and moderately risk-averse merchants.[63] American banks, unlike their German counterparts, did not promote new enterprise; instead, they serviced the needs of existing, proven enterprises. One reason that critics have rejected the supply-leading hypothesis is that supply-leading banks were unprofitable at the outset. Because few nascent industries existed, profitable lending opportunities were few. Such banks, then, would survive only with large subsidies or by outright state ownership.

Several states provided such subsidies and several others operated state-owned banks. Although Schumpeter and Gerschenkron constructed their theories around a supply-leading institution modeled on the Credit Mobilier, most of these early American banks fit into their frameworks in a way not envisioned by either. The Bank of Kentucky and the Bank of the State of Tennessee were two of several banks formed in the early nineteenth century, wholly owned by the state, whose charge was to extend low-cost credit to farmers so that their states' agricultural potential could be quickly realized. Although these were not a type of institution envisioned by Schumpeter or Gerschenkron, they nevertheless promoted the development of commercialized agriculture, a first step on the path to economic modernity.

Institutions, such the Bank of Kentucky, initially extended most of their credit in traditional sectors (e.g., agriculture and commerce) but gradually altered their portfolios as economic conditions changed and new industries arose. In this way, banks generated enough revenue even from the outset to minimize the state subsidy. Governments, nonetheless, provided a multitude of indirect subsidies: corporate status and limited liability; the right of summary diligence, in which creditors could seize a delinquent debtor's assets without the formality of a court hearing; promises of perpetual or limited monopolies; and the right to create and issue liabilities under unusually favorable conditions. Once a bank was firmly established, the economy reasonably monetized, the state well populated, and agriculture commercialized, the state could release market forces in the financial sector by chartering new banks or spinning off the formerly state-owned enterprise.

If such a modified supply-leading hypothesis is an accurate representation of the antebellum experience, each state's banking choices had far-reaching ramifications for subsequent economic growth. Finance alone was not the wellspring of economic development, but it was likely to have been a contributing factor. Western and southern states were acting appropriately in their encouragement of banking. More monetized economies with adequate credit supplies generally grew more rapidly than less monetized, credit-short economies.[64]

Just as economic theory can provide a justification for state intervention in banking based on theories of public goods, externalities, and economic development, political theory can generate a similar justification based on a contemporary republican impulse that historians label the "commonwealth ideal."[65] The commonwealth ideal holds that the state should take an active part in promoting the general welfare of the community. Because some contemporaries believed that banks provided nearly universal benefits, and because privately owned corporations chartered in newly settled regions were unable to raise enough capital to operate on the desired scale, the state stepped in, providing capital, corporate privilege, and a host of other entitlements. Laissez-faire was fine up to a point, but when the implications of a strict free market philosophy did not accord with political ideals, it was quickly abandoned.

Given the strong emotions surrounding state intervention in the antebellum economy, state ownership and subsidization were not universally beloved. Jefferson's political philosophy attracted adherents throughout the antebellum era. As late as 1849, Governor Seabrook of South Carolina disapproved of the Bank of the State of South Carolina, despite the bank's 30-year record of service to the state. He called the bank a dangerous, pernicious, and anti-Republican institution, an anomaly in a state whose legislative delegation had denounced the Second Bank of the United States as an unnatural linking of economy and polity. Moreover, Seabrook did not see the sense of providing farmers with "unusual facilities for commanding money."[66]

When Seabrook expressed this opinion, South Carolina was already the second most monetized economy in the South and the sixth most monetized economy in the United States. In per capita bank credit, South Carolina rivaled New York and Louisiana and trailed behind only southern New England. In some sense, Seabrook was correct. It may not have been logical for the state to own a bank in a reasonably developed, monetized economy. We can only speculate whether Seabrook would have taken a similar stance

30 years earlier or if he lived closer to the frontier. The depression of the late 1830s and early 1840s, massive bank failures during the same period, and the rise of radical anticorporatism during the Jacksonian era turned many against close state-bank involvement. A sizable fraction of the electorate, however, still accepted the principle that the state owed its citizens sound money and cheap credit—fundamental elements of the commercial infrastructure. If it took the state to supply them, so be it.

State commitment to the commonwealth ideal was never more apparent than during the economic tough times of the early 1820s and early 1840s. When the post war boom turned bust in 1819, 63 western banks quickly closed and Kentucky witnessed the emergence of a political coalition made up of landowning debtors who lobbied the legislature for relief. Relief advocates lobbied for inflationary banking in order to reduce the debt burdens taken on during the previous expansion. The old Bank of Kentucky responded to these calls, partly to ward off legislative interference, by suspending specie payments and announcing that it would expand its note issues to reinflate.[67]

The bank's commitment to suspension and reinflation was weak at best, largely because a number of the bank's more conservative directors opposed the policy.[68] Directors of the Louisville branch, mostly conservative merchants, initially refused to suspend payments and did only after explicit orders were forwarded from the parent office in Frankfort, a town of minimal commercial importance but site of the state capital. Conservative directors called a special meeting and demanded that the bank retrench by gradually reducing discounts and circulation and bolstering specie reserves to prepare for speedy resumption. Directors of the rural branches, not surprisingly, called for additional relief measures: easy credit, expanded note issues, and continued suspension. Sound banking policy favored the Louisville minority, but politics and the farmers' needs dictated a more lenient credit and monetary policy.

John Adair, the relief candidate, won the gubernatorial election and a majority of both houses were pledged to sweeping relief reforms.[69] The legislature's policy was built on two pillars. The first was a state-owned bank with a real commitment to reinflation. The second, a series of stay laws that created a virtual moratorium on debt collections. The Bank of the Commonwealth of Kentucky was chartered in the 1820 legislative session. All Kentucky residents, particularly heavily mortgaged landholders and indebted farmers, were eligible for up to $1,000 in loans so that they could discharge their debts without sacrificing their land at ruinously low prices.[70] The Bank of the Commonwealth was not required to redeem its notes in specie, but the notes were made legal tender for all debts due to the state. Lands owned by the state south of the Tennessee River were pledged for the final redemption of the bank's notes. Finally, to ensure that the new bank would protect indebted landholders, a replevy law was enacted that required creditors to accept the bank's notes in payment of an existing debt or to forgo collection for up to two years.

The twin relief measures created a rift in Kentucky politics that persisted throughout the decade. When existing courts found most of the relief program unconstitutional, the 1820/21 relief legislature created an entirely new judicial system and appointed judges sympathetic to the relief program. The old (antirelief) and new (prorelief) courts operated side by side and created legal confusion, acrimony, and dissent.[71] Proreliefers were adamant enough to convince William Gouge that they would defend their courts and their program "with powder and ball" if necessary.[72]

The October 1821 legislative session brought a second wave of relief measures. The Bank of the Commonwealth, which had not issued its legal maximum of banknotes, was instructed to immediately issue an additional $500,000, but it was also told to start retrenching by August 1822 to prepare for the resumption of specie payments.[73] State land agents were instructed to sell lands securing the bank's paper to assure its commitment to specie redemption. At the same time, the legislature continued its earlier stay laws. No attached property could be sold by creditors if it brought less than 75 percent of its fair value (defined by a board of assessors) at auction. Imprisonment for debt was also suspended, except in cases of fraud.

The relief system's legal and economic record was mixed. Federal courts limited some parts of the stay laws, particularly when the laws pitted non-resident creditors and resident debtors. In *Wayman v. Southard*, U.S. Chief Justice John Marshall blasted Kentucky's claim that the federal judiciary had an obligation to respect all relevant state laws when deciding a case, and he struck down most of Kentucky's debt moratorium laws.[74] What surprised many contemporaries was the Court's willingness to condone the Bank of the Commonwealth. Questions concerning whether the bank violated the constitutional ban on state bills of credit naturally arose. The bank was established by and for the state, under the direction of 12 directors all appointed by the state, and operated without a mandate to redeem its notes in specie. Some contemporary legal experts drew parallels between the Bank of the Commonwealth and a Missouri loan office that the Court struck down in 1830.[75] In *Briscoe v. The Bank of the Commonwealth*, the U.S. Supreme Court held that the bank did not fall under the constitutional proscription, even though it was a wholly state-owned institution whose note issues were ultimately secured by state lands.[76] Hammond argues that the decision was as timid as any handed down by the high court.[77] The Court's timidity, if that's what it was, may reflect its struggle with fine legal distinctions or the simple fact that, had the Court struck down the Bank of the Commonwealth, worse financial chaos may have followed because at least a half-dozen other states had chartered similar institutions.

The important issue is not whether the Bank of the Commonwealth's notes were de facto bills of credit, but whether the bank achieved the social and economic objectives set for it. "It has long been recognized," writes Thomas Berry, "that enforcement of a dollar contract after a major [unanticipated] decline of prices is highly inequitable and that sale of the debtor's property to fulfill such a contract is even more undesirable, especially if such a sale takes place under temporarily unfavorable conditions."[78] Although exact declines in land prices between 1818 and 1820 cannot be determined, it is well known that land prices typically fell about 50 percent and recovered very slowly thereafter. The overall western price level followed the same pattern, as did the market value of the notes of the Bank of the Commonwealth. In September 1821, its notes traded for about 67 cents on the dollar; by April 1822, they declined to about 55 cents. Berry argues that the nearly equal declines in the general price level and the market value of the Bank of the Commonwealth's notes left creditors in the same position they would have been in had the recession and deflation not occurred.[79] Similarly, Gouge argued that the only equitable solution was to adjust individual contracts to reflect changes in the purchasing power of money.[80] But changes in the purchasing power of money in the face of invariant contract prices would have accomplished the same end, and it may have done so at a lower cost. Gouge's solution would have required renegotiation on a massive scale, with a considerable amount of costly litigation as the likely outcome. Depreciating the purchasing power of money accomplished the same object, albeit indiscriminately.

The commonwealth ideal was not singularly Kentuckian. In the throes of the depression of the early 1820s, Tennessee passed a series of stay laws and chartered the State Bank of Tennessee. With a capital of $1 million supplied by the state itself, the bank extended small loans to landholding debtors.[81] Unlike Kentucky's relief program, however, Tennessee's was short lived. William Carroll, antirelief candidate and political ally of Andrew Jackson, prevailed in the gubernatorial election and quickly dismantled most of the relief program. The State Bank was not closed until 1830 and then only because the bank's cashier absconded, revealing a $140,000 cash shortage.

Other states instituted their own variants of Kentucky's relief program. In 1821, Illinois enacted a number of stay laws that delayed foreclosures for up to two years and chartered the State Bank of Illinois, modeled after Kentucky's Bank of the Commonwealth.[82] The bank's $500,000 capital was wholly subscribed by the state and divided among five branches located throughout the state. It was allowed to issue $1 to $20 notes receivable for all state and county taxes. The bank loaned up to $100 on unsecured promissory notes and $1,000 on notes collateralized by mortgages. All loans matured in one year but would be renewed upon payment of 10 percent of the original principal. In this way, one-tenth of the bank's circulation would be repaid each year for ten years, at which time the bank would cease to exist.

Ohio also passed replevy laws, preventing hasty liquidations at fire-sale prices, but refused to charter a relief bank.[83] Louisiana, on the other hand, chartered two distinct relief banks. In 1818, the state subscribed to one-quarter of the Louisiana State Bank's $2 million capital. Credit problems in the early 1820s changed the bank's lending and it began extending loans with maturities beyond 180 days at 8 percent interest.[84] When the Louisiana State Bank's lending failed to meet demand, the state chartered the Bank of Louisiana, which was required to loan at least $2 million to distressed planters.[85]

During the depression of the early 1840s, relief measures were again called for and many states returned to the model established 20 years earlier. Illinois enacted stay laws on debt collections and moratoria on foreclosures, but the U.S. Supreme Court struck them down as unconstitutional.[86] Kentucky's legislators chose not to enact a new wave of replevy laws but pressured the state's existing banks to extend more loans. When the banks balked, the state senate directed the standing Joint Committee on Banks to report on the possibility of establishing a state-owned bank like the Bank of the Commonwealth that had been liquidated in the 1830s. Recalling the credit and monetary dislocations surrounding the highly politicized Bank of the Commonwealth, Kentucky's existing banks finally agreed to assist troubled farmers in return for an act legalizing the suspension of specie payments. The state's three branch banks increased their aggregate circulation by about $1 million and made loans of less than $500 at maturities of 220 days that were subject to 120-day renewals as long as 20 percent of the original loan amount was repaid at each renewal. Extant records show that the Bank of Kentucky extended $100,000 in such loans in the state's 7th congressional district and $102,500 in the 3rd district. Kentucky's policy effectively balanced farmers' and financiers' demands. Farmers needed additional credit to avoid foreclosure; financiers demanded retrenchment after any short-term expansion.[87] The banks' relief lending relieved distress, but it was canceled in 19 months, allowing banks to prepare for resumption in a rational, timely manner.

While Kentucky considered but never chartered a new state-owned bank, Tennessee did. The Bank of Tennessee differed markedly from its predecessor, the Bank of the State of Tennessee. Believing that lending solely to debt-strapped farmers had been the cause of the earlier bank's downfall, the legislature made the new bank a hybrid institution.[88] In the short term, it focused on mortgage lending, but it was to lend about one-half of its funds on pure commercial paper. The bank's capital was supplied by the state and the legislature chose its directors. In true commonwealth ideal fashion, the bank's profits were used to finance common schools (about $100,000 annually) and colleges ($18,000). Moreover, the state was authorized to issue $4 million in bonds to finance internal improvement projects, and the bank, like the Bank of the State of South Carolina, was responsible for both interest and principal. Whether in inception or in execution, the Bank of Tennessee turned out to be a huge success. It remained profitable throughout the remainder of the antebellum era, despite being saddled with the state's bonded debt. The Civil War, not financial mismanagement, doomed the Bank of Tennessee.

Wholly or partially state-owned banks, however much they represented the commonwealth ideal, created two potential problems for the states that chartered them. First, they undermined incentives to foster competitive banking. Although state subsidization may have been necessary in the earliest stages of development, economic growth and financial development eventually undermined such banks' intellectual foundation. Founded with the express purpose of enhancing the commonweal, their success increased the demand for financial services that a state truly committed to the common welfare would sanction. On one hand, the state was presumably obliged to look out for the public interest. On the other, the state held a significant pecuniary stake in an existing bank, and chartering one or more competitors would cut into the state bank's profits.

It is, indeed, curious that when faced with this dilemma, most states appeased calls for expansion and competition. Despite owning one-fifth of the monopoly the Bank of Virginia founded in 1804, Virginia chartered the Farmers Bank in 1812 and the Exchange Bank in 1837 and allowed them both to establish branches in towns where the Bank of Virginia already operated. The state did not allow genuine competition until the early 1850s, after it had sold its bank shares. South Carolina, Louisiana, and Tennessee also allowed entry despite close connections to their banks. Although it seems counterintuitive, competition may have enhanced a state bank's standing. Competition lowered lending rates, but it also provided a check on the state bank's operations. As Schweikart notes, competition "left little room for the state to engage in financial shenanigans with its own institution."[89]

A second problem with state-owned banks was that the state faced a potentially large contingent liability. Well-run banks provided a steady stream of dividend income to the state. A poorly run one drained the treasury. While the Bank of the State of South Carolina and the Bank of Tennessee were successful institutions, state banks in Alabama, Mississippi, Arkansas, Illinois, Georgia, and Florida failed. Did it make sense for the state to renege on its liabilities in the same way a private debtor could through a bankruptcy procedure? Private debtors imposed losses because their negative net worth position was irreversible in the short run. States did not face the same problem. They could tax. Taxes were politically unpleasant, but it was political suicide (in most instances) for a legislator to inform his bank-creditor constituents to accept a loss. Because constituents holding the failed bank's claims preferred to spread a loss among all taxpayers, legislators did, too. Thus, the state's contingent liability lost its contingency. It became very real.

Moreover, even a casual reading of the results of state ownership implies that the lack of market forces and the prevalence of political forces induced inefficient behaviors. When the Bank of the State of Alabama was established, there was an immediate crush of requests from every legislator to locate a branch in his district whether or not it was economic to place one there.[90] Moreover, the state capital and the main office of the bank were moved from Cahawba to Tuscaloosa to further erode the remaining political influence of the Royalists, whose strongholds were in northern Alabama. Thus, the bank became farther removed from a place of economic consequence. At the same time, debtor groups forced the state to abandon its right to inspect the bank's books, leaving it with no effective regulator. The state also protected its institution from outside competition. It did everything it could to undermine the integrity of the widely respected Bank of Mobile, short of repealing its charter, and it mercilessly attacked other interlopers. Although the state pressed the bank for revenues to replace direct taxation, the bank did not face the same kind of profit incentives facing traditional commercial banks.

Alabama's strategy of creating and protecting a favored lender worked well enough during good times, but the panic of 1837 quickly exposed the cracks in the bank's foundation. Unable to collect on most of its loans and unable to meet debts payable in New York City, the bank began speculating on cotton. Its speculations probably violated its charter, but it was soon so fully engrossed in the speculation that the bank could not have easily extracted itself even if told to do so. When the speculation soured, the politicians needed a scapegoat, and blame was laid on excessive borrowing by the bank's officers and directors. When the cotton speculation became public, depositors ran the bank, worsening its already unfavorable reserve position. Finally, when former employees revealed the extent to which officers were afforded generous overdrafts, it was apparent that the bank's days were numbered. By 1839, Alabama's taxpayers were left on the hook for the bank's deficit.

All of this is reminiscent of the U.S. savings and loan crisis of the 1980s. Freed from market forces, the bank took risks that market-oriented banks (like the Bank of Mobile) refused. Moreover, the implicit insurance provided by the state government encouraged the bank to engage in inefficient go-for-broke strategies in an effort to save itself. Finally, the lack of basic regulation of even the most rudimentary sort provided the opportunity for bank officers to engage in criminal or near-criminal fraud.

Thus, states that chose to establish state-owned banks walked a tightrope. On one hand, they had to recognize the potentially large contingent liability. Alabama was presented with a large bill. Georgia, too, was forced to pay more than $500,000 of the Central Bank of Milledgeville's net worth shortfall in 1845. Safeguards, from the basic (such as the right to inspect the bank's books) to the more complex (such as appointing a bank's directors) to allowing competitive forces to direct the bank's activities, were required to mitigate the state's potential liability. On the other hand, the state had to be willing to relinquish its favored position when it became clear that its role as venture capitalist was no longer necessary or desired.

It was also requisite for the state to understand the real nature of its actions and act appropriately. Some banks, like the Bank of the State of South Carolina and the State Bank of Indiana, were designed as long-term solutions to long-standing problems: long-term agricultural credit in the former case and short-term commercial credit in the latter. Because they were expected to solve problems over a long period, these banks' missions were well conceived; appropriate institutions with appropriate safeguards were established. In other instances, such as those involving the Bank of the Commonwealth (1820–1834) and the State Bank of Illinois (chartered in 1819, repealed in 1821), banks were hastily thrown together without a clear mission other than lending to the legal limit as quickly as possible to reinflate the economy. It is not surprising, therefore, that these banks became political and economic liabilities. With no real incentive to fund borrowers with projects likely to provide a positive return, these banks allocated funds on some other (usually politically motivated) basis.

These banks were organized to minimize the transfer of property when economic conditions would have otherwise dictated wholesale liquidation. Such liquidation, of course, would have been inefficient and would have imposed unnecessary hardship on a large percentage of the population. To the extent that hastily chartered relief banks avoided inefficient foreclosure and liquidation, they served their purpose. In the end, then, we cannot declare relief banks unsuccessful. Some eventually failed with large losses assumed by taxpayers, but they also reinflated economies and allowed for a more orderly disposal of property. Determining whether the net benefits were positive will require further research, but we are forced to accept the proposition that, on net, state-owned banks, even the relief banks of the early 1820s and early 1840s, advanced the commonweal.

Concluding Remarks

Beginning in the 1820s and continuing through the antebellum era, southerners grew increasingly tied to cotton agriculture. People in the Old Northwest grew increasingly dependent on a market-oriented agriculture based on corn and pork. It is not particularly surprising, then, that the primary sources of income became the basis for banking. The West was, relatively speaking, land rich and capital poor. In the public mind, all that was needed to bring this land under plow, to make it productive and its inhabitants wealthy, was capital. And the regions' banks found ways to supply it. "Although broad categorization runs the risk of deemphasizing or ignoring idiosyncratic features," notes Schweikart, "the patterns of southern regulatory development generally tended to encourage either competition and little state activity on the one hand or heavy state involvement and control on the other."[91] States in the Old Northwest followed similarly dichotomous strategies, sometimes alternately pursuing one then the other.

Despite regional differences in topography, industrial mix, and culture, banks everywhere were expected to contribute to a region's economic development. Regardless of exact organizational form, banks achieved their objective in several ways. They acted as the prototypical intermediaries, facilitating the flow of funds from savers to investors. They monetized the economy. They financed various infrastructure projects, which allowed for more-rapid, more-efficient movement of goods between regions that, in turn, fostered regional specialization and the potential to capture the benefits of regional comparative advantages. They prevented the inefficient liquidation of assets during crises.

Contemporary southerners and westerners recognized, though often vaguely and indistinctly, the link between financial and economic growth. Thus, where private capital was in short supply, the state stepped in, sometimes to augment private capital, sometimes to act in its stead. The commonwealth ideal was alive and well as states took responsibility for promoting the general welfare of their citizenry. In the earliest stages of development, the ideal found its expression in the subsidization of banks in the same way that states subsidized other forms of infrastructure. In time, the relationship was reversed. When the state subsidized banks in their formative period, they were later called on to finance other forms of infrastructure—roads, canals, railroads, and so forth. This turnabout often benefited banks, but it just as often eroded their soundness.

Such failures did not result from the violation of some immutable formulation of sound banking. They often resulted from bad timing, such as being chartered in 1837 or being asked to do what was unlikely to succeed in any case, like subsidize an unprofitable canal. Moreover, banks were expected to simultaneously accomplish the contradictory objectives of sound currency and liberal credit. It was the banks' responsibility to walk the fine line and lean one way or the other depending on current sentiment and both long- and short-term expectations. That banks did not always succeed should not be a surprise. What is surprising is the general success of the majority of these regions' banks. Though western banks were sometimes found wanting, their shortcomings were excusable in that they were "instrumental in assisting aggressive, enterprising men to transform, at a very rapid rate, a primitive agricultural economy" into a more modern, more productive one.[92]

Banks were, in fact, very much an exception. In his study of nineteenth-century Wisconsin, Lawrence Friedman finds that when western states wanted to act on their interventionist impulses, they found themselves constrained by institutional factors. In most instances, states were forced to adopt mechanisms that relied neither on bureaucracy (because they did not yet exist) nor on direct subsidization through taxes (because the ability to collect taxes was limited).[93] Thus, Harry Scheiber observes that states that attempted to administrate subsidy programs typically failed miserably.[94] He notes a few exceptions, like the Erie Canal administrators, but they were few. State-sponsored banks provide a mixed tale: some succeeded, some failed, and some achieved a measure of success for a brief time. That states turned to banks was logical. Bank bureaucracy was relatively small, and banks—the good ones, at least—were able to support themselves with minimal direct and continuing subsidies. States injected initial capital and then turned the banks out to do their business. In Virginia, the outcome was a system of "broad regulations, liberal powers, freedom of action, and few restrictions. The final result was a banking system which merited and won the entire confidence of the people."[95]

10

Property Banking, Free Banking, and Branch Banking

Because well-managed commercial banks quickly became profitable and self-sufficient, they required few continuing direct subsidies. Usually, the only state encouragement needed was an initial injection of capital. Thereafter, the state could step back and, like other shareholders, decide how to spend the dividends. The commonwealth ideal sanctioned limited government intervention, and such intervention, when prudent and limited in scope, generally proved beneficial. One perceived shortcoming with the implementation of the commonwealth ideal was that its benefits were too narrowly distributed. Merchants became the primary beneficiaries because they became the banks' principal clients. Farmers and planters resented this favoritism. Agriculture, after all, formed the backbone of the southern economy, so agriculture, argued farmers, should receive at least equal access to credit.

These sentiments brought the commonwealth ideal to full flower in the 1830s. No longer content to act as limited partners or venture capitalists to fledgling but promising enterprises, four southern states provided direct subsidies to an untested and highly speculative financial venture. These so-called property or plantation banks were capitalized through the sale of government-guaranteed bonds and provided long-term mortgage credit to farmers and planters. The objective, of course, was to stimulate agricultural production by reducing the costs of farm or mortgage credit. There was nothing inherently faulty with these plans. Today, there are a host of familiar mortgage credit institutions that subsidize home and land ownership. Nevertheless, these property banks all failed, imposing large losses to both bond and note holders. Plantation banks failed for a number of reasons, but not because they operated contrary to the essential nature of intermediation.

249

Not surprisingly, the failure of several large institutions soured southern legislators on banking. Some states imposed a moratorium on new bank charters; others adopted one implicitly simply by refusing to charter new banks. Within a decade, however, it became apparent that continued economic expansion demanded extended credit facilities. In the 1850s, a number of southern and western states turned to free banking. New York's favorable experience with free banking prompted its importation into such widely different places as Wisconsin and Tennessee, Indiana, and Louisiana. Although nominally modeled after New York's 1838 law, each state tinkered with the system, adapting it and modifying it to meet local needs and preferences.

Because free banking came in different guises, it operated better and worse according to how it was modified. Traditional tales overwhelmingly cast it in a bad light. As Logan Esary noted, the wildcat "banker from Owl Creek has usually been thought worthy of a full length portrait."[1] Recent research, however, shows that the South and West were not overrun with wildcats. A few sprung up when conditions favored them, but free banks failed for the same reasons other banks failed. The type of banking often had little to do with it. "In Ohio and Tennessee," writes Bray Hammond, "banking had been neither conspicuously bad nor conspicuously good, and free banking did not change the record materially."[2]

The defining characteristic of southern and western banking was branch banking, and it was conspicuously good. Branch banking not only made it economic to open branches in areas too small or not yet sufficiently developed commercially to support an independent bank, but it also facilitated mutual support and cooperation. A small number of large banks forced banks to recognize their strategic, competitive, and cooperative interdependence. Although this may have led to collusion and cartelization in the industry, there is little evidence to suggest that it did. Networks of a few large banks came together during financial crises to provide support and mutual guarantees that steeled them against the buffeting storms. Thus, southern and western systems experienced fewer failures and less disruption of the payments system during crises than northern banking systems.

King Cotton, the Commonwealth Ideal, and Property Banks

Economic expansion in the late 1820s and early 1830s induced a marked increase in banking in the South and West. And, consistent with the commonwealth ideal, there was an escalation in state involvement. Between 1827 and 1835, Ohio chartered 14 banks; Louisiana, 11; Florida, Georgia, and Michigan, 10 each; South Carolina, 5; Kentucky, Tennessee, Mississippi, and North Carolina, 3 each; and Virginia, Wisconsin, Illinois, and

Indiana, 1 each. Table 10.1 shows how rapidly some state and regional economies were monetized. Virginia and South Carolina, long-settled states, experienced 2.8 and 6.5 percent average annual increases in per capita money, respectively, between 1820 and 1840. Residents of newly settled states, like Indiana at 6.8 percent, saw slightly higher per capita money growth rates. Few places, however, experienced more growth in terms of average annual growth rates and in absolute amounts than Louisiana (7.9 percent and $20.25), Florida ($\infty$ percent and $14.15), and Mississippi (8.4 percent and a remarkable $47.93). The common thread linking the latter three was that they chartered property banks, which placed cotton at the heart of the financial sector.

Cotton production exploded after 1800. By 1831, domestic consumption exceeded 90 million pounds. The value of exports exceeded $50 million in 1834 and there was little to suggest that demand would soon slow. Prices were volatile, rising and falling in long swings throughout the antebellum era, but agricultural productivity increased secularly throughout the era, so real income from cotton trended upward. As southerners focused even more on cotton, it insinuated itself into business generally and into banking particularly. Cotton drove credit demand; by the mid-1830s, it was driving credit supply. Four states—Arkansas, Florida, Louisiana, and Mississippi—chartered banking institutions collateralized by cotton land and slaves.

Like other southern states, Florida embraced a combination of government-subsidized plantation banks that operated alongside government-subsidized commercial banks, as well as wholly private commercial lenders. With a capital of $1 million raised through the sale of government-guaranteed bonds collateralized by mortgages on plantations and slaves, the Union Bank was Florida's largest, but not only, subsidized institution.[3] Within a year, the bank's capital was increased to $3 million, with the added $2 million raised through additional bond sales. Prime, Ward and King of New York and Thomas Biddle & Company of Philadelphia brokered the sale of the first bond issue in New York City and Philadelphia.[4] When sales of the $2 million issue of 1834 languished in the Northeast, London and Amsterdam brokers placed most of the bonds at 95 percent of par or better.

Planters became shareholders by tendering a mortgage, which gave them the right to borrow up to two-thirds of its value. The Union Bank's charter required subscription books to be opened throughout the state, but they were opened only in Pensacola, Tallahassee, and Marianna.[5] Although the bank's organizers may have violated the charter by not taking subscription outside of Florida's panhandle, it was probably due to pragmatism rather than corruption. In 1833, about 40,000 people lived in Florida and about one-fifth of them lived in Leon County (Tallahassee area). St. Augustine was the only heavily populated place where subscription books were not opened. Even though some families took large stakes—like John and Robert Gamble, who subscribed to a combined 1,348 shares—ownership was rea-

Table 10.1 Bank Money per Capita by State and Region, 1820–1860

Region/State	1820	1830	1840	1850	1860
NEW ENGLAND	$7.14[a]	$9.56	$11.36	$15.99	$26.72
MIDDLE ATLANTIC	2.61[b]	7.71	9.08	15.46	22.77
SOUTH ATLANTIC	5.51	4.39	7.26	10.00	11.29
Virginia	4.18	4.53	7.34	8.97	10.18
North Carolina	1.06[c]	2.10	3.38	4.30	6.53
South Carolina	2.94	3.48	10.80	16.98	21.60
Georgia	10.59[d]	7.52	7.76	12.91	11.78
Florida	0.00	0.00	14.15	0.00	2.06
OLD NORTHWEST	0.60	1.41	4.69	4.80	4.95
Ohio	0.26[e]	0.28	3.74	7.27	4.76
Indiana	1.19	1.47	4.65	3.91	4.94
Illinois	0.85	5.86	9.09	1.93	5.45
Wisconsin	0.00	0.00	3.59	3.24	8.49
Michigan	0.00	1.53	2.36	2.10	0.74
OLD SOUTHWEST	4.85	3.65	14.98	7.35	13.74
Kentucky	4.07	0.80	5.66	8.34	15.92
Tennessee	2.79[f]	0.33	6.53	4.72	8.44
Mississippi	11.09	7.33	59.02	0.27	0.28
Alabama	2.80	2.42	12.43	4.81	12.12
Louisiana	5.23[g]	4.49	25.48	24.70	44.29
Missouri	5.96	8.18	3.37	5.77	8.63

Notes: [a]Bank money figure from 1823; population from 1820. [b]Bank money figures for New York, Delaware, and Maryland from 1819. [c]Bank money figure from 1819. [d]Bank money figure for Georgia from 1821. [e]Bank money figure for Ohio from 1819. [f]Bank money figure for Tennessee from 1821. [g]Bank money figure for Louisiana from 1819. Regions are defined as follows. New England: Maine, New Hampshire, Vermont, Massachusetts, Rhode Island, and Connecticut; Middle Atlantic: New York, New Jersey, Pennsylvania, Delaware, Maryland, and District of Columbia.

Sources: Fenstermaker, Development, appendix B; U.S. Comptroller of the Currency, Annual Report (1876); U.S. Census Office, Compendium, table VIII.

sonably dispersed. In 1840, about one-sixth of all free males over 21 years old and residing in Leon County owned shares.

In addition to the Union Bank, Florida also partly subsidized the Bank of Pensacola and the Southern Life Insurance and Trust Company of St. Augustine. The territory, then, had an aggregate indebtedness of $3.9 million, all of which had underwritten the territory's financial infrastructure. Despite accomplishing the twin goals of facilitating dispersed ownership and widening geographic credit facilities, these banks faced vehement opposition. When Jacksonian, antibank Democrats took control of Florida's territorial legislature, they issued a series of scathing reports in 1840 and 1841 that accused the banks of violating their charters, making unsound

loans, worsening social and economic inequality, and subsidizing speculation.[6] A later report insisted that Florida was not responsible for the bonds;
Congress was. Congress had reviewed and authorized an unconstitutional
act, so the nation's, rather than the new state's, taxpayers should be on the
hook. Repudiationist sentiment grew, and in 1841, the governor vetoed a
bill that would have closed the Union Bank and repudiated the debt. The
issue lingered until 1853 when an arbitrator determined that the bonds had
not been issued by an agent of the United States, a decision that effectively
endorsed repudiation.

Few states matched Louisiana's involvement in and subsidization of
banking and credit, especially agricultural credit. After a decade of relative
stasis in the state's banking industry, the sector grew rapidly in the 1830s
when Louisiana chartered three distinct types of banks. It chartered traditional commercial banks that extended credit to artisans and merchants and
financed inventories and working capital, as well as the export of staple
crops. It also chartered the improvement banks discussed in chapter 9 that
financed specific infrastructure projects, like canals, hotels, and railroads.
The cornerstone of Louisiana's 1830s banking policy, however, was its plantation banks.

Louisiana's economy was unlike any other in the lower South. Like other
southern states, Louisianans remained committed to slavery, plantation agriculture, and the production of export staples. Unlike those other states,
Louisiana had a strategically located port that developed into a major international trading center. By 1840, New Orleans had over 100,000 residents, or more than 29 percent of the state's total population, which made
Louisiana the most urbanized state in the union.[7] Moreover, New Orleans'
commercial sector resembled those of New York or Philadelphia rather than
Charleston or Mobile. Outside New Orleans, however, Louisiana was distinctly southern. Such difference created social, political, and economic tensions between rural Louisiana and New Orleans. Economic differences
came to the fore in banking policy. All of Louisiana's banks operated in
New Orleans and, although several operated rural branches, all focused on
short-term mercantile lending. Planters viewed these rural branches as little
more than mechanisms designed to mobilize rural savings for the benefit of
urban merchants.

Between 1827 and 1833, Louisiana chartered three plantation banks in
response to planter complaints of credit rationing. The first was the Consolidated Association of Planters.[8] It raised its capital by taking in $2 million
in mortgages, which served as collateral for bonds issued by the bank at 5-,
10-, and 15-year maturities. No dividends were paid. All profits were chan-
neled into a sinking fund to meet interest and principal repayment on the
bonds. Planters tendering mortgages could borrow up to 50 percent of the
value of the mortgages. The bank intended to sell its bonds in Europe, but
it found foreign capitalists reluctant to invest in an unfamiliar derivative
security. Because the bank's bonds were unsalable, the state stepped in and

issued $2.5 million in state-issued bonds carrying the same mortgage collateral, as well as a state guarantee. These bonds were quickly taken up by European investors.

The Consolidated Association was a quick success, which induced the chartering of the Union Bank in 1832. The Union Bank established eight branches, and its $7 million capital was financed through the sale of $8 million in state bonds, collateralized by mortgages on improved, cultivated land, revenue-producing buildings, and slaves.[9] Mortgagors were allowed to borrow up to one-half of the value of their mortgaged property.

The Union Bank also proved exceedingly popular, and its capital was quickly oversubscribed. To meet the demand for mortgage loans, Louisiana chartered the Citizens Bank in 1833.[10] Encouraged by the success of the Consolidated Association and the Union Bank, the Citizens Bank followed a more ambitious plan. Its authorized capital was $12 million, secured through the sale of bonds collateralized by mortgages and slaves. Legislators anticipated that the success of the Consolidated Association would overcome investor concerns with derivative mortgage securities, but their optimism was unfounded.

As with the Consolidated Associations original bonds, the Citizens Bank found European investors unwilling to buy up its mortgage-based bonds. The state again stepped in and issued its own on the bank's behalf. By this time, however, investor enthusiasm had waned and the bank's European agent found it difficult to market the bonds. In mid-1836, Hope & Company of Amsterdam informed the bank that the Amsterdam market was saturated and suggested that the focus shift to the London and Paris markets. In August, the Citizens Bank's board of directors authorized Hope & Company to alter $3 million in bonds so that interest could be paid in Amsterdam, London, or Paris, rather than at Hope & Company's office in Amsterdam alone.[11]

Allegations of financial shenanigans surrounding the sale of the bonds reduced demand. The bank's directors denied any wrongdoing, but the City Bank of New Orleans refused to accept the Citizens Bank's notes until the latter agreed to an independent audit of its accounts. In May 1837, the Citizens' board invited the state treasurer, as well as the presidents of five other New Orleans banks, to inspect its books.[12] Questions surrounding the bank's bond sales continued, however. In June, critics alleged that Hope & Company and Hope's London agent received unusually large commissions (kickbacks) and that the Citizens' own president was a partner in the London agent, a charge he denied.[13]

By 1837, the aggregate paid-in capital of Louisiana's 16 banks exceeded $39 million. About $20 million of that was raised in England and Europe (mostly Holland) through the sale of state-guaranteed bonds. Another $7 million was sold in the United States, mostly in Boston, New York, and Philadelphia.[14] The results of state intervention were unmistakable. By 1840, Louisiana was the most credit-rich, most monetized state in the nation (see table 10.1).[15] Louisianans, with more than $25 per capita, made more use of bank-supplied currency than residents in either Massachusetts ($21.18) or Rhode Island ($20.71). Its use of bank-supplied credit and money outstripped that of either the Middle Atlantic or the South Atlantic region by a factor of three or more. Thus, the Old Southwest's plantation banks "became one of the most important agencies for capital import into the United States" during the 1830s.[16] With a combination of commercial, improvement, and plantation banks, George Green writes that Louisiana's system "was an effective financial intermediary, mobilizing domestic and foreign savings and channeling them to Louisiana's credit-thirsty agriculture, commerce, and social-overhead projects."[17]

Despite some allegations of wrongdoing leveled at the region's banks, Philadelphia's investors enthusiastically purchased southern bank shares and banknote brokers purchased notes at relatively low rates. Table 10.2 provides share prices for three southern banks and banknote discounts for seven during the midcentury depression. Panel A of table 10.2 juxtaposes share prices of three distinct types of southern banks: an improvement bank (the Canal Bank), a plantation bank (the Planters Bank), and a partly state-owned commercial bank (the Bank of Kentucky). Although these banks do not capture the totality of the region's banking experience, they are broadly representative of how investors and banknote brokers viewed these kinds of banks.

Share prices suggest that investors bid up the price of Planters Bank shares in response to Mississippi's bond guarantee. Its shares sold at a premium over both the Canal Bank and the Bank of Kentucky. Trading in all shares ceased during the depths of the depression. When it resumed, growing repudiationist sentiments in Mississippi alarmed investors, which drove Planters Bank share values down markedly. Prices of Canal Bank and Bank of Kentucky shares also declined, but not as sharply. It is notable, and probably not coincidental, that state ownership (as in the Bank of Kentucky) proved a better guaranty of banks than bonds carrying the faith and credit of the state.

Banknote discounts, provided in panel B of table 10.2, show that banknote broker opinion mirrored investor opinion. Notes of the Canal Bank and the Bank of Kentucky maintained their values throughout the panic and the suspension of specie payments. Note discounts also show that brokers could discriminate among different banks because the prices they paid for notes of Louisiana's three plantation banks diverged after 1842. Notes of the Union Bank, which remained solvent and profitable throughout the depression, sold at considerably higher prices than those of the barely solvent Consolidated Association and Citizens Bank. Banknote brokers never had very high opinions of the plantation banks of Mississippi or Florida. These banks' notes traded at substantial discounts up to 1839, and most brokers refused to accept them at any price after the suspension of specie payments.

Although states promised their full faith and credit to the repayment of

Table 10.2 Share Prices and Banknote Discounts in Philadelphia for
Selected Southern Banks, Quarterly, 1835–1844

A: Share Prices

Year.Qtr	Canal Bank New Orleans	Planters Bank of Natchez	Bank of Kentucky
1835.1	$109.50	$118.25	$na
1835.2	111.50	127.50	108.00
1835.3	105.00	118.50	89.00
1835.4	104.50	121.00	93.00
1836.1	102.00	121.00	101.67
1836.2	100.00	124.00	102.85
1836.3	92.00	115.00	88.13
1836.4	90.00	122.50	80.00
1837.1	95.00	118.00	80.00
1839.3	na	53.00	na
1839.4	70.00	55.00	50.00
1840.1	70.00	24.00	50.00
1840.2	70.00	23.00	57.00
1840.3	70.00	19.00	57.00
1840.4	70.00	14.00	57.00
1841.1	70.00	11.00	na
1841.2	60.00	10.00	50.00
1841.3	53.00	8.00	50.00
1841.4	45.00	5.00	50.00
1842.1	na	na	na
1842.2	na	na	47.00
1842.3	10.00	1.50	42.00
1842.4	10.00	1.00	43.50
1843.1	10.00	1.00	47.00
1843.2	16.00	5.00	62.00
1843.3	21.00	na	66.00
1843.4	42.50	3.00	75.00
1844.1	40.50	3.00	71.00
1844.2	na	5.00	75.00
1844.3	38.75	7.00	73.00
1844.4	36.50	6.00	73.25

B: Banknote Discounts

Year. Qtr	Bank of Ky.	Union Bank Fla.	Canal Bank La.	Planters Bank Fla.	Consolidated Association La.	Citizens Bank La.	Union Bank La.
1835.1	—[a]%	na%	3%	4%	3%	na%	3%
1835.2	2	7	1.5	4	1.5	1.5	1.5
1835.3	2	10	2	3	2	2	2
1835.4	2	10	2.5	3	2.5	2.5	2.5
1836.1	2.5	10	4	5	4	4	na
1836.2	2.5	10	4.5	10	4.5	4.5	na
1836.3	2.5	—	4.5	5	4.5	4.5	na
1836.4	3	20	4	5	4	4	na
1837.1	3	20	6	8	6	6	6
1837.2	6	—	ns[b]	ns	ns	ns	ns
1837.3	4.5	—	10	18	10	10	10
1837.4	3.5	15	3	18	3	3	3
1838.1	na	20	na	na	na	na	na
1838.2	3.5	20	8	20	8	8	8
1838.3	2	15	4	8.5	4	4	4
1838.4	2.5	—	2.5	8.5	2.5	2.5	2.5
1839.1	3.5	—	2	7	2	2	2
1839.2	3.5	—	4	—	4	4	4
1839.3	5.5	—	5.5	12.5	5.5	5.5	5.5
1839.4	4	—	2	12.5	2	2	2
1840.1	4.5	—	1	—	1	1	1
1840.2	4.5	—	3.5	—	3.5	3.5	3.5
1840.3	4	—	1.5	—	1.5	1.5	1.5
1840.4	4	—	1.5	—	1.5	1.5	1.5
1841.1	7.5	—	6	—	6	6	6
1841.2	6.5	—	5	—	5	5	5
1841.3	6.5	—	3	—	3	3	3
1841.4	6.5	—	5	—	5	5	5
1842.1	10.5	—	—	—	—	—	—
1842.2	4	—	na	—	na	na	na
1842.3	2.5	—	60	—	75	75	75
1842.4	2.5	—	2	—	35	30	2
1843.1	2	—	2	—	35	40	2
1843.2	1	—	2.5	—	35	40	2.5
1843.3	1.5	—	2	—	50	40	2
1843.4	1.5	—	1	—	45	40	1
1844.1	1	—	0.5	—	40	45	0.5
1844.2	1.5	—	1.5	—	40	45	1.5
1844.3	1.5	—	1.5	—	25	25	1.5
1844.4	1.5	—	1	—	20	20	1

Notes: [a] signifies that brokers purchased notes of these banks only when accompanied by a letter of reference. [b] No sale, which means that brokers refused to purchase these notes at any discount. na implies not available or not reported. All data are from end of quarter.

Source: Bicknell's, various issues 1835–1844.

the bank bonds, they made no explicit provisions for the bonds' retirement other than the banks' profits. By underwriting financial intermediaries, states assumed massive contingent liabilities that lost their contingency in the late 1830s and early 1840s. During the financial panics in 1837 and 1839 through 1842, bank profits failed even to meet the scheduled interest payments. As the bonds fell into default, state governments were called to make good on them.

Mississippi refused. Mississippi's checkered banking experience reached its nadir in the early 1840s. Of the state's 25 banks in 1837, only 2 continued after 1841. The year 1841 marked the beginning of a pitched political battle over its defunct plantation banks: the Union Bank and the Planters Bank of Natchez. A legislative committee recommended that the state honor its bank bonds. The governor recommended repudiation, a sentiment with wide popular appeal. Because foreigners held most of the bonds, Democrats argued that Mississippians could shift the costs of the banks' failures abroad with few domestic consequences. In 1842, Mississippi repudiated its debt, which, as Larry Schweikart notes, "placed the state on the international defaulters' list."[18] When the state went looking to sell bonds during the Civil War, it was sharply rebuffed. It could not sell bonds again until after the Civil War.

Florida joined Mississippi on the international defaulters' list. Between 1839 and 1845, Florida's Democrats won several antibank, anticorporate political victories. They repealed the charters of three banks; discouraged entrepreneurs from starting new ones; and, after a long fight following an 1841 referendum, repudiated nearly $4 million in territorial bonds in 1842.[19] Foreign lenders also rejected Florida's Civil War bond issues.

Faced with the largest contingent liability of any of the plantation bank states but unwilling to repudiate, Louisiana developed several strategies to retire its debt. In 1843, it allowed delinquent debtors to pay off their debts in bank bonds. Because Louisiana had not paid interest on its bonds for more than two years, they sold below par, which made them an attractive option for many planters and factors. They sold cotton in England or Europe, bought depreciated bonds, and tendered them to the state, which accepted them at par. Nevertheless, this plan retired only a small portion of the state's outstanding $22 million bond issues. Liquidating the banks and retiring the bonds proved to be a source of consternation for more than 40 years.[20] As late as 1913, a portion of the bonds was refunded, and some bonds were still unredeemed as late as 1935, fully a century after they had been issued.

Information in table 10.2 shows the market's reaction to repudiation debates. Shares in the Planters Bank of Natchez (recall that the the state issued bonds to finance two-thirds of its $3 million capital) traded at $118 in March 1837. As with other southern bank shares, active trading ceased for two years. When trading resumed, Planters Bank shares traded at $53, less than one-half of their price two years earlier. When the repudiation debate began in earnest in 1840, the bank's shares fell sharply. By the end of 1842, they traded for just $1 per share. Although Canal Bank shares also declined sharply after 1842, they did not drop as precipitously as Planters Bank shares. With no threat of repudiation in Kentucky, Bank of Kentucky shares traded below par but at a sizable premium over notes of banks whose states threatened repudiation. Even though it was clear by 1840 that the Citizens Bank and the Consolidated Association were bankrupt, Louisiana's commitment to honor its obligations kept these banks' notes trading at discounts reflecting their expected liquidation value.

What was the cause of the plantation banks' collapse? One contemporary considered property banks a hybrid of a "state loan office and an ordinary banking business,"[21] which Fritz Redlich contends was an "unfortunate combination of incompatible functions."[22] Even these banks' organizers, officers, and directors were sometimes dissatisfied with the banks' hybrid nature. Minute books of the Citizens Bank show that Edmund Forstall, the bank's president, was never comfortable with the bank's mixed mission.[23] He was more comfortable with pure commercial banking and attributed the bank's failure to its unnatural combination of mortgage and commercial lending. Like many other bankers of his era, Forstall believed in real-bills banking. As an insider, Forstall surely recognized that the bulk of these banks' lending was indeed commercial, if not purely real-bills, in nature. Perhaps he was offering excuses instead of explanations for his bank's failure.

Irene Neu's claim that these banks became nearly "indistinguishable from ordinary banks that served the commercial community" is overstated, but these banks did come under the control of New Orleans merchants.[24] Although these banks' capital was raised through mortgages supplied by planters for the benefit of planters, the banks were an ingenious device used by New Orleans merchants to increase and control the state commercial banking capital. In fact, the author of the Consolidated Association's act, a wealthy New Orleans merchant, encouraged subscriptions from wealthy planters who generally distrusted commercial banks. Moreover, the strongest legislative support for these banks came not from rural parishes but from a bloc of New Orleans legislators.

Published balance sheets show that shareholders (mortgagors) borrowed the 50 percent of the capital allotted to them, but they were not the principal borrowers. In January 1840, the Consolidated Association, with a capital of $2.5 million, was owed $1.3 million on mortgages and nearly $2 million by commercial borrowers. At the Union Bank, mortgages totaled $3.2 million and commercial loans totaled $6.2 million. Only at the Citizens Bank did mortgage lending ($5.1 million) exceed short-term commercial lending ($4.1 million).[25] Even here, the bank made every effort to diversify its portfolio. The bank's minute books reveal that by 1836, most day-to-day lending, about $200,000 per week on average, was done on domestic and foreign exchange. Relatively few new mortgages were taken up after the initial capital subscription.

By itself, hybridization fails to explain why these banks failed. Even regular commercial banks extended long-term mortgage credit, albeit in smaller amounts. Why, then, the unfortunate end? George Green identifies three potential explanations.[26] First, property banks were inherently unsound, being built on a misguided idea of easy credit based on illiquid security. Second, though sound in conception and structure, the banks were mismanaged. Third, though well conceived and well executed, the banks came into being at an inopportune time that made them especially vulnerable. Green argues that most historians accepted the first explanation. Most contemporaries accepted a combination of the first and second, leaning more toward the second. Green accepts the third. Mortgage borrowers were concentrated in export-oriented staple agriculture. Commercial borrowers, too, relied on the same staples. Although the banks were nominally diversified between agricultural and commercial credit and between mortgage and real-bills lending, the diversification was illusory. When cotton prices tumbled, both sectors were hard hit. Additionally, these banks were cursed with the misfortune of simple bad timing. Chartered only a few years before the crises of the late 1830s, they were not given enough time to solidify their positions, establish reputations, and construct truly diversified portfolios. However, the Union Bank's experience shows that even a young bank could survive. It was forced into liquidation in 1844, not because it was insolvent, but because politicians turned against it. The Union Bank, in fact, generated sufficient revenue throughout the depression to meet interest payments on its bonds.

Facing either an unexpected tax liability or repudiation and discredit, legislators and their constituents grew disenchanted with all banks. Throughout most of the 1840s, Louisiana forbade the chartering of any new or the rechartering of any existing banks. Radical, antibank Democrats came into power in several other states and reversed Whig and even moderate Democratic banking policies. Even where radical, antibank sentiment failed to take hold, the experiences of the early 1840s left legislators reluctant to liberally charter new banks. Bank formation slowed everywhere and came to a complete standstill in some places. By the early 1850s, however, most states recognized a growing demand for banking and responded, many with free banking.

Western Populism and Free Banking On and Off the Frontier

In the depression era, westerners and southerners developed a distaste for banks, particularly state-sponsored banks. Nearly every state assembly debated some sort of antibank legislation.[27] Antibank sentiment peaked in the early 1840s and more than a handful of states prohibited new or renewed bank charters. By almost any measure, banking services and intermediation declined sharply during the 1840s. Between 1840 and 1850, bank money per capita fell by 26 cents in Michigan, 35 cents in Wisconsin, 74 cents in Indiana, 78 cents in Louisiana, $1.81 in Tennessee, $7.16 in Illinois, $7.62 in Alabama, and an astounding $58.75 in Mississippi (see table 10.1). Among western states, only Ohio, Kentucky, and Missouri witnessed modest increases in banking services.

Economic expansion required credit, currency, and intermediary services. The 1840's "revulsion to banks" left most states with inadequate banking facilities in 1850.[28] Clearly, growth in banking services did not keep up with increases in population, improved acreage, agricultural output, real per capita income, or any other available measure of contemporary economic activity. Credit was rationed in the early 1850s and interest rates in the Old Southwest and, especially, the Old Northwest exceeded rates in the eastern United States by about a full percentage point, a substantial difference in an economy characterized by integrated regional capital markets.[29]

A variety of extralegal bankers partially mitigated the credit and money crunch. Florida provides a telling example. When antibank Democrats took control in the 1840s, they reversed previous Whig bank policies. A wave of antibank laws passed up to 1845 discouraged domestic bank formation, but Florida could not or did not prohibit out-of-state banks from operating inside its borders. About a dozen agencies of New York City, Charleston, and Savannah banks, as well as at least 14 private banks, opened in Florida between 1845 and 1853.[30] While private banks, extralegal banks, and agencies mitigated the ill effects of inadequate banking facilities, few operated on a sufficient scale to replace legitimate commercial banks. In the 1850s, legislators developed an attraction toward what had repulsed them in the 1840s. Some states began issuing new charters. Others instituted free banking.

By 1860, 18 states had enacted New York–style free banking. Four others enacted bond-secured note issue and liberalized chartering (see table 10.3). Free banking spread for any number of reasons, but a combination of insufficient intermediation and Jacksonian populism that took root in the South and, especially, the West were the driving forces. In the 1840s and 1850s, as Redlich notes, free banking grew into the favored system. "Percolating westward," he writes, "it suddenly became the banking idea of the day. Free Banking represented so perfectly the underlying spirit of the period that everybody seemed to have been just waiting for the formula."[31]

Still, there was an approximate 15-year lag between passage of the first free banking law in the late 1830s and its widespread adoption in the early 1850s. Legislative prudence may have been the cause. As ideologically appealing as free banking's laissez-faire underpinnings were, pragmatic legislators may have demanded evidence of free banking's successes and fail-

Table 10.3 States Enacting Free Banking or Bond-Secured
Note Issue

State	Year	State	Year
Michigan[a]	1837	Connecticut	1852
Georgia	1838	Indiana	1852
New York	1838	Tennessee	1852
Ohio[b]	1845	Wisconsin	1852
Alabama	1849	Florida	1853
Kentucky[b]	1850	Louisiana	1853
Illinois	1851	Michigan	1857
Massachusetts	1851	Iowa	1858
Ohio	1851	Minnesota	1858
Vermont	1851	Missouri[b]	1858
Virginia[b]	1851	Pennsylvania	1860

Notes: [a]Law revoked in 1840. [b]Allowed bond-secured note issue and liberalized chartering but did not allow true free entry.

Source: Rolnick and Weber, "Free Banking," p. 12.

ures before embracing it. Others remained wary. Legislative committees in Virginia, for example, discussed free banking as early as 1837 but delayed action until 1851. Even then, the state retained its chartering privilege, but it granted them liberally and required new banks to provide bond collateral.[32] New York's experience undoubtedly converted some skeptics. After a rocky start, New York experienced a long stretch with few failures, regular if uneven financial growth, and relative calm outside the rarely noted recession of 1848.

Although New York's experience is, perhaps, the most discussed free banking episode, it was not the country's first. Shortly after Michigan gained statehood in 1837, it adopted a free banking law modeled after a bill then under consideration in New York.[33] Michigan's and New York's free banking laws differed in important respects. Michigan's act provided for 100 percent mortgage collateral for note issues. New York lawmakers discussed mortgage collateral but eventually allowed only one-half of a bank's notes to be secured by mortgages. Problems with mortgage security were manifold. Market values of real estate could quickly and unexpectedly decline in response to exogenous macroeconomic shocks. Declines in land values, therefore, could just as quickly erase a bank's net worth. Furthermore, any attempt to realize on the collateral during a general downturn would drive prices lower, further undermining a bank's position. There were also problems at the outset in valuing mortgages. In the absence of well-organized derivative security markets, valuations were subjective, highly idiosyncratic, prone to sharp revaluation, and open to fraud. Although these difficulties could arise in New York, they were less systemically problematic because most areas eastern and southern New York were long-settled regions with reasonably thick mortgage markets and established property values. Michigan, on the other hand, was recently settled, with land and mortgages traded in thin, highly speculative markets.

Michigan's problems were compounded by a nationwide suspension of specie payments shortly after its free banking statute was adopted. However, this gave Michigan's prospective bankers a singularly lucrative opportunity to establish banks without facing the usual convertibility constraint.[34] With the dual incentives of overvalued (or difficult to value) mortgages and suspended specie payments, banks quickly sprung up. In January 1837, Michigan had 9 banks; by December, it had 18; and by the end of February 1838, it had 40. Hugh Rockoff notes that most of these banks were "dubious affairs" from which generations of banking historians drew lessons about the confluence of laissez-faire and banking. What many of these historians neglected was that banks were organized during a general suspension of specie payments, so they were freed from an important monitoring mechanism— the ability to maintain specie convertibility. Historians may have failed to recognize the incentive effect, but Michigan's legislators did not. They amended the 1837 act in 1838 so that existing banks could legally continue without immediately resuming specie payments, but new banks were required to open with convertible notes.

The amendments came too late, however. By September 1839, only 9 banks remained and the average holder of a failed bank's notes recovered about 60 cents on the dollar.[35] Rockoff and Gerald Dwyer argue that the shortcomings of lax oversight and a poorly worded law may have been overcome had markets been operative. Gary Gorton argues that banknote markets quickly arbitraged on fundamental differences between the market and par value of free bank notes.[36] Because Michigan was on the frontier, information disseminated slowly. Nevertheless, contemporary banknote reporters made people aware of their low assessment of these banks. By August 1837, large-denomination Michigan banknotes sold at substantial discounts, higher discounts than those of notes of comparable banks in other states.[37] Small-denomination notes were unsalable at any price. Young banks, of all types, had difficulty circulating notes at par because they had not yet developed reputations, and Michigan's free banks were stalked by what F. A. Hayek calls the "thousand hounds" of the press.[38] The market, often sooner rather than later, punished poor portfolio allocations and quickly drove bad banks from the market.

A wave of free banking laws passed in the 1850s with uneven results; even Michigan reinstated their law in 1857. Hammond provides a negative interpretation of most states' experiences. He argues that bank fraud was so widespread, so endemic to the whole system, that people living in states without banks were probably better off than people living in the free banking states of Michigan, Wisconsin, Indiana, and Illinois.[39] Would residents of free banking states really have been better off without banks? We can, of course, stand Hammond's interpretation up against the empirical evidence. One way to address this is to consider whether banks enhanced economic growth. Theorists and financial historians argue that banks positively influence economic growth and Howard Bodenhorn shows that financial development correlates positively with subsequent economic growth in antebellum America, including the Old Northwest.[40]

A more often adopted approach is to, first, determine losses suffered by note holders and, second, determine the extent to which these losses resulted from a breach of the contractual promise to redeem due to legitimate business failure and the extent to which note holder losses resulted from fraud.[41] Although it probably provided little comfort to a note holder to discover that his loss resulted from legitimate business error rather than fraud, the implications for the continued functioning of the payments system were momentous. If rampant fraud was the principal cause of bank failure, people would quickly stop using bank-supplied currency. The benefits of banking on the frontier would have been stillborn. If miscalculation was the known cause, the use of bank currency would have been suboptimal relative to a no-failure case, but it would not vanish.

In the first three years of Indiana's free banking law, 68 banks opened. Only 38 survived to the law's third anniversary. Fully 87 percent of Illinois' free banks closed by 1861, and most of these failed in the sense that they could not redeem their notes at par. Of the 108 free banks operating in Wisconsin at the beginning of 1861, 36 failed and another 15 closed before the end of 1863. These experiences were atypical in many respects, but they have become the basis for analyzing free banking.

Why did these banks fail in clusters? The traditional explanation was wildcat banking. To determine if wildcatting was important, we need an operative definition of a wildcat. Arthur Rolnick and Warren Weber adopt a straightforward definition: a bank that remained in operation for less than one year and failed to redeem its notes at par. Andrew Economopoulos adds a third feature: inaccessible location.[42] Although these definitions miss some of the fundamental elements of the traditional wildcatting hypothesis, they nevertheless serve as useful definitions in that they capture the essential nature of wildcatting, namely, starting a bank with the lone intention of capturing one-time gains from arbitraging on a difference between the par value of note issues and the market value of collateral bonds. In effect, wildcat bankers purchased bonds at prices significantly below par, but they were able to secure notes equal, or nearly equal, to the par value of the bonds. They then issued notes, purchased easily hidden assets, and absconded with the proceeds of a fraudulent note issue.

Using this last definition, Rolnick and Weber, as well as Economopoulos, show that wildcatting was not the driving force behind free bank failures in Indiana, Illinois, and Wisconsin. Minnesota's bad free banking experience, on the other hand, may have been and probably was a classic case of wildcatting. The state auditor accepted most Minnesota bonds at par even when they were selling at about 20 percent of par value.[43] Seven of nine Minnesota bank failures satisfy the twin conditions of nonpar redemption of notes upon closure and a life span of one year or less. Note holders recovered less than 30 cents on the dollar. As long as these banks circulated their notes at par, it is evident that Minnesota's free banks profitably arbitraged on differentials between the par and market values of collateral bonds and, in so doing, defrauded the note-holding public.

It seems unlikely that seven failures—even spectacular failures, which these were not—would prompt such a sturdy myth. What made the myth of the wildcat so hardy were the recurrent waves of failures. With one exception, they did not occur simultaneously, so contemporaries may have simplistically linked these waves with wildcatting. Of 24 Indiana free bank failures, for example, 21 were nominally consistent with one or more elements of the wildcat definition, but evidence on the price of Indiana collateral bonds suggests that wildcatting was not particularly profitable. Between May 1852 and August 1854, when most free banks failed, bond prices never fell below 95 percent of par.[44] Such a small spread seems unlikely to have prompted widespread wildcatting. And although most free bank failures in Illinois and Wisconsin occurred in a brief period, the evidence there fails to confirm the wildcatting hypothesis.

The question lingers: why did bank failures occur in clusters? The Rolnick-Weber-Economopoulos hypothesis, discussed in chapter 8 in a New York context, attributes free bank failures to falling asset prices. They argue that periods of falling bond prices correlate with clusters of free bank failures. Free bank failures in Illinois and Wisconsin clustered in 1861. The driving force was the collapse in bond prices, especially bonds of southern states, in the early days of the Civil War. Because many of these states' banks collateralized their note issues with Louisiana, Missouri, Tennessee, and Virginia securities, the outbreak of hostilities made it unlikely that northern holders would receive scheduled interest payments. It was likely, as well, that southern states would repudiate bonds held by the enemy. Bond prices plummeted. Bank portfolios deteriorated. Note holders cashed out. Free banks failed in bunches. By forcing banks to hold portfolios top-heavy with state bonds, free banking exposed banks to excessive term structure and interest rate risk. In the Illinois and Wisconsin instances, it exposed them to significant default risk, not unlike that experienced by money-center banks during the LDC debt crises in the 1970s and 1980s.

Rolnick, Weber, and Economopoulos thus attribute free bank failures to declining asset prices that undermined the banks' net worth, which induced runs and bank closings. As discussed in chapter 8, this explanation has not gone unchallenged. It may be applicable to the Illinois and Wisconsin experiences if the outbreak of hostilities in 1861 was a mostly unanticipated, purely exogenous event, which is highly debatable. It is less clear that it explains the Indiana experience.

Free banking was established in Indiana in May 1852, but it was early 1853 before bank openings began in earnest. By the end of 1853, however, 28 free banks closed. In 1854, 34 more closed. Many writers blamed wild-catting, an explanation that fails to hold up to scrutiny. Rolnick and Weber blame falling prices of Indiana bonds, which collateralized most Indiana free bank note issues. Their explanation seems plausible enough, but they do not provide a serious test of the hypothesis. They do not know the exact dates that banks failed. They narrow failure dates to sometime between July 1854 and January 1855, the same period in which bond prices were falling. But because they cannot precisely date the timing of free bank failures, Rolnick and Weber cannot provide compelling evidence that bond price declines were truly exogenous. It is possible, even probable, that the bond price declines in this instance are the result of rather than the catalyst for the free bank failures. As the banks closed, the state auditor threw over $1.2 million in Indiana bonds and about $250,000 in securities of other states on a thin market. The natural and expected result was rapidly declining bond prices.

Iftekhar Hasan and Gerald Dwyer offer an alternative explanation, one that provides little support for either the wildcatting or falling asset price hypothesis.[45] Instead of bond price declines being the exogenous force, they were endogenous to the failures themselves. In May 1854, Ohio enacted a law prohibiting the circulation of small-denomination banknotes issued by out-of-state banks after October 1854. With a fine of $100 per infraction, the penalty for violating the act was prohibitively steep, so Cincinnati's bankers met in early summer to coordinate the return of small-denomination Indiana banknotes and acquire specie, especially small coins, in return.

Between December 1853 and December 1854, the modal discount on Indiana banknotes increased from 1.5 percent to 25 percent, reflecting the sharp decrease in demand for Indiana notes generally, and small-denomination notes particularly.[46] Knowing that substantial volumes of their notes circulated in Ohio, forward-looking Indiana bankers should have anticipated a sharply declining demand for their notes. Declining demand for banknotes would decrease the demand for collateral bonds. A decrease in demand would drive down the price, which eroded the free banks' net worth. Moreover, as the notes came back for redemption, one method of bolstering a bank's reserves was to sell collateral bonds. This act increased the supply of bonds, which further reduced the value of the free banks' portfolios. Thus, the decline in bond prices was at least partly endogenous. Hasan and Dwyer show that the prices of Kentucky, Pennsylvania, and Ohio bonds all declined in the second half of 1854, but none experienced as sharp a decline as Indiana bonds, which lost nearly 25 percent of their value in about four months.

Hasan and Dwyer conclude that Indiana's free bank failures did not result from an asymmetric information–driven bank run (extrinsic uncertainty). That is, note holders did not change their opinion of bank solvency based on some irrelevant event. Instead, note holder demand changed as a result of a very relevant event—the change in Ohio's law—that adversely affected free banks (intrinsic uncertainty). In this case, informed note holders understood how this exogenous event affected certain banks. About one-half of Indiana's free banks failed in the second half of 1854, and it is likely that most of these relied inordinately on the circulation of small-denomination banknotes, most of which circulated in Ohio. Future research should determine how many.

Where are we, then, in understanding why free banks failed? Since the mid-1980s, the traditional wildcatting hypothesis has been displaced with the Rolnick-Weber-Economopoulos falling asset price explanation. Although the latter is, in many respects, a more satisfying explanation than the traditional tale, it, too, is not fully adequate. One important issue that Rolnick, Weber, and Economopoulos fail to address is that chartered bank failures do not rise concurrently and proportionately with free bank failures. As Rockoff notes, it is difficult to imagine a scenario in which banks fail in large numbers when asset prices are rising. Thus, the falling asset price explanation begs the question of why free banks were more susceptible to failure than chartered banks when asset prices were falling. Exogenous shocks that reduced the public's confidence in the ability of states, with the authority to tax, to repay their debts (which would have contributed to falling bond prices) must have had similar effects on the public's confidence in the ability of private borrowers to meet their obligations. Why, then, did proportionately more free than chartered banks fail?

One possibility is that free bank portfolios were less opaque than chartered bank portfolios. Bond-collateral requirements may have made free bank portfolios more transparent, hence more easily valued by informed market participants. Because collateral bonds could be continuously marked to market, note holders were able to value a substantial fraction of free bank portfolios. Bond-collateral requirements designed to increase consumer confidence in banks may have had the perverse and counterintuitive effect of making them more susceptible to runs by increasing their transparency. Holders of a chartered bank's notes might have suspected the bank's insolvency; holders of a free bank's notes were sure of it.

Moreover, it was likely that many of these small free banks were insider affairs with relatively undiversified portfolios even beyond the collateral bond holdings. Loan portfolios are notoriously opaque, but they are less so if a bank's loans are concentrated among a relatively small, easily identifiable group of borrowers. If some note holders could easily observe the projects undertaken with a bank's funds, they could exercise their own judgment on the value of a bank's portfolio and act accordingly. This counterintuitive interpretation implies that large chartered banks, whose portfolios were more difficult to mark to market, were less susceptible to runs by panicky note holders precisely because their portfolios were opaque.

A second possibility is that the chartering process itself, though prone to favoritism and corruption, created public confidence in banks. The costs associated with a charter were substantial and, although these costs were sunk and thus should not have affected decision making, it is unlikely that bankers would quickly and willingly walk away from a bank. Because it took several years, perhaps even decades, to fully amortize the chartering costs, consumers knew that bankers faced incentives to persist and more readily accepted chartered bank notes even in the face of substantial exogenous shocks. By demanding a substantial sunk cost, chartering requirements eliminated fly-by-night operators, which meant that it took large exogenous shocks to shake public confidence in a chartered bank. Note holders were less sure about free bankers. This may explain why New England banks continued to take out legislative charters even after free banking was instituted. It also helps explain why bond-collateral note issue combined with legislative chartering in Ohio, Kentucky, and Virginia demonstrated much lower failure rates than pure free banking enacted elsewhere.

A third possible explanation recognizes that free bankers may have been recklessly overleveraged.[47] Contemporaries argued that virtually anyone with a few dollars in his pocket and an ability to borrow a few more could start a free bank. With a combination of his own funds and some borrowed money, the prospective banker bought state bonds and received banknotes that were used to buy still more bonds, for which he received more banknotes that were used to pay off the original loan. In such a case, the new banker was operating under a staggering debt burden. His ratio of capital to notes was 1:1.

Why would anyone establish such a bank? Dwyer shows that a banker could parlay a minimal personal investment into a fairly substantial investment in government bonds. The banker's incentive was not to establish a fraudulent bank and quickly abscond. Instead, as long as he kept his bank afloat, he received the interest on the bonds. This type of bank was just a highly leveraged arbitrageur. The risks associated with these institutions, as with any highly leveraged investment strategy, were very high and depended on fairly stable bond prices. A sharp decline in bond prices would cause the banker to be called on to increase his investment or reduce his note issue. Both reduced the leverage ratio and the bank's profitability. A sharp rise in bond prices would raise the opportunity cost of holding bonds in a locked-in collateral security account, and the banker would voluntarily close his bank to capture the capital gains.

Rockoff offers a fourth explanation for why free banks failed more often than chartered banks. He argues that financial entrepreneurs near the frontier formed expectations about the potential demand for banking services with substantial error.[48] It has long been recognized that infant businesses suffer high rates of infant mortality.[49] Studies in the industrial organization literature suggest that when entrepreneurs are unsure about their probability of success, they enter the business at suboptimal sizes. Boyan Jovanovic, for instance, develops a model in which potential entrants are assumed to know the mean and standard deviation of all similar firms' costs, but they cannot calculate their own individual expected value.[50] After paying a non-recoverable entry fee, each firm receives noisy signals about its true costs that induces it to either expand, contract, or exit. It follows that industries with high rates of entry also exhibit high rates of concurrent exit, a finding that conflicts with the standard textbook tale of optimal-sized firms entering when equilibrium output expands, exiting when it contracts, and never doing both simultaneously. Exit rates lag entry rates, but the two are largely concurrent. Moreover, there is little evidence that hazard rates for young, nonfinancial firms are driven primarily by macroeconomic shocks. Industry-specific features, notably profitability, rather than general macro factors drive entry and exit.[51]

Western free banks failed in large numbers because credit demands, as well as the bankers' capabilities, were highly uncertain. In long-settled regions, credit demand was better known and the chartering process, whatever its shortcomings, may have proved an effective filter for differentiating between high- and low-capability bankers. Potential bankers with low expected capabilities were unlikely to labor through the convoluted chartering process. Moreover, the large scale at which chartered banks entered relative to free banks meant that chartered banks were better able to weather some early setbacks that free banks may not have survived. The features of large scale and sizable initial net worth gave organizers an early opportunity to observe managerial capabilities and replace poor managers if necessary. Closely held, small free banks entered with less net worth and rarely survived early managerial missteps.

Modern research largely overturns the long-held wildcatting theory of free bank failures. Based on extant evidence, perhaps 10 percent of bank failures were consistent with the wildcatting hypothesis. Rolnick and Weber assert that this finding "should not be interpreted as indicating that no questionable banking practices occurred in the Free Banking Era. No doubt there were some. The conclusions which should be drawn from our analysis is that these practices were not responsible for the vast majority of free bank failures."[52]

With the wildcatting hypothesis put to rest, discussions of free banking can now focus on its successes, as well as its shortcomings. As the foregoing discussion makes clear, there was no single reason why free banks failed, just as there was no one dimension along which they succeeded. As Rockoff notes, free banking took several incarnations and none was inherently more stable than others; understanding free banking compels us to examine how the idea was put into practice in each case.[53] The essential question with which legislators struggled was how to simultaneously ensure confidence in the banking and payments system and preserve the benefits of competition and free entry. "The mechanisms available for this purpose in the antebellum period were limited by institutional constraints such as the gold standard and by the vision of legislators."[54] The available evidence supports an interpretation in direct opposition to Hammond's. Antibank legislation did not improve the welfare of the people. In many respects, it made them worse off. With banks unable to open and control indigenous sources of credit and money, people in bankless states, like Iowa and Texas, were reduced to relying on extralegal, often illegal, sources. What makes free banking look so bad is that loss rates are calculable from extant sources. Loss rates that sometimes exceeded 30 cents on the dollar are staggering. What we do not know is whether the people of bankless Iowa suffered larger or smaller losses on circulating media supplied by extralegal and illegal sources. The records simply do not exist to determine these losses, and it may well be that they exceeded losses elsewhere. It is clear that free banking was not successful in every aspect, but it represented a bold attempt to solve the dual demands of free competition and stable credit.

Branch Banking Networks, Mutual Guarantees, and Stability in the Storm

In some regards, what made the South and West distinctive was how they modified what they imported. For instance, the commonwealth ideal motivated northeastern legislators, but perhaps not as strongly as it motivated legislators in the South and West. Free banking, too, was largely an eastern import. Branch banking, however, was uniquely southern and western. New York allowed two banks with one branch each. Pennsylvania condoned, even encouraged, branching by two Philadelphia banks. Both opened a handful of branches but either closed or sold most of them within a short time. Banks to the south and west of Pennsylvania, on the other hand, operated extensive branch networks. When the Army of the Potomac marched into Virginia, the state's two largest banks operated nearly a score of branches. So did Kentucky's three dominant banks. Tennessee's Planters Bank, Union Bank, and the Bank of Tennessee each had about five branches. Ohio and Indiana each operated networks of semiautonomous, mutually insured banks. Branch bank networks also arose in the Carolinas, Georgia, Louisiana, Mississippi, and Illinois for a time.

Branch banking was attractive because, as George Starnes notes regarding Virginia, small and scattered pools of capital were consolidated into institutions that spread their benefits more broadly than a similar number of small, undercapitalized banks would have. When these pools of private capital were supplemented with direct state support and either implicit or explicit guarantees, public confidence in most of these banks was enhanced. Confidence, in turn, encouraged use of bank money, which reinforced the banks' intermediary abilities.

Many writers claim that branching allowed for more-diversified portfolios relative to those attainable by unit banks. Lawrence White, for instance, argues that in regard to northern banks:

> unit banking restrictions are likely to have prevented banks from op-
> timally diversifying their portfolios, because bank lending in that day
> was largely limited by transactions costs to borrowers in the neigh-
> borhood of the bank. Unit banking tied the solvency of banks too
> closely to the fortunes of particular industries that happened to be
> located in the town in which the bank was authorized to operate.[55]

White's characterization of nineteenth-century banking markets relies on a long-standing assumption that local or, at least, regional banking markets were segmented and nonintegrated. That is, he assumes that unit bankers in, say, southwestern Pennsylvania did not or could not lend in Baltimore, Philadelphia, or New York. They certainly didn't lend in Richmond, Charleston, or New Orleans. On this score, White's characterization is clearly incorrect. Unit banks in the northeastern United States (and else-where) could and did diversify their portfolios through a variety of mech-anisms. Connecticut's unit banks were repeatedly reprimanded by the state's bank commissioners for buying too many commercial bills in New York City, bills that may have been drawn against lumber, cotton, tobacco, and wheat bound for export, and any number of manufactured goods com-ing from Europe and England.[56] But Connecticut bankers' extraregional lending was not narrowly focused on Wall Street's active commercial paper market. During the depression of the early 1840s, Connecticut's banks ab-sorbed losses arising from lending in Alabama and Ohio. Developments in the South during this period so concerned the directors of the Phoenix Bank of Hartford that they sent two men on a tour of the South to investigate the bank's southern borrowers. Eventually, however, the bank wrote off more than $15,000 in southern loans.

Similarly, Lance Davis finds that New England textile mills borrowed regularly from both local and New York City banks.[57] Mill owners gained access to more and better funding sources and nonlocal banks found an effective source of portfolio diversification, both geographic and sectoral. Most rural banks developed respondent relationships with banks in regional banking centers, such as Baltimore, Pittsburgh, Hartford, Providence, Rich-mond, Charleston, and Louisville. These regional money center banks, in turn, maintained close ties with banks in national money centers, such as New York, New Orleans, Philadelphia, and Boston. Such money center cor-respondents bought and sold commercial paper for their respondents, col-lected exchange, made remittances, and even engaged in some limited clear-ing operations. Moreover, most money center banks had agents in London, Liverpool, Amsterdam, and Paris who could remit or collect foreign exchange drawn on a wide variety of imports and exports. Unit banks un-doubtedly loaned mostly to local borrowers. Any bank of any size could, if it chose, diversify until the incremental costs and benefits were equalized. Transaction costs were not so prohibitive as to impede some degree of diversification.

Even banks that chose not to interact with commercial center agents and buy up commercial paper could diversify in a limited way. Massachusetts bank commissioners reported in 1852 that several banks hired agents who traveled through the countryside discounting promissory notes for merchants, innkeepers, farmers, and artisans. The commissioners condemned the practice, arguing that banks "have a locality to which their operations are designed to be confined."[58] By 1859, the practice had spread and agents of Massachusetts country banks were increasingly moving into State Street (Boston's financial district) to buy commercial paper. Davis Dewey, along with many other banking historians, takes a dim view of these practices. He labels banks with traveling agents "saddle-bag" banks and argues that they had a single purpose: to disperse a bank's notes as widely as possible to slow redemption.[59] He fails to recognize that, by the mid-1850s, the Suffolk system had effectively eliminated this as a motivation, at least for New England's unit banks.

Outside New England, dispersing banknotes may have slowed redemptions and reduced reserve holdings, but diversification and the exploitation of better lending opportunities outside the locality of a bank surely remained strong motivators. Dewey and other banking historians often fail to recognize that banknotes were not circulated for the sake of circulating them. They were circulated in return for valuable consideration, namely, the acquisition of interest-earning assets. That is what the directors of the Bank of East Tennessee (Knoxville) had in mind, in September 1851, when they directed the bank's cashier to remit up to $5,000 to a Memphis agent to buy "good Bills upon New Orleans, having not more than 90 days to run."[60] In October, another $10,000 was remitted to the Memphis agent. Later the same month, $1,000 was sent to the Louisville firm of Moussart & Company to buy commercial paper (bills of exchange) payable in New York City.[61] The Bank of East Tennessee's exchange operations continued to grow, and in May 1853, it appointed the American Exchange Bank of New York City its eastern collection agent. By circulating its banknotes in Memphis and Louisville, the Bank of East Tennessee may have been able to extend more credit on a given reserve base, but diversification was likely to have been a driving force as well. Minutes of the directors' meetings fail to reveal which, if either, motivated the policy, but it is likely that both played a part.

Just as unit banking did not preclude diversification, branch banking did not guarantee it. Branching facilitated geographic diversification, but it did not ensure industrial or sectoral diversification. The previously discussed plantation banks provide a case in point. Despite branching statewide and mixing long-term mortgage lending with short-term commercial lending, portfolios of plantation banks were highly dependent on the fortunes of the cotton market. Short-term bills were drawn on cotton shipments. Long-term mortgages were effectively collateralized with cotton production, present and future. When cotton prices declined in the late 1830s, hard-hit commercial and mortgage borrowers were unable to meet their obligations. Banks that sought sectoral, maturity, and geographic, diversification—like the Bank of Virginia, which operated urban and rural branches and loaned to merchants, artisans, and agriculturalists—thrived in good times and outlasted the bad ones. Branch banks that failed to follow similar strategies failed in economic downturns.

The real advantage of branch banking in the antebellum South and West became most evident, perhaps, during financial crises. Charles Calomiris and Schweikart argue that intrabank and interbank cooperation arose among branch banks during the panic of 1857.[62] Such cooperation, especially interbank cooperation, promoted banking stability in the face of small but sharp financial shocks. The panic of 1857 followed the course of a classic financial crisis. Securities markets had softened, particularly the market for western railroad securities, but had not seen a broad decline. Banks were profitable and their portfolios were neither stronger nor weaker than usual. Nevertheless, unit banks suffered inordinate losses and failures compared to branch banks.

Traditional explanations of the panic credit the failure of the Ohio Life Insurance and Trust Company as the spark. Ohio Life engaged in limited commercial banking, but it acted as a remitting correspondent for several Ohio banks through its New York City office. During the 1850s, Ohio Life developed a sound reputation and paid about 8 percent dividends per annum. Swept up in the railroad craze of the mid-1850s, the company's New York manager, Edward Ludlow, invested nearly three-quarters of the bank's assets in railroad securities. When some of these railroads experienced financial troubles, Ohio Life's portfolio declined proportionately. Eventually, the bank was forced to suspend. Although Ludlow's activities just prior to the company's suspension remain clouded, their consequences are clear.

Ohio Life's failure was not the precipitating cause of the panic. It did, however, set already nervous investors on edge. Its failure, combined with sharp declines in the prices of western railroad shares, made bank creditors increasingly uneasy because they could not readily determine which banks and to what extent they were invested in these securities. Asymmetric information problems led to the kind of intrinsic uncertainty discussed in chapter 9. Recall that intrinsic uncertainty theories of bank panics hold that panics occur because bank creditors are aware that an adverse shock has caused the deterioration of bank portfolios but they cannot determine its precise incidence. Depositors and note holders may, as a result, engage in an indiscriminant bank run.

The sequence of events in mid- to late 1857 conforms to the intrinsic uncertainty hypothesis. Between late July and mid-September, informed traders drove up the discount on country banknotes in both Philadelphia and New York. Such an increase in risk perceptions among informed traders prompted some note holders and depositors to convert bank liabilities to specie. Country banks faced specie drains and drew on their city correspondents, straining city banks and reducing their reserve positions. City banks responded by refusing to renew brokers' loans (i.e., loans to securities dealers and traders collateralized by stocks and bonds), which forced brokers to sell stocks at depreciated prices, driving them into default. Bank creditors witnessed these defaults and failures and accelerated their specie demands. A full-fledged run erupted in mid-October and New York City banks followed banks in Philadelphia and Boston that had suspended a few weeks earlier. The failure of Ohio Life was a harbinger, but the root cause of the panic was the "declining fortunes of western railroads and declines in western land values, along with the concentration of asset risk and reserve drain in New York City."[63]

Ironically, a panic of western origin (western railroads and Ohio Life) was mostly eastern in consequence. It was the highly reputable banking systems of New York and New England that suspended specie payments. The banking systems of the South and West, with a "general reputation . . . for free and easy banking," generally did not.[64] Among these regions' banking systems, the Bank of the State of Ohio, the State Bank of Indiana, the banks of Kentucky, and about one-half of South Carolina's banks maintained note convertibility and deposit redemptions. The common thread was these banks' branch networks.

Hammond argues that the small number of large banks in these systems allowed them to act in concert and avoid the worst effects of the crisis, but he does not identify any specific actions taken in concert.[65] Calomiris and Schweikart do. Ohio banks avoided a general suspension of specie payments in 1857 and 1858 despite their close affiliation with the failed Ohio Life. They avoided suspension and failure because the mutually insured branches of the State Bank of Ohio cooperated with one another and with the state's independent and free banks. The 31 offices of the State Bank of Ohio were not branches in the traditional sense; rather, they formed a federation of independent banks under the supervision of the State Board of Control, which supervised and regulated each member. Although each bank was semiautonomous, each was proportionately responsible for the liabilities of the other 30 members. Mutual liability could have exposed the banks to greater rather than less risk because the notes of any member were redeemable at any and all others.[66] Unusually large or unanticipated redemption demands could thus threaten one or more members.

The Board of Control, however, insulated its members from the panic in two ways. First, the board transferred assets of the failed Ohio Life to its creditor banks. In effect, its subordinated the claims of Ohio Life's other creditors to the State Bank. Ohio Life's assets were liquidated during the panic to bolster the member banks' reserves. Second, the board and its members exceeded their mandate to act as a mutual guarantee system designed to reimburse creditors of failed members and became a system of mutual liquidity insurance. Under the board's guidance, relatively strong banks supplied reserves to weak or vulnerable banks. In September and October 1857, four troubled banks received a total of $56,000 in reserves from other members, and none of the State Banks' members failed.

Moreover, the benefits of Ohio's State Bank network transcended the system itself. Because it was able to maintain banknote and deposit convertibility, it fostered confidence in the state's independent and free banks as well. Ohio's banks were pressed by panicky creditors. Between November 1856 and February 1858, specie holdings at Ohio's independent banks declined by 14.6 percent and specie holdings at the State Bank members declined by 14.4 percent, but reserves at the state's free banks actually increased by 2.6 percent.[67] Even though reserve positions deteriorated, they actually improved relative to outstanding circulation. Circulation at Ohio's independent banks declined by 57.8 percent; State Banks members, 27.7 percent; and free banks, 42.6 percent. A significant factor that allowed the independent and free banks to weather the storm was a 31.4 percent increase in debts due to the State Bank. Apparently, the State Bank of Ohio not only redistributed reserves within the system, but it also supplied reserves to nonmember banks to stem potential runs. Contraction was the order of the day, but mass failure was not. In the end, only one of Ohio's 54 banks failed during the panic.

Indiana's experience stands in contrast to Ohio's. Of 32 free banks operating before the panic, only 18 remained afterward. Rolnick and Weber attribute the failures to falling bond prices, but the real problem may have been the absence of an effective coordinating mechanism like that existing in Ohio. The State Bank of Indiana, a federation of semiautonomous banks like the State Bank of Ohio, maintained specie payments throughout the panic. There is no extant evidence that this bank developed a mutual liquidity guarantee system like that developed in Ohio, but actual or potential intrabank transfers likely mollified note holder and depositor concerns.[68]

Despite its own success in weathering the panic, the State Bank of Indiana was either unable or unwilling to assist the state's free banks. Calomiris and Schweikart attribute its unresponsiveness to the poor reputation of Indiana's free banks.[69] Although this was certainly a factor, a more proximate cause for its inaction was that its charter was due to expire in December 1857, and it was winding down. It was calling loans, retiring its circulation, and liquidating other assets; thus, it was in no position to take the lead and coordinate interbank arrangements outside of its own narrow circle.

Milton Friedman and Anna Schwartz, among many others, argue that liquidity problems like those that develop during financial panics are unlikely to remain confined to a small subset of the banking sector.[70] Difficulties at one bank give rise to depositor and note holder fears about the liquidity or solvency of other institutions. Bank runs are potentially contagious. Systemwide crises can be averted only if bank creditors can be reassured about the safety and liquidity of their currency holdings. An individual bank may be able to offer that reassurance by borrowing from other banks, using its sound assets as collateral, and meeting the redemption demands of panicked creditors. If the panic is systemic, however, interbank borrowing will not avert crisis or suspension of convertibility. An outside source of base money is required to bolster confidence in the banks and to stem a run. The usual prescription is a central bank with the power to create base money.

The experience of states employing self-regulating, mutual guarantee banks suggests that central banking is just one of many potential solutions to liquidity crises. Mutual guarantee pacts created incentives to monitor among those best suited to monitor banks (namely, other banks) and to lend support or even pool resources during a panic. In good times, the mutual guarantee system aligned the incentive to regulate with the authority to regulate. The mutual guarantee made it in each member's best interest to establish an effective means to watch over and discipline other members. Economists call such systems incentive compatible because each party faces incentives compatible with the group's best interest. In bad times, this built-in monitoring, surveillance, and support system could be employed to reassure nervous creditors. By reallocating resources, depositors and note holders were placated, and once the unusually pressing demand had passed, members were well positioned to correct exposed deficiencies.

Although bank federations in Ohio and Indiana held out the possibility that private institutions could maintain public confidence in the payments system during a financial crisis, they did not provide prima facie evidence that lenders of last resort are unnecessary. The Ohio and Indiana federations maintained convertibility among relatively small subsets of the region's (or certainly the nation's) banking sector. As the number of banks expands and as the geographic distance between them widens, effective monitoring becomes increasingly costly. Because banks interact less often, incentives to monitor are reduced. Thus, the optimal size of an efficacious mutual coinsurance federation may be too small to protect the payments system on a national scale. The lender of last resort function may, then, be best viewed as a public good because the prevention of one inefficient, run-induced bank closing makes all other banks better off.[71] As with most public goods, private suppliers provide a suboptimal quantity of such services. As a result, a lender of last resort, whether government sponsored or not, may be justified.

Although no southern state adopted a mutual guarantee system, the South's extensive branching networks achieved similar results during the panic. No branch bank in Virginia, North Carolina, South Carolina, Kentucky, Missouri, Tennessee, or Louisiana failed. In fact, Calomiris and Schweikart note that Kentucky, Alabama, and Louisiana actually witnessed bank *entry* during the panic period.[72] Nowhere was branch banking's strength better demonstrated than in Virginia. In 1852, Virginia enacted a modified form of free banking that allowed entry of small unit banks. Although the state's six branch banks suspended specie payments during the panic (mostly because banks in Philadelphia, New York, and Boston drew large amounts of specie from southern banks after they had already suspended), none failed. Two independent banks failed, but most others experienced declining fortunes.[73] Public confidence in the state's well-managed branch banks remained strong. Confidence in the smaller, younger independent banks evaporated rapidly.

In part, the performance of southern branch banks during the panic reflected a long-standing cooperation between banks and their borrowers. Northern banks, after having suspended specie payments themselves, raided southern banks that maintained convertibility. Faced with the choice of suspending or dramatically curtailing credit, banks and merchants opted for suspension. Merchants wrote newspaper editorials and legislative memorials supporting the banks' actions and declaring their continued willingness to accept the banks' notes at par. Even though suspension of specie payments disrupted the smooth operation of the payments system, the disruption was less severe than a serious credit crunch and a number of bank failures.[74] Suspension relieved debtors because it encouraged loan recontracting. Banks were freed from short-term liquidity constraints and borrowers were freed from selling assets at fire-sale prices to meet their debts. Suspension gave banks breathing room and the time to focus on long-term solvency rather than short-term liquidity.

Garnering the support of merchants and politicians was, of course, critical, but establishing a system of intrabank and interbank cooperation was fundamental. Branch systems decreased the cost of intrabank cooperation dramatically. Constant monitoring by a parent office kept branches in line during economic expansions and could rationally reallocate resources to exploit emerging profit opportunities. During panics, these same mobilizing abilities were used to avert crisis. "In times of panic," notes Starnes, "funds can be used more efficiently under the branch system. It is not likely that all the branches of a large bank will be pressed for funds at the same time, and assistance can be rendered to any members in distress by the mother bank and the other branches."[75]

Cooperation among otherwise competing banks was also important during a crisis. Branch networks with fewer parties to the negotiations were more likely to enter into mutually beneficial agreements. In October 1857, for example, Charleston's banks agreed to receive each other's notes at par, "effectively expanding the supply of reserves by making notes as good as gold for interbank transactions."[76] The South's reliance on large branching networks facilitated ad hoc cooperation. Not only did the small number of banks diminish the costs of reaching an agreement, but they also reduced the costs of monitoring the agreements. In the Northeast, by way of contrast, the large number of small banks made agreement prohibitively expensive.

Even if an agreement had been reached, the costs were high and the benefits were too small and too widely dispersed for incentive-compatible cooperation to arise.

Hard-Won Cooperation in the 1830s: Lessons Learned and Not Forgotten

The successful interbank cooperation observed by Calomiris and Schweikart may have represented the culmination of long experience punctuated by more failures than successes. Georgia and South Carolina stand out as cases of failed southern interbank cooperation during the crisis of the late 1830s. In both 1837 and 1839, Savannah's and Augusta's large banks attempted to establish regular interbank settlements, but interior banks refused to join in because they feared that the urban banks would use the system to limit country bank note issues.[77]

In South Carolina, similar attempts to establish interbank cooperation never materialized. In 1838, the legislature grew concerned with the quality of the state's bank-supplied currency. Notes of several banks circulated below par and it was believed that unsound practices had caused the depreciation. A legislative resolution instructed the Bank of the State of South Carolina to take any measures necessary to return all of the state's banks' notes to par.[78] The bank made several efforts to control banknote issues, but the bank's policing actions were unpopular. Any effort the bank made to appease legislators excited the wrath of the other banks. W. A. Clark notes that financiers made efforts, independent of legislative dictates, to "save the weaker banks from going to wall by cooperation among the stronger."[79] Ultimately, South Carolina's banks failed to cooperate.

Banks in other places learned to cooperate. In early March 1837, Herman Briggs & Company of New Orleans, one of the nation's largest cotton brokerages, failed following a sharp decline in cotton prices. J. L. & S. Joseph, merchants and cotton brokers in New York City, failed as soon as news of the Briggs failure arrived. Although the failure of Briggs & Company was not the proximate cause of the panic of 1837, it did, like the failure of Ohio Life in 1857, signal a change in business sentiment.[80] For the next month, bank creditors grew increasingly jittery. New Orleans banks suspended specie payments in April, and the Dry Dock Bank of New York City was run on 8 May 1837. Within the next two days, most of the city's other banks suspended. Within a few days, Philadelphia and Baltimore banks followed suit.

Many interior banks maintained specie payments even in the face of sharp depletions of their reserves. Kentucky banks were one such case. Although closely tied to New Orleans, Kentucky banks worked hard to maintain specie payments even after New Orleans banks suspended. In fact, Kentucky banks sustained their pre-panic levels of loans and circulation through the spring and summer of 1837. Between 31 January and 30 April, the banks actually increased their specie reserves by $178,000. Trouble struck in late summer, however. A legislative committee investigating the Northern Bank of Kentucky reported that it appeared "from the cash book, and the evidence of the teller, that an unprecedented run upon the bank, for specie, began in August last; that the run was very heavy during the whole of the following month" and finally abated in mid-October.[81] Despite the length and severity of the run, the Northern Bank obtained enough specie to meet all redemption calls.

From whence did that specie originate? Clearly, the Northern Bank did not rely on its New Orleans or Philadelphia correspondents. They were engaged in their own liquidity scramble. The Northern Bank's ostensible rival, the Bank of Kentucky, turned out to be its last and best ally. The Bank of Kentucky, unlike the Northern Bank, was not run and it continued to augment its specie holdings through 1837. When the Northern Bank faced certain embarrassment, the Bank of Kentucky came to its aid. Figure 10.1 plots monthly amounts *due from other banks* (interbank lending) at the Bank of Kentucky and amounts *due to other banks* (interbank borrowing) at the Northern Bank between January 1837 and December 1838. Although the legislative committee dated the run's onset in August, it apparently began in July. Even as early as April, the Bank of Kentucky supported the Northern Bank. The simultaneous spikes in the two series, however, occur in July as the Northern received massive support from the Bank of Kentucky

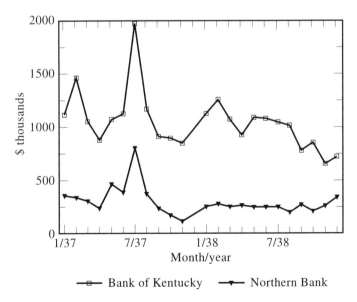

Figure 10.1 Interbank Transfers between Kentucky Banks, 1837–1838. Sources: Kentucky, *Senate Journal* (1837/38, 1838/39).

(and, perhaps, other banks as well). Once the run was stemmed, the Northern Bank gradually paid down its interbank indebtedness.

Louisiana's banks also supported one another during the panic. On 12 April 1837, shortly after New Orleans banks suspended payments, the banks' presidents met to develop strategies for interbank cooperation and clearing and labeled themselves the Board of Presidents.[82] They agreed to accept each other's notes on deposit, to not pay out other banks' notes, to engage in daily note exchanges, and to settle weekly in bills of exchange drawn on New York or London. In addition, each bank agreed to place a weekly balance sheet on public view in the lobby of the Union Bank. On each Sunday morning, the bank presidents were to meet to review the statements and determine strategy for the upcoming week. At the 12 April conference, each president promised to expand his bank's loans by 10 percent. This was, of course, a correct response. The best response to a financial crisis is to increase credit availability and pump liquidity into the system. The issue was whether or for how long these 16 banks could maintain a unified front if economic conditions continued to deteriorate.

The Citizens Bank was the first to crack. When the president laid the board's directive before the Citizens' directors on the afternoon of 12 April, they conceded to all of the terms except one: they refused to accept the notes of the Atchafalaya Railroad Bank. The following day, the Board of Presidents acquiesced to Citizens' refusal, probably because they planned to jointly finance the importation of $1.5 million in specie from Cuba using the Citizens' Havana agent.[83] Other than the single concession made to the Citizens Bank, any bank found not abiding by the agreement was to be immediately ejected from the coalition and its notes were to be refused by the other banks.

One day later, on 14 April, the board's resolve was put to the test when the New Orleans Gas Light and Banking Company was caught paying out notes of other banks, a direct violation of the agreement. On threat of expulsion, it stopped paying out other banks' notes. The Citizens Bank complained that daily settlements were not punctual. Its directors resolved to ignore the agreement. The bank's cashier was "instructed to cause the other local Bank notes to be paid at this counter."[84] Further, on 15 April, the Citizens' directors ignored the agreement to expand its loans by 10 percent. In fact, its directors resolved that all outstanding 60-day notes would be renewed, but only as long as at least 10 percent of the note was paid. Notes running 120 days would be renewed only with a 20 percent reduction in value. This action took some pressure off existing debtors, but it effectively reduced the volume of currency and liquidity. On 22 April, the Citizens Bank agreed to continue with the earlier specie importation resolution, but on 25 April, it rejected a plan to issue large-denomination banknotes ($100, $500, and $1,000) to facilitate interbank clearings.[85]

In mid-May, a second crack appeared in the coalition. An article, originally published in a Baltimore newspaper and reprinted in New Orleans, claimed that the Citizens Bank had violated its charter and that the bank's European agents were themselves in dire straits. The following day, the directors of the City Bank of New Orleans informed the Board of Presidents and the Citizens Bank that it would no longer accept the latter's notes. Moreover, the City Bank called for an independent audit of the Citizens' books. The Citizens Bank shot back, calling the reports "absurd & ridiculous."[86] In retaliation, the Citizens Bank rejected notes of the City Bank. With the entire coalition about to fall apart, cooler heads convinced the Citizens Bank's directors that an independent audit was, in fact, a very good idea. Within a week, it invited the presidents of the Union Bank, the Mechanics & Traders Bank, the Commercial Bank, and the Louisiana State Bank, as well as the state treasurer, to inspect the bank and publish their findings.[87] Noticeably absent, however, was a representative of the City Bank.

After having its own reputation pilloried, the Citizens Bank's directors came to recognize the importance of cooperation and joint action; thereafter, they were more willing to fully participate in the coalition. However, even after the audit cleared the Citizens Bank of any obvious wrongdoing, several other banks supported the ejection of the Citizens from the coalition. Still others demanded that the Citizens alone resume specie payments to prove its condition. Doing so, of course, would have doomed it to failure. The dissenting voices surely recognized this but nevertheless felt it more important to exact some vengeance rather than protect the coalition as a whole.

In late May, the Board of Presidents began hammering out an agreement under which stronger banks would support weaker ones. Also discussed were several methods to reinflate the local economy and avoid the rapidly escalating debt-deflation problem. The board was, as Green notes, trying to establish a joint lender of last resort.[88]

All New Orleans banks adopted the board's resolutions. As such, every bank agreed to accept the notes of all others in amounts consistent with the normal course of trade. In addition, troubled banks were granted extraordinary allowances. The Citizens Bank, for example, agreed to take in up to $50,000 of the Carrollton Bank's notes provided that the Carrollton remitted an equal amount of good, short-term commercial paper.[89] The Huntsville Bank of Alabama, which operated a large New Orleans agency, was similarly allowed to expand its drawing rights at the Citizens Bank. Acting in unison, New Orleans banks followed Walter Bagehot's recommendation for central banks, namely, to rediscount all good commercial paper and increase liquidity until the public's demand for currency was sated.[90]

Once a basic agreement was finally established, the banks could turn to the most pressing issue: the growing debt-deflation problem and the looming possibility of massive debtor insolvencies. The banks struck an accord whereby strong banks agreed to increase credit and currency issues while weak banks gradually contracted. With each bank circulating notes equal in value to 20 percent of its paid-in capital, public confidence would increase (because strong banks would increase their issues and weak banks would contract) and the aggregate circulation would expand. On 22 May, the Canal Bank (a highly regarded bank) was asked to increase its circulation from its current $316,000 to $700,000. At the same time, the Carrollton Bank (a troubled bank with a poor reputation) was asked to reduce its circulation by $54,000. If the city's banks had abided by the agreement, their aggregate circulation would have increased by more than $1.5 million. In so doing, they would have reversed the local deflation and alleviated the growing real burden faced by bank debtors.

However, the banks failed to meet the agreed-upon circulations, due more to the extent of the economic downturn than to an inability to cooperate. As the recession deepened, the minute books of the Citizens Bank filled up with discussions of how best to deal with delinquent debtors. References to Herman Briggs & Company cropped up repeatedly well into 1838. After several attempts to strike an accord with Briggs and various other companies connected with Briggs, the Citizens Bank's attorney was finally instructed to commence suit on Briggs's protested notes.[91] On 28 August, that directive was belayed, allowing Briggs an additional period to provide an alternative schedule of repayments. On 31 August, Briggs offered $60,000 in settlement. The directors rejected it. In December, the bank was still haggling with Briggs's attorneys and Briggs was again offered an additional term to develop an acceptable repayment schedule.

Other, less notable, creditors requested similar forbearance. Fry & Company's $15,000 debt was extended, and the company agreed to pay $5,333 in three installments due as much as 18 months beyond the original maturity. Another debtor repaid his loan in 530 bales of cotton and a mortgage payable in 24 months. Even while its own debtors requested leniency and patience, the Citizens' creditors were growing increasingly impatient. The bank had asked its London agent, F. de Lizardi & Company, to hold £43,000 in sterling bills drawn by New Orleans cotton brokers and endorsed by the bank. Instead of heeding the bank's instructions, however, de Lizardi remitted the bills to the Bank of England, which demanded immediate payment from the Citizens Bank.[92] It was likely that New Orleans' other banks faced similar difficulties.

Had the panic been short lived, the banks' cooperative agreement may have averted any bank failure. The recession's longevity, however, eventually wore down the strong banks that could no longer support weak or embarrassed ones. Between 1838 and 1842, eight Louisiana banks, with combined capital in excess of $38 million, closed. Despite the eventual collapse of the Board of Presidents and the failure of so many banks, the city's banks showed that they were capable of cooperation and mutual support.

The point of cooperation never was, and should not have been, to subvert the market process and shore up insolvent, inefficient banks. Instead, it was designed to avert the failure of solvent and efficient, but illiquid, banks. In that regard, it largely succeeded.

In 1837, southern banks were unable to cooperate to the same extent that they did in 1857, but the earlier instance may have been a learning experience. Even the limited cooperation among southern banks in 1837 stood in stark contrast to the lack of cooperation among northern banks. Philadelphia banks, for example, faced most of the same issues faced by New Orleans banks, namely, credit contraction, massive note holder redemptions and depositor withdrawals, and a number of weak banks in need of support from strong ones. Disagreements over interbank clearing mechanisms blocked agreement. Whereas New Orleans banks quickly agreed to accept each other's notes, Philadelphia banks failed to reach a similar agreement. Two of Philadelphia's fifteen banks refused to accept the notes of any others. Only six banks agreed to accept and exchange each other's notes, but clearings apparently occurred irregularly. A resolution adopted by the six cooperating banks provided that interest could be charged on interbank balances whenever they exceeded $25,000.[93]

In the early 1840s, the failures of the Girard Bank and the Bank of the United States of Pennsylvania occurred amid rumors of fraud and failed cotton speculations. These closings threatened to prompt a run on Philadelphia's other banks. The remaining banks established a Bank League pledged to mutual support and cooperation and the banks agreed to jointly provide as much as $500,000 to support a bank being run. When the Moyamensing Bank was run, the group came to its defense. However, in March 1842, when the legislature demanded all the state's banks to resume payments after a suspension, the Bank League was unable to provide the resources to support its members. Anticipated by nearly everyone, a run materialized and the Bank League's resources were insufficient to stem it. Unable to secure enough specie independently, the Mechanics Bank and the Manufacturers and Mechanics Bank of Philadelphia, as well as the Bank of Penn Township in the southern suburbs, were forced to close within days of resumption. Nine of Philadelphia's fifteen banks survived the depression, but all did so without the sort of cooperation found in New Orleans. The Girard Bank and the Bank of the United States of Pennsylvania were clearly insolvent when they closed, but evidence on the other four banks is less clear. It is likely that they succumbed more to liquidity than solvency shortfalls.

Why were northern banks unable to form the same sorts of mutual support coalitions that emerged in the South? Economists usually point to the large number of small banks in the North and the small number of large banks in the South. With so many potential members, the costs of forming and policing mutually acceptable agreements were prohibitive. Despite the logical appeal of this argument, it fails to fully explain the northern experience. Recall that New Orleans had 16 cooperating banks. Of Philadelphia's 15 banks, only 6 entered into the original 1837 pact of cooperation and support. The inability of Philadelphia's banks to support one another during tough times undoubtedly resulted from the hard terms they offered each other in good times. Schwartz and Donald Adams document how Philadelphia's earliest banks worked diligently to derail the formation of new banks, to raise the costs of their charters, and to undermine them once they opened. Not surprisingly, such actions on an incumbent's part led to hostility and mutual distrust. These sentiments set the tone for interbank relations, undermining any possibility of cooperation during tough times. Banks entangled in long-standing battles were unlikely to rush to one another's aid during a liquidity crunch. The cost of negotiating an agreement was not just a function of the number of banks involved. It was also a function of those banks' relational histories. Long-term enemies were unlikely allies, no matter the threat posed by a common danger.

This is not to argue that incumbent banks in the South welcomed new rivals with open arms, but tales of recurrent bank wars so common among northern banks are not found in the histories of southern banks. It may have been that state involvement and intervention had some effect. Having a financial stake in several competing banks, southern legislators may have appointed bank directors more likely to cooperate than to do battle. A remarkable feature of the southern branch system was that legislators did not relegate particular banks to particular geographic markets, thereby creating small monopolies. As a result, most southern branch banks overlapped, competing in several markets.

In Virginia, for example, the Bank of Virginia, the Farmers Bank of Virginia, and the Exchange Bank all operated branches in Richmond, Petersburg, Fredericksburg, and Norfolk. When the legislature became convinced that a particular town deserved a bank, it amended the charters of several banks to encourage each to open a branch in that place. In 1860, for example, Virginia provided that five different banks could open a branch in Parkersburgh, four could open a branch in Abingdon, five in Harrisville, seven in Marion, four in Huntersville, and five in Liberty.[94] Because they were so geographically connected and so extensively intertwined in other respects, these banks engaged in a sort of genial competition. The downside to this sort of competitive structure, of course, was that it facilitated collusion and cartelization of the banking industry. Although this was a very real possibility, indirect evidence, such as interest rates, profit rates, and dividend rates, fails to demonstrate that effective cartels formed. Rates of return on bank capital or bank assets in Virginia and elsewhere in the South Atlantic were not significantly higher than in the Northeast. Although this is not sufficient, by itself, to refute collusive behavior, it does suggest that southern consumers received the benefits of interbank cooperation without paying an excessive price.

Concluding Remarks

The commonwealth ideal was alive and well throughout the antebellum United States, but it was expressed in banking policy most vehemently in the Old South and the Old Northwest. Where private capital alone was lacking, the state stepped in to deepen financial markets and broaden produce markets. In the earliest stages of development, the commonwealth ideal found expression in the form of subsidized banks and transportation facilities. Once rudimentary systems were put in place, states turned to subsequent concerns.

The pinnacle of the commonwealth ideal was the plantation bank. Directly underwritten by states, plantation banks in Mississippi, Florida, Arkansas, and Louisiana provided cheap credit to planters. These states marketed some of the earliest derivative securities, state bonds guaranteed by mortgages tendered to state-sponsored banks. Although the banks claimed no responsibility for these debts, the bonds sold only when they carried an implicit governmental guarantee. Investors discovered only after the fact that the guarantees offered by Florida, Mississippi, and Arkansas weren't worth much. Despite these banks' poor record, they served their purpose. They made funds available for land improvements and other investments that eventually increased aggregate welfare.

A second defining feature of southern and western banking was widespread adoption of free banking, even while states continued to support and stake chartered banks. Although free banking was not as successful in the West as it was in New York, it was unfair, as Logan Esary contended, to characterize western banking by the "wildcat banker from Owl Creek."[95] Without a doubt, wildcatting existed. But it makes little sense to judge western bankers as a group by the actions of a few wildcatters.

Modern research has mostly overturned the traditional belief that free bank failures resulted from fraud. Rather, they were caused by the same factors that caused other businesses, including banks, to fail. Unrealistic expectations, unknown and untested entrepreneurial capabilities, entry at insufficient scale, excessive infant mortality, bad timing, exogenous macroeconomic shocks, and unresponsive or ill-advised legislative requirements all caused free banks to fail. No consensus has yet been reached on the proportionate contribution of each of these causes, but few still argue that wildcatting was the principal, or even an important, cause of bank failures.

Although studies of free banking continue to proliferate, an emerging literature is redirecting attention toward the beneficial aspects of banking structures unique to the South and West. Green, Calomiris, and Schweikart, among others, argue that southern branch banks performed their intermediary functions and potentially vitiated the worst effect of most financial panics, namely, the collapse of the payments system. Large, geographically dispersed branch networks provided intrabank mutual guarantees and facilitated interbank cooperation. When the panic of 1857 struck, these banks banded together and avoided the kind of financial disruption experienced in the Northeast.

Interbank cooperation, like that observed in 1857, was learned, however. Previous attempts to cooperate proved less successful. Whether the different experience in 1857 resulted from specific lessons 20 years earlier or whether the cooperative agreement was placed under less stress by a shorter-lived panic remains an open question. Nevertheless, southern branch banks and western bank federations were able to coordinate their activities, but northern banks could not. Part of the explanation is the lower costs of forming and policing agreements among small groups of banks in the South. The nature of interbank rivalry and competition also played a part. Bank managers were no less prone to animosity, resentment, and distrust than anyone else. The cutthroat nature of competition in some markets stood in the way of cooperative solutions to common concerns.

11

Assessing America's Early Banks

America's early banks are reminiscent of the beaks of Darwin's finches. They all appeared with slight variation, yet they all served the same purpose. Just as there was no optimal ornithological trait, there was no optimal banking system. Whether a particular system succeeded or failed depended on more than its structural predicates: free entry versus restrictive chartering, branching versus unit banking, bond collateral versus insurance funds, mutual guarantees versus shareholder liability, single versus double versus unlimited liability. A banking system's success or failure depended on a host of institutional, political, cultural, and industrial influences that determined what a particular system's banks did. Were they expected to strictly adhere to commercial or real-bills lending? Were they expected to provide mortgage loans? Were they expected to support an incumbent political machine? Were they expected to become good members of a federation of mutually supporting branches? Were they expected to fight their way into a highly competitive market with a number of aggressive incumbents determined to protect their turf?

The traditional prescription for success—the real-bills hypothesis—was no guarantee of success. Among the many shortcomings and fallacies inherent in the theory, perhaps its most glaring weakness was that, in its simplest form, it operated on only a single margin despite the fact that banks made choices across many. Even if banks had been effectively constrained to short-term commercial lending, there is no reason to believe that fewer or smaller bank failures would have occurred. In a related vein, Thomas Hellman, Kevin Murdock, and Joseph Stiglitz note that the imposition of capital requirements (even risk-based capital requirements) will not single-handedly eliminate moral hazard and inefficient risk taking.[1] They argue that capital requirements may eliminate inefficient risk taking, but the required capital would be unreasonably high. There is no efficient outcome consistent with strictly capital-based regulation.

In other words, prudential bank regulations could not focus on a single bank choice variable. Because banks maximized across numerous margins—capital, specie reserves, loan types, deposit rates, loan rates, and so forth—effective regulation had to instruct (but perhaps not direct) bankers about acceptable tradeoffs. When states liberalized bank entry, they limited some activities and set broad boundaries. Most imposed capital leverage ratios, the most common being that loans could not exceed three times paid-in capital. A few imposed specie reserve requirements.[2] All faced usury limits. Free bankers held prescribed portfolios of government bonds and mortgages. Variations were limited only by the imagination and insight of the legislators who wrote the regulations. Ultimately, the decentralized federal polity gave states the space to experiment, something they did enthusiastically. In the end, deciding if an experiment was worthwhile depended on whether it achieved its objectives. A second issue is how banks affected macroeconomic performance, a subject to which we now turn.

Banks and the Macroeconomy

At the risk of oversimplifying sometimes complex theses, the historiography of early American banking centers around the theme that banks and money are special. Banks are unlike suppliers of other commodities and thus should be subject to more and different regulatory oversight than producers of commonplace goods. Historical studies of banking, from William Gouge's *Short History of Paper Money and Banking in the United States* (1833) through Bray Hammond's *Banks and Politics in America from the Revolution to the Civil War* (1957), accept a well-entrenched, stylized reality: caught up in the recurrent boom-bust cycles of primitive capitalist economies, banking services outraced economic activity in the boom, which fueled speculative frenzies through inflationary currency creation that further encouraged inefficient risk taking by entrepreneurs; in the bust, sharp credit and monetary contraction created a debt-deflation cycle that accelerated the downward recessionary spiral. Legitimate and illegitimate businesses alike filed for bankruptcy. Most banks suspended; some failed. After a long period of retrenchment and a brief period of quiescence, the cycle began anew. The central message of Hammond's influential, Pulitzer Prize–winning book was "that the government had to regulate banking and that the more centralized the system, the better."[3]

The 20-year periodicity of panics in 1819, 1837, and 1857 that largely coincided with peaks in bank formation and expansion lent credence to the traditional interpretation. Public land sales increased from just 285,000 acres in 1810 to more than 3.4 million acres in 1818 and 2.9 million in

1819. The following year, the speculative bubble burst.[4] Land sales contracted sharply, falling to 652,000 acres in 1823. As the bubble was blown up, the number of banks tripled from 102 in 1810 to 338 in 1818.[5] When it burst, bank failures mounted so that only 267 remained in 1822. The economic expansion of the 1810s, punctuated by the panic of 1819, is said to have exposed a basic inconsistency inherent in a number of state banking systems: continuous specie convertibility and the liberal extension of long-term agricultural credit.[6]

Not having learned hard lessons in the 1810s, the 1830s provided the United States a second opportunity to observe the outcome of too-liberal banking policies. The banking sector was relatively quiescent in the 1820s. It was 1828 before the United States had as many banks as it had in 1818. The year 1827, on the other hand, ushered in a decade of unprecedented financial experimentation and liberalization. Louisiana helped set the tone for the era when it chartered the Consolidated Association of Planters in 1827, a bank capitalized by state bonds collateralized with mortgages on farms and slaves. Three other southern states followed. Jackson's veto of the Second Bank's recharter encouraged liberal bank chartering as states scrambled to replace its credit facilities. Free banking was the culmination of a decade-long call for freer entry.

Once again, a sustained agricultural boom was one of the driving forces behind bank formation. Between 1829 and 1836, the prices of farm products increased by nearly 51 percent while the overall price level increased just 18 percent.[7] This change in relative prices markedly increased returns to land investment and land improvements. In 1829, the federal government sold about 1.2 million acres of public land. In 1836, it sold more than 20 million acres. The volume of private sales is unknown, but contemporary descriptions of accelerated turnover rates and rampant land speculation indicate that it was of a similar order of magnitude.

Traditional interpretations of the era attribute the land speculation, in part, to the banks. Between 1827 and 1837, the number of banks doubled from 333 to 729. Although many banks eschewed agricultural credit, many others offered it in abundance. In fact, two notable financial innovations of the period—the plantation banks and free banks discussed in chapter 10— either directly or indirectly fostered land investment and commercialized agriculture. Both types of banks sprung up in areas generally devoid of adequate, or even any, banking facilities and catered to a largely agricultural clientele. As such, at least one-half to two-thirds of their portfolios were long-term assets, mostly mortgages.

Contemporaries and historians have generally criticized these banks because they routinely violated real-bills prescriptions; namely, responsible banks limited themselves to short-term lending that financed real (typically wholesale) transactions. Banking history, therefore, has been written from the perspective of what Richard Sylla calls the soundness orthodoxy.[8] According to this orthodoxy, real-bills lending curbed speculative excesses because credit and monetary expansion occurred only in response to an expanding base of tangible goods. Land was an inappropriate basis for currency and monetary creation because it broke the connection between economic development and money growth, leading to inflation at best and to speculation at worst. The flaws in real-bills reasoning are detailed in chapter 3. Similarly, Edwin Perkins argues that the soundness orthodoxy was employed by many banking historians to scare modern bankers straight.[9] By demonstrating the consequences of excessive risk taking and blatant violations of best-available banking practices, these writers hoped to influence bank and bank regulator behavior.

Modern research into the pace and pattern of nineteenth-century U.S. economic growth makes it possible to stand the traditional interpretation up against some statistical evidence. An important strand of the traditional interpretation is that the banking sector overreacted to macroeconomic events, which added fuel to both upturns and downturns. Figure 11.1 indicates that banking growth and economic growth occurred concurrently. The rapid increase in the number of banks in the 1810s was, it appears, a case of sectoral catch-up. After that, the two series move together, consistent with Raymond Goldsmith's observation that most countries experienced a "rough parallelism" between economic and financial growth.[10] The figure also provides some limited evidence in favor of the growth-inducing effects of banking.[11] Rapid growth in the number of banks in the 1820s preceded the economic expansion of the 1830s; even more-rapid growth in the banking sector in the 1830s preceded a long period of unprecedented growth

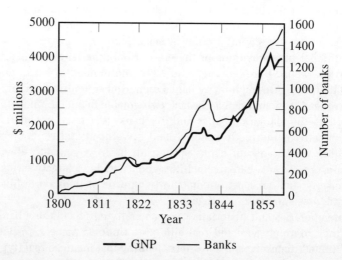

Figure 11.1 Number of Banks and Gross National Product (in current dollars). Sources: Fenstermaker, *Development*; U.S. Comptroller of the Currency, *Annual Report* (1931); Berry, *Revised Annual Estimates*.

between 1843 and 1857. Although this evidence is not conclusive, the data do not support the contention that the expansion of the financial sector in the 1810s, 1830s, and 1850s was disproportionate to growth in aggregate economic activity or the source of macroeconomic instability.

Even though growth in the number of banks did not outrace economic fundamentals, it is possible, of course, that money and credit creation grew disproportionately as banks increased their leverage ratios. Figure 11.2 details the specie leverage ratio; that is, the number of dollars of banknotes and deposits supported by a dollar of specie reserves (in effect, the inverse of the reserve ratio). Relative to a flat 40-year trend, the 1830s stand out as a period of markedly increased specie leverage, implying that banks were either using their reserves more efficiently or accepting greater liquidity risks. It was more likely that banks were taking on greater risks. The credit crunch induced by Nicholas Biddle, president of the Second Bank of the United States, 1833–1834 exposed the nonsustainability of the banks' attempts to spread their reserves more thinly. Yet, they returned to these levels soon after the Second Bank's closing. Finally, the panic of 1837 initiated a nearly decade-long reduction in the ratio. The low point was in 1843 with a halving of the ratio from its peak. After the depression of the 1840s, the specie leverage ratio returned to and largely fluctuated around its long-term trend value. The years just prior to the panic of 1857 saw an increase in

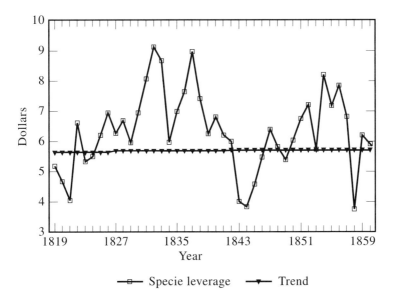

Figure 11.2 Specie Leverage Ratio. Note: Calculated as total circulation plus deposits divided by specie reserves. Sources: Fenstermaker, *Development*; U.S. Comptroller of the Currency, *Annual Report* (1931).

the leverage ratio similar to but smaller than that of the 1830s. Banks seemingly took on riskier positions during the economic expansions of the 1830s and the 1850s.

Capital leverage ratios (i.e., the number of dollars of loans supported by a dollar of capital) presented in figure 11.3 tell a similar tale. Over the course of the antebellum era, banks learned how to safely arbitrage a greater volume of loans out of a given capital. As with specie leverage ratios, banks clearly accepted greater risks in the 1830s; otherwise, they did not deviate significantly from the trend. Even though capital leverage ratios in the 1830s were high by historical standards, they were quite low by modern standards. The importance of this ratio, of course, is that it provides a measure of how well-insulated bank creditors were from losses due to bank failure. The lower the ratio, the more insolvency risk borne by shareholders. The higher the ratio, the more insolvency risk borne by bank creditors.

What was happening in the 1830s to encourage banks to increase their risk exposure? Banks were responding to the profit motive. Between 1829 and 1835, bank profits rose. One factor driving the increased profits was a decline in short-term interest rates relative to long-term rates. Such a shift effectively decreased the banks' funding costs (i.e., they could borrow more cheaply) while their lending rates increased. A similar sequence emerged

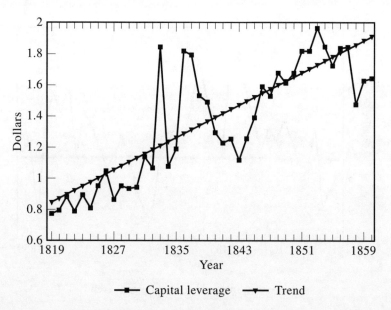

Figure 11.3 Capital Leverage Ratio. Note: Calculated as total loans and discounts divided by total paid-in capital. Sources: Fenstermaker, *Development*; U.S. Comptroller of the Currency, *Annual Report* (1931).

in the late 1840s and early 1850s, with bank profits rising as short-term rates fell relative to long-term rates. It is not surprising, then, that the early 1830s and early 1850s witnessed bank entry and increased leverage ratios. Rising profits on arbitraging on differences between short-and long-term rates induced entry and expansion as bankers strived to capture these profits.

The downside to these increasing short-long interest spreads was narrowing spreads in the late 1830s and late 1850s. Unexpected increases in relative short-term rates put banks that had expanded their mortgage or other long-term lending under pressure. Modern studies of financial intermediation note that mortgage lending was not inherently destabilizing, but it could be if banks were not sufficiently diversified or if there was a substantial maturity mismatch in the lenders' portfolios. A fundamental concern for mortgage lenders was that they intermediated short-term liabilities into long-term assets (e.g., banknotes and deposits into mortgages), which exposed them to so-called interest rate or term-structure risk.

A sudden and sharp increase in the short-term interest rate effectively raised the costs of attracting funds while the nominal return on a mortgage portfolio was fixed in the short run. It was profitable, perhaps, to attract 30-day deposits paying 3 percent interest per annum and to lend on 12-, 18-, or 24-month mortgages at 6 percent per annum. If short-term rates rose sharply relative to long-term rates, say to 7 percent, the mortgage portfolio became unprofitable. Lenders paid more for funds than their portfolios generated in revenues. An increase in short-term rates to, perhaps, 5 percent may have been sufficient to make the mortgage portfolio unprofitable once the costs of intermediation were included. The evidence suggests that banks may have actually derived a short-term advantage from a small rise in the relative price of short-term credit, but sustained and sharp increases in relative short-term rates eventually took a toll and drove bank profits down. In the early 1840s, bank profits fell dramatically in response to rising short-term rates.[12] For banks with sizable mortgage portfolios, extended periods of high relative short-term rates eventually drove them into insolvency.

Thus, the past century of scholarship has focused inordinate attention on these periods of failure. Did bankers get caught up in a speculative bubble? Almost certainly. Did legislators also get caught up in the bubble? Almost certainly. Were liberal chartering policies, including free banking, and unprecedented state intervention, including dedicated and heavily subsidized mortgage banks, uncalled for or even counterproductive? Almost certainly not. Earlier chartering systems were prone to the same sort of enthusiastic excesses as more-liberal systems. A fundamental difference, however, was that earlier chartering systems were more prone to corruption and bribery.

Moralistic arguments aside, there are good reasons to dislike corruption, especially institutionalized corruption. Some economists argue that corruption can be benign. Looked upon as part of a Coasian bargaining process, corruption is little more than a bureaucrat and a private agent negotiating their way to an efficient allocation of property rights.[13] As long as the bribery game is competitive and the corrupt official awards the license to the highest bidder, allocative efficiency is maintained, only now the producer's surplus lines the pockets of the corrupt official rather than the pockets of the winning bidder's shareholders.

When the participants in this game do not have complete and symmetric information, however, the outcome may not be efficient. First, the briber and the bribee may not be able to come to terms because the briber has an incentive to understate anticipated future rents or profits. Knowing this, the bribee faces an incentive to overstate his demands on the briber. Even the simplest bargaining models show that when strike prices do not overlap, trade will not occur. Second, corrupt bargains are generally not enforceable. Third, and perhaps most relevant to early American banking markets, the bribee may refuse to deliver what was promised. In many instances, prospective bankers offered substantial bribes to legislators in return for the property right to a monopoly in banking in a particular place. In nearly as many instances, and often within a short time, the bargain was reneged on when the legislators, able to extract an additional bribe from a potential competitor for the first mover, chartered a second bank.

Some may be inclined to argue Mancur Olson's contention, namely, that eventually bribery and corruption became so institutionalized that corrupt legislators acted more like "stationary" than "roving" bandits, and that the distortionary effects of the exactions of a stationary bandit were more akin to taxation than bribery.[14] Still, the need to conceal the corruption in most instances led to greater distortions than above-board taxation. It may, for example, have been more efficient to have a number of modest banks operating in each of Pennsylvania's towns, like Lancaster, Reading, Chester, and so on, than to have a handful of very large banks operating in Philadelphia. Because the likelihood that the corruption would be discovered increased with the number of corrupt acts, it made sense to limit the number of charters to a few large ones. Thus, corruption had potentially large negative consequences for static efficiency.

Was corruption likely to negatively affect economic growth as well? Pranab Bardhan notes that any bribe payment aimed at obtaining an operating license surely reduced the incentive to invest.[15] Additionally, the redirection of productive resources from investment to legislator consumption had detrimental effects on growth rates. More insidious yet was that as bribes increased, profit rates on productive investment fell relative to rent seeking, which tended to encourage the latter. Kevin Murphy, Andrei Shleifer, and Robert Vishny argue that rent seeking exhibited increasing returns and that growth slowed by rent seeking tended to induce additional rent seeking, and so on in a vicious cycle.[16] Slow growth tended to reduce the returns to entrepreneurship relative to rent seeking. The induced marginal increase in rent seeking, in turn, reduced the returns to entrepreneurship, which further reduces growth.

The American pattern of corrupt bank chartering seemingly followed the trend observed in other places (much more serious research is needed in this area before anything other than circumstantial evidence can be brought to bear on this issue, however).[17] Bardhan argues that, in general, there was a negative correlation between corruption and growth. In some countries, however, an initial burst of growth may have worsened corruption before it got better. Why would corruption increase in the early stages of economic growth? As the economy grew, it tended to grow more complex, and public officials confronted more opportunities to extract rent from newly emerging industries and sectors, like banking and finance, particularly through the granting of monopoly franchises. Despite this upsurge in official corruption in the early stages of economic development, development ultimately generated forces antagonistic to corruption. Extended periods of growth raised the returns to entrepreneurship relative to rent seeking, which redirected activity in socially beneficial ways. Increased economic activity also afforded the opportunity to raise civil servant salaries, thereby reducing incentives to solicit bribes. Most important, however, may have been the emergence of a working or middle class that found corruption distasteful and demanded reform. Political histories of free banking, for example, make clear that it was politically popular precisely because it represented a break from past corrupt chartering practices.

It was important for banks to elicit the widest possible confidence in their abilities to intermediate, to supply currency, and to provide credit. The history of American banking, seen appropriately, is a story of that pursuit. Early on, chartering served two purposes. It allowed legislators to extract (either individually or in unison) some of the rents earned by monopoly banks, but it was also an exercise in reputation formation. A charter was nothing less than a legislative imprimatur. It served notice that someone had assessed the capabilities of the applicants and had found them adequate. When chartering fell in disrepute, either because it encouraged corruption or because it infringed on the inherent rights of individuals to pursue a profession of their choice, legislators searched for mechanisms to maintain confidence in the system. Bond-secured note issue under free banking, collateralized state bonds under plantation banking, mutual guarantee networks like those in Indiana and Ohio, and direct insurance programs like those in New York and Vermont were all designed to secure note holder confidence. Even the Suffolk system was, in some measure, a franchise operation that imposed common procedural rules, which allayed consumer distrust. That some of these structures were more successful than others is not surprising. Different forms were adopted to achieve common ends, and a priori it was difficult to determine which ones would be relatively more successful.

Such groping about for appropriate structures allowed the banking sector to grow and flourish in the antebellum era. With fewer banks, capital accumulation would have been a slower, more grinding process than it actually was, and the pace of economic development would have followed a different path. Most theories of economic growth focus on nexus of capital accumulation and savings. Both must increase, or take on different forms, for growth to occur. A remarkable feature of most modern theories is that they ignore the role of financial intermediaries, even though they are an integral part of any market economy because they facilitate savings and investment. Rondo Cameron argues that any number of "social, psychological, or economic changes may take place to persuade society to desire to save a significantly larger proportion of its net product, [but] the existence or introduction of financial institutions will be necessary to make that decision effective."[18] George Tucker, the first professor of economics at the University of Virginia, was more blunt: "Credit enters so largely into the dealings and concerns of every civilized community [developed economy]," he wrote "that, if any large part of its operations were suddenly suspended, the whole machinery of society would be at a stand."[19]

Notes

Chapter 1

1. Diamond, "Financial Intermediation," and Ramakrishan and Thakor, "Information Reliability."

2. King and Levine, "Financial Intermediation," "Finance and Growth," and "Finance, Entrepreneurship, and Growth;" and Levine, "Financial Development."

3. Bodenhorn, *History*, chapter 2.

4. Barro, "Economic Growth"; and Barro and Sala-i-Martin, "Convergence across States" and "Convergence," discuss convergence.

5. Appleton, *Examination*, p. 29.

6. Green, "Louisiana" and *Finance and Economic Development*.

7. See White (ed.), *Free Banking*, 3 vols., for an introduction to the free banking literature in the Austrian tradition.

Chapter 2

1. Anonymous, *Defence*, pp. 21–22.

2. Wainwright, *History*, pp. 9–13.

3. Schwartz, "Beginning," pp. 426–28.

4. Stokes, *Chartered Banking*, pp. 15–16.

5. Gallatin, *Writings*, I, p. 129.

6. Stokes, *Chartered Banking*, pp. 16–17.

7. Quoted in Golembe, *State Banks*, p. 53 note.

8. Hammond, *Banks*, p. 579.

9. Hammond, *History*, I, p. 334; Seavoy, *Origins*, p. 84.

10. Starnes, *Sixty Years*, pp. 33–34.

11. Ibid., pp. 43–44.

12. Hammond, *Banks*, p. 146.

13. Lamoreaux and Glaisek, "Vehicles"; Lamoreaux, *Insider Lending*, pp. 59–62.

14. Buchanan, "Rent Seeking," pp. 6–8.

15. Landes and Posner, "Trademark Law," p. 267.

16. Reiffen and Patterson, "Rise."

17. Schwartz, "Beginning," pp. 429–30.

18. Wainwright, *History*, p. 244.

19. Rajan, "Past," p. 536.

20. Shleifer and Vishny, "Large Shareholders" and "Survey," p. 754.

21. Shleifer and Vishny, "A Survey," p. 754.

22. Ibid., p. 755.

23. Ibid., p. 760.

24. Redlich, *Molding*, p. 17.

25. U.S. House *Executive Doc. No. 77*, pp. 102–19.

26. Baskin and Miranti, *History*, p. 74.

27. Ibid., pp. 107–8.

28. Chadbourne, *History*, pp. 31–32.

29. Gallatin, *Writings*, III, p. 419.

30. New York, *Assembly, Doc. No. 59* (1831), p. 30.

31. New York, *Assembly, Doc. No. 74* (1835), p. 24.

32. New York, *Assembly, Doc. No. 80* (1836), p. 15.

33. Chadbourne, *History*, p. 12.

34. Anonymous, *Bank Bills*, p. 5.

35. Lamoreaux and Glaisek, "Vehicles," pp. 511–12.

36. Hammond, *Banks*, p. 302.

37. Ibid., p. 124.

38. Bagehot, *Lombard Street*, p. 214; Gallatin, *Writings*, III, pp. 380–81.

39. American State Papers, *Finance*, III, p. 588.

40. Ibid.

41. Hammond, *Banks*, p. 468.

42. Citizens Bank, *Minute Books*, 6 August 1838.

43. Gras, *Massachusetts First National Bank*, p. 77.

44. Bagehot, *Lombard Street*, p. 259.

45. Redlich, *Molding*, p. 118.

46. Bagehot, *Lombard Street*, p. 174.

47. Redlich, *Molding*, pp. 34–35.

48. Chadbourne, *History*, p. 58.

49. Coase, "Nature."

50. Amartya Sen quoted in Klamer, "A Conversation," p. 147.

51. Blair, *Ownership*, p. 19.

52. Jensen and Meckling, "Theory," p. 308.

53. Smith, *Inquiry*, p. 233; Berle and Means, *Modern Corporation*.

54. Berle and Means, *Modern Corporation*, p. 122.

55. See, for example, Stiglitz, "Credit Markets," p. 141.

56. Fama, "Agency Problems"; Fama and Jensen, "Agency Problems"; and "Separation"; Easterbrook, "Two Agency-Cost Explanations"; Shleifer and Vishny, "Survey."

57. This work builds on the earlier contracting literature of Alchian and Demsetz, "Production"; and Jensen and Meckling, "Theory."

58. Fama and Jensen, "Separation," pp. 303–4.

59. Fama and Jensen, "Agency Problems," pp. 331–32.

60. Ibid., p. 293.

61. Bank of Tennessee, *Charter*, p. 6, provided that the governor appoint all 12 directors for two-year terms. By comparison, the governor appointed 3 of 11 directors at the Bank of Kentucky.

62. Duke, *History*, p. 37.

63. Philadelphia Bank, *By-Laws*, p. 3; Bank of Chester County, *Minute Book*, 3 November 1814.

64. Bank of Chester County, *Minute Book*, 22 November 1814–31 October 1815.

65. Bank of Tennessee, *Minute Book*, 11 October 1860.

66. Bank of East Tennessee, *Minute Book*, 23–29 September 1851.

67. Citizens Bank, *Minute Books*, 30 May 1836.

68. Ibid., 2 June 1836.

69. Bank of Chester County, *Minute Book*, 3 November 1814.

70. Starnes, *Sixty Years*, p. 100.

71. Hollis and Sweetman, "Higher Tier Agency Problems."

72. Calculated from information in Hubert, *Merchants' National Bank*, pp. 14, 143–44, and Warren and Pearson, *Prices*.

73. Virginia, "Report," p. 11. Professor Tucker (author of *Theory of Money and Banks*) was the highest paid faculty member. All other professors were paid $750 per three-term academic year.

74. Ibid.

75. Jensen and Meckling, "Theory," pp. 328–29.

76. Modigliani and Miller, "Cost." Modigliani received the Nobel Prize in Economic Science in 1985; Miller in 1990. The Nobel committee, in both instances, mentioned their 1958 contribution.

77. Blair, *Ownership*, p. 36.

78. Brealey and Myers, *Principles*, p. 412.

79. This remains a common textbook explanation. Ross, Westerfield, and Jordan, *Essentials*, pp. 361–73.

80. Myers, "Capital Structure Puzzle," apparently originated the term.

81. Baskin and Miranti, *History*, p. 158.

82. Ibid.

83. Stiglitz, "Credit Markets," p. 143.

84. Easterbrook, "Two Agency-Cost Explanations," pp. 653–54.

85. Ibid., p. 654.

86. Dewatripont and Tirole, "Efficient Governance Structure," pp. 24–25.

87. Campbell and Kracaw, "Information Production," pp. 877–78.

88. Ibid., p. 879.

89. Baskin and Miranti, *History*, p. 255.

90. Ibid., p. 19.

91. Shleifer and Vishny, "Survey," pp. 752–53.

92. *Union Bank v. Campbell* (1843), 4 Humphreys 394–99.

93. *Johnson v. Churchwell* (1858), 1 Head 146–49.

94. *Marr v. Bank of West Tennessee* (1867), 4 Coldwell 479.

95. Ibid., 479.

96. Baskin and Miranti, *History*, p. 51.

97. Quoted in ibid., p. 191.

98. The coefficient of variation is calculated as the standard deviation divided by the mean. This procedure standardizes values when comparing two variables with different means and variances. In this case, the dividend return is measured as dividend payment divided by paid-in capital; profit rates equal dividend payout plus tax payments plus changes in retained earnings all divided by total earning assets.

99. Atack and Rousseau, "Business Activity," pp. 156–57.

100. Fama and Jensen, "Agency Problems," p. 339.

101. Dewatripont and Tirole, "Efficient Governance Structure," p. 33.

102. Ibid., p. 31; and Ramakrishan and Thakor, "Information Reliability," provide theoretical support for this position.

103. Diamond and Dybvig, "Bank Runs," provide theoretical support for this position. Advocates of this theory are too numerous to list here.

104. Calomiris and Kahn, "Role."

105. Gorton, "Reputation Formation"; Bodenhorn, "Small Denomination Banknotes" and "Quis Custodiet."

106. Gorton, "Reputation Formation."

107. Bodenhorn, "Quis Custodiet."

108. Bodenhorn, "Small Denomination Banknotes."

109. Smith, *Inquiry*, pp. 305–13.

110. Ibid., pp. 820–24.

111. Dewatripont and Tirole, "Efficient Governance Structure," p. 26.

112. Chandler, *Visible Hand*.

113. Bodenhorn and Haupert, "Was There a Note Issue Conundrum" and "Note Issue Paradox."

Chapter 3

1. Fama, "What's Different"; Diamond, "Monitoring."

2. Redlich, *Molding*, p. 116.

3. James, *Money*, pp. 59–60.

4. Adams, *Finance*, p. 92.

5. Tucker, *Theory*, p. 189.

6. Ibid., p. 166.

7. Lamoreaux, *Insider Lending*, p. 105.

8. Moulton, "Commercial Banking," p. 639.

9. Dunbar, *Theory*, pp. 29–30.

10. Hammond, *Banks*, pp. 676–77.

11. Diamond, "Debt Maturity Structure."

12. Sargent and Wallace, "Real-Bills Doctrine."

13. Thornton, *Enquiry*, pp. 253–56. Humphrey, "Mercantilists," pp. 65–70, presents a critical examination of Thornton's arguments.

14. Bernanke, "Non-Monetary Effects"; Bernanke and Gertler, "Agency Costs."

15. Fisher, "Debt-Deflation Theory."

16. Green, *Finance*, pp. 117–34, offers a similar interpretation.

17. Some banks required endorsers (consignors) on single-name paper, but the basic feature of the credit was unchanged.

18. Report of the Bank of Kentucky, U.S. House, *Executive Doc. No. 79*, p. 762.

19. Bodenhorn, *History*, chapter 5, outlines the evolution of antebellum bill markets.

20. Dunbar, *Theory*, p. 115.

21. Gouge, "Commercial Banking," pp. 316–17.

22. The records of the Citizens Bank of New Orleans show that the bank bought several thousand dollars in sterling-denominated bills every week. It purchased lesser amounts payable in French francs and Dutch guilders.

23. Nevins, *History*, p. 15; Hammond, "Long and Short Term Credit," p. 89.

24. Nevins, *History*, p. 15.

25. Redlich, *Molding*, p. 7.

26. Ibid., p. 65.

27. Hammond, *Banks*, p. 75.

28. Schumpeter, *Theory* and *Capitalism*. Kirzner, "Entrepreneurial Discovery," provides an Austrian interpretation of the competitive process, which shares several features with Schumpeter's view.

29. This section draws heavily on Bodenhorn, "Private Banking" and "Engine."

30. Schumpeter, *Theory*, chapter 3.

31. Rosenberg, "On Technological Expectations," p. 525.

32. Kirzner, "Entrepreneurial Discovery," p. 64.

33. Sylla, "American Banking."

34. The contemporary pamphlet literature is massive and the real-bills debate can be traced back to the classical-mercantilist debates in the late eighteenth century. It was reincarnated in the Currency School–Banking School debates of the early to mid–nineteenth century and continued into the Keynesian debates of the mid–twentieth century. White, *Free Banking*, and Humphrey, "Mercantilists," offer modern interpretations of the banking and monetary consequences of real-bills theory and policy.

35. Moulton, "Commercial Banking," p. 641.

36. Ibid., pp. 657–58.

37. Ibid., p. 487.

38. Adams, *Finance*.

39. Davis, "New England Textile Mills."

40. No claim is made that this is a representative sample of early American banks. It is simply a sample of banks whose records survive, were located, and were investigated. Given its nonrandom nature (unless survivability is random, which is possible), the conclusions are highly tentative. A similar sample might generate a completely different view of antebellum lending practice, though that seems unlikely.

41. Bodenhorn, "Engine," provides more detailed evidence on the Black River Bank.

42. Loveland Paddock owned 90 percent of the capital stock; his two eldest sons each owned 5 percent. His youngest son was not brought into the business. Bodenhorn, "Free Banking" and "Engine," details the bank's history.

43. An attempt was made to link borrowers at the Bank of Cape Fear to a decennial manuscript census, but prior to 1850 it is difficult to ascertain occupations with any certainty. Borrower characteristics, however, generally implied farm and plantation ownership.

44. Moulton, "Commercial Banking," pp. 706–7.

45. Holdsworth, *Financing*, p. 199.

46. Concerns about long-term lending among modern banking theorists (unlike nineteenth-century commentators) focuses not so much on how quickly a bank could realize on its loans, but on the explicit risks of financing short-term debt with long-term assets. Using short-term debt to finance long-term assets opens banks up to term structure and interest rate risks. These risks came to the fore in the U.S. savings and loan crisis in the 1980s.

47. One of the Black River Bank's most frequent borrowers in the late 1850s, Nelson Plato, was a livestock broker and drover who rarely renewed a bill.

48. Again, no claim is made that these banks' portfolios are representative of all banks.

49. This explanation is offered and justified in Bodenhorn, "Private Banking."

50. Ashton, *Industrial Revolution*, p. 73.

51. Puth, *American Economic History*, p. 248.

52. Smith, *Inquiry*, book ii, chapter i.

53. Deane, "Role of Capital," pp. 355–56.

54. Pollard, "Fixed Capital," pp. 301–2.

55. Deane, "Role," pp. 357–58.

56. Sokoloff, "Investment," pp. 548–50.

57. Callender, "Early Transportation," p. 150.

58. Pollard, "Fixed Capital," pp. 307–8.

59. Sylla, "American Banking," p. 220.

60. Quoted in Wyatt, "Rise," p. 32.

61. Ibid., p. 33.

62. Ibid., pp. 33–34.

63. Branch & Company Records, *Bill Books*.

64. Horton, *Geographical Gazetter*, p. 778.

65. Ibid.

66. Emerson, *Our County*, p. 364.

67. Ibid. p. 365.

68. Black River Bank, *Discount Book #3*.

69. Emerson, *Our County*, p. 360; Black River Bank, *Discount Book #3*.

70. Emerson, *Our County*, p. 335; Black River Bank, *Discount Book #3*.

71. Diamond, "Financial Intermediation"; Ramakrishan and Thakor, "Information Reliability"; and Fama, "What's Different."

72. Diamond, "Monitoring."

73. Fama, "What's Different."

74. Townsend, "Optimal Contracts."

75. Petersen and Rajan, "Benefits" and "Effect."

76. Boot and Thakor, "Moral Hazard."

77. Sharpe, "Asymmetric Information."

78. Ibid. p. 1070.

79. Rajan, "Insiders" and "Past"; Berlin, "For Better."

80. Rajan, "Past," p. 536.

81. The results are derived from a regression (unreported) that controls for several other factors likely to affect loan rates, including loan size, maturity, consignors, place of payment, and so forth.

82. These estimates are based on a regression of the natural logarithm of loan amounts on a constant, place of payment, maturity, renewal, number of endorsers, and quarterly seasonal dummies, in addition to the number of previous borrowings and its square. Most of the coefficients were significant at usual levels; the adjusted R-square was 0.40; the regression F-statistic was 146.2.

83. Mokyr, *Lever.*

Chapter 4

1. A recent example is Friedman and Schwartz, "Has the Government," pp. 50–51.

2. Stokes, *Chartered Banking,* pp. 2–4; Gras, *Massachusetts First National Bank,* pp. 25–27.

3. Quoted in Hasse, *History of Banking,* p. 15.

4. Field, "Sectoral Shift"; Hekman, "Product Cycle."

5. Davis, "New England Textile Mills," pp. 22–24.

6. This remains true today. The emergence of small-scale community banks coincident with the consolidation through merger of large regional banks reflects the information-intensive, idiosyncratic nature of bank lending. Large banks offer standardized contracts to those meeting predetermined criteria. For those unable to meet the criteria, community banks offer credit in smaller amounts and at higher interest rates. Broaddus, "Bank Merger Wave," p. 9.

7. Stokes, "Public and Private," p. 283.

8. Rothenberg, "Emergence," pp. 787–88.

9. Martin, *Century.* Between 1800 and 1830, 16 banks, 17 insurance companies, and 6 manufacturing firms went public in Boston.

10. Fenstermaker, *Development,* appendix A.

11. Davis, *Currency,* pp. 76–79.

12. Ibid., pp. 85–86, 89, 98–101.

13. Hasse, *History of Money,* p. 6.

14. Smith, *Inquiry,* p. 406.

15. Redish, "Why Was Specie."

16. Davis, *Currency,* p. 85.

17. Ibid., p. 102.

18. Chadbourne, *History,* pp. 10–11.

19. Quoted in Davis, *Currency,* p. 143.

20. Langguth, *Patriots,* pp. 31–32.

21. Spencer, *First Bank,* pp. 8–9.

22. Gras, *Massachusetts First National Bank,* pp. 22–23.

23. Reed, *Sketch,* p. 5.

24. Citizen, *Village Bank,* pp. 9–10.

25. Reed, *Sketch,* pp. 6–7.

26. Weiss, "Issue," pp. 777–78.

27. Quoted in Stokes, *Chartered Banking,* p. 3.

28. Ibid., p. 9.

29. Knox, *History*, p. 371.

30. Stokes, *Chartered Banking*, p. 9.

31. Dorr's Rebellion of 1841–1842 arose out of protests against Rhode Island's original constitution (1663) that disqualified adult males who did not own $134 in land (about one-half of the adult male population in the mid-1830s). Dorr organized an unsanctioned convention that drafted a new constitution, held a popular election, and seated a legislature in opposition to the official one. When Dorr went to Washington and New York in search of support for the government, the governor called out the militia to put it down. Upon his return, Dorr organized an unsuccessful attack on the Providence Arsenal. After a few skirmishes, Dorr's followers disbanded, his lieutenants surrendered, and Dorr was captured and sentenced to life imprisonment. He was released within a year. Schlesinger, *Age*, pp. 411–17; Foner and Garraty, *Reader's Companion*, p. 916.

32. *Hunt's Merchants' Magazine* 3 (November 1840), p. 413.

33. Economopoulos, "Impact."

34. Rhode Island, *Acts and Resolves* (Oct. 1835).

35. Massachusetts, "True Abstract" (1830–1834).

36. Gras, *Massachusetts First National Bank*, p. 97.

37. Humphrey, "Cost Dispersion," p. 28.

38. Barth, *Great Savings and Loan Debacle;* Kane, *S & L Insurance Mess;* and White, *S & L Debacle.*

39. Mester, "Traditional and Nontraditional Banking," pp. 546–47.

40. Gorton and Haubrich, "Loan Sales."

41. Mester, "Traditional and Nontraditional Banking," p. 561.

42. Quoted in Dewey, *State Banking*, p. 142.

43. Burpee, *First Century*, p. 54.

44. Hasse, *History of Money*, p. 38.

45. Chadbourne, *History*, pp. 35–37.

46. Knox, *History*, p. 360.

47. Reed, *Sketch*, pp. 11–13.

48. Stokes, "Public and Private Finance," p. 274.

49. Quoted in ibid., p. 273.

50. Whitney, *Suffolk Bank*, pp. 3–4.

51. Dewey, *State Banking*, p. 49.

52. Parsons, *History*, pp. 6–7.

53. Hasse, *History of Banking*, pp. 21–23.

54. Massachusetts, *Report of a Committee* (1809).

55. Massachusetts, *Report of the Committee* (1811).

56. Massachusetts, *Report of the Committee* (1811).

57. Appleton, *Defence*, p. 34.

58. Ibid., p. 35.

59. Clark, "Economies"; Gilligan and Smirlock, "Empirical Study."

60. Lamoreaux, "Banks," Information Problems," and *Insider Lending.*

61. Lamoreaux, "Banks," pp. 65–52. Vatter, "Industrial Borrowing," anticipated some of Lamoreaux's findings. Lockard, *Banks*, argues that Lamoreaux's insider model does not adequately describe banks in Massachusetts' Connecticut River valley. He finds evidence that credit facilities at banks in the valley were not dominated by insiders, but he draws these conclusions from the records of two savings banks and two commercial banks. It is not clear that Lockard's

sample is representative, so Lamoreaux's interpretation stands pending more evidence.

62. Lamoreaux and Glaisek, "Vehicles," p. 507.

63. Lamoreaux, "Information Problems," pp. 166–67.

64. Stokes, *Chartered Banking*, p. 29.

65. Lamoreaux and Glaisek, "Vehicles," pp. 512–20.

66. Ibid., p. 506.

67. Rhode Island, *Acts and Resolves* (January 1837), pp. 89–92.

68. Dewey, *State Banking*, p. 187.

69. Quoted in Stokes, *Chartered Banking*, pp. 43–44.

70. Lamoreaux, "Information Problems," p. 164.

71. Calomiris, "Comment," p. 197. New England was a net exporter of short-term capital in the antebellum era. Scarcity is a relative term. Credit is always scarce; what matters is relative scarcity.

72. Jensen and Meckling, "Theory," p. 313.

73. Shleifer and Vishny, "Large Shareholders," p. 463; "Survey," p. 760.

74. Fama and Jensen, "Separation," p. 307.

75. Greif, "Cultural Beliefs," p. 913.

Chapter 5

1. Fenstermaker, *Development;* Temin, *Jacksonian Economy.*

2. Gorton, "Reputation Formation"; and Bodenhorn, "Quis Custodiet."

3. Redlich, *Molding*, p. 67, is representative. This characterization should be accepted skeptically given that there were relatively few country banks operating between 1800 and 1810.

4. Quoted in Chadbourne, *History*, pp. 41–42.

5. Dewey, *State Banking*, p. 74.

6. Ibid., pp. 80–81; and Redlich, *Molding*, p. 68.

7. Gras, *Massachusetts First National Bank*, p. 75.

8. Trivoli, *Suffolk Bank*, p. 13.

9. The New England Bank's dividend rate exceeded the average by only two-tenths of 1 percent in 1814 and nine-tenths of 1 percent in 1815. Martin, *Century*, p. 97.

10. Redlich, *Molding*, p. 72.

11. Ibid., p. 71.

12. Knox, *History*, p. 367.

13. *Niles' Register* (16 June 1821); quoted in Dewey, *State Banking*, p. 83.

14. Knox, *History*, p. 365.

15. Rolnick, Smith, and Weber, "Lessons," p. 13.

16. Calomiris and Kahn, "Efficiency," p. 771.

17. Dewey, *State Banking*, p. 85.

18. Root, "New England Bank Currency," p. 279.

19. Statements made by bank commissioners in the antebellum era need to be read cautiously. Regulatory capture was very real because it was common for the banks themselves to elect bank commissioners and many commissioners were retired bankers.

20. Chadbourne, *History*, pp. 44–45.

21. Simonton, *Maine*, p. 25.

22. Calomiris and Kahn, "Efficiency," p. 777.

23. Whitney, *Suffolk Bank*, pp. 23–25.

24. Hasse, *History of Banking*, pp. 22–23.

25. Lake, "End," p. 197.

26. Ibid., pp. 203–4.

27. Rolnick, Smith, and Weber, "Lessons."

28. Myers, *New York Money Market*, provides a description of New York's clearing system.

29. Calomiris and Kahn, "Efficiency," p. 767.

30. Hammond, *Banks*, p. 554.

31. Redlich, *Molding*, p. 72.

32. Schweikart, "U.S. Commercial Banking," pp. 606–7.

33. Hammond, *Banks*, p. 552.

34. Lake, "End," p. 188.

35. Redlich, *Molding*, pp. 74–75.

36. Fenstermaker and Filer, "Impact," pp. 36–39.

37. Walker, *History*, pp. 67–68.

38. Lake, "End," pp. 189–90.

39. Mullineaux, "Competitive Monies," pp. 886–87, 891–93.

40. Calomiris and Kahn, "Efficiency," p. 772.

41. Ibid., pp. 773–74.

42. This is an application of Calomiris and Kahn, "Role."

43. Simonton, *Maine*, p. 61.

44. *Bicknell's*, 28 January 1840.

45. Smith and Weber, "Private Money Creation," p. 627.

46. Ibid., p. 656.

47. Ibid., p. 653.

48. Bodenhorn, "Capital Mobility."

49. Hammond, *Banks*, p. 554.

50. Rockoff, "Suffolk System," p. 454.

51. Economides, "Economics," p. 676.

52. Economides and White, "Networks," p. 652.

53. Saloner and Shepard, "Adoption," p. 480.

54. Mester, "Efficient Production," p. 18, recognizes this for airlines operating hub and spoke networks.

55. McAndrews, "Network Issues," p. 18.

56. Henriet and Moulin, "Traffic-Based Cost Allocation," p. 332.

57. This discussion draws heavily on Lacker, Walker, and Weinberg, "Fed's Entry," pp. 16–18.

58. Ibid., p. 18.

59. Henriet and Moulin, "Traffic-Based Cost Allocation," pp. 334–35.

60. Ibid., pp. 343–45.

61. McAndrews, "Network Issues"; and Weinberg, "Organization."

62. Rolnick, Smith, and Weber, "Lessons," show that the Suffolk generated profits far greater than other Boston banks.

63. Weinberg, "Organization," p. 25.

64. This and the next paragraph follow the discussion in Weinberg, "Organization," p. 38.

65. Redemption by mail was not unheard of, but it was avoided in antebellum America. Given the risks of returning banknotes through the mail, the sending bank often tore the banknotes in half, sending the halves in separate packages. Postal redemption thus proved expensive to all involved, including the issuing bank that effectively lost the use of the torn banknotes and had to have new ones printed. To modern ears, this sounds like a trivial cost, but paper was expensive in early America. It was commonplace to find banknotes printed on the blank side of recycled paper.

66. Myers, *New York Money Market*.

67. Economides, "Network Externalities," pp. 212–13, 221, argues that in the face of significant network externalities, a monopolist may have an incentive to invite competition. The intuition is that the monopolist cannot convince potential members that it will expand the network to an efficient size because monopolists profit by restricting output. With competition in provision of the network good, potential members are more likely to subscribe to a network, which expands network size and, under appropriate conditions, implies larger profits for the former monopolist. The Suffolk used nonmarket mechanisms, namely, threats and coercion, to overcome the monopoly problem.

68. Bodenhorn, "End," provides evidence that the Suffolk exploited economies of scale in banknote clearing.

69. Calomiris and Kahn, "Efficiency," make this argument.

70. Weinberg, "Organization," pp. 26–27.

71. Ibid., p. 34.

72. Saloner and Shepard, "Adoption," p. 480.

73. Gorton, "Clearinghouses."

74. Mullineaux, "Competitive Monies," labels this the Suffolk I era.

75. Smith and Weber, "Private Money Creation," p. 650, provide a calculation suggesting that the subsidy would have taken the form of below-market rates on overdrafts, but the rate could not have been less than 0.83 percentage points below the market loan rate. The subsidy was small indeed. If a country bank was overdrawn by more than its permanent deposit (a Suffolk-mandated limit), the subsidy could not have exceeded $16.60 per annum for a bank with $100,000 in capital. The subsidy was considerably smaller than this because the Suffolk did not allow the overdraft to run for longer than a week or two. The effective subsidy, with only periodic overdrafts, was more likely to have amounted to less than $5 per annum, perhaps less.

76. Whitney, *Suffolk Bank*, pp. 23–25.

77. Tables detailing the calculation of these figures are available from the author on request.

78. Whitney, *Suffolk Bank*, p. 45.

79. Lacker, Walker, and Weinberg, "Fed's Entry."

80. Ibid, p. 11.

Chapter 6

1. Hammond, *Banks*, p. 556.

2. Gallatin, *Writings*, vol. III, p. 408.

3. Bryan, *History*, p. 134.

4. Larson, *Jay Cooke*; Perkins, *Financing Anglo-American Trade*; Adams, *Finance*; Sylla, "Forgotten Men"; Schweikart, "Private Bankers"; and Bodenhorn, "Private Banking," present case studies of the activities of various early American private bankers.

5. James, "Bank," p. 58.

6. Ibid., p. 57.

7. Lewis, *History*, p. 14.

8. Ibid. pp. 26–30.

9. Ibid., pp. 41–42.

10. Schwartz, "Beginning," p. 418.

11. Lewis, *History*, p. 54.

12. Hammond, *Banks*, pp. 53–54.

13. Lewis, *History*, pp. 54–72.

14. Domett, *History*, pp. 5–6.

15. Letter from Hamilton to J. B. Church, 10 March 1784, quoted in ibid., pp. 6–7.

16. Nevins, *History*, pp. 1–4.

17. Quoted in Domett, *Bank of New York*, p. 18.

18. Bryan, *History*, pp. 17–18.

19. Quoted in James, "Bank of North America," p. 64.

20. Bryan, *History*, pp. 17–20.

21. Schwartz, "Beginning," p. 426.

22. Wainwright, *History*, p. 10.

23. Ibid.

24. Bodenhorn, "Entry."

25. Lewis, *History*, p. 152.

26. Quoted in Domett, *Bank of New York*, p. 42.

27. Ibid., p. 55.

28. Ibid., p. 56.

29. *Bankers' Magazine* (3), September 1848, p. 138.

30. Helderman, *National and State Banks*, p. 11; Chaddock, *Safety Fund Banking System*, pp. 233–34.

31. Wright, "Artisans."

32. Fenstermaker, *Development*, table A-21.

33. Pennsylvania, *Senate Journal* (1842). The large value of notes of the Girard and Moyamensing banks was due to these banks' imminent closings, and the fact that they had not resumed specie payments.

34. Myers, *New York Money Market*, pp. 94–97.

35. Gorton, "Clearinghouses," pp. 277–79.

36. Gorton and Mullineaux, "Joint Production," p. 459.

37. Myers, *New York Money Market*, p. 97.

38. Gorton and Mullineaux, "Joint Production," pp. 461–62.

39. Gorton, "Clearinghouses," pp. 280–81.

40. Bryan, *History*, pp. 23–24.

41. Ibid., p. 42.

42. Fenstermaker, *Development*, table A-14.

43. Bryan, *History*, pp. 15–16, 79–80.

44. Daniels, *Pennsylvania*, pp. 91–92.

45. Dewey, *State Banking*, pp. 125–26.

46. Fenstermaker, *Development*, table A-24.

47. Holdsworth, *Financing*, p. 204.

48. Huertas and Silverman, "Charles E. Mitchell," pp. 93–94.

49. Holdsworth, *Financing*, pp. 137–39.

50. Ibid., pp. 265–66, 304–5.

51. Ibid., p. 140.

52. Daniels, *Pennsylvania*, pp. 148–49.

53. Ibid., pp. 151–53.

54. Krooss, "Financial Institutions," pp. 113–14.

55. *Connecticut Courant*, 17 May 1814, quoted in Woodward, *Hartford Bank*, p. 102.

56. Rates of return to equity were calculated from balance sheets reported by the banks. Earnings were calculated as dividends plus taxes plus changes in retained earnings from year t to $t + 1$. Equity was capital plus retained earnings in year $t + 1$. Thus, the rate of return was earnings $(t + 1)$ / equity $(t + 1)$. Underlying data from Pennsylvania, *House Journal* (1820, 1821).

57. We must be careful in drawing too-sweeping conclusions from this information. Historians like to relate these stories and use them as evidence of bankers ignorant of even contemporary banking practice and thus incompetent. Clearly, such bankers existed. But so too did responsible, informed, and educated bankers. My own experience with the records of the Bank of Chester County (Pennsylvania), the Black River Bank of Watertown (New York), and Thomas Branch & Company of Petersburg (Virginia) finds that some bankers kept detailed records, which were used to make informed decisions about credit and other banking policies.

58. Holdsworth, *Financing*, pp. 373–74.

59. Pennsylvania, *House Journal* (1819–1829).

60. Gibbons, *Banks*, p. 179.

61. Quoted in James, "Bank," pp. 63–64.

62. Schumpeter, *Capitalism*.

63. Livingood, *Philadelphia-Baltimore Trade Rivalry*, pp. 5–6.

64. Paine, *The Independent Gazette*, 12 March 1787, quoted in ibid., p. 8.

65. Livingood, *Philadelphia-Baltimore Trade Rivalry*, p. 11.

66. Quoted in ibid., p. 19.

67. Taylor, *Transportation Revolution*, p. 44.

68. Ibid., pp. 44–45; and Livingood, *Philadelphia-Baltimore Trade Rivalry*, p. 22.

69. Wainwright, *History*, p. 84.

70. Daniels, *Pennsylvania*, p. 66.

71. *Bicknell's*, various issues, 1841–1845.

72. Wainwright, *History*, pp. 84–85.

73. Lewis, *History*, pp. 100–106.

74. Ibid., p. 106.

75. The year 1844 was chosen because that was the first year for which the commonwealth's auditor, who compiled the bank's annual reports, requested and systematically reported information on outstanding relief issues.

76. Bryan, *History*, pp. 44–46.

77. Goldsmith, *Financial Structure*, p. 48.

Chapter 7

1. Calomiris, D. " 'Vulnerable' Economies," p. 238.

2. Calomiris, "Deposit Insurance," pp. 10–11.

3. Fisher, "Debt-Deflation Theory"; Bernanke, "Non-Monetary Effects"; Bernanke and Gertler, "Agency Costs."

4. Temin, *Jacksonian Economy*.

5. Calomiris, "Is Deposit Insurance Necessary?" p. 287.

6. Hammond, *History*, p. 337.

7. Chaddock, *Safety Fund Banking System*, p. 247.

8. New York Assembly, *Journal* (1818), p. 15, quoted in ibid., p. 248. Hammond, *Banks*, pp. 149–64; and Seavoy, *Origins*, chapters 3 and 4, provide descriptions of the politics surrounding bank chartering in early New York.

9. Chaddock, *Safety Fund Banking System*, pp. 252–55.

10. Root, "New York Bank Currency," p. 288.

11. Lincoln, *Messages*, vol. III, p. 241.

12. Hammond, *History*, p. 334.

13. Root, "New York Bank Currency," p. 288.

14. Chaddock, *Safety Fund Banking System*, p. 260.

15. Letter from Abijah Mann to A. C. Flagg, 28 January 1868, quoted in Flagg, *Banks*, p. 37.

16. As far as I am aware, no one has collected information on assessments and payments made by shareholders of failed antebellum banks. Evidence from the National Banking Era shows that recoveries averaged between 40 and 70 percent. It seems likely, pending evidence to the contrary, that recoveries in the antebellum era were of a similar order of magnitude.

17. "An Act to Create a Fund for the Benefit of the Creditors of Certain Monied Corporations and for Other Purposes," reprinted in *Albany Argus*, 6 April 1829.

18. New York, "Annual Report" (1831), p. 31.

19. Fenstermaker, *Development*, appendix B. Not all demand liabilities were insured because a few banks chartered prior to 1829 had not yet sought charter renewals.

20. New York, "Annual Report" (1832).

21. New York, "Annual Report" (1836), pp. 14, 46–47.

22. Ibid., pp. 4–11.

23. New York, "Report of a Committee" (May 1837), pp. 6–7.

24. *Shipping and Commercial List*, 25 February, 29 April, 29 July, and 26 August 1837.

25. Golembe, "Deposit Insurance Legislation," p. 190.

26. Root, "New York Bank Currency," pp. 292–93.

27. FDIC, *First Fifty Years*, p. 15.

28. Chaddock, *Safety Fund Banking System*, p. 333.

29. Ibid., p. 337.

30. Ibid., pp. 328–30.

31. Bodenhorn, "Engine," provides insights into how one upstate New York banker diversified his portfolio in the late antebellum era. It seems unlikely that many diversification opportunities were available in the early 1830s, especially in smaller, more-remote villages.

32. Weiss, "U.S. Labor Force Estimates."

33. Estimates based on author?s calculations (available on request) from statistics reported in ibid. and Weiss, "Long-Term Changes."

34. Wright, "Bank Ownership," finds that agricultural loans made up an important part of early New York bank loan portfolios.

35. Calculated from index numbers reported in Warren and Pearson, *Prices*, table 3, p. 25.

36. Fenstermaker, *Development;* U.S. Comptroller of the Currency, *Annual Report* (1876); U.S. Census Office, *Compendium* (1870).

37. Diamond and Dybvig, "Bank Runs"; and Dewatripont and Tirole, "Efficient Governance Structure."

38. Flannery, "Using Market Information," pp. 277–78.

39. "An Act to Create a Fund for the Benefit of the Creditors of Certain Monied Corporations and for Other Purposes," reprinted in *Albany Argus*, 6 April 1829.

40. Lincoln, *Messages*, vol. IV, pp. 33–34.

41. New York, *Assembly Doc. No. 172* (1841), p. 4.

42. Ibid., p. 7.

43. Flannery and Sorescu, "Evidence."

44. Flannery, "Using Market Information," provides a review of the recent literature.

45. Kane, "Who."

46. Goldberg and Hudgins, "Response."

47. Park and Peristiani, "Market Discipline," p. 363.

48. Calomiris and Kahn, "Role."

49. Kahn and Roberds, "Demandable Debt."

50. Gorton, "Reputation Formation," p. 350.

51. Bodenhorn, "Quis Custodiet."

52. Calomiris, "Deposit Insurance" and "Is Deposit Insurance Necessary?"; and Calomiris and Schweikart, "Panic."

53. Kane, *S & L Insurance Mess;* White, *S & L Debacle;* Barth, *Great Savings and Loan Debacle.*

54. Walter, "Can a Safety Net Subsidy," p. 10.

55. Marcus and Shaked, "Valuation"; and Pennachi, "Reexamination."

56. FDIC, *First Fifty Years*, table 2.3, p. 23.

57. FDIC, *Annual Report* (1996), p. 109.

58. Both the FDIC and the Savings Association Insurance Fund (SAIF) now charge zero premiums to low-risk institutions.

59. U.S. Comptroller of the Currency, *Annual Report* (1876), pp. CII–CV.

60. Bodenhorn, "Faith." These values are consistent with the banks' ownership of their own banking houses and the property surrounding them with, perhaps, a few small undivested foreclosures.

61. New York, "Annual Report," (1835–1840).

62. Kane, *S & L Insurance Mess*, p. 4.

63. Kane, "High Cost."

64. New York, "Communication from W.L. Marcy," pp. 4–23.

65. *Albany Argus*, 6 February 1840. Comments in the *Argus* must be read knowing that it was closely allied with the state's Democratic Party, so its criticisms may have been overly harsh.

66. Osterberg and Thomson, "Depositor-Preference Laws;" and Osterberg, "Impact."

67. Osterberg and Thomson, "Depositor-Preference Laws," p. 14.

68. Ibid., p. 15.

69. Ibid., p. 16.

70. Calomiris, "Deposit Insurance," p. 13.

71. Sylla, "Early American Banking," pp. 112–13.

72. Calomiris, "Deposit Insurance," p. 25.

73. Ibid., p. 25.

Chapter 8

1. Dwyer, "Wildcat Banking," pp. 1–2.

2. King, "On the Economics," p. 129.

3. Friedman, *Program*, p. 6.

4. Miller, *Banking Theories*, p. 150.

5. Dowd, "U.S. Banking," p. 149.

6. Although the term "monopoly" may not be accurate in the strictly technical sense, banks in the first half of the nineteenth century had local monopolies to the extent that one bank's effective loan or circulation territory did not overlap another's. Sylla, "Federal Policy," provides an analysis of this for postbellum banking markets. The Bank of Albany, for example, was chartered in 1792 and held a local monopoly until the entry of the New York State Bank in 1803. The Mohawk Bank of Schenectady (1807) held its local monopoly for 25 years until the entry of the Schenectady Bank (1832). Fenstermaker, *Development*, table A-21.

7. Hammond, *Banks*, p. 577.

8. Seavoy, *Origins*, p. 54.

9. Ibid., p. 60.

10. Ibid., pp. 47–48.

11. Ibid., p. 90.

12. Ibid., p. 106.

13. Flagg, *Banks*, pp. 7–8.

14. Seavoy, *Origins*, pp. 106–7. This was an extreme real-bills position, operating under the presumption that real bills represented the safest short-term investments.

15. Cooper, *Lectures*, p. 157.

16. Carey, *Credit System*, p. 118; Hildreth, *Letter*, p. 12.

17. Flagg, *Banks*, pp. 7–8.

18. Redlich, *Molding*, p. 189.

19. Hammond, *Banks*, p. 338, made a similar argument. He argued that Jacksonians advocated free entry into banking for "the good, earthy reason that it was a fine way to make money."

20. Flagg, *Banks*, pp. 15–16, 22, 24.

21. Miller, *Banking Theories*, p. 147; Redlich, *Molding*, p. 191.

22. Redlich, *Molding*, pp. 192–96.

23. Hammond, *Banks*, pp. 577–79.

24. Seavoy, *Origins*, chapter 6; and Hammond, *Banks*, pp. 585–92, provide a chronicle of the court battles over free banking.

25. Hammond, *Banks*, p. 572.

26. Ibid., p. 596.

27. King, "On the Economics," pp. 139–43.

28. New York, *Assembly Doc. No. 29* (1842).

29. *Albany Argus*, 27 February 1850.

30. New York, *Assembly Doc. No. 3* (1861).

31. New York, *Assembly Doc. No. 6* (1853).

32. New York, *Assembly Doc. No. 3* (1861).

33. Hammond, *Banks*, pp. 597–98.

34. Rolnick and Weber, "Explaining," p. 49.

35. Quoted in Hammond, *Banks*, p. 597.

36. Ibid.

37. Rolnick and Weber, "Free Banking," p. 11.

38. Carr and Mathewson, "Unlimited Liability," pp. 766–84.

39. Ng, "Free Banking Laws," pp. 877–89.

40. Bodenhorn, *History*, table 2.1, p. 63.

41. Sylla, "Early American Banking."

42. Economopoulos and O'Neill, "Bank Entry," p. 1080.

43. Bodenhorn, "Business Cycle," pp. 531–35.

44. Rockoff, "Free Banking Era," pp. 157, 160.

45. New York, *Assembly Doc. No. 69* (1833); Pennsylvania, *Senate Journal* (1833); Virginia, *House Documents* (1833).

46. New York, *Assembly Doc. No. 34* (1843); Virginia, *House Documents* (1843); Pennsylvania, *Senate Journal* (1843).

47. Bodenhorn, "Entry."

48. Rolnick and Weber, "Free Banking," p. 15.

49. Rolnick and Weber, "Causes," pp. 272–73.

50. Redlich, *Molding*, p. 199.

51. Rockoff, "Free Banking Era," p. 149.

52. Gorton, "Pricing," p. 61.

53. Goodhart, "Are Central Banks," pp. 16–17.

54. Gorton, "Banking Theory," p. 271. The former types of models follow from the model developed in Diamond and Dybvig, "Bank Runs."

55. Rolnick and Weber, "Inherent Instability," pp. 881–82.

56. Goodhart, "Are Central Banks," p. 17.

57. Rolnick and Weber, "Causes," table 7, pp. 284–85.

58. Dwyer, "Wildcat Banking," p. 7.

59. King, "On the Economics," pp. 147–48.

60. White, "Regulatory Sources," pp. 892–93; Rolnick and Weber, "Free Banking," "Causes," and "Inherent Instability."

61. Rolnick and Weber, "Causes," p. 274.

62. Gorton, "Banking Theory," p. 268.

63. Rockoff, "Lessons," p. 98.

64. Rockoff, "Institutional Requirements," p. 625.

65. Rolnick and Weber, "Banking Instability"; Hasan and Dwyer, "Bank Runs."

66. Hasan and Dwyer, "Bank Runs," pp. 281, 283.

67. Rockoff, "Institutional Requirements," p. 623.

68. Rockoff, "Lessons," p. 98.

69. Gorton, "Reputation Formation"; and Haupert, "Investment."

70. Rockoff, "Lessons," p. 100.

71. Bell, "Profit," offered the original scholarly contribution.

72. Bodenhorn and Haupert, "Was There a Note Issue Conundrum" and "Note Issue Paradox."

73. Cagan and Schwartz, "National Bank Note Puzzle."

74. Champ, "Underissue"; and Kuehlwein, "National Bank Note Controversy."

75. Bodenhorn and Haupert, "Was There a Note Issue Conundrum," table 2, p. 707.

76. Bell, "Profit"; and Goodhart, "Profit."

77. 11 Peters 326 (1837).

78. Hammond, *Banks*, p. 107.

79. 11 Peters 348 (1837).

80. *Veazie Bank v. Fenno*, 8 Wallace 549 (1870).

81. Seavoy, *Origins*, chapter 6.

82. *Thomas v. Dakin*, 22 Wendell 2 (1839).

83. *Shipping and Commercial List*, 9 November 1839.

84. *Warner v. Beers*, 23 Wendell 103 (1840).

85. *People v Assessors of Niagara*, 7 Hill 504 (1841); see also *People v. Assessors of Watertown*, 1 Hill 618 (1841).

86. Quoted in Hammond, *Bank*, p. 587.

87. Redlich, *Molding;* Golembe, "Deposit Insurance Legislation."

88. Bodenhorn and Haupert, "Note Issue Paradox," pp. 691–92.

89. White and Selgin, "*Laissez-Faire* Monetary Thought," p. 35.

90. Smith, *Rationale*, p. 150. This was also a motivating factor in the choice to finance additional lending through deposits rather than through currency expansion. Bond-to-note arbitrage was not costless, as the model of perfect arbitrage assumes.

91. Cited in Miller, *Banking Theories*, p. 147. Lord may have been discussing the cyclical rather than the seasonal elasticity of the currency, but neither he nor Miller makes it clear that he was.

92. Bryan, *History*, p. 18.

93. This closely follows White, "Regulatory Sources," p. 896.

94. Bogue, *Money*, p. 25.

95. Cagan, "First Fifty Years," p. 20.

96. Benston, "Does Bank Regulation," p. 207.

97. New York, *Assembly Doc. No. 34* (1843).

98. Benston, "Does Bank Regulation," p. 223. See Barth, *Great Savings and Loan Debacle;* Kane, *S & L Insurance Mess;* and White, *S & L Debacle*, for careful studies of the causes and consequences of the thrift crisis.

99. Gorton, "Reputation Formation" and "Pricing"; and Bodenhorn, "Quis Custodiet."

100. Redlich, *Molding*, pp. 187–89.

101. Friedman, *Program;* Hayek, *Denationalization*. White, *Free Banking*, collects the more important contributions of the modern free banking school. It must be kept in mind, however, that New York's free banking was not strictly "free" in the sense used by the modern school. New York's system imposed a

host of restrictions that modern free bankers argue should be eliminated to achieve financial services efficiency.

102. Redlich, *Molding*, p. 188.

103. Hammond, *Banks*, pp. 598–99.

104. Ibid., p. 599.

105. Sylla, *American Capital Market*, p. 36.

106. Bodenhorn, *History*, chapters 2 and 3.

107. Sylla, "Early American Banking," pp. 108–9.

108. Quoted in Hammond, *Banks*, p. 594.

109. Hughes, *Governmental Habit Redux*.

Chapter 9

1. Schweikart, *Banking*, pp. 3, 12–13, 20–21.

2. Ibid., pp. 34–37.

3. Quoted in ibid., pp. 143–44.

4. See ibid., pp. 140–44; Green, *Finance*; Caldwell, *Banking History*.

5. Trescott, *Financing*, pp. 10–11.

6. Starnes, *Sixty Years*, p. 26.

7. Fenstermaker, *Development*, appendix A.

8. Dewey, *State Banking*, p. 138.

9. Hammond, "Banking," Schweikart, *Banking*, pp. 91–92.

10. Govan, "Banking," p. 164.

11. Quoted in ibid., p. 164.

12. Quoted in Golembe, *State Banks*, p. 196.

13. Bodenhorn, *History*; Golembe, *State Banks;* and Parker, "Finance."

14. Dewey, *State Banking*, p. 160.

15. Schweikart, *Banking*, pp. 101–2.

16. South Carolina, *Compilation*, p. 428.

17. Quoted in Woodman, *King Cotton*, p. 4.

18. Ibid., p. 34.

19. Weiss, "U.S. Labor Force Estimates," tables 1A.1 and 1A.9; Esary, *State Banking*, p. 228.

20. Quoted in Golembe, *State Banks*, p. 103.

21. Ransom and Sutch, *One Kind*, provide an account of postbellum debt-peonage debate. Rothstein, "Ante-Bellum Wheat"; and Roeder, "Merchants," offer parallel interpretations of the antebellum era. Green, *Finance*, pp. 28–30, offers an opposing interpretation.

22. Bateman and Weiss, *Deplorable Scarcity*.

23. Nisbit, "Interest Rates"; Ghate, "Interaction."

24. Nisbit, "Interest Rates," p. 81.

25. Green, *Finance*, pp. 29–30.

26. Starnes, *Sixty Years*, p. 127.

27. Woodman, *King Cotton*, p. 41.

28. Atack and Passell, *New Economic View*, p. 153.

29. Starnes, *Sixty Years*, pp. 58–59.

30. Ibid., pp. 57–63.

31. Ibid., pp. 70–72.

32. Ibid., pp. 81–84.

33. Virginia, *House Documents* (1839).

34. Starnes, *Sixty Years*, pp. 81–84, 101–2, 108.

35. Lesesne, *Bank*, pp. 25–26.

36. Ibid., pp. 33–36.

37. Schweikart, *Banking*, p. 230.

38. Clark, *History*, pp. 142–43.

39. Ibid., pp. 135–40.

40. The notes of these banks typically sold at greater discounts than notes of others. See *Bicknell's* or other banknote reporters from the era for banknote prices.

41. Green, *Finance*, pp. 24, 30.

42. Caldwell, *Banking History*, pp. 51–52.

43. Fenstermaker, *Development*, appendix A–12.

44. Redlich, *Molding*, pp. 205–8; Hammond, *Banks*, pp. 680, 690, indirectly criticizes these banks by portraying the 1842 Louisiana banking act as a return to sound principles.

45. Green, *Finance*, pp. 30, 34.

46. Green, "Louisiana," p. 228.

47. Gendreau and Prince, "Private Costs," pp. 8–9.

48. Social rates of return from Fishlow, *American Railroads*; and Ransom, "Social Returns"; as reported in Atack and Passell, *New Economic View*. Social rates of return were based on the following assumptions: (1) $1 million investment in infrastructure project completed in year 0 that provided no benefits prior to completion; (2) social rate of return in terms of reduced transportation costs of 11 percent per annum; (3) bank failure in year 10 taking six years to liquidate, imposing $83,333 ($500,000/6) in costs per year; (4) bank provided no social benefits outside financing the project (i.e., depositors and note holders received no uncompensated transaction or liquidity benefits—this assumption biases the break-even social rate of return upward because private benefits were surely at least as large as the dividends paid by the bank); (5) assumed constant of 6.5 percent social discount rate; (6) assumed 20-year useful life of the infrastructure project (an underestimate that upwardly biases the break-even social rate of return); (7) $3 million in liabilities outstanding is generous (which increases bank failure costs and also biases the break-even rate of return upward). A higher break-even social rate of return implies a less useful project.

49. Huntington, *History*, p. 124.

50. Golembe, *State Banks*, p. 187.

51. Ibid., pp. 239–40.

52. Atack and Passell, *New Economic View*, pp. 166, 168.

53. Adams, "Role," p. 237.

54. Dewey, *State Banking*, p. 35.

55. Starnes, *Sixty Years*, pp. 27–30.

56. Esary, "State Banking," p. 298.

57. McCulloch, *Men*, pp. 114–15.

58. Callender, "Early Transportation," p. 111. For a review of the literature appearing between about 1940 and 1971, see Scheiber, "Government." Jonathan Hughes's *Governmental Habit Redux* remains one of the best interpretations of the era by an economic historian.

59. This discussion draws heavily on Bodenhorn, *History*, pp. 214–16.

60. Quoted in Duke, *History*, p. 9.

61. Gerschenkron, *Economic Backwardness*, especially chapter 2.

62. Schumpeter, *Theory*, chapter 3.

63. Larson, *Jay Cooke*, pp. 86–87.

64. Bodenhorn, *History*, pp. 73–80.

65. See Scheiber, "Government," and sources therein for a general statement of the doctrine. McPherson, *Battle Cry,* discusses its connection to banking. Royalty, "Banking"; Mallalieu and Akural, "Kentucky Banks"; and Duke, *History,* discuss it within the context of Kentucky banking.

66. Quoted in Clark, *History*, p. 255–56.

67. The old Bank of Kentucky was a partly state-owned institution chartered in 1806 and closed in 1822. The new Bank of Kentucky was a partly state-owned institution founded in 1834.

68. Royalty, "Banking," pp. 94–95.

69. Ibid., p. 96.

70. Duke, *History*, pp. 18–19.

71. Freyer, "Negotiable Instruments," pp. 450–51.

72. Gouge, *Short History*, pp. 131–32.

73. Royalty, "Banking," p. 99.

74. 10 Wheaton 46–47 (1825).

75. *Craig v. State of Missouri*, 4 Peters 410–65 (1830).

76. 11 Peters 257–350 (1837).

77. Hammond, *Banks*, p. 107.

78. Berry, *Western Prices*, p. 394.

79. Ibid., p. 402.

80. Gouge, *Short History*, pp. 126, 132.

81. Abernathy, "Early Development," pp. 319–20.

82. Root, "States," p. 234.

83. Huntington, *History*, p. 72.

84. Green, *Finance*, pp. 19–20.

85. Ibid., p. 113.

86. Mallalieu and Akural, "Kentucky Banks," pp. 302–3.

87. Duke, *History*, pp. 97–99.

88. Abernathy, "Early Development," pp. 322–23.

89. Schweikart, *Banking*, p. 99.

90. See Schweikart, *Banking*, pp. 148–58; and Brantley, *Banking*, vol. I, for the details of the Bank of Alabama's establishment and collapse.

91. Schweikart, *Banking*, p. 50.

92. Golembe, *State Banks*, pp. 239–40.

93. Friedman, *Contract Law*, p. 150.

94. Scheiber, "Government," pp. 141–42.

95. Starnes, *Sixty Years*, p. 129.

Chapter 10

1. Esary, "State Banking," p. 219.

2. Hammond, *Banks*, p. 617.

3. Abbey, "Union Bank," pp. 208–9.

4. Ibid., pp. 212–13.

5. Ibid., pp. 211–12.

6. Ibid., pp. 222–23.

7. Green, "Louisiana," p. 200.

8. Caldwell, *Banking History*, p. 46.

9. Ibid., pp. 47–48.

10. Ibid., p. 49.

11. Citizens Bank, *Minute Books*, 22 August 1836.

12. Ibid., 27 May 1837.

13. Ibid., 29 June 1837.

14. Caldwell, *Banking History*, pp. 53–54.

15. Mississippi is excluded because its 1840 figure of $59.02 per capita resulted from two large, short-lived banks and a small aggregate population. The post-1840 collapse in Mississippi's banking sector provides further evidence that the 1840 value is not indicative of Mississippi banking.

16. Redlich, *Molding*, p. 206.

17. Green, *Finance*, p. 17.

18. Schweikart, *Banking*, p. 53.

19. Ibid., pp. 41, 171–74.

20. Caldwell, *Banking History*, pp. 67–68.

21. Quoted in Green, "Citizens Bank," p. 59.

22. Redlich, *Molding*, p. 208.

23. Citizens Bank, *Minute Books*, 3 September 1838.

24. Neu, "J.B. Moussier," p. 553.

25. U.S. House, *Executive Doc. No. 111*, p. 709.

26. Green, "Citizens Bank," p. 67.

27. Sharp, *Jacksonians*; and Shade, *Banks*, chapter 6, discuss the politics of free banking.

28. Shade, *Banks*, p. 145.

29. Bodenhorn, *History*, pp. 128–41.

30. Schweikart, *Banking*, p. 41.

31. Redlich, *Molding*, p. 202.

32. The charters of Virginia's first few banks extended several pages, laying out in detail the rights and responsibilities of bankers. Beginning in 1851, the Virginia legislature chartered several banks in a single act, which typically ran little more than 10 or 11 paragraphs. See, for example, "An Act to Incorporate the Bank of the Old Dominion, the Bank of Commerce at Fredericksburg, and the Mechanics and Traders Bank of the City of Norfolk," Virginia, *Acts of Assembly* (1850/51), pp. 45–47.

33. Dwyer, "Wildcat Banking," pp. 6–7.

34. Rockoff, "Institutional Requirements," p. 622.

35. Rockoff, "New Evidence," pp. 886–87.

36. Gorton, "Reputation Formation" and "Pricing."

37. Berry, *Western Prices*, p. 444.

38. Hayek, *Denationalization*, pp. 44–45.

39. Hammond, *Banks*, p. 626.

40. Bodenhorn, *History*, chapter 2.

41. Dwyer, "Wildcat Banking," p. 2.

42. Rolnick and Weber, "Causes"; Economopoulos, "Illinois Free Banking Experience."

43. Rolnick and Weber, "Causes," pp. 276–77.

44. Ibid., pp. 278–79.

45. Hasan and Dwyer, "Bank Runs."

46. Ibid., pp. 277–78.

47. Dwyer, "Wildcat Banking," pp. 9–12.

48. Rockoff, "New Evidence," p. 888.

49. Churchill, "Age," showed that one-half of all businesses established between 1946 and 1955 were either sold or closed within two years. Hazard rates at other times and in other places are similar (Caves, "Industrial Organization," pp. 1954–55). It is likely that failure rates among early American businesses, including banks, were of the same order of magnitude.

50. Jovanovic, "Selection."

51. Bodenhorn, "Business Cycle," provides evidence that macroeconomic factors influenced but did not drive entry into five antebellum banking markets. More studies are needed of entry and exit decisions of financial firms.

52. Rolnick and Weber, "Causes," p. 290.

53. Rockoff, "New Evidence," p. 888.

54. Ibid.

55. White, "Regulatory Sources," p. 895.

56. Burpee, *First Century*, p. 54.

57. Davis, "New England Textile Mills."

58. Quoted in Dewey, *State Banking*, p. 141.

59. Ibid., p. 103.

60. Bank of East Tennessee, *Minute Book*, 30 September 1851.

61. Ibid., 3 October 1851, 16 October 1851.

62. Calomiris and Schweikart, "Panic." See also Calomiris, "Deposit Insurance."

63. Calomiris and Schweikart, "Panic," pp. 818–19.

64. Rockoff, "Lessons," pp. 90–91.

65. Hammond, *Banks*, p. 712.

66. Calomiris and Schweikart, "Panic of 1857," p. 826.

67. U.S. House, *Executive Doc. No. 87* pp. 236–41; U.S. House, *Executive Doc. No. 107* pp. 286–91.

68. Hugh McCulloch's (*Men*, p. 134–35) discussion of the panic era does not reveal bank policy during the period.

69. Calomiris and Schweikart, "Panic," pp. 828–29.

70. Friedman and Schwartz, "Has the Government," pp. 53–54.

71. Rockoff, "Institutional Requirements," p. 630.

72. Calomiris and Schweikart, "Panic," p. 830.

73. Virginia, *House Documents* (1857–1860). Percentage declines in most measures, including loans, deposits, circulation, and dividends, were substantially larger among the state's independent banks.

74. See Gorton, "Bank Suspension," for a discussion of bank suspensions.

75. Starnes, *Sixty Years*, p. 28.

76. Calomiris and Schweikart, "Panic," p. 830.

77. Govan, "Banking," pp. 177–78.

78. Lesesne, *Bank*, pp. 41–42. See South Carolina, *Reports* (1838), pp. 116–17, for the details of the resolution.

79. Clark, *History*, p. 224.

80. Although there are a number of explanations for the panics of 1837 and 1839, Peter Temin (*Jacksonian Economy*) offers the most widely accepted modern interpretation. Unlike traditional explanations that focused on the failure of the Bank of the United States of Pennsylvania, Jackson's specie circular, the "pet bank" system, and the actions of the Independent Treasury, Temin attributes the panics to the Bank of England's contractionary policy that prompted specie outflows, creating a widespread liquidity scramble among U.S. banks. Schweikart, *Banking*, chapter 1, takes issue with some of Temin's interpretations.

81. U.S. House, *Executive Doc. No. 79*, p. 766.

82. Citizens Bank, *Minute Books*, 12 April 1837.

83. Ibid., 13 April 1837.

84. Ibid., 14 April 1837.

85. Ibid., 14 April–26 April 1837.

86. Ibid., 24 May 1837.

87. Ibid., 27 May 1837.

88. Green, "Louisiana," p. 212.

89. Citizens Bank, *Minute Books*, 6 May–12 June 1837.

90. Bagehot, *Lombard Street*.

91. Citizens Bank, *Minute Books*, 24 August–11 December 1837.

92. Ibid., 21 September–26 October 1837.

93. Wainwright, *History*, p. 42.

94. *Bankers' Magazine* (July 1860), pp. 38–39.

95. Esary, "State Banking," p. 219.

Chapter 11

1. Hellman, Murdock, and Stiglitz, "Liberalization," p. 148.

2. Economopoulos, "Impact."

3. Schweikart, "U.S. Commercial Banking," p. 606.

4. Smith and Cole, *Fluctuations*, p. 185.

5. Fenstermaker, *Development*, pp. 13, 68.

6. Russell, "U.S. Currency System," p. 49.

7. Warren and Pearson, *Prices*, table 3.

8. Sylla, "American Banking."

9. Perkins, *American Public Finance*, p. 267.

10. Goldsmith, *Financial Structure*, p. 48.

11. See King and Levine, "Finance and Growth," and "Finance, Entrepreneurship, and Growth"; and Bodenhorn, *History*, chapter 2, for theoretical and empirical investigations of the links between financial and economic growth.

12. The U.S. savings and loan crisis of the 1980s grew out of a similar sequence of events. See Barth, *Great Savings and Loan Debacle*; Kane, *S & L Insurance Mess*; and White, *S & L Debacle*, for detailed studies of the era. Briefly, they find that sizable increases in short-term interest rates quickly made savings and loan banks unprofitable and, because relative short-term rates remained high for long periods, many savings and loan banks were driven into insolvency.

13. Bardhan, "Corruption," p. 1322.

14. Olson, "Dictatorship."
15. Bardhan, "Corruption," pp. 1327–28.
16. Murphy, Shleifer, and Vishny, "Why is Rent-Seeking."
17. Bardhan, "Corruption," p. 1329.
18. Cameron, "Theoretical Bases," p. 4.
19. Tucker, *Theory*, p. 127.

Bibliography

Articles and Books

Abbey, Kathryn T. "The Union Bank of Tallahassee: An Experiment in Territorial Finance." *The Florida Historical Quarterly* (April 1937), pp. 207–31.

Abernethy, Thomas P. "The Early Development of Commerce and Banking in Tennessee." *Mississippi Valley Historical Review* 14:3 (Dec 1927), pp. 311–25.

Adams, Donald R., Jr. "Wage Rates in the Early National Period: Philadelphia, 1785–1830." *Journal of Economic History* 28:3 (September 1968), pp. 404–17.

———. "Some Evidence on English and American Wage Rates, 1790–1830." *Journal of Economic History* 30:3 (September 1970), pp. 499–520.

———. "The Role of Banks in the Economic Development of the Old Northwest." In *Essays in Nineteenth Century Economic History: The Old Northwest*, pp. 208–45. Edited by David C. Klingaman and Richard K. Vedder. Athens: Ohio University Press, 1975.

———. *Finance and Enterprise in Early America: A Study of Stephen Girard's Bank, 1812–1831*. Philadelphia: University of Pennsylvania Press, 1978.

Alchian, Armen A., and Harold Demsetz. "Production, Information Costs, and Economic Organization." *American Economic Review* 62:5 (December 1972), pp. 777–95.

Anonymous (Nathan Appleton). *Bank Bills or Paper Currency and the Banking System of Massachusetts with Remarks on Present High Prices*. Boston: Little, Brown and Company, 1856.

Anonymous (Nathan Appleton). *A Defence of Country Banks; Being a Reply to a Pamphlet Entitled 'An Examination of the Banking System of Mas-*

sachusetts,' in Reference to the Renewal of the Bank Charters. Boston: Stimpson and Clapp, 1831.

Appleton, Nathan. An Examination of the Banking System of Massachusetts. Boston: Stimpson and Clapp, 1831.

Ashton, T. S. The Industrial Revolution, 1760–1830. Oxford: Oxford University Press, 1969.

Atack, Jeremy, and Peter Passell. A New Economic View of American History. New York: W.W. Norton & Company, 1994.

Atack, Jeremy, and Peter Rousseau. "Business Activity and the Boston Stock Market, 1835–1869." Explorations in Economic History 36:2 (April 1999), pp. 144–79.

Bagehot, Walter. Lombard Street: A Description of the Money Market. New York: Charles Scribner's Sons, 1906.

Bank of Tennessee. The Charter of the Bank of Tennessee, passed January 19, 1838, Together with All Laws Altering or Amending any of its Provisions Passed Since that Date. Nashville, Tenn.: privately printed, 1854.

Bardhan, Pranab. "Corruption and Development: A Review of the Issues" Journal of Economic Literature 35:3 (September 1997), pp. 1320–46.

Barro, Robert J. "Economic Growth in a Cross-Section of Countries" Quarterly Journal of Economics 106 (May 1991), pp. 407–43.

Barro, Robert J., and Xavier Sala-i-Martin. "Convergence across States and Regions." Brookings Papers on Economic Activity (1991), pp. 107–58.

———. "Convergence." Journal of Political Economy 100 (April 1992), pp. 223–51.

Barth, James R. The Great Savings and Loan Debacle. Washington, D.C.: American Enterprise Institute Press, 1991.

Baskin, Jonathan Barron, and Paul J. Miranti, Jr. A History of Corporate Finance. Cambridge: Cambridge University Press, 1997.

Bateman, Fred, and Thomas Weiss. A Deplorable Scarcity: The Failure of Industrialization in the Slave Economy. Chapel Hill: University of North Carolina Press, 1981.

Bell, Spurgeon. "Profit on National Bank Notes." American Economic Review 2:1 (March 1912), pp. 38–60.

Benston, George J. "Does Bank Regulation Produce Stability? Lessons from the United States." In Unregulated Banking: Chaos or Order?, pp. 207–32. Edited by Forrest Capie and Geoffrey E. Wood. New York: St. Martin's Press, 1991.

Berle, Adolph A., Jr., and Gardiner C. Means. The Modern Corporation and Private Property. New York: Commerce Clearing House, 1932.

Berlin, Mitchell. "For Better or Worse: Three Lending Relationships," Federal Reserve Bank of Philadelphia. Business Review (Nov.–Dec. 1996), pp. 1–10.

Bernanke, Ben S. "Non-Monetary Effects of the Financial Crisis in the Propagation of the Great Depression." American Economic Review 73:3 (June 1983), pp. 257–76.

Bernanke, Ben S., and Mark Gertler. "Agency Costs, Net Worth, and Business Fluctuations," American Economic Review 79:1 (March 1989), pp. 14–31.

Berry, Thomas Senior. *Western Prices before 1861: A Study of the Cincinnati Market*. Cambridge: Harvard University Press, 1943.

——. *Revised Annual Estimates of American Gross National Product: Preliminary Estimates of Four Major Components of Demand, 1789–1889*. University of Richmond, Bostwick Paper No. 3, 1978.

Blair, Margaret M. *Ownership and Control: Rethinking Corporate Governance for the Twenty-First Century*. Washington, D.C.: The Brookings Institution, 1995.

Bodenhorn, Howard. "Entry, Rivalry and Free Banking in Antebellum America." *Review of Economics and Statistics* 72:4 (November 1990), pp. 682–86.

——. "Capital Mobility and Financial Integration in Antebellum America." *Journal of Economic History* 52:3 (Sept 1992), pp. 585–610.

——. "Faith, Hope and Coinsurance: Bank Liability Insurance, Moral Hazard, and the New York Safety Fund System." Unpublished manuscript, St. Lawrence University, June 1993.

——. "The Business Cycle and Entry into Early American Banking." *Review of Economics and Statistics* 75:3 (August 1993), pp. 531–35.

——. "Small Denomination Banknotes in Antebellum America." *Journal of Money, Credit, and Banking* 25:4 (November 1993), pp. 812–27.

——. "The End of the Suffolk System: A Reappraisal." Unpublished working paper, 1996.

——. "Private Banking in Antebellum Virginia: Thomas Branch & Sons of Petersburg." *Business History Review* 71:4 (Winter 1997), pp. 513–42.

——. "Free Banking and Financial Entrepreneurship in Nineteenth Century New York: The Black River Bank of Watertown." *Business and Economic History* 27:1 (Fall 1998), pp. 102–14.

——. "Quis Custodiet Ipsos Custodes?" *Eastern Economic Journal* 24:1 (Winter 1998), pp. 7–24.

——. "An Engine of Growth: Real Bills and Schumpeterian Banking in Antebellum New York." *Explorations in Economic History* 36:3 (July 1999), pp. 278–302.

——. *A History of Banking in Antebellum America: Financial Markets and Economic Development in an Age of Nation Building*. Cambridge: Cambridge University Press, 2000.

Bodenhorn, Howard, and Michael Haupert. "Was There a Note Issue Conundrum in the Free Banking Era?," *Journal of Money, Credit, and Banking* 27:3 (August 1995), pp. 702–12.

——. "The Note Issue Paradox in the Free Banking Era." *Journal of Economic History* 56:3 (September 1996), pp. 687–93.

Bogue, Allan G. *Money at Interest: The Farm Mortgage on the Middle Border*. Ithaca, N.Y.: Cornell University Press, 1955.

Boot, Arnould W. A., and Anjan V. Thakor. "Moral Hazard and Secured Lending in an Infinitely Repeated Credit Market Game." *International Economic Review* 35:4 (November 1994), pp. 899–920.

Brantley, William H. *Banking in Alabama, 1816–1860*. 2 vols. Birmingham, Ala.: privately printed, 1961, 1967.

Brealey, Richard, and Stewart C. Myers. *Principles of Corporate Finance*, 4th ed. New York: McGraw-Hill, 1991.

Broaddus, J. Alfred, Jr. "The Bank Merger Wave: Causes and Consequences." Federal Reserve Bank of Richmond *Economic Quarterly* 84:3 (summer 1998), pp. 1–11.

Bryan, Alfred C. *A History of State Banking in Maryland.* Baltimore, Md.: Johns Hopkins University Press, 1899.

Buchanan, James M. "Rent Seeking and Profit Seeking." In *Toward a Theory of the Rent-Seeking Society*, pp. 3–15. Edited by James M. Buchanan, Robert D. Tollison, and Gordon Tullock. College Station: Texas A&M Press, 1980.

Burpee, Charles W. *First Century of the Phoenix National Bank of Hartford.* Hartford, Conn.: privately printed, 1914.

Cable, John Ray. *The Bank of the State of Missouri.* Studies in History, Economics and Public Law, vol. 52, no. 2. New York: Columbia University Press, 1923.

Cagan, Phillip. "The First Fifty Years of the National Banking System—An Historical Appraisal." In *Banking and Monetary Studies*, pp. 15–42. Edited by Deane Carson. Homewood, Ill.: Richard D. Irwin, 1963.

Cagan, Phillip, and Anna J. Schwartz. "The National Bank Note Puzzle Reinterpreted" *Journal of Money, Credit, and Banking* 23:3 (August 1991), pp. 293–307.

Caldwell, Stephen A. *A Banking History of Louisiana.* Baton Rouge: Louisiana State University Press, 1935. (Reprint edition, New York: Arno Press, 1980).

Callender, G. S. "The Early Transportation and Banking Enterprises of the States in Relation to the Growth of Corporations." *Quarterly Journal of Economics* 27 (1903), pp. 111–62.

Calomiris, Charles W. "Deposit Insurance: Lessons from the Record." Federal Reserve Bank of Chicago *Economic Perspectives* 13 (May/June 1989), pp. 10–30.

———. "Is Deposit Insurance Necessary? A Historical Perspective" *Journal of Economic History* 50:2 (June 1990), pp. 283–95.

———. "Comment." In *Inside the Business Enterprise: Historical Perspectives on the Use of Information*, pp. 195–203. Edited by Peter Temin. Chicago: University of Chicago Press, 1991.

———. "Do 'Vulnerable' Economies Need Deposit Insurance? Lessons from U.S. Agriculture in the 1920s." In *If Texas Were Chile: A Primer on Banking Reform*, pp. 237–314. Edited by Philip L. Brock. San Francisco: ICS Press, 1992.

Calomiris, Charles W., and Charles Kahn. "The Role of Demandable Debt in Structuring Optimal Banking Arrangements." *American Economic Review* 81:3 (June 1991), pp. 497–513.

———. "The Efficiency of Self-Regulated Payment Systems: Learning from the Suffolk System." *Journal of Money, Credit, and Banking* 28:4 (November 1996), pp. 766–97.

Calomiris, Charles W., and Larry Schweikart. "The Panic of 1857: Origins, Transmission, and Containment" *Journal of Economic History* 51:4 (December 1991), pp. 807–34.

Cameron, Rondo. "Theoretical Bases of a Comparative Study of the Role of Financial Institutions in the Early Stages of Industrialization." In *Fi-

nancing Industrialization, vol. I, pp. 1–20. Edited by Rondo Cameron. Brookfield, Vt.: Edward Elgar, 1992.

Campbell, Tim S. and William A. Kracaw. "Information Production, Market Signalling and the Theory of Financial Intermediation," *Journal of Finance* 35 (September 1980), pp. 863–82.

Carey, Henry C. *The Credit System in France, Great Britain, and the United States*. Philadelphia: 1838.

Carr, Jack L., and G. Frank Mathewson. "Unlimited Liability as a Barrier to Entry." *Journal of Political Economy* 96:4 (August 1988), pp. 766–84.

Caves, Richard E. "Industrial Organization and New Findings on the Turnover and Mobility of Firms." *Journal of Economic Literature* 36:4 (December 1998), pp. 1947–82.

Chadbourne, Walter W. *A History of Banking in Maine, 1799–1930*. Orono: University of Maine Press, 1936.

Chaddock, Robert E. *The Safety Fund Banking System in New York, 1829–1866*. Washington, D.C.: Government Printing Office, 1910.

Champ, Bruce. "The Underissue of National Banknotes During the Period 1875–1913." Unpublished working paper, University of Western Ontario (May 1990).

Chandler, Alfred. *The Visible Hand: The Managerial Revolution in American Business*. Cambridge, Mass.: Belknap Press of Harvard University Press, 1977.

Churchill, Betty C. "Age and Life Expectancy of Business Firms." *Survey of Current Business* 35:12 (1955), pp. 15–19.

Citizen. *The Village Bank at Danvers. A Glance at its History with Other Relevant Matter, for the Consideration of the Stockholders and the Community Interested*. Boston: McIntire & Moulton, 1862.

Clark, Jeffrey A. "Economies of Scale and Scope at Depository Financial Institutions: A Review of the Literature." Federal Reserve Bank of Kansas City *Economic Review* 73:8 (September/October 1988), pp. 16–33.

Clark, W. A. *The History of Banking Institutions Organized in South Carolina Prior to 1860*. Columbia: The Historical Commission of South Carolina, 1922.

Coase, Ronald H. "The Nature of the Firm." *Economica* 4 (November 1937), pp. 386–405.

Cooper, Thomas. *Lectures on the Elements of Political Economy*. Columbia, S.C.: D. E. Sweney, 1826.

Daniels, Belden L. *Pennsylvania: Birthplace of Banking in America*. Harrisburg: Pennsylvania Bankers Association, 1976.

Davis, Andrew McFarland. *Currency and Banking in the Province of the Massachusetts Bay*. New York: Publications of the American Economic Association, Third Series, May 1901.

Davis, Lance E. "The New England Textile Mills and Capital Markets: A Study of Industrial Borrowing, 1840–1860," *Journal of Economic History* 20:1 (March 1960), pp. 1–30.

Deane, Phyllis. "The Role of Capital in the Industrial Revolution," *Explorations in Economic History* 10 (summer 1973), pp. 349–64.

Dewatripont, Mathias, and Jean Tirole. "Efficient Governance Structure: Implications for Banking Regulation." In *Capital Markets and Financial In-*

termediation, pp. 12–35. Edited by Colin Mayer and Xavier Vives. Cambridge: Cambridge University Press, 1993.

Dewey, Davis R. *State Banking Before the Civil War*. Washington, D.C.: Government Printing Office, 1910.

Diamond, Douglas. "Financial Intermediation and Delegated Monitoring." *Review of Economic Studies* 51 (1984), pp. 392–414.

———. "Debt Maturity Structure and Liquidity Risk." *Quarterly Journal of Economics* 106 (1991), pp. 709–37.

———. "Monitoring and Reputation: The Choice between Bank Loans and Directly Placed Debt." *Journal of Political Economy* 99 (1991), pp. 689–720.

Diamond, Douglas, and Philip Dybvig. "Bank Runs, Deposit Insurance, and Liquidity." *Journal of Political Economy* 91 (June 1983), pp. 401–19.

Domett, Henry W. *A History of the Bank of New York, 1784–1884*. New York: privately published, n.d.

Dowd, Kevin. "U.S. Banking in the 'Free Banking' Period. In *Laissez-Faire Banking*, pp. 149–79. Edited by Kevin Dowd. London: Routledge, 1993.

Duke, Basil W. *History of the Bank of Kentucky, 1792–1895*. New York: Arno Press, 1980 (reprint of Louisville: J.P. Morton, 1895).

Dunbar, Charles F. *The Theory and History of Banking*. New York: G.P. Putnam's Sons, 1929.

Dwyer, Gerald P., Jr. "Wildcat Banking, Banking Panics, and Free Banking in the United States." Federal Reserve Bank of Atlanta *Economic Review* 81:3 (December 1996), pp. 1–20.

Easterbrook, Frank H. "Two Agency-Cost Explanations of Dividends." *American Economic Review* 74:4 (September 1984), pp. 650–59.

Economides, Nicholas. "Network Externalities, Complementarities, and Invitations to Enter." *European Journal of Political Economy* 12:2 (September 1996), pp. 211–33.

———. "The Economics of Networks." *International Journal of Industrial Organization* 14:6 (October 1996), pp. 673–99.

Economides, Nicholas, and Lawrence J. White. "Networks and Compatibility: Implications for Antitrust." *European Economic Review* 38:3 (April 1994), pp. 651–62.

Economopoulos, Andrew. "Illinois Free Banking Experience." *Journal of Money, Credit, and Banking* 20:2 (May 1988), pp. 249–64.

Economopoulos, Andrew J. "The Impact of Reserve Requirements on Free Bank Failures." *Atlantic Economic Journal* 14 (December 1986), pp. 76–84.

Economopoulos, Andrew, and Heather O'Neill. "Bank Entry during the Antebellum Period." *Journal of Money, Credit, and Banking* 27:4 (November 1995, part I), pp. 1071–85.

Emerson, E. C., editor. *Our County and Its People: A Descriptive Work on Jefferson County, New York*. Boston: Boston History Company, 1898.

Esary, Logan. "State Banking in Indiana, 1814–1873." *Indiana University Studies No. 15*. Bloomington: Indiana University Press, 1912.

Fama, Eugene F. "Agency Problems and the Theory of the Firm," *Journal of Political Economy* 88 (April 1980), pp. 288–307.

———. "What's Different about Banks?" *Journal of Monetary Economics* 6 (January 1985), pp. 29–39.

Fama, Eugene F., and Michael C. Jensen. "Separation of Ownership and Control." *Journal of Law and Economics* 26 (June 1983), pp. 301–25.

———. "Agency Problems and Residual Claims." *Journal of Law and Economics* 26 (June 1983), pp. 327–49.

Federal Deposit Insurance Corporation. *The First Fifty Years: A History of the FDIC, 1933–1983.* Washington, D.C.: FDIC, 1984.

Fenstermaker, J. Van. *The Development of American Commercial Banking: 1782–1837.* Kent, Ohio: Kent State University Bureau of Economic and Business Research, 1965.

Fenstermaker, J. Van, and John E. Filer. "Impact of the First and Second Banks of the United States and the Suffolk System on New England Bank Money, 1791–1837." *Journal of Money, Credit, and Banking* 18:1 (February 1986), pp. 28–40.

Field, Alexander James. "Sectoral Shift in Antebellum Massachusetts: A Reconsideration." *Explorations in Economic History* 15:2 (April 1978), pp. 146–71.

First Annual Directory for the city of Petersburg to which is Added a Business Directory for 1859. Petersburg, Va.: George E. Furd, 1859.

Fisher, Irving. "The Debt-Deflation Theory of Great Depressions." *Econometrica* 1 (October 1933), pp. 337–57.

Fishlow, Albert. *American Railroads and the Transformation of the Ante-Bellom Economy.* Cambridge: Harvard University Press, 1965.

Flagg, A. C. *Banks and Banking in the State of New York from the Adoption of the Constitution in 1777 to 1864.* Brooklyn, N.Y.: Rome Brothers, 1868.

Flannery, Mark J. "Using Market Information in Prudential Bank Supervision: A Review of the U.S. Empirical Evidence." *Journal of Money, Credit, and Banking* 30:3 (August 1998, part I), pp. 273–305.

Flannery, Mark J., and Sorin M. Sorescu. "Evidence of Bank Market Discipline in Subordinated Debenture Yields: 1983–1991." *Journal of Finance* 51 (September 1996), pp. 1347–77.

Foner, Eric, and John A. Garraty, editors. *The Reader's Companion to American History.* Boston: Houghton Mifflin Company, 1991.

Freyer, Tony A. "Negotiable Instruments and the Federal Courts in Antebellum American Business." *Business History Review* 50:4 (winter 1976), pp. 435–55.

Friedman, Lawrence M. *Contract Law in America: A Social and Economic Case Study.* Madison: University of Wisconsin Press, 1965.

Friedman, Milton. *A Program for Monetary Stability.* New York: Fordham University Press, 1959.

Friedman, Milton, and Anna J. Schwartz. "Has the Government Any Role in Money?" *Journal of Monetary Economics* 17 (1986), pp. 37–62.

Gallatin, Albert. *The Writings of Albert Gallatin.* Edited by Henry Adams. 3 vol. New York: Antiquarian Press Ltd., 1960.

Gendreau, Brian C., and Scott S. Prince. "The Private Costs of Bank Failures: Some Historical Evidence." Federal Reserve Bank of Philadelphia *Business Review* (March/April 1986), pp. 3–14.

Gerschenkron, Alexander. *Economic Backwardness in Historical Perspective.* Cambridge: Harvard University Press, 1962.

Ghate, P. B. "Interaction between the Formal and Informal Financial Sectors: The Asian Experience." *World Development* 20 (June 1992), pp. 859–72.

Gibbons, J. S. *The Banks of New York, Their Dealers, the Clearing House, and the Panic of 1857.* New York: D. Appleton & Company, 1859.

Gilligan, Thomas W., and Michael L. Smirlock. "An Empirical Study of Joint Production and Scale Economies in Commercial Banking." *Journal of Banking and Finance* 8:1 (1984), pp. 67–77.

Godfrey, Carlos Emmar. *The Mechanics Bank, 1834–1919, Trenton in New Jersey: A History.* Trenton, N.J.: privately printed, 1919.

Goldberg, Lawrence G., and Sylvia C. Hudgins. "Response of Uninsured Depositors to Impending S&L Failures: Evidence of Depositor Discipline." *Quarterly Review of Economics and Finance* 36 (fall 1996), pp. 311–25.

Goldsmith, Raymond W. *Financial Structure and Development.* New Haven, Conn.: Yale University Press, 1969.

Golembe, Carter H. "The Deposit Insurance Legislation of 1933: An Examination of its Antecedents and Purposes." *Political Science Quarterly* 76: 2 (June 1960), pp. 181–200.

———. *State Banks and the Economic Development of the West.* New York: Arno Press, 1978.

Goodhart, Charles A. E. "Profit on National Banknotes." *Journal of Political Economy* 73 (October 1965), pp. 516–22.

———. "Are Central Banks Necessary?" In *Unregulated Banking: Chaos or Order?* pp. 1–21. Edited by Forrest Capie and Geoffrey E. Wood. New York: St. Martin's Press, 1991.

Gorton, Gary. "Bank Suspension of Convertibility." *Journal of Monetary Economics* 15:2 (March 1985), pp. 177–93.

———. "Banking Theory and Free Banking History: A Review Article." *Journal of Monetary Economics* 16 (1985), pp. 267–76.

———. "Clearinghouses and the Origin of Central Banking in the United States." *Journal of Economic History* 45:2 (June 1985), pp. 277–83.

———. "Reputation Formation in Early Bank Note Markets." *Journal of Political Economy* 104:2 (April 1996), pp. 346–97.

———. "Pricing of Free Bank Notes." *Journal of Monetary Economics* 44:1 (August 1999), pp. 33–64.

Gorton, Gary, and Donald J. Mullineaux. "The Joint Production of Confidence: Endogenous Regulation and Nineteenth Century Commercial-Bank Clearinghouses." *Journal of Money, Credit, and Banking* 19:4 (November 1987), pp. 457–68.

Gorton, Gary B., and Joseph G. Haubrich. "Loan Sales, Recourse and Reputation: An Analysis of Secondary Loan Participations." Unpublished manuscript: Wharton School, University of Pennsylvania, May 1987.

Gouge, William M. *A Short History of Paper Money and Banking in the United States.* Philadelphia: T.W. Ustick, 1833.

———. "Commercial Banking." *Hunt's Merchants' Magazine and Commercial Review* 8 (April 1843), pp. 313–21.

Govan, Thomas P. "Banking and the Credit System in Georgia, 1810–1860." *Journal of Southern History* 4 (May 1938), pp. 164–84.

Gras, N. S. B. *The Massachusetts First National Bank of Boston, 1784–1934.* Cambridge: Harvard University Press, 1937.

Green, George D. "The Citizens Bank of Louisiana: Property Banking in Troubled Times, 1833–1842." *Papers of the Fifteenth Annual Meeting of the Business History Conference.* Bloomington: Indiana University, 1968.

———. *Finance and Economic Development in the Old South: Louisiana Banking, 1804–1861.* Stanford, Calif.: Stanford University Press, 1972.

———. "Louisiana, 1804–1861." In *Banking and Economic Development: Some Lessons from History*, pp. 199–231. Edited by Rondo Cameron. New York: Oxford University Press, 1972.

Greif, Avner. "Cultural Beliefs and the Organization of Society: A Historical and Theoretical Reflection on Collectivist and Individualist Societies." *Journal of Political Economy* 102:5 (October 1994), pp. 912–50.

Hammond, Bray. "Long and Short Term Credit in Early American Banking." *Quarterly Journal of Economics* 49 (November 1934), pp. 79–103.

———. "Banking in the Early West: Monopoly, Prohibition, and Laissez Faire." *Journal of Economic History* 8 (May 1948), pp. 1–24.

———. *Banks and Politics in America from the Revolution to the Civil War.* Princeton, N.J.: Princeton University Press, 1957.

Hammond, Jabez. *The History of Political Parties in the State of New York.* 3 vols. Syracuse, N.Y.: Hall, Mills & Company, 1852.

Hasan, Iftekhar, and Gerald P. Dwyer, Jr. "Bank Runs in the Free Banking Period." *Journal of Money, Credit, and Banking* 26:2 (May 1994), pp. 271–88.

Hasse, William F., Jr. *A History of Banking in New Haven, Connecticut.* New Haven, Conn.: privately printed, 1946.

———. *A History of Money and Banking in Connecticut.* New Haven, Conn.: privately printed, 1957.

Haupert, Michael. "Investment in Brand Capital: Evidence from the Free Banking Era." *American Economist* 35:2 (Fall 1991), pp. 73–80.

Hayek, F. A. *The Denationalization of Money.* London: Institute for Economic Affairs, 1976.

Hekman, John S. "The Product Cycle and New England Textiles," *Quarterly Journal of Economics* 94:4 (June 1980), pp. 697–717.

Helderman, Leonard. *National and State Banks: A Study of Their Origins.* Boston: Houghton Mifflin, 1931.

Hellman, Thomas F., Kevin C. Murdock, and Joseph E. Stiglitz. "Liberalization, Moral Hazard in Banking, and Prudential Regulation: Are Capital Requirements Enough?" *American Economic Review* 90:1 (March 2000), pp. 147–165.

Henriet, Dominique, and Herve Moulin. "Traffic-Based Cost Allocation in a Network." *RAND Journal of Economics* 27:2 (summer 1996), pp. 332–45.

Hildreth, Richard. *Letter to His Excellency, Marcus Morton, on Banking and the Currency.* Boston, 1840.

Holdsworth, John Thom. *Financing an Empire: History of Banking in Pennsylvania.* Chicago: S.J. Clarke Publishing Company, 1928.

Hollis, Aidan, and Arthur Sweetman. "Higher Tier Agency Problems in Financial Intermediation: Theory and Evidence from the Irish Loan Funds." Unpublished working paper, University of Calgary, August 1999.

Horton, W. H. *Geographical Gazetter of Jefferson County, New York, 1684–1890*. Syracuse, N.Y.: Syracuse Journal Company, 1890.

Hubert, Philip G., Jr. *The Merchants' National Bank of the City of New York: A History of its First Century Compiled from Official Records at the Request of the Directors*. New York: privately printed, 1903.

Huertas, Thomas F., and Joan L. Silverman. "Charles E. Mitchell: Scapegoat of the Crash?" *Business History Review* 60:1 (spring 1986), pp. 81–103.

Hughes, Jonathan R.T. *The Governmental Habit Redux*. Princeton, N.J.: Princeton University Press, 1991.

Humphrey, David B. "Cost Dispersion and the Measurement of Economies in Banking." Federal Reserve Bank of Richmond *Economic Review* 73:3 (May/June 1987), pp. 24–38.

Humphrey, Thomas M. "Mercantilists and Classicals: Insights from Doctrinal History." Federal Reserve Bank of Richmond *Quarterly Review* 85:2 (spring 1999), pp. 55–82.

Huntington, Charles Clifford. *A History of Banking and Currency in Ohio before the Civil War*. Ohio Archaeological and Historical Publications. Columbus, Ohio: F.J. Heer Printing Company, 1915.

James, F. Cyril. "Bank of North America and the Financial History of Philadelphia." *Pennsylvania Magazine of History and Biography* 64:1 (January 1940), pp. 56–96.

James, John A. *Money and Capital Markets in Postbellum America*. Princeton, N.J.: Princeton University Press, 1978.

Jensen, Michael C., and William H. Meckling. "Theory of the Firm: Agency Costs and Ownership Structure." *Journal of Financial Economics* 3:4 (October 1976), pp. 305–60.

Jovanovic, Boyan. "Selection and the Evolution of Industry." *Econometrica* 50:3 (1982), pp. 649–70.

Kahn, Charles M., and William Roberds. "Demandable Debt as a Means of Payment: Banknotes versus Checks." *Journal of Money, Credit, and Banking* 31:3 (August 1999, part 2), pp. 500–525.

Kane, Edward J. "Who Should Learn What from the Failure and Delayed Bailout of the ODGF?" Federal Reserve Bank of Chicago *Proceedings from a Conference on Bank Structure and Competition* (1987), pp. 306–26.

———. "The High Cost of Incompletely Funding the FSLIC Shortage of Explicit Capital." *Journal of Economic Perspectives* 3:1 (fall 1989), pp. 31–47.

———. *The S & L Insurance Mess: How did it Happen?* Washington, D.C.: Urban Institute Press, 1989.

King, Robert G. "On the Economics of Private Money." *Journal of Monetary Economics* 12 (1983), pp. 127–58.

King, Robert G., and Ross Levine. "Finance and Growth: Schumpeter Might Be Right." *Qaurterly Journal of Economics* 108 (August 1993), pp. 717–37.

———. "Finance, Entrepreneurship, and Growth," *Journal of Monetary Economics* 32 (December 1993), pp. 513–42.

———. "Financial Intermediation and Economic Development." In *Capital Markets and Financial Intermediation*, pp. 156–96. Edited by Colin Mayer and Xavier Vives. Cambridge: Cambridge University Press, 1993.

Kirzner, Israel. "Entrepreneurial Discovery and the Competitive Market Process: An Austrian Approach." *Journal of Economic Literature* 35:1 (March 1997), pp. 60–85

Klamer, Arjo. "A Conversation with Amartya Sen." *Journal of Economic Perspectives* 3:1 (winter 1989), pp. 135–50.

Klebaner, Benjamin. *American Commercial Banking: A History*. Boston: Twayne Publishers, 1990.

Knox, John Jay. *A History of Banking in the United States*. New York: Bradford Rhodes & Company, 1903.

Krooss, Herman E. "Financial Institutions." In *The Growth of American Seaport Cities, 1790–1825*, pp. 104–38. Edited by David Gilchrist. Charlottesville: University of Virginia Press, 1967.

Kuehlwein, Michael. "The National Bank Note Controversy Reexamined." *Journal of Money, Credit, and Banking* 24:1 (February 1992), pp. 111–26.

Lacker, Jeffrey M., Jeffrey D. Walker, and John A. Weinberg. "The Fed's Entry into Check Clearing Reconsidered." Federal Reserve Bank of Richmond *Economic Quarterly* 85:2 (spring 1999), pp. 1–32.

Lake, Wilfred. "The End of the Suffolk System." *Journal of Economic History* 7:4 (December 1947), pp. 183–207.

Lamoreaux, Naomi R. "Banks, Kinship, and Economic Development: The New England Case," *Journal of Economic History* 46:3 (Sept 1986), pp. 647–667.

———. "Information Problems and Bank's Specialization in Short-Term Commercial Lending: New England in the Nineteenth Century." In *Inside the Business Enterprise: Historical Perspectives on the use of information*, pp. 161–195. Edited by Peter Temin. Chicago: University of Chicago Press, 1991.

———. *Insider Lending: Banks, Personal Connections, and Economic Development in Industrial New England*. Cambridge: Cambridge University Press, 1994.

Lamoreaux, Naomi R., and Christopher Glaisek. "Vehicles of Privilege of Mobility? Banks in Providence, Rhode Island, during the Age of Jackson." *Business History Review* 65:4 (autumn 1991), 502–27.

Landes, William M., and Richard A. Posner. "Trademark Law: An Economic Perspective." *Journal of Law and Economics* 30 (October 1987), pp. 265–309.

Langguth, A. J. *Patriots: The Men Who Started the American Revolution*. New York: Simon and Schuster, 1988.

Larson, Henrietta. *Jay Cooke: Private Banker*. Cambridge: Harvard University Press, 1936.

Lesesne, J. Mauldin. *The Bank of the State of South Carolina*. South Carolina Tricentennial Commission. Columbia: University of South Carolina Press, 1970.

Levine, Ross. "Financial Development and Economic Growth: Views and Agenda." *Journal of Economic Literature* 35:2 (June 1997), pp. 688–726.

Lewis, Lawrence, Jr. *A History of the Bank of North America, The First Bank Chartered in the United States.* Philadelphia: J.B. Lippincott & Company, 1882.

Lincoln, Charles Z. *Messages from the Governors*, vols. 3 and 4. Albany, N.Y.: J.B. Lyon & Company, 1909.

Livingood, James Weston. *The Philadelphia-Baltimore Trade Rivalry, 1780–1860.* Harrisburg, Pa.: Pennsylvania Historical and Museum Commission, 1947.

Lockard, Paul A. *Banks, Insider Lending and Industries of the Connecticut River Valley of Massachusetts, 1813–1860.* Unpublished Ph.D. dissertation, University of Massachusetts, 2000.

Mallalieu, William C., and Sabri M. Akural. "Kentucky Banks in the Crisis Decade: 1834–1844." *Register of the Kentucky Historical Society* 65 (1967), pp. 294–303.

Marcus, Alan J., and Israel Shaked. "The Valuation of FDIC Deposit Insurance Using Option-Pricing Estimates." *Journal of Money, Credit, and Banking* 16:4 (November 1984, part I), pp. 446–60.

Margo, Robert A., and Georgia C. Villaflor. "The Growth of Real Wages in Antebellum America: New Evidence." *Journal of Economic History* 47:4 (December 1987), pp. 873–95.

Martin, Joseph G. *A Century of Finance.* Boston: privately printed, 1898. (Reprint edition, New York: Greenwood Press, 1969.)

McAndrews, James J. "Network Issues and Payments Systems." Federal Reserve Bank of Philadelphia *Business Review* (November/December 1997), pp. 15–24.

McCulloch, Hugh. *Men and Measures of Half a Century.* New York: Charles Scribner's Sons, 1888.

McPherson, James M. *Battle Cry of Freedom: The Civil War Era.* New York: Oxford University Press, 1988.

Mester, Loretta J. "Efficient Production of Financial Services: Scale and Scope Economies." Federal Reserve Bank of Philadelphia *Business Review* (January/February 1987), pp. 15–25.

———. "Traditional and Nontraditional Banking: An Information-Theoretic Approach," *Journal of Banking and Finance* 16:3 (1992), pp. 545–66.

Miller, Harry E. *Banking Theories in the United States before 1860.* Cambridge: Harvard University Press, 1927. (Reprint edition, Clifton, N.J.: Augustus M. Kelly Publishers, 1972.)

Modigliani, Franco, and Merton Miller. "The Cost of Capital, Corporation Finance and the Theory of Investment." *American Economic Review* 48 (June 1958), pp. 261–97.

Mokyr, Joel. *Lever of Riches: Technological Creativity and Economic Progress.* New York: Oxford University Press, 1990.

Moulton, H. G. "Commercial Banking and Capital Formation." *Journal of Political Economy* 26: (1918), pp. 484–508, 638–63, 705–31, 849–81.

Mullineaux, Donald J. "Competitive Monies and the Suffolk Bank System: A Contractual Perspective." *Southern Economic Journal* 53 (April 1987), pp. 884–98.

Murphy, Kevin M., Andrei Shleifer, and Robert W. Vishny. "Why Is Rent-Seeking So Costly to Growth?" *American Economic Review* 83:2 (May 1993), pp. 409–14.

Myers, Margaret G. *The New York Money Market: Volume I, Origins and Development.* New York: Columbia University Press, 1931.

Myers, Stewart C. "The Capital Structure Puzzle." *Journal of Finance* 39 (July 1984), pp. 575–92.

Neu, Irene D. "J.B. Moussier and the Property Banks of Louisiana." *Business History Review* 35 (winter 1961), pp. 550–57.

Nevins, Allan. *History of the Bank of New York and Trust Company, 1784 to 1934.* New York: privately printed, 1934.

Ng, Kenneth. "Free Banking Laws and Barriers to Entry into Banking, 1838–1860." *Journal of Economic History* 48:4 (December 1988), pp. 877–89.

Nisbit, Charles. "Interest Rates and Imperfect Competition in the Informal Credit Markets of Rural Chile." *Economic Development and Cultural Change* 16 (October 1967), pp. 73–90.

Olson, Mancur. "Dictatorship, Democracy, and Development." *American Political Science Review* 87:3 (September 1993), pp. 567–75.

Osterberg, William P. "The Impact of Depositor Preference Laws." Federal Reserve Bank of Cleveland *Economic Review* 32:3 (quarter 3, 1996), pp. 2–11.

Osterberg, William P., and James B. Thomson. "Depositor-Preference Laws and the Cost of Debt Capital." Federal Reserve Bank of Cleveland *Economic Review* 35:3 (quarter 3, 1999), pp. 10–20.

Park, Sangkyun, and Stavros Peristiani. "Market Discipline by Thrift Depositors." *Journal of Money, Credit, and Banking* 30:3 (August 1998, part 1), pp. 347–64.

Parker, William N. "The Finance of Capital Formation in Midwestern Development, 1800–1910." In *American Economic Development in Historical Perspective*, pp. 168–76. Edited by Thomas Weiss and Donald Schaefer. Stanford, Calif.: Stanford University Press, 1994.

Parsons, *A History of Banking in Connecticut.* New Haven, Conn.: Yale University Press, 1935.

Pennachi, George C. "A Reexamination of the Over- (or Under-) Pricing of Deposit Insurance." *Journal of Money, Credit, and Banking* 19:3 (August 1987), pp. 340–60.

Perkins, Edwin J. *Financing Anglo-American Trade: The House of Brown, 1800–1880.* Cambridge: Harvard University Press, 1975.

———. *American Public Finance and Financial Services, 1700–1815.* Columbus: Ohio State University Press, 1994.

Petersen, Mitchell A., and Raghuram G. Rajan. "The Benefits of Lending Relationships: Evidence from Small Business Data." *Journal of Finance* 49:1 (March 1994), pp. 3–37.

———. "The Effect of Credit Market Competition on Lending Relationships." *Quarterly Journal of Economics* 110:2 (May 1995), pp. 407–43.

Philadelphia Bank. *By-Laws of the Philadelphia Bank; Together with Rules and Regulations for the Government of the Board of Directors in Conducting the Business thereof as a Deliberative Body.* Philadelphia: William F. Geddes, 1843.

Pollard, Sidney. "Fixed Capital in the Industrial Revolution in Britain." *Journal of Economic History* 24:3 (September 1964), pp. 299–314.

Puth, Robert C. *American Economic History*, 3d ed. Fort Worth, Tex.: Dryden Press, 1993.

Rajan, Raghuram G. "Insiders and Outsiders: The Choice between Informed and Arm's-Length Debt." *Journal of Finance* 47:4 (September 1992), pp. 1367–400.

———. "The Past and Future of Commercial Banking Viewed through an Incomplete Contract Lens." *Journal of Money, Credit, and Banking* 30:3 (August 1998, part 2), pp. 524–50.

Ramakrishan, Ram, and Anjan Thakor. "Information Reliability and a Theory of Financial Intermediation," *Review of Economic Studies* 52 (1984), pp. 415–32.

Ransom, Roger. "Social Returns from Public Transport Investment: A Case Study of the Ohio Canal." *Journal of Political Economy* 78:5 (September 1970), pp. 1041–60.

Ransom, Roger, and Richard Sutch. *One Kind of Freedom: The Economic Consequences of Emancipation.* Cambridge: Cambridge University Press, 1977.

Redish, Angela. "Why Was Specie Scarce in Colonial Economies? An Analysis of the Canadian Currency, 1796–1830." *Journal of Economic History* 44:3 (September 1984), pp. 713–28.

Redlich, Fritz. *The Molding of American Banking: Men and Ideas.* 2 parts. New York: Johnson Reprint Company, 1968.

Reed, George B. *Sketch of the Early History of Banking in Vermont.* Boston: privately printed, 1879.

Reiffen, David, and Maggie Patterson. "The Rise and Retreat of the Market for Joint-Stock Shares Revisited: The Effect of the Bubble Act in Eighteenth Century England." *Journal of Economic History* 50:1 (March 1990), pp. 163–71.

Richmond, Petersburg, Norfolk, and Portsmouth Business Directory, 1859–1860. Richmond, Va.: William F. Bartlett, 1859.

Rockoff, Hugh. "The Free Banking Era: A Reexamination." *Journal of Money, Credit, and Banking* 6 (1974), pp. 141–67.

———. "New Evidence on Free Banking in the United States." *American Economic Review* 75:4 (September 1985), pp. 886–89.

———. "Institutional Requirements for Stable Free Banking." *Cato Journal* 6:2 (fall 1986), pp. 617–34.

———. "Suffolk System." In *The Encyclopedia of American Economic History*, pp. 453–454. Columbia, S.C.: Bruccoli Clark Layman, 1990.

———. "Lessons from the American Experience with Free Banking." In *Unregulated Banking: Chaos or Order?* pp. 73–109. Edited by Forrest Capie and Geoffrey E. Wood. New York: St. Martin's Press, 1991.

Roeder, Robert E. "Merchants of Ante-Bellum New Orleans." *Explorations in Entrepreneurial History* 10 (April 1958), pp. 113–22.

Rolnick, Arthur J., and Warren E. Weber. "Free Banking, Wildcat Banking, and Shinplasters." Federal Reserve Bank of Minneapolis *Quarterly Review* 6 (fall 1982), pp. 10–19.

———. "The Causes of Free Bank Failures: A Detailed Examination." *Journal of Monetary Economics* 14 (October 1984), pp. 267–91.

———. "Banking Instability and Regulation in the U.S. Free Banking Era." Federal Reserve Bank of Minneapolis *Quarterly Review* 9 (summer 1985), pp. 2–9.

———. "Inherent Instability in Banking: The Free Banking Experience." *Cato Journal* 5:3 (winter 1986), pp. 877–90.

———. "Explaining the Demand for Free Bank Notes." *Journal of Monetary Economics* 21:1 (August 1988), pp. 47–71.

Rolnick, Arthur J., Bruce D. Smith, and Warren E. Weber. "Lessons from a Laissez-Faire Payments System: The Suffolk Banking System (1825–58)." Federal Reserve Bank of Minneapolis *Quarterly Review* 22:3 (summer 1998), pp. 11–21.

Root, L. Carroll. "New York Bank Currency: Safety Fund vs. Bond Security." *Sound Currency* 2 (February 1895), pp. 285–308.

———. "States as Bankers." *Sound Currency* 2 (April 1895), pp. 221–51.

———. "New England Bank Currency." *Sound Currency* 2 (June 1895), pp. 254–83.

Rosenberg, Nathan. "On Technological Expectations," *Economic Journal* 86 (1976), pp. 523–35 (reprinted in *Inside the Black Box*).

Ross, Stephen A., Randolph W. Westerfield, and Bradford D. Jordan. *Essentials of Corporate Finance*. Chicago: Irwin, 1996.

Rothenberg, Winifred. "The Emergence of a Capital Market in Rural Massachusetts, 1730–1838." *Journal of Economic History* 45:4 (December 1985), pp. 781–808.

Rothstein, Morton. "The Antebellum South as a Dual Economy: A Tentative Hypothesis." *Agricultural History* 41:4 (1967), pp. 373–82.

Royalty, Dale. "Banking and the Commonwealth Ideal in Kentucky, 1806–1822." *Register of the Kentucky Historical Society* 77 (1979), pp. 91–107.

Russell, Steven. "The U.S. Currency System: A Historical Perspective." Federal Reserve Bank of St. Louis *Review* 73:5 (September 1991), pp. 34–61.

Saloner, Garth, and Andrea Shepard. "Adoption of Technologies with Network Effects: An Empirical Examination of the Adoption of Automated Teller Machines." *RAND Journal of Economics* 26:3 (autumn 1995), pp. 479–501.

Sargent, Thomas J., and Neil Wallace. "The Real-Bills Doctrine versus the Quantity Theory: A Reconsideration." *Journal of Political Economy* 90 (December 1982), pp. 1212–36.

Scheiber, Harry N. "Government and the Economy: Studies of the 'Commonwealth' Policy in Nineteenth-Century America." *Journal of Interdisciplinary History* 3:1 (summer 1972), pp. 135–51.

Schlesinger, Arthur M., Jr. *The Age of Jackson*. New York: Book Find Club, 1945.

Schumpeter, Joseph A. *The Theory of Economic Development: An Inquiry into Profit, Capital, Credit, Interest, and the Business Cycle*. Translated by Redvers Opie. Cambridge: Harvard University Press, 1934.

———. *Capitalism, Socialism and Democracy*, 3d ed. New York: Harper & Row, 1950.

Schwartz, Anna Jacobson. "The Beginning of Competitive Banking in Philadelphia, 1782–1809." *Journal of Political Economy* 55 (October 1947), pp. 417–31.

Schweikart, Larry. "Private Bankers in the Antebellum South." *Southern Studies* 25 (summer 1986), pp. 125–34.

———. *Banking in the American South from the Age of Jackson to Reconstruction* Baton Rouge: Louisiana State University Press, 1987.

———. "U.S. Commercial Banking: A Historiographical Survey." *Business History Review* 65:4 (autumn 1991), pp. 606–61.

Seavoy, Ronald E. *The Origins of the American Business Corporation, 1784–1855: Broadening the Concept of Public Service during Industrialization.* Westport, Conn.: Greenwood Press, 1982.

Second Annual Directory for the City of Petersburg to Which Is Added a Business Directory for 1860. Petersburg, Va: George E. Furd, 1860.

Shade, William G. *Banks or No Banks: The Money Issue in Western Politics, 1832–1865.* Detroit: Wayne State University Press, 1972.

Sharp, James Roger. *The Jacksonians versus the Banks: Politics in the States after the Panic of 1837.* New York: Columbia University Press, 1970.

Sharpe, Steven. "Asymmetric Information, Bank Lending and Implicit Contracts: A Stylized Model of Customer Relationships." *Journal of Finance* 45 (1990), pp. 1069–87.

Shleifer, Andrei, and Robert W. Vishny. "Large Shareholders and Corporate Control." *Journal of Political Economy* 94:3 (June 1986), pp. 461–88.

———. "A Survey of Corporate Governance." *Journal of Finance* 52:2 (June 1997), pp. 737–83.

Simonton, William G. *Maine and the Panic of 1837.* Unpublished master's thesis, University of Maine, 1971.

Smith, Adam. *An Inquiry into the Nature and Causes of the Wealth of Nations.* New York: Modern Library, 1937.

Smith, Bruce D., and Warren E. Weber. "Private Money Creation and the Suffolk Banking System." *Journal of Money, Credit, and Banking* 31:3 (August 1999, part 2), pp. 624–59.

Smith, Vera. *The Rationale of Central Banking and the Free Banking Alternative.* Indianapolis: Liberty Press, 1990. (Reprint of *The Rationale of Central Banking.* London: P.S. King & Son, 1936.)

Smith, Walter Buckingham, and Arthur Harrison Cole. *Fluctuations in American Business, 1790–1860.* Cambridge: Harvard University Press, 1935.

Sokoloff, Kenneth L. "Investment in Fixed and Working Capital during Early Industrialization: Evidence from U.S. Manufacturing Firms." *Journal of Economic History* 44:2 (June 1984), pp. 545–56.

Spencer, Charles Jr. *The First Bank of Boston, 1784–1949.* New York: Newcomen Society, 1949.

Starnes, George T. *Sixty Years of Branch Banking in Virginia.* New York: Macmillan Company, 1931.

Stiglitz, Joseph E. "Credit Markets and the Control of Capital." *Journal of Money, Credit, and Banking* 17:2 (May 1985), pp. 133–52.

Stokes, Howard Kemble. *Chartered Banking in Rhode Island, 1791–1900.* Providence, R.I.: Preston & Rounds Company, 1902.

———. "Public and Private Finance." In *State of Rhode Island and Providence Plantations at the End of the Century: A History*, vol. III, pp. 173–322. Edited by Edward Field. Boston: Mason Publishing Company, 1902.

Sylla, Richard. "Federal Policy, Banking Market Structure, and Capital Mobilization in the United States, 1863–1913." *Journal of Economic History* 29:4 (December 1969), pp. 657–86.

———. "American Banking and Growth in the Nineteenth Century: A Partial View of the Terrain." *Explorations in Economic History* 9 (1971), pp. 197–227.

———. *The American Capital Market, 1846–1914: A Study of the Effects of Public Policy on Economic Development.* New York: Arno Press, 1975.

———. "Forgotten Men of Money: Private Bankers in Early U.S. History." *Journal of Economic History* 36:1 (March 1976), pp. 173–88.

———. "Early American Banking: The Significance of the Corporate Form." *Business and Economic History* 14:1 (March 1985), pp. 105–23.

Taylor, George Rogers. *The Transportation Revolution, 1815–1860.* New York: Holt, Rinehart & Winston, 1966.

Temin, Peter. *The Jacksonian Economy.* New York: W.W. Norton & Company, 1969.

Thornton, Henry. *An Enquiry into the Nature and Effects of the Paper Credit of Great Britain* (1802). Edited by F. A. von Hayek. London: George Allen & Unwin, 1939.

Townsend, Robert. "Optimal Contracts and Competitive Markets with Costly State Verification." *Journal of Economic Theory* 21 (October 1979), pp. 265–93.

Trescott, Paul B. *Financing American Enterprise: The Story of Commercial Banking.* New York: Harper & Row, 1963.

Trivoli, George. *The Suffolk Bank: A Study of a Free–Enterprise Clearing System.* London: The Adam Smith Institute, 1979.

Tucker, George. *The Theory of Money and Banks Investigated.* Boston: C.C. Little and J. Brown, 1839 (reprinted New York: Greenwood Press, 1968).

Vatter, Barbara. "Industrial Borrowing by the New England Textile Mills, 1840–1860: A Comment," *Journal of Economic History* 21:2 (June 1961), pp. 216–221.

Wainwright, Nicholas B. *History of the Philadelphia National Bank.* Philadelphia: William F. Fell Company, 1953.

Walker, Amasa. *History of the Wickaboag Bank.* Boston: Crosby, Nichols & Company, 1857.

Walter, John R. "Can a Safety Net Subsidy Be Contained?" Federal Reserve Bank of Richmond *Economic Quarterly* 84:1 (winter 1998), pp. 1–20.

Warren, George F. and Frank A. Pearson. *Prices.* New York: John Wiley & Sons, 1933.

Watertown, North Watertown, and Juhelville Business and Residence Directory for 1856–57. Watertown, NY.: J.D. Huntington, 1856.

Weinberg, John A. "The Organization of Private Payments Networks." Federal Reserve Bank of Richmond *Economic Quarterly* 83:2 (spring 1997), pp. 25–43.

Weiss, Roger W. "The Issue of Paper Money in the American Colonies,

1720–1774," *Journal of Economic History* 30:4 (December 1970), pp. 770–84.

Weiss, Thomas. "U.S. Labor Force Estimates and Economic Growth, 1800–1860." In *American Economic Growth and Standards of Living before the Civil War*, pp. 19–75. Edited by Robert E. Gallman and John Joseph Wallis. Chicago: University of Chicago Press, 1992.

——. "Long-Term Changes in U.S. Agricultural Output per Worker, 1800–1900." *Economic History Review* 46:2 (May 1993), pp. 324–41.

White, Lawrence H. "Regulatory Sources of Instability in Banking." *Cato Journal* 5:3 (winter 1986), pp. 891–97.

——. *Free Banking*, 3 vols. Brookfield, Vt.: Edward Elgar, 1993.

White, Lawrence H., and George A. Selgin. "*Laissez-Faire* Monetary Thought in Jacksonian America." In *Perspectives on the History of Economic Thought*, vol 4., pp. 20–39. Edited by Donald E. Moggridge. Aldershot, England: Edward Elgar, 1990.

White, Lawrence J. *The S & L Debacle: Public Policy Lessons for Bank and Thrift Regulation*. New York: Oxford University Press, 1991.

Whitney, David R. *The Suffolk Bank*. Cambridge, Mass.: Riverside Press, 1878.

Woodman, Harold D. *King Cotton and His Retainers: Financing and Marketing the Cotton Crop of the South, 1800–1925*. Lexington: University of Kentucky Press, 1968.

Woodward, P. H. *One Hundred Years of the Hartford Bank*. Hartford, Conn.: Case, Lockwood, & Brainerd, 1892.

Wright, Robert. "Bank Ownership and Lending Patterns. *Business History Review* 73 (spring 1999), pp. 40–60.

Wright, Robert E. "Artisans, Banks, Credit, and the Election of 1800." *The Pennsylvania Magazine of History and Biography* 122, no. 3 (July 1998), 211–39.

Wyatt, Edward A. "Rise of Industry in Ante-Bellum Petersburg." *William and Mary Quarterly* Second Series 17 (October 1937), pp. 1–36.

Archival Sources

Bank of Cape Fear, Hillsborough Branch. *Records, 1815–1846*. Southern Historical Collection of the Manuscripts Department, University of North Carolina. Chapel Hill, North Carolina.

Bank of Charleston. *Records*. Division of Archives and Special Collections. Robert Scott Small Library, College of Charleston. Charleston, South Carolina.

Bank of Chester County (Pennsylvania). *Minute Book, 1814–1825*. Chester County Historical Society.

Bank of Chester County *Discount Book*. Chester County Historical Society.

Bank of East Tennessee (Knoxville). *Minute Book, 1844–1858*. Records of the Bank of Tennessee, Microfilm #3. State Library of Tennessee. Nashville, Tennessee.

Bank of Gallatin. *Discount Book, 1822–1824*. Records of the Bank of Tennessee, Microfilm #3. State Library of Tennessee. Nashville, Tennessee.

Bank of Tennessee. *General Check Ledger*. Record Group Number 47.

Records of the Bank of Tennessee. State Library of Tennessee. Nashville, Tennessee.

Bank of Tennessee, Memphis Branch. *Minute Book, 1858–1862*. Record Group Number 47. Records of the Bank of Tennessee, Microfilm #3. State Library of Tennessee. Nashville, Tennessee.

Black River Bank. *Black River Bank Records* (1855–1859). Jefferson County Historical Society. Watertown, New York.

Black River Bank. *Discount Books #2 and #3*. Jefferson County Historical Society. Watertown, New York.

Branch & Company Records. *Bill Books, 1845–1858*. Virginia Historical Society. Richmond, Virginia.

Citizens Bank of Louisiana. *Minute Books and Records, 1833–1868*. Records of Ante-Bellum Southern Plantations from the Revolution through the Civil War. Series H. Selections from the Howard Tilton Memorial Library, Tulane University and the Louisiana State Museum Archives. Microfilm reels 13–17. Frederick, Md.: University Publications of America.

State Bank of New Brunswick. *Protested Notes, 1852–1853*. Division of Archives, Alexander Library, Rutgers University. New Brunswick, New Jersey.

United States. Census Office. Eighth Census (1860). Manuscript censuses for Tennessee and Virginia.

Government Documents

American State Papers. *Finance* 6 vols. Washington, D.C.: Gales and Seaton, 1824–1828.

Federal Deposit Insurance Corporation. *Annual Report*. (1996).

Indiana. State Bank of Indiana. *Report of the State Bank of Indiana and Condition of its Branches to the Governor*. Indianapolis: Austin H. Brown, 1853.

Massachusetts. General Court. *Report of a Committee of the Massachusetts Senate to Investigate the Affairs of the Penobscot Bank* (December 1809).

Massachusetts. General Court. *Report of the Committee Relative to the Penobscot Bank* (1811).

Massachusetts. General Court. "True Abstract of the Returns of Several Banks to the Secretary of the Commonwealth." Boston (1820, 1827, 1830–1835, 1845, 1846, 1855).

New York. General Assembly. "Annual Report of the Bank Commissioners." *Assembly Document No. 59* (January 1831).

New York. General Assembly. "Annual Report of the Bank Commissioners." *Assembly Document No. 70* (January 1832).

New York. General Assembly. "Annual Report of the Bank Commissioners." *Assembly Document No. 69* (January 1833).

New York. General Assembly. "Annual Report of the Bank Commissioners." *Assembly Document No. 74* (January 1835).

New York. General Assembly. "Annual Report of the Bank Commissioners." *Assembly Document No. 80* (January 1836).

New York. General Assembly. "Annual Report of the Bank Commissioners." *Assembly Document No. 78* (January 1837).

New York. General Assembly. "Report of a Committee Appointed to Investigate the Banks." *Assembly Document No. 328* (May 1837).

New York. General Assembly. "Annual Report of the Bank Commissioners." *Assembly Document No. 71* (January 1838).

New York. General Assembly. "Annual Report of the Bank Commissioners." *Assembly Document No. 101* (January 1839).

New York. General Assembly. "Annual Report of the Bank Commissioners." *Assembly Document No. 44* (January 1840).

New York. General Assembly. "Communication from W. L. Marcy, Receiver of the City Bank of Buffalo, Transmitting a Report Pursuant to a Resolution of the Assembly of the 22d January." *Assembly Document No. 144* (February 1841).

New York. General Assembly. "Report of the Bank Commissioners, in Answer to a Resolution of the Assembly of the 23d of February, in Relation to the Wayne County Bank, and to the Safety Fund." *Assembly Document No. 172* (March 1841).

New York. General Assembly. "Annual Report of the Bank Commissioners." *Assembly Document No. 29* (January 1842).

New York. General Assembly. "Annual Report of the Bank Commissioners." *Assembly Document No. 34* (January 1843).

New York. General Assembly. "Annual Report of the Superintendent of the Banking Department." *Assembly Document No. 6* (January 1853).

New York. General Assembly. "Annual Report of the Superintendent of the Banking Department." *Assembly Document No. 15* (January 1854).

New York. General Assembly. "Annual Report of the Superintendent of the Banking Department." *Assembly Document No. 10* (January 1855).

New York. General Assembly. "Annual Report of the Superintendent of the Banking Department." *Assembly Document No. 4* (January 1856).

New York. General Assembly. "Annual Report of the Superintendent of the Banking Department." *Assembly Document No. 5* (January 1857).

New York. General Assembly. "Annual Report of the Superintendent of the Banking Department." *Assembly Document No. 4* (January 1858).

New York. General Assembly. "Annual Report of the Superintendent of the Banking Department." *Assembly Document No. 5* (January 1859).

New York. General Assembly. "Annual Report of the Superintendent of the Banking Department." *Assembly Document No. 3* (January 1860).

New York. General Assembly. "Annual Report of the Superintendent of the Banking Department." *Assembly Document No. 3* (January 1861).

Pennsylvania. *House Journal* (1819–1829, 1832, 1839–1841).

Pennsylvania. *Senate Journal* (1819–1831, 1833–1838, 1841–1852).

Rhode Island. General Assembly. "Abstract of Returns from the Several Banks in the State of Rhode Island, made to the General Assembly." *Acts and Resolves* 1820, 1827, 1835–1845, 1848, 1850, 1855, 1858, 1860.

South Carolina. *Reports and Resolutions of the General Assembly of South Carolina* (1838 1844, 1852–1854, 1860, 1865).

South Carolina. *A Compilation of All the Acts, Resolutions, Reports and Other Documents in Relation to the Bank of the State of South Carolina.* Columbia, S.C., 1848.

U.S. Census Office. 8th Census (1860). *A Compendium of the Eighth Census.* Washington, D.C.: Government Printing Office, 1862.

U.S. Census Office. 9th Census (1870). *A Compendium of the Ninth Census.* Washington, D.C.: Government Printing Office, 1872.

U.S. Comptroller of the Currency. *Annual Report of the Comptroller of the Currency.* Washington, D.C.: GPO, 1876.

U.S. Comptroller of the Currency. *Annual Report of the Comptroller of the Currency.* Washington, D.C.: GPO, 1931.

U.S. House. 25th Congress, 2d Session. *Executive Document No. 79.*

U.S. House. 26th Congress, 2d Session. *Executive Document No. 111.*

U.S. House. 30th, 1st. Session. *Executive Document No. 77.*

U.S. House. 32d, 1st. Session. *Executive Document No. 122.*

U.S. House. 33d Congress, 2d Session. *Executive Document No. 82.*

U.S. House. 34th Congress, 1st Session. *Executive Document No. 102.*

U.S. House. 34th Congress, 3d Session. *Executive Document No. 87.*

U.S. House. 35th Congress, 1st Session. *Executive Document No. 107.*

U.S. House. 36th Congress, 2d Session. *Executive Document No. 77.*

Virginia. General Assembly. *House Documents* (1820–1860).

Virginia. General Assembly. "Report of the University of Virginia," *House Document No. 11* (1845/46)

Virginia. General Assembly. *House Journal* (1821/22).

Virginia. General Assembly. *Acts of Assembly* (1850/51).

Periodicals

Albany Argus, various issues, 1829–1860.

Bankers' Magazine, various issues, 1847–1860.

Bicknell's Counterfeit Detector, Banknote Reporter, and General Price Current, various issues, 1835–1858.

Hunt's Merchants' Magazine, various issues, 1840–1861.

Niles' Rigister, 16 June 1821.

Shipping and Commercial List, various issues, 1837–1839.

Index

accommodation paper, 56
Adair, John, 240
Adams, Donald, 54, 284
Adams, Samuel, 77
adverse selection, 8, 66, 67, 83, 157, 181, 183
agency
  costs, 25, 26, 30, 31, 34, 35, 36, 92, 94, 106
  problems, 26, 33, 83, 84, 93, 94
  relationship, 25
Agricultural Bank of Pittsfield, 114
Agricultural and Manufacturing Bank of Carlisle, 140
agriculture
  banks, 85
  credit, 253, 289
  lending, 165, 220
Albany Regency, 187
American Exchange Bank, 135, 194, 272
American Philosophical Society, 146
Appleton, Nathan, 88, 89
Aqueduct Association, 135
Army of the Potomac, 270
Ashton, T. S., 60
Associated Banks of Boston, 99
Atack, Jeremy, 38

Atchafalaya Railroad and Banking Company, 232, 280
Augusta Bank, 97

Bagehot, Walter, 23, 281
Bangor Bank, 20
bank
  capital, 19, 21
  commissioners, 160, 161, 165, 167, 168, 169, 176, 178, 191, 194
  failure, 8, 19, 184, 189, 240
  liability insurance, 123, 155, 156, 166, 169, 183, 184
  runs (*see also* runs), 48, 106, 107, 119, 121, 122, 129, 136, 137, 155, 156, 180, 182, 275
  war, 190
Bank of Albany, 312n.6
Bank of America of New York, 14, 50
Bank of Buffalo, 161, 162, 176, 178
Bank of Cape Fear, 54, 56, 302n.43
Bank of Charleston, 57, 58, 59
Bank of Chester County, 29, 30, 56, 309n.57
Bank of Commerce, 197
Bank of the Commonwealth of Kentucky, 234, 240, 241, 242, 243, 246

Bank of East Tennessee, 29, 37, 272
Bank of England, 126, 156, 157, 165,
    205, 282, 320n.80
Bank of Gallatin, 54, 56
Bank of Indiana, 274
Bank of Kentucky, 28, 48, 234, 236, 238,
    240, 243, 255, 259, 279
Bank of Louisiana, 243
Bank of Maryland, 74, 130, 131
Bank of Massachusetts, 130
Bank of Mobile, 245
Bank of Mutual Redemption, 96, 101,
    102, 117
Bank of New York, 24, 52, 129, 130,
    133
Bank of North America, 8, 13, 23, 47,
    77, 126, 127, 128, 129, 130, 131,
    132, 133, 145, 149, 222
Bank of Northern Liberties, 142
Bank of Penn Township, 135, 283
Bank of Pennsylvania, 131, 132, 141,
    142, 142, 148, 222, 234
Bank of Pensacola, 252
Bank of Pittsburgh, 141, 142
bank profits, 201, 202
Bank of the State of Alabama, 30, 244
Bank of the State of New York, 128
Bank of the State of Ohio, 274
Bank of the State of South Carolina,
    224, 230, 239, 243, 244, 246, 278
Bank of the State of Tennessee, 236,
    238, 243
Bank of Tennessee, 29, 57, 58, 65, 70,
    243, 244, 270
Bank of the United States of
    Pennsylvania, 153, 283
Bank of the Valley of Virginia, 228
Bank of Virginia, 15, 31, 42, 59, 220,
    222, 228, 234, 235, 236, 244, 273,
    284
bankers' bank, 96
banking panic, 184, 205
banknote
    brokers, 40, 41, 43, 96, 97, 98, 107,
        115, 135, 156, 170, 255
    discount, 98, 99, 100, 103, 105, 106,
        115, 116, 122
    redemption war, 103
bankruptcy, 34, 35, 48, 87

banks
    and capital formation, 54
    commonweal, 78
    economic growth, 3, 45, 52, 53, 54,
        57, 62, 143, 153, 157, 222, 223, 227,
        233, 239, 247, 264
Bardhan, Pranab, 294, 295
Baring Bank, 197
Baskin, Joathan, 38
Bath Bank, 20
Bell, Spurgeon, 209
Benston, George, 215
Berle, Adolph, 26
Berlin, Mitchell, 67, 68
Bernanke, Ben, 156
Berry, Thomas, 242
Biddle, Nicholas, 22, 143, 191, 291
bilateral exchange, 113, 115
bills
    of credit, 74, 75, 79, 125, 126, 128,
        143, 241
    of exchange, 29, 30, 49, 50, 51, 56,
        82, 125, 186, 190, 224, 234, 280
    of lading, 49, 50
Black River Bank, 54, 56, 57, 59, 63, 64,
    65, 68, 69, 71, 302n.47, 309n.57
Blackstone Canal Bank, 85
Blackwell, John, 74
board of directors, 22, 24, 27, 28, 29, 31
Bodenhorn, Howard, 40, 41, 42, 43,
    171, 199, 201, 209, 211, 216, 264
Bogue, Allan, 214
bond collateral, 212, 213, 214, 268
bond collateral requirements, 206, 267
bond-secured note issue, 5, 6, 159, 181,
    184, 209, 212, 218, 261, 295
bonus, 17
bonus payments, 158
Boot, Arnould, 66
Boston, Norwich and New London
    Railroad Company, 86
Boston Exchange Office, 98
Branch, Thomas, 63
branch banking, 6, 9, 113, 215, 243,
    250, 270, 272, 273, 276
    in Pennsylvania, 141–42
branch network, 227, 235, 274, 276, 277
Branch and Sons (see Thomas Branch
    and Sons)

branches, 232, 240, 242, 245, 253, 287
Breck, Samuel, 147
bribery, 14, 15, 188, 293, 294
Briscoe v. The Bank of the
    Commonwealth, 241
Briscoe v. Bank of Kentucky, 210
brokers' loans, 274
Bronson, Isaac, 189
Brown, John, 80
Bryan, Alfred, 124, 139
Bubble Act, 77
Budd, Thomas, 125
Burr, Aaron, 13, 134
Butchers and Drovers Bank, 140, 141

Cagan, Philip, 209, 214
Calhoun, John C., 230
Callenders, G. S., 62, 235
Calomiris, Charles, 40, 91, 100, 101,
    103, 106, 107, 157, 169, 170, 171,
    172, 174,181, 273, 274, 275, 276,
    278, 285
Cameron, Rondo, 296
Canal Bank, 259, 282
canals, 8
capital, 13, 20, 24
    installment payments, 20
    leverage ratios, 292
    requirements, 174
Carey, Henry, 189
Carr, Jack, 198
Carrollton Bank, 281, 282
cartels, 284
cashiers, 23, 24, 28, 30, 31, 129, 143,
    168, 242, 280
central bank, 205, 217, 236
Central Bank of Milledgeville, 245
central banking, 276
Chaddock, Robert, 134, 157
Champ, Bruce, 209
Chancellor Livingston, 128, 129
Chandler, Alfred, 42
Charleston-Hamburg Railroad, 230
charter mongering, 15
chartering, 6, 14, 16, 17
    liberalized in New England, 199
chartering bonus, 15
charters, 11, 12, 15, 186
Chemical Bank, 135, 187, 188

Chesapeake and Delaware Canal, 147,
    148
Chesapeake and Ohio Canal, 147
chief executive officer, 28
circulation period, 101
Citizens Bank of Louisiana, 23, 30
Citizens Bank of New Orleans, 254,
    255, 259, 280, 281, 282, 301n.22
City Bank of Baltimore, 138
City Bank of Buffalo, 176, 177
City Bank of New Haven, 86
City Bank of New Orleans, 254, 281
Civil War, 231, 244, 258, 265
Clark, W. A., 278
Clay, Henry, 219
clearing
    operations, 155
    services, 66
    system, 99
clearinghouses, 8, 112, 115, 135, 136,
    137
    certificates, 135, 136
clearings, 103, 112, 113
    banknotes, 94, 95
    bilateral, 96
    gross, 135
    interbank, 108
    net, 135
Clinton, DeWitt, 157, 186
closed corporations, 93
Coase, Ronald, 25
coinage, 75
coinsurance, 8, 107, 159, 173
collateral, 45, 48, 49, 56, 66, 67, 81,
    125, 132, 137, 139, 180, 184, 185,
    188, 189, 191, 192, 193, 194, 198,
    202, 206, 207, 208, 212, 216, 253,
    254, 276
    bond, 195, 196, 209, 264, 266, 287
    mortgage, 85, 203, 217, 262
Colman, John, 76
Columbia Bank and Bridge Company,
    231
Commercial Bank of Buffalo, 162, 176,
    178
Commercial Bank of Natchez, 50
Commercial Bank of New Orleans, 281
Commercial Bank of New York City,
    162

commercial paper, 18, 43, 44, 48, 53, 67, 69, 70, 82, 83, 136, 141, 237, 243, 271, 272
commonweal, 90, 244, 246
commonwealth ideal, 9, 239, 242, 243, 247, 249, 250, 270, 285
Compagnie des Indes, 20
Connecticut River Banking Company, 85
Consolidated Association of Planters, 253, 254, 255, 259, 289
contagion, 185, 207
contagious runs (see also runs), 205
continental currency, 78, 126
contingent fund, 29
convertibility, 275, 276, 289
Cooper, Thomas, 188, 189
Corn Exchange Bank, 140, 141
Cornwallis, Lord, 127
corporate governance, 12, 18, 24, 25, 35, 39, 41
corporate hierarchies, 7
corporate privilege, 222
correspondence networks, 113
correspondent relationships, 113, 114
corruption, 293, 294, 295
costly state verification, 66
cotton factor, 50
credit crunches, 48, 277
Credit Mobilier, 238
credit rationing, 226
cross-subsidization, 111, 112, 117, 118, 119
Cumberland Road, 147, 152, 153
Currency Act of 1765, 126
currency inelasticity, seasonal, 212

Davis, Lance, 54, 73, 271
Deane, Phyllis, 61
debt repudiation, state, 206
debt-deflation, 48, 166, 288
  problems, 156, 281
debt-peonage, 225
deflation, 47, 48
demand-following hypothesis, 238
Democrats, 190, 210, 219, 220, 229, 252, 258, 260, 261
deposit
  certificates of, 82
  core, 82
  preference laws, 179
deposit insurance, 156, 169, 181
  implicit subsidy, 174, 177
  and risk taking, 174
Derby Bank, 86
Dewatripont, Mathias, 36, 39, 41, 166
Dewey, Davis, 272
Diamond, Douglas, 47, 166
discount committee, 140
disintermediation, 156, 205, 206, 215
disputes, sectional and partisan, 13
diversification, 25
dividends, 34, 35, 36, 38, 39, 84, 88, 90, 92, 127, 130, 133, 143, 152, 158, 195, 201, 216, 234, 235, 253, 273, 284, 300n.98
  smoothing, 38
Dorr, Thomas, 81
Dorr's Rebellion, 81, 304n.31
Dry Dock Bank, 135, 278
Dry Dock Company, 135
Dunbar, Charles, 46
Dwyer, Gerald, 206, 207, 208, 215, 263, 266, 268
Dybvig, Philip, 166

Easterbrook, Frank, 26, 35, 36
economic growth, 4, 43, 52
Economides, Nicholas, 109
economies of scale, 96, 113
  and scope, 89, 103
Economopoulos, Andrew, 167, 199, 202, 264, 265
engines of growth, 128
English East India Company, 20
entry barriers, 198, 199
Equal Righters, 191
Equal Rights Party, 190
Erie Canal, 147, 148, 161, 164, 178, 227, 230, 247, 228
Esary, Logan, 224, 250, 285
Exchange Bank of Providence, 13, 38
Exchange Bank of Virginia, 244, 284
Exchange and Banking Company, 232
exchange brokers, 141

factorage system, 225, 226
factors, 50, 57, 226, 227, 258

Fama, Eugene, 26, 30, 93
Farmer Bank of Lancaster, 140
Farmers Bank of Bucks County, 143
Farmers Bank of Maryland, 138
Farmers Bank of Virginia, 15, 59, 228,
    234, 244, 284
Farmers and Drovers Bank, 140
Farmers and Mechanics Bank of
    Frederick, 140
Farmers and Mechanics Bank of
    Philadelphia, 57, 139
Farmers and Mechanics Bank of
    Pittsburgh, 140
Farmers and Mechanics Bank of
    Rahway, 140
Farmers and Merchants Bank of
    Baltimore, 152
Farmers and Millers Bank of
    Hagerstown, 140
Farminton Canal, 86
Federal Deposit Insurance Corporation
    (FDIC), 8, 156, 174, 175, 179
Federal Reserve, 120
Federal Reserve Board, 120
Federal Savings and Loan Insurance
    Corporation, 8
Federalist, 13, 14, 132, 133, 189, 219
Fenstermaker, J. Van, 105
Filer, John, 105
financial
    experimentation, 6
    fixed capital, 56
    innovation, 123, 124
    oligarchy, 78
    panics, 107, 155, 275, 285
    stability, 104
First Bank of the United States, 13, 14,
    22, 80, 128, 131, 133, 142, 145, 157,
    219, 234, 235
Fisher, Irving, 48, 156, 157, 166, 217
Fishlow, Albert, 233
fixed capital, 61, 62
    investment, 54
fixed investment, 57
Flagg, A. C., 188, 189
Flannery, Mark, 169
foreign exchange, 260, 271
Forman, Joshua, 158, 159, 181, 189
Forstall, Edmund, 259

fractional reserve banking, 130
fractional reserves, 40, 205, 214
Francis, Tench, 23, 24
Franklin Bank of Baltimore, 152
Franklin Bank of Cincinnati, 14
fraud, 12, 21, 24, 31, 33, 37, 145, 157,
    158, 177, 181, 184, 185, 189, 197,
    202, 215, 216, 241, 262, 263, 264,
    283, 285
free bank failures, 265
free banking, 5, 8, 9, 123, 154, 181, 183,
    184, 185, 186, 190, 191, 195, 197,
    198, 199, 200, 201, 204, 206, 208,
    211, 214, 215, 217, 218, 220, 222,
    229, 235, 250, 260, 261, 262, 263,
    265, 268, 270, 277, 285, 289, 295,
    314n.101
Free Banking Act, 159, 192, 197, 198,
    210
Free Banking Act of 1838, 185
Free Banking Act, 1840 amendments,
    196
Free Banking Act, 1846 amendments,
    197
Free Banking era, 213, 269
free banks, 274
free entry, 192
free incorporation, 218
free rider problem, 18
Friedman, Lawrence, 247
Friedman, Milton, 185, 217, 275
Fry & Company, 282

Gallatin, Albert, 14, 21, 123, 188, 189,
    235
General Society of Mechanics and
    Tradesmen, 140
Gerschenkron, Alexander, 9, 238
Gertler, Mark, 156
Gibbons, J. S., 143
Girard, Stephen, 54
Girard Bank, 283
Glaisek, Christopher, 15, 22, 90
Goldburg, Lawrence, 169
Goldsmith, Raymond, 152, 290
Golembe, Carter, 211, 233
Goodhart, Charles, 205, 209
Gorton, Gary, 40, 41, 42, 170, 203, 204,
    206, 208, 216, 263

Gouge, William, 50, 51, 241, 242, 288
government supervision, 166
governmental oversight, 155
Gras, N. S. B., 23
Great Northern Railroad, 221
Green, George, 232, 255, 281, 285
Green County Bank, 135
Greif, Avner, 93
Grocers Bank, 140
gross clearing, 99, 112

Hallowell and Augusta Bank, 20
Hamilton, Alexander, 24, 126, 129, 133, 134, 217, 219
Hamilton, James Alexander, 190
Hammond, Bray, 22, 47, 52, 53, 104, 108, 112, 123, 144, 192, 196, 197, 203, 210, 223, 241, 250, 263, 264, 270, 274
Hampshire and Hampton Canal, 86
Hartford Bank, 74
Harvard College, 74
Hasan, Ifekhar, 207, 208, 215, 266
Haupert, Michael, 43, 208, 209, 211
Hayek, F. A., 217, 263
Haynes, Robert Y., 230
Helderman, Leonard, 134
Hellman, Thomas, 287
Henriet, Dominique, 112
Herman Briggs & Company, 277, 282
hierarchical structure, 26, 27, 28, 33, 42
hierarchies, 30
Hildreth, Richard, 189
Hiwasse Railroad, 230
Hollis, Aidan, 31
Hope & Company, 254
Hudgins, Sylvia, 169
Hughes, Jonathan, 218
Huntsville Bank, 281

Iddings, Caleb, 144
improvement banks, 232, 233, 253, 255
industrial
   credit, 57
   lending, 59
inelastic currency, 186, 218
inflation, 47, 48
information asymmetries, 11, 17, 18, 25, 35, 38, 47, 66, 70, 194, 202, 205, 273
   problems, 65, 82, 91, 105, 106
information costs, 226
infrastructure, 6, 9, 43, 124, 187, 230, 231, 233, 234, 236, 240, 247, 252
insider lending, 91
insurance companies, 92
interbank
   balances, 283
   clearings, 280, 283
   coinsurance, 106
   cooperation, 113, 165, 273, 277, 280, 284, 286
   deposits, 173
   relationships, 113
   settlements, 101, 278
internal improvements, 8, 146, 147, 221, 227, 228, 229, 233

Jackson, Andrew, 210, 219, 242, 289
Jacksonian era, 240
Jacksonian populism, 261
Jacksonian populists, 190
James, F. Cyril, 145
James and Kanawha Canal, 227, 229
James River and Kanawha Company, 228
Jefferson, Thomas, 14, 86, 217, 219, 235, 239
Jensen, Michael, 26, 30, 33, 93
joint-stock banking, 198
junk bonds, 43
J. L. & S. Joseph, 278

Kahn, Charles, 40, 100, 101, 103, 106, 107, 169, 170
Kane, Edward, 169, 177
Kennebec Bank, 20
King, E. M. W., 29
King, Robert, 184, 206
kinship networks, 7
Kuehlwein, Michael, 209

Lacker, Jeffrey, 111
Lake, Wilfred, 105
Lamoreaux, Naomi, 15, 22, 46, 89, 90, 91, 92
Lancaster Trading Company, 142

Lancaster Turnpike, 146
Land Bank, 76, 77
land banks, 74, 126, 129, 133, 225
land speculation, 161
Larson, Henrietta, 238
Law, John, 20
Leather Manufacturers Bank of New
    York City, 140, 141
lemons, 184, 185
lender of last resort, 182, 276, 281
Lenow, James, 29
Liability
    double, 158, 159, 164, 197, 198
    limited, 80, 190, 196, 198, 238
    triple, 159
    unlimited, 80, 129, 138, 159, 190,
       198, 287
Lincoln Bank, 99
line of credit, 84
liquidity, 25, 40, 46, 80, 82
Lizardi & Company, 282
Loco-Focos, 190, 191
logrolling, 158
long-term relationships, 45
Lord, Eleazor, 190, 212
Louisiana State Bank, 243, 281
Louisville, Cincinnati and Charleston
    Railroad, 230
Louisville Bank, 234
Lovanovic, Boyan, 268
Ludlow, Edward, 273
Lumbermans Bank, 140, 141

MacVickar, John, 189
Manhattan Company, 134, 135, 222
Manhattan Fire Insurance Company,
    190
Manufacturers Bank of Bellville, 140
Manufacturers and Mechanics Bank,
    135, 283
Marietta and Susquehanna Trading
    Company, 142
Marr v. Bank of West Tennessee, 37
Marshall, John, 241
Massachusetts Bank, 23, 52, 74, 78
Mathewson, Frank, 198
McAndrews, James, 112
McCulloch, John Ramsey, 189
McDougall, Alexander, 129

McHenry, James, 130
McLane Report, 61
Means, Gardiner, 26
Mechanics Bank of Baltimore, 140
Mechanics Bank of New Haven, 86
Mechanics Bank of New York, 140
Mechanics Bank of Newark, 140
Mechanics Bank of Patterson, 141
Mechanics Bank of Philadelphia, 135,
    137, 140, 283
Mechanics and Traders Bank, 281
Meckling, William, 33
merchant bankers, 77
merchant banking, 125
Merchant's Bank of New York, 14, 31
Merrill, Samuel, 225
Metropolitan Bank, 194
Mexican crisis, 205
Miller, Harry, 185, 189
Miller, Morton, 34, 35
Miners Bank of Pottsville, 140
Miranti, Paul, 38
Modigliani, Franco, 34, 35
Modigliani-Miller theorem, 37
Mohawk Bank of Schenectady, 312n.6
monetary stability, 221
monitoring, 12, 18, 19, 24, 26, 27, 29,
    30, 31, 33, 35, 36, 39, 40, 42, 43,
    45, 66, 67, 83, 92, 93, 94, 107, 113,
    169, 171, 174, 175, 216, 218, 263,
    276
    and demandable debt, 169, 170
    muted incentives, 173
monopoly, 17
monopoly profits, 16
moral hazard, 45, 66, 71, 82, 106, 157,
    181, 287
Morris, Robert, 125, 126, 127
mortgages, 48, 52, 57, 74, 75, 76, 85,
    128, 140, 161, 165, 176, 192, 193,
    194, 217, 224, 225, 230, 232, 234,
    235, 242, 243, 251, 254, 259, 260,
    263, 171, 173, 282, 285, 287, 288,
    289, 293
    credit, 9, 249
    lending, 220
Moulin, Herve, 112, 122
Moulton, H. G., 46, 53, 54, 57, 62
Moussart & Company, 272

Moyamensing Bank, 135, 283
Mullineaux, Donald, 105, 106
Murdock, Kevin, 287
Murphy, Kevin, 294
mutual coinsurance, 276
mutual cooperation, 283
mutual guarantee banks, 276
mutual guaranty system, 8, 10
Myers, Margaret, 135

Nantucket Bank, 21
National Banking Act of 1863, 10, 209
National Banking Act of 1864, 10
National Banking Era (1863–1913), 209,
    232, 310n.16
National City Bank, 141
National Road, 236
net-clearing system (*see also* clearings,
    net), 99
network, 7, 8, 97, 108, 113, 117, 122
  banknote discounts, 121
  clearings, 113
  common costs, 110, 111
  effects, 111
  externalities, 110, 112, 114, 307n.67
  links and nodes, 109, 110
  node, 114
  star, 109, 110
  two-way, 109
Neu, Irene, 259
New England Bank, 98, 99, 100
New Haven Bank, 72
New Hope Bank and Bridge Company,
    231
New London Society for Trade and
    Commerce, 75
New Orleans Canal and Banking
    Company, 231
New Orleans Carrollton Railroad and
    Banking Company, 232
New Orleans Gas Light and Banking
    Company, 232, 280
New Orleans Improvement and Banking
    Company, 232
New Orleans and the Jackson Railroad,
    221
New York Chemical Manufacturing
    Company, 135, 187

New York City Bank Clearinghouse
    Association, 96
New York Manufacturing Company,
    135, 187
New York State Bank, 312n.6
Ng, Kenneth, 198, 199, 202
Nisbit, Charles, 226
Northern Bank of Kentucky, 234, 279,
    280
Northwestern Bank of Virginia, 228
note holder preference, 179, 180
note issue seasonality, 9
note-issue paradox, 9, 209

Ohio Canal, 227, 233
Ohio Deposit Guaranty Fund, 169
Ohio Life, 274, 278
Ohio Life Insurance and Trust
    Company, 273
Ohio Life and Trust Company, 136
Ohio State Board of Control, 274
Olson, Mancur, 294
Omnibus Banking Act of 1814, 142,
    143, 144
O'Neill, Heather, 199, 202
Osterberg, William, 179
overdrafts, 117

Paddock, Loveland, 63, 301n.42
Paine, Thomas, 146
panic, 156, 166, 273, 277
panic of 1819, 155, 157, 158, 289
panic of 1837, 155, 291, 320n.80
panic of 1839, 155, 156, 320n.80
panic of 1857, 155, 180, 197, 273, 291
paper
    double-named, 48, 49, 50, 84
    single-named, 48, 49, 50, 52
par check collection, 120
Park, Sangkyun, 169
partnerships, 11, 12, 37, 68, 125, 128,
    138, 198
Pawtuzet Bank, 91
payment system network, 108, 112, 119
payment systems, 155, 156, 166, 183,
    197, 220, 269, 277, 285
pecking order theory, 34, 35
Pennsylvania Bank, 13, 17

Pennsylvania Main Line Canal, 147, 153, 277
Penobscot Bank of Bucksport, 86, 87
Peristiani, Stavros, 169
Perkins, Edwin, 290
pet bank, 320n.80
Petersen, Mitchell, 66, 68
Philadelphia Bank, 13, 17, 29, 131, 132, 141, 142
Phoenix Bank of Hartford, 83, 271
Phoenix Bank of New York, 135, 187
Phoenix Bank of Providence, 38
Pittsburgh Manufacturing Company, 142
plantation banks, 9, 220, 249, 251, 253, 255, 258, 259, 272, 285, 289, 295
Planters Bank of Natchez, 255, 258, 259, 270
political connections, 178
Pollard, Sidney, 62
Portage Rail Road, 147
Prime, Ward and King, 251
principal-agent problem, 33
private bankers, 11, 49, 125, 138, 141
private banking, 63, 139, 188, 198
private banks, 54, 189, 190, 191, 198, 228, 261
Privy Council, 125
profits, 216
promissary notes, 48, 49, 52, 56, 125, 138, 186, 190, 242, 272
property banks, 251, 260
proprietorships, 11, 68, 128
Providence Bank, 13, 38, 74, 80, 90, 91
Puth, Robert, 60

Quaker merchants, 127
Quinebaug Bank, 86

Raguet, Condy, 143, 189
railroads, 147
Rajan, Raghuram, 66, 67, 68
Real Estate Bank of Baltimore, 139
Real Estate Bank of Frederick, 139
real-bills, 45, 46, 48, 57, 62, 158, 159, 217, 221, 225, 259, 260, 287, 289, 290, 301n.34
  doctrine, 7, 44, 45, 46, 52
  and fallacy of composition, 47

lending, 56
policy, 47
redemption war, 131, 137
Redlich, Fritz, 23, 52, 53, 98, 104, 112, 123, 145, 189, 203, 211, 217, 236, 259, 261
Regency, 194
Regency's Safety Fund, 191
regulatory forbearance, 177, 178, 182
relationships, 65, 66, 67, 68, 70, 71
  and bank loan rates, 68
Relief Act of 1841, 149
relief banks, 246
relief notes, 149, 150
renewals, 47, 56, 85, 140
renewed loans, 54
rent seeking, 16, 17, 294
replevy laws, 240, 242, 243
Republican, 13, 14, 132, 133, 191, 219
Republican Party, 186, 187
repudiation, 148, 253, 258, 265
reputation formation, 40
reserve ratios, 107, 291
reserve requirements, 81, 137, 185, 198, 288
restraining acts, 188, 189, 190
restraining laws, 198
retained earnings, 34, 35, 39, 44, 195
Ricardo, David, 189, 218
Ritchie, Thomas, 219
Rives, William, 220
Roberds, William, 169, 170
Rockoff, Hugh, 108, 197, 201, 202, 203, 207, 208, 215, 263, 267, 268, 269
Roeder, Robert, 225
Roger Williams Bank, 14
Rolnick, Arthur, 103, 202, 203, 206, 207, 208, 215, 265, 266, 267, 269, 275
Rothenberg, Winifred, 74
Rothstein, Morton, 225
Rousseau, Peter, 38
runs (see also bank, runs), 82, 169, 207, 214, 215, 265, 266, 267, 273, 274, 276, 280, 283

Safety Fund, 8, 156, 157, 159, 160, 164, 165, 167, 168, 171, 172, 174, 176, 177, 178, 179, 180, 181, 183, 190, 211, 216

Safety Fund Act, 160, 161, 181
Safety Fund Act, 1842 amendments, 162
Safety Fund System, 154, 166
salaries, bank, 31, 33
Saloner, Garth, 110, 114
Sargent, Thomas, 47
savings banks, 92
savings and loan crisis of the 1980s,
    174, 245
Scheiber, Harry, 247
Schenectady Bank, 312n.6
Schumpeter, Joseph, 9, 53, 63, 64, 145,
    238
Schwartz, Anna, 131, 209, 275, 284
Schweikart, Larry, 223, 230, 244, 246,
    258, 273, 274, 275, 276, 278, 285
Seavoy, Ronald, 210
Second Bank of the United States, 14,
    112, 128, 143, 190, 191, 239, 289,
    291
sectional rivalries, 146
Selgin, George, 212
separation of ownership and control,
    24, 25
Seton, William, 24, 129
shareholders, large, 18, 19, 92, 94
Sharpe, Steven, 67, 68
Shepard, Andrea, 110, 114
shirking, 12, 25, 26, 27, 33, 42
Shleifer, Andrei, 18, 92, 294
Shoe and Leather Bank, 140
Silver Bank, 76
small-denomination banknotes, 84, 220,
    266
Smith, Adam, 25, 41, 61, 75, 189, 218
Smith, Bruce, 103, 107, 116
Sokoloff, Kenneth, 62
solvency, 46
Sorescu, Sorin, 169
soundness orthodoxy, 289, 290
South Royalton Bank, 120
South Sea Bubble, 20
South Western Rail Road Bank, 230, 231
Southern Life Insurance and Trust
    Company, 252
specie
    circular, 320n.80
    convertibility, 263
    leverage ratio, 291, 292

redemption, 99
shortage, 75
Starnes, George, 227, 270, 277
State Bank of Albany, 14
State Bank of Boston, 84
State Bank of Illinois, 242, 246
State Bank of Indiana, 224, 225, 235,
    246, 275
State Bank of New Brunswick, 54
State Bank of Ohio, 275
State Bank of Tennessee, 242
state-owned banks, 6, 85
state ownership of bank shares, 84
stay laws, 240, 241, 242, 243
sterling bills, 282
Steuart, James, 218
Stiglitz, Joseph, 287
stock notes, 20, 21, 22, 90
Stokes, Howard Kemble, 73, 81
subordinate debt, 179
subsidization, implicit, 183
Suffolk Bank, 7, 85, 96, 98, 99, 100,
    101, 102, 104, 106, 107, 108, 112,
    114, 115, 116, 117, 119, 120, 121
    as franchisor, 106
Suffolk system, 7, 94, 96, 97, 103, 108,
    112, 114, 117, 123, 272, 295
    and money supply, 105
    as protocentral bank, 104, 108
summary execution, 81
summary judgment, 158
summary process, 80
sunspot, 205
supply-leading hypothesis, 238, 239
suspension of specie payment, 48, 148
Susquehanna and Tidewater Canal, 148
Sweetman, Arthur, 31
Sylla, Richard, 53, 63, 199, 202, 217,
    218, 289

tax rates, 89
taxes on banks, 88
Taylor, George Rogers, 147
Taylor, John, 219
Temin, Peter, 156
Thakor, Anjan, 66, 68
Thomas Biddle & Company, 251
Thomas Branch & Company, 309n.57

Thomas Branch and Sons, 54, 55, 57, 59, 63
Thomson, James, 179
Thornton, Henry, 47
Tirole, Jean, 36, 39, 41, 166
tobacco warehouse receipts, 130
trade acceptance, 49
trade credit, 226
transaction costs, 25
transparency, 207, 218, 267
Tremont Bank, 98
Trescott, Paul, 221
Tucker, George, 31, 46, 52, 53, 296

underissue of notes, 186
Union Bank of Boston, 84
Union Bank v. Campbell, 37
Union Bank of Florida, 251, 253, 254
Union Bank of Georgia, 259
Union Bank of Louisiana, 50, 221, 255, 260, 280, 281
Union Bank of Mississippi, 258
Union Bank of Tennessee, 270
Union Canal, 147, 148
unit banking, 287
unit banks, 271, 272, 273, 277
usury, 128, 168, 215, 288

Van Buren, Martin, 158, 186, 187, 190, 210
Vishny, Robert, 18, 92, 294
voting rights, 18, 19

Wainwright, Nicholas, 132
Walker, Amasa, 105
Walker, Jeffrey, 111
Wallace, Neil, 47
War of 1812, 186
Ward, Thomas Wren, 197
Washington Bank, 85
Waterville Bank, 20, 176
Wayman v. Southard, 141
Wayne County Bank, 168
Weber, Warren, 103, 107, 116, 202, 203, 206, 207, 208, 215, 264, 265, 266, 267, 269, 275
Weinburg, John, 111, 112, 122
West Greenwich Farmers Bank, 80
Whigs, 191, 219, 220, 260, 261
White, Lawrence H., 5, 206, 212, 213, 271
wildcat banking, 264
wildcat banks, 202
wildcats, 203, 204, 250
wildcatting, 208, 211, 216, 264, 265, 266, 267, 269, 285
Willing, Thomas, 130, 145
Woodman, 227
Worcester Bank, 100, 119
working capital, 46, 54, 57, 60, 61, 62, 71
Wright, Robert, 134

zombie banks, 177